THE
AMERICAN AUTOMOBILE
A CENTENARY

This edition first published in the United States in 1992 by
SMITHMARK Publishers, a division of U.S. Media Holdings, Inc.,
16 East 32nd Street, New York, NY 10016.

3rd Printing 1996

First published in the United Kingdom 1995 by Prion Books Ltd.,
32-34 Gordon House Road, London NW5 1LP

SMITHMARK books are available for bulk purchase for sales
promotion and premium use. For details write or call the manager
of special sales, SMITHMARK Publishers, 16 East 32nd Street,
New York, NY 10016 (212) 532-6600.

ISBN 0-7651-9631-X

Printed in Hong Kong

HALF TITLE
Henry Ford and his 1898 Quadricycle

TITLE PAGE
Bill Porter and his 1995 Buick Riviera

THE
AMERICAN AUTOMOBILE
A CENTENARY

Nick Georgano

with photographs by
Nicky Wright

SMITHMARK

TABLE OF CONTENTS

TABLE OF CONTENTS

1929 PACKARD CUSTOM 645 DIETRICH
OWNER: DUKE DAVENPORT (PHOTO NICKY WRIGHT)

Of all twentieth-century artifacts none is more quintessentially American than the automobile. Germany may have been the birthplace of the automobile and France its cradle, but it was in America that the car first became a part of the lives of ordinary people, and an important contributor to the economy. Although overtaken in recent years by Japan, for eight decades the United States led the world in auto manufacture, passing France in 1906 with an output of 33,200 passenger cars. Automobiles of American manufacture or design have been sold in every country of the world, even in those with opposing political ideologies. The Soviet tractor, car, and truck industry could not have come into existence without the help of Ford; even the architect of the vast Gorki plant was a Ford man, Albert Kahn. The first Chinese trucks of the 1930s used American-made components, while the Jeep Cherokee-based Beijing BJ was China's second largest production car in 1990. The auto industries of Australia, South Africa, and most Latin American countries were founded on American designs. Mass-production was brought to Europe by Ford and, later, General Motors. In 1919 two-fifths of all the motor vehicles on British roads were Fords, made in the company's Manchester plant.

What is more, almost all the associated aspects of an auto-centered world which we now take for granted originated in the United States — electric traffic lights, parking meters, multilane highways, multistory car parks, and motels, as well as some almost exclusively American ideas such as drive-in movies, restaurants, and banks. It is a cliché to say that the automobile revolutionized the way of life of millions of Americans, but today we often forget just how drastic that revolution was. Take vacations, for instance. Up to the third decade of this century, most working-class families in cities and farming communities never dreamed of taking a vacation. Ownership of an automobile, which became widespread between 1920 and 1930, enabled them to takes short trips away from home, even if only for a weekend. The lure of the big outdoors took Americans by storm; cooking and washing far from modern conveniences became a welcome challenge, while a bed was often no more than a plank propped between two running boards. Hardship was, if anything, an attraction: "We cheerfully endure wet, cold, mosquitoes, blackflies and sleepless nights just to touch naked reality once more," said one of Henry Ford's traveling companions.

It has been estimated that the inhabitants of North America collectively spend 62,000 years a week in their cars. It has also been said that 20 percent of Americans are conceived in automobiles. A few are also born in them, and alas many die in them. Some individualists even choose to be buried in them. And greater mobility has improved the breed — inbreeding in country districts ended once cars became widespread. "The farmer's boy found that he could court the lady of his choice even if she lived fifty miles away. He could select his mate from the whole wide world" (*Middletown: a Study in Contemporary American Culture*, 1929).

The part played by the auto industry in the American economy is no less striking. More than 2.5 million U.S. citizens earn their living from manufacturing, selling, or repairing motor vehicles, or ministering to them with gasoline and other fuels. Thousands of others are involved in the building and maintenance of the country's highways. In fact the economic health of the nation is closely tied to the success or failure of the industry centered on Detroit. A close watch is kept on the Goodyear display on the road from the airport into Detroit which registers each time a car is completed. In a good year it clicks down every second of every working day.

To squeeze 100 years of history, some 4,000 makes of automobile, and an output of about 1.757 billion units into 288 pages has inevitably meant compression and summary, but I have tried to achieve a balance between the technical, social, and personal factors that have created the American automobile in all its variety. All the significant models have been included, as well as many that were interesting.

Detailed credits are given elsewhere, but I would like to pay tribute to the magnificent photography of my friend Nicky Wright, without whom this book would never have existed.

Nick Georgano, 1992

1900 MOBILE STEAMER ▼

OWNERS: MARK AND TOOTSIE ACCOMAZZO (PHOTO NICKY WRIGHT)

CHAPTER ONE

PRECURSORS AND PIONEERS

1805 – 1900

"It ran no faster than an old man could walk . . . but it did run."

Charles Duryea, 1893

IT WAS REPORTED IN 1803 that there were no more than six steam engines in America, while Britain boasted several hundred — the Industrial Revolution came late. The United States was still largely a country of farmers and merchants; manufactured goods were imported or made in small home-based workshops, and for long-distance travel rivers were much more suitable than roads. It was not an encouraging climate for inventing motor vehicles of any kind, yet Nathan Read of Warren, Massachusetts, produced drawings for a steam carriage as early as 1790, and actually gained an audience with George Washington to expound his ideas. Fifteen years later a self-propelled vehicle actually ran on the streets of Philadelphia.

Oliver Evans (1755–1819) was probably America's leading engineer in the eighteenth century, author of the definitive work on milling technology, *The Young Millwright and Miller's Guide*, still the standard work in the 1860s. James Watt's interest in steam was sparked by a tea kettle, Evans' by a heated gun barrel with water in it. If one end of the gun barrel was sealed with tightly packed wadding and the other end heated in a fire, after a while the wadding blew out as loudly as if

the barrel had been filled with gunpowder. Surely, the young Evans thought, here was a power that could be harnessed usefully. Although he later built stationary engines to grind plaster of paris and saw marble, his first thoughts were of steam-powered wagons and boats. In 1805 he realized his ambitions in a rather unusual way.

The Philadelphia Board of Health, impressed by several Evans engines working in the city, commissioned him to build a steam-powered dredger to remove silt from the docks on the Delaware River. For this Evans designed a new engine which used steam supplied at a pressure of 120 pounds per square inch in a cylinder of 5 inches bore and 19 inches stroke. This was mounted in flat-bottomed barge 30 feet long and 12 feet wide driven by a paddle wheel at the stern; the mud was to be brought up by a chain of buckets. The machine was built in Evans' yard at Market and Ninth Street, about half a mile from the Delaware and 1½ miles from the River Schuylkill where it was eventually launched. The fact that it went the long way round to reach water and that Evans christened it Orukter Amphibolos (Amphibious Digger) indicate that he intended it to travel on land, at least temporarily. Perhaps, since nobody had commissioned a road vehicle

from him, he saw this as the only way to achieve an ambition that had absorbed him for more than 30 years. He hoped that Orukter would demonstrate that the self-propelled carriage was a practical proposition.

For the journey from workshop to river Evans fitted a simple rope drive from the end of the crankshaft to the rear axle; the paddle wheel was not to be installed until Orukter entered the water. The wheels broke under the weight of the vehicle after a few yards, but the workmen volunteered to make a new set of wheels and axles in their own time. The machine left the works successfully on July 13, 1805, the first time a vehicle had moved under its own power on the streets of an American city.

Evans could not resist taking his creation to Centre Square (now the site of City Hall) where stood two enormous atmospheric beam engines, installed by the Englishman Benjamin Latrobe for pumping water. Like Watt, Latrobe was scornful of high-pressure steam and had made no secret of his contempt for Evans' theories, so it must have been sweet revenge for Evans to parade his comparatively small machine under his detractor's nose. And parade he did, for Orukter attracted so much attention from the crowd that it circled Centre Square for three days. Spectators who had the money were asked to contribute 25 cents, but the less affluent were not turned away (at the time, a workman's daily wage was around 90 cents). Half the receipts went to Evans and half to the workmen who had given their evenings free of charge.

After three days on display, Orukter clanked and rattled its way down Market Street to the Schuylkill, where it settled into the water. The rope drive to the wheels was disconnected, and when the tide had floated the barge from its undercarriage the paddle wheel was installed and Orukter began its maiden voyage, down the Schuylkill, up the Delaware to Dunks Ferry, New Jersey, and back to Philadelphia, a distance of nearly 45 miles. It could not begin its work until the dredging equipment had been fitted, and this caused endless problems. Three years later Orukter had still not done a day's work. The Board of Health tried to blame Evans, but he retaliated and eventually received in full his payment of $5,000, although the Board never had a satisfactory dredger. After all the excitement in Centre Square, it is a sad anticlimax to record Orukter's obituary in the minutes of the Board of Health for June 9, 1809: "The Committee appointed to superintend the sale of the Mud Machine reported that they had received twenty seven dollars for Pig Iron sold to James Ash June, and four dollars ten cents for bricks sold to Mr. Hamilton, both articles taken out of said Mud Machine."

Evans continued to make high-pressure stationary engines, selling licenses to other manufacturers. Although he never made another moving vehicle, he did not abandon his dreams. In 1812 he wrote: "The time will come when people will travel in stages moved by steam engines, from one city to another, almost as fast as birds fly.... A carriage will set out from Washington in the morning, the passengers will breakfast in Baltimore, dine in Philadelphia and sup in New York the same day." And so they did, eventually, but not until a century later.

▶ WISCONSIN'S FIRST STEAM CAR WAS "THE SPARK" OF 1871, DESIGNED BY A PROFESSOR OF PHYSICS, H.S. CARHART, AT THE SUGGESTION OF HIS BROTHER DR. J.W. CARHART. THE BOILER WAS MADE BY THE BUTTON FIRE ENGINE WORKS OF WATERFORD, NEW YORK; MUCH OF THE REST OF THE ENGINEERING WAS THE WORK OF RACINE'S J. I. CASE COMPANY. IT RAN SUCCESSFULLY, ALTHOUGH WITH MUCH NOISE, AND INSPIRED THE STATE OF WISCONSIN TO OFFER A $10,000 PRIZE SEVEN YEARS LATER.
STATE HISTORICAL SOCIETY OF WISCONSIN

THE STEAM PASSENGER CAR

On both sides of the Atlantic early experimenters were concerned with the utility of the road vehicle. The ancestor of them all, Nicolas Cugnot's *fardier* of 1770, was a gun tractor, Orukter was a dredger, and nearly all the British vehicles of the 1820s and 1830s were buses or stage coaches. In 1826 Thomas Blanchard of Springfield, Massachusetts, built an eight-seater steam carriage, and 14 years later the first self-propelled fire engine, by Hodge, ran on the streets of New York. Passenger cars for pleasure rather than commerce did not begin to appear until the next decade. The honor of being the first American to offer vehicles for sale belongs to New Yorker John Kenrick Fisher, who formed the American Steam Carriage Company. In 1853 the company advertised steamers with a promised speed of 15mph on good gravel roads at the then very high price of $2,000. Sadly, it seems, nobody bought.

Four years after Fisher's advertisements another New Yorker, Richard Dudgeon, built a steam passenger car, but this was destroyed by fire. He built a second machine in 1866 and this has survived to the present day. It looks like a small locomotive, with a bench seat on either side of the boiler. The engine consists of two single cylinders, each driving a rear wheel; these, like those at the front, are of solid red cedar wood, with iron tires.

▼ THE TWO COMPETITORS GREEN BAY AND OSHKOSH IN THE 1878 200-MILE RACE. THE GREEN BAY WAS THE FASTER BUT RAN INTO A CULVERT, GIVING THE PRIZE TO THE OSHKOSH WHICH AVERAGED 6mph. THIS DRAWING WAS MADE MANY YEARS AFTER THE EVENT AND MAY NOT BE AN ACCURATE REPRESENTATION OF THE VEHICLES.
STATE HISTORICAL SOCIETY OF WISCONSIN

▲ THE SECOND STEAM CAR BUILT BY RANSOM OLDS, THIS DATES FROM 1890. IT HAD A FLASH BOILER, LIQUID FUEL, AND AN OUTPUT OF 4hp. IT WAS SOLD TO A CLIENT IN INDIA, BUT HE NEVER TOOK DELIVERY AS IT WAS LOST AT SEA.
OLDSMOBILE HISTORY CENTER

Steering is by a centrally-pivoted front axle, which seems to have been a bugbear of the Dudgeon down the ages. No one but its builder could master it and even he once ran into a barber shop at Oyster Bay. When the Dudgeon was tried out in the 1950s, historian Phil Dumka reported that it seemed to need 50 turns from lock to lock, "slower than an oil tanker," and that driver Joe Knowles "...wore himself out correcting for the drift, then correcting for the correction." This was in a journey of less than 1 mile.

Dudgeon used his car for some time in New York City, for business journeys and for taking his family to church, but eventually the noise and smoke so scared the horses that the police ordered him off the city streets. He also got on the wrong side of Tammany Hall politicians, who retaliated in the way they thought would hurt Dudgeon most. He then took his car to his country home at Locust Valley, Long Island, where he continued his experiments. Presumably country horses were no more pleased with his machine than city ones, but at least there were fewer of them.

From the 1860s onward steam cars multiplied across the United States, although few achieved more than fleeting local fame. Despite their dedication, their inventors seldom received any financial reward and were frequently the despair of their families. Sometimes they despaired themselves. John Gore of Brattleboro, Vermont, weary of complaints from the neighbors and the restriction of having to have a boy walk in front of his car ringing a bell, one day inadvertently ran his machine into a ditch, climbed out, and said that as far as he was concerned the thing could stay there. He walked home and the engine was later removed for a local bakery.

Most of these pioneer cars were light steam buggies, although some were heavier wagons, such as that built in Quincy, Massachusetts, in 1861 by Louis Badger. Intended for hauling granite, it also carried the West Quincy Brass Band on occasion, although most local people thought it was no match for a good team of oxen. The most extraordinary invention was the Steam Man, patented in 1870 by Zadoc P. Dederick and Isaac Grass of Newark, New Jersey. This was a life-size figure of a man, complete with top hat, with a boiler inside his jacket and a two-cylinder engine behind his back which worked his legs by a very complex system of cranks. The ingenious inventors even gave their man two speeds forward and two in reverse. He would only function when attached to a cart or carriage. One might be forgiven for doubting that he ever functioned at all, but the famous gasoline car pioneer Charles E. Duryea said in later years that he definitely saw the Steam Man in action.

The most persistent builder of steam cars in America was Sylvester Hayward Roper of Roxbury, Massachusetts. His first vehicle was announced in *Scientific American* in 1863, but may well have been completed earlier. The front portion was a two-passenger horse buggy, behind which was a vertical boiler producing a pressure of up to 60 pounds per square inch (half that of Evans' boiler of nearly 60 years before) and a 2hp engine. Roper later sold the machine to a fairground promoter, the self-styled Professor W.W. Austen, who exhibited it under his own name at numerous fairs in New England and other East Coast states from 1865 to at least 1870, possibly later. With a claimed top speed of 30mph, it was a great draw at circuses, and was frequently matched against the fastest horse the neighborhood could offer. Roper subsequently built about ten other vehicles, including two steam motorcycles. The first of these, made in 1869, was a crude-looking velocipede with iron tires, but in 1894 he produced a very neat-looking machine with a tiny water tube boiler and a marine-type two-cylinder engine of 2 x 4 inches fitted into the frame of a standard Columbia bicycle, driving the rear wheel directly from the connecting rods. When turning at only 200rpm, this engine gave a theoretical top speed of 60mph. Whether the machine ever attained this is not known, but Roper was traveling pretty fast when he crashed his machine at Boston's Charles River Track and was instantly killed. This was in 1896, when he was aged over 60. Ironically, Austen had met his death at the same track two years earlier when he collided with another steamer, almost certainly the first two-car accident in American history.

Most of the early steamers originated from New England, but there were exceptions. Wisconsin's first self-propelled vehicle, built in 1871, was the idea of Racine resident Dr. J.W. Carhart, with design by his brother H.S. Carhart, a professor of physics at Northwestern University and Michigan State University. Construction was mainly by the J. I. Case Company, still famous for their agricultural equipment, and automobile builders from 1911 to 1927. Named "The Spark," the Carhart machine had a large vertical boiler behind the buggy-like seat and was very noisy. The doctor recalled in later years that no racing car of 1914 could exceed the decibels emitted by "The Spark," and that "...we usually had the street entirely to ourselves, for when they had seen it the citizens were unanimous in predicting that The Spark would blow up."

In 1878 the State of Wisconsin offered a prize of $10,000 for "a cheap and practical substitute for the use of horses and other animals on the highway and farm." The contestants had to complete a 200-mile journey, and although seven entered only two showed up at the start line in Green Bay. One was called, appropriately, the Green Bay, although built in the nearby community of Wequiock, and the other was the Oshkosh from the city of that name. Both were heavy vehicles, the Green Bay turning the scales at 14,255 pounds, about a third heavier than the Oshkosh. Both pulled trailers carrying fuel and water. The Green Bay was the faster, but its

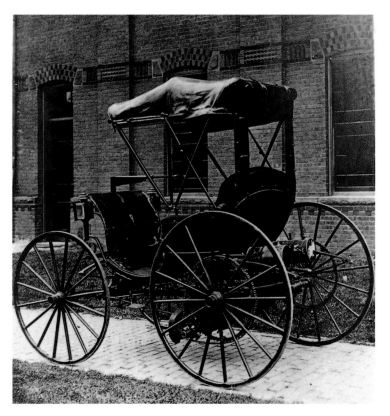

driver/builder E. P. Cowles ran it into a culvert and had to stop for repairs, so, in true hare and tortoise fashion, the Oshkosh plodded on to win at an average spread of just over 6mph. The State tried to deny the Oshkosh builders the prize on the grounds that a speed of 6mph did not make the machine practical, but after some argument its builders were awarded half the money.

Other pioneer steamers included those of Elijah Ware of Bayonne, New Jersey, who built several between 1861 and 1867, one of which he sold to a Canadian Roman Catholic priest living on Prince Edward Island. Priced at $300, this was almost certainly the first American-built vehicle to be exported. George Alexander Long of Northfield, Massachusetts, and Lucius Copeland of Phoenix, Arizona, and later Camden, New Jersey, both made steam-powered tricycles based on Columbia bicycles between 1880 and 1890, while mass-production pioneer Ransom Eli Olds made two steamers, with three and four wheels, in 1887 and 1890 respectively. The Philion steamer from Akron, Ohio, had an interesting background; Achille Philion was a French-born circus artist who married an Akron girl, Belle Melvin, and built his small four-wheeled car to publicize the circus in the parades that announced its arrival in town. Begun in 1887, it was not completed until 1892. By 1904 Philion was operating a movie theater and many years later his car featured in such movies as *The Magnificent Ambersons* and *Excuse My Dust.*

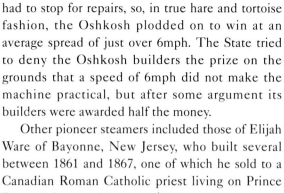

◄ THE FIRST DURYEA CAR, AS MODIFIED IN JANUARY 1894. SOON AFTERWARD FRANK DURYEA BEGAN WORK ON HIS SECOND CAR, AND THE PIONEER WAS PUT INTO STORAGE UNTIL 1920, WHEN IT WAS RESCUED BY INGLIS M. UPPERCU AND PRESENTED TO THE UNITED STATES NATIONAL MUSEUM.

MOTOR VEHICLE MANUFACTURERS' ASSOCIATION

THE ARRIVAL OF GASOLINE AND ELECTRIC POWER

The claim to the title of America's First Gasoline Car has been disputed many times, but the first to give rise to a car manufactured for sale was undoubtedly that of the brothers Frank and Charles Duryea.

The Duryea brothers were born in Illinois, Charles in 1861 and Frank in 1869, but were living in Springfield, Massachusetts, when they began work on their first car. In later years there was a lot of undignified controversy between the brothers and their families about who was really responsible for the car's design. It seems that the original idea was Charles', that the initial construction work was perhaps shared between the brothers, but that after Charles' departure to Peoria, Illinois, in September 1892 development work was solely that of Frank. Charles was perhaps disillusioned with the slow progress on the car, which would not run at all after nearly a year's work, and anyway he had a successful bicycle business in Peoria to look after. Frank continued, alone, with financial assistance from Erwin F. Markham; the car was running by February 1893 and in September was ready for road trials.

The body and frame of this first Duryea were those of a horse-drawn buggy purchased secondhand for $70, and the engine was a horizontal single-cylinder unit of 1,302cc which developed a theoretical 4hp. Features included low-tension ignition and a spray carburetor. Transmission was by friction drive. The car's first recorded run on public roads took place on September 21, 1893. Frank recorded in a letter to Charles: "...have tried it finally and thoroughly, and have quit trying until some changes are made." Presumably it did not run very well, and the next known trial did not take place until November 10, when the *Springfield Morning Union* recorded that the car ran up and down two streets, then "stopped short, refusing to move. Investigation revealed that the bearing had been worn smooth by the friction, and a little water sprinkled upon it put it in working condition again." Incidentally, although the news item referred to a "vehicle operated by gasoline," the headline read "An Electric Carriage Tried in Springfield." This was not untypical of the confusion spread by journalists of the day, who had

▲ ELWOOD P. HAYNES IN HIS FIRST CAR, COMPLETED IN 1894 (ALTHOUGH HE LATER CLAIMED IT WAS MADE A YEAR EARLIER).

MOTOR VEHICLE MANUFACTURERS' ASSOCIATION

▼ ANOTHER VIEW OF THE FIRST HAYNES, WITH ITS MAKER AT THE TILLER, NEXT TO A LARGE TOURING MODEL OF 1908.

MOTOR VEHICLE MANUFACTURERS' ASSOCIATION

little idea of even the basic workings of the automobile. Many years later Charles Duryea said of one of these early trials: "It ran no faster than an old man could walk, but it did run."

Further changes were made during the winter of 1893/4, but the following year Frank was working on a new design with spur gear drive to the rear axle. He sent drawings to Charles, who applied for a patent which was granted on June 11, 1895. Unfortunately Charles made no mention of his brother on the application, which bears the title C.E. Duryea, Road Vehicle. This poor treatment of his brother was continued when he described Frank merely as the "operator" of the car which won the *Chicago Times-Herald* race in November 1895. He circulated a photograph of himself at the wheel of the car in Springfield the previous summer, but at the time it was taken Charles had not yet learned to drive. His part in the great race was limited to a ride in a sleigh.

Self-publicists often fare better than dedicated engineers, but in the long run Frank earned more from the automobile than Charles did. Together they set up the Duryea Motor Wagon Company in Springfield, but built no more than 13 cars between 1895 and 1898, then went their separate ways. Charles then organized several companies which made cars of his own highly eccentric design; from 1902 to 1906 these had three-cylinder engines mounted at the rear behind the seat, and tiller steering, although by this time most other auto makers had gone over to wheel steering. Among the advantages Charles claimed for the tiller was that it only occupied one hand, so that the other could hold a passenger's waist, a good five-cent cigar, or, in inclement weather, an umbrella. He later made a solid-tired high-wheel buggy called the Buggyaut, and cyclecars with three or four wheels called the Gem. That was until 1916, after which he wrote technical books and articles until his death in September 1938. While it would not be true to say that he died a pauper, he was certainly not a rich man. Frank, on the other hand, designed a car which was taken up by the Stevens Arms & Tool Company as the Stevens-Duryea. The car grew increasingly large and expensive, and in 1915 the company was sold to Westinghouse, Frank's share of the proceeds being $0.5 million dollars, which enabled him to live comfortably for the rest

of his long life. He died in February 1967, seven months before his 98th birthday.

The Duryeas were not the only engineers who tinkered with road vehicles. In Anderson, Indiana, John William Lambert built a three-wheeled car in 1891, but it was destroyed in a fire before manufacture could begin. Two years later Elwood P. Haynes (1857–1925), field superintendent of the Indiana Natural Gas & Oil Company, purchased a single-cylinder two-stroke Sintz marine engine with the intention of using it in a road vehicle. He approached the Riverside Machine Works in Kokomo, Indiana, which was run by the Apperson brothers, Elmer and Edgar, asking them to build the car for him. This they did, and on July 4, 1894, the car was ready for testing. The makers were so afraid of ridicule that they had it towed by horses out of town for testing. The car had a spur gear transmission with three forward speeds but no reverse, a foot-operated throttle, and tiller steering. A few similar cars were turned out over the next four years, although Haynes kept his job with the gas and oil company, and the Appersons continued with general engineering work. In 1898 they formed the Haynes-Apperson Automobile Company and began turning out cars at the rate of one every two or three weeks. By this time Haynes had decided that he wanted to be a pioneer, so he not only discounted the part the Appersons had

played in his first car, but predated it by a year, claiming it was made in 1893, when it was only an idea in his head. The Lambert car was also a problem to him, having been made in the same state, so he visited William Lambert and asked him not to object if he called his vehicle "America's First Car." Lambert agreed, and although he subsequently made cars under his own name, he never referred to his three-wheeler of 1891. Haynes does not seem to have worried about the Duryea brothers, probably figuring that they were too busy arguing with each other to notice his claim.

There were other pioneers, some of whom pre-dated the Duryeas, such as Gottfried Schloemer and Frank Toepfer who built a car in Milwaukee in 1892. Like Haynes, they used a Sintz engine, and the car was tested, but they never made another. Even earlier was William Morrison of Des Moines, Iowa, who built a seven-passenger electric car in 1890. The electric buggy, as he called it, took part in a parade in September 1890, attracting nationwide publicity through magazines such as *Scientific American*. This prompted more than 16,000 inquiries, and it took Morrison and his partner Louis Schmidt all their time just to open the mail. They soon gave up reading the letters, simply opening them for the sake of the postage stamps enclosed, which filled two bushel baskets.

Morrison had no intention of becoming a car manufacturer, although he may have built a few more vehicles to test his batteries. He sold his buggy to Harold Sturges, who entered it in the 1895 *Chicago Times-Herald* race. As late as 1907 Morrison declared: "I wouldn't give ten cents for an automobile for my own use."

In Philadelphia Henry Morris and Pedro Salom also made electric cars which they called Electrobats. At first, each car carried its own name, in the manner of railroad locomotives or ships, Crawford Wagon, Fish Wagon, Skeleton Wagon, and so on, but they soon ran out of names and for 1896 their vehicles were simply called Electrobats. They had front drive, and many were used as taxicabs in Philadelphia and New York.

CHICAGO TIMES-HERALD RACE

In the early 1890s America's various automobile pioneers were working largely in ignorance of each other and well out of the gaze of the general public, but in 1895 most of the inventors just mentioned, plus many others, were brought together through America's first automobile contest. This was the idea of H.H. Kohlsaat, publisher of the *Chicago Times-Herald* newspaper, who had been inspired by the French contests from Paris to Rouen and to Bordeaux in 1894 and 1895 respectively. He thought that a similar event in America would act as a catalyst to arouse interest in the horseless carriage, and also bring useful publicity to his newspaper.

The event was announced on July 9, 1895, with the entry list closing on September 13. The race was to take place on November 2. A total of 89 entries was received, but 30 pleaded that they could not be ready in time, so the contest was postponed to Thanksgiving Day, November 28. Even then only 11 announced that they would actually start, and of these five failed to make it to the start line for various reasons. The actual starters were a Duryea, an Electrobat, the five-year-old Morrison electric entered by Harold Sturges, and three cars based more or less on the German Benz. Late November was far from an ideal time to hold a contest in Chicago, and the cars were hampered by slushy snow for most of the 54-mile journey from Jackson Park to Evanston and back. Only two

cars completed the course, the Duryea in first place, followed by a Mueller-Benz. Large crowds turned out to see the start, but their enthusiasm did not last for 11 hours of a chilly November day. As Gerald Rose, the British chronicler of early auto racing, wrote: "The Duryea...passed through the dark and snowy streets almost unobserved."

The prize money was $5,000, of which $2,000 went to the Duryeas, $1,500 to the H. Mueller Company, and $500 each to Macy's department store for its Benz and to Sturges, even though their cars did not complete the course. The rest of the money went to other entrants, even those who did not reach the start line, for various technical points, while Morris and Salom were awarded a gold medal for their Electrobat, for its "safety, ease of control, absence of noise, vibration, heat or odor, cleanliness and general excellence of design and workmanship."

The *Times-Herald* event may not have been a brilliant success, but it did attract a great deal of public attention to the new vehicles. It was certainly more useful to the cause than the next contest, the race organized in May 1896 by the

New York magazine *Cosmopolitan*, between the city and Irvington. Of the six starters, only the Duryea completed the course, its time of 7 hours 13 minutes over 60 miles being a great improvement over the 10 hours 23 minutes for the 54 miles of the Times-Herald race. The failure of its competitors, which included three other Duryeas, a Carlos Booth, and an Armstrong electric, prompted the following rhyme:

Six horseless carriages entered for a drive,
Wheel came off one, and then there were five,

Five horseless carriages, racing as before,
Chain slipped on one, and then there were four;

Four horseless carriages, speeding merrily,
Bicycle ran into one, and then there were three;

Three horseless carriages came to a hill,
Hill stayed right where it was, so the drivers had to get off and push, and that was why the time between City Hall and Irvington for the prize of 3,000 dols., offered by a magazine, was not what it

might have been if there had not been any hill there.

The poem appeared in *The Wheel*, a leading bicycle magazine, which explains the disparaging sentiments about automobiles. In fact the cyclists who set out to follow the cars reached Irvington ahead of them.

The Duryea distinguished itself later in the year when it was the first car to arrive at the conclusion of the famous London to Brighton run held in England in November. There were no more important races held in America for a number of years.

AN INDUSTRY GETS GOING

The year 1896 was of great significance in the history of the American automobile, not least because it was then that the French word "automobile" first came into common use in American publications. Before that, "horseless carriage" was the most common term, although motocycle was also used, and America's first trade journal, published by H.H. Kohlsaat, was entitled *The Motocycle (Automobile) Maker & Dealer*. A better-known and longer-lived journal, *The Horseless Age*, appeared a month later, in November 1895, and was published until May 1918.

The year 1896 was also the first in which more than one car was made from the same design; the Duryeas turned out 13 examples of what must be called America's first production car, and the first known purchaser was George H. Morill Jr. of Norwood, Massachusetts. It is not known if any other car makers actually sold cars in 1896, but several noteworthy experimenters built their first vehicles. The first to be made in the motor capital, Detroit, was the work of Charles Brady King (1868–1957), who had made his engine in 1894, and hoped to have a car ready for the *Times-Herald* race. The engine was unusual in having four cylinders,

▶ THE DURYEA FACTORY AT SPRINGFIELD, FROM WHICH 13 CARS EMERGED DURING 1896, MAKING IT THE FIRST MOTOR VEHICLE MANUFACTURING PLANT IN THE UNITED STATES.

MOTOR VEHICLE MANUFACTURERS' ASSOCIATION

when most of his rivals had not ventured beyond one, or at most two. Unable to compete in the Chicago contest, King contented himself with riding as an official umpire on the Mueller-Benz (and driving it for the final hour), but in March 1896 his car was ready and made its first trials on the city's streets. Following in hot pursuit on a bicycle was a young electrical engineer named Henry Ford.

Charles King, in fact, played an important part in the building of the first Ford car, for he obtained some of its components, such as the chain for transmitting power to the rear wheels. Ford, like all the other builders of his day, had no ready-made components to work with. The cylinders for his engine came from a length of scrap pipe from a

DAIMLER MOTOR CO., - Steinway, Long Island City, N. Y

Duryea Motor Wagon Company,

SPRINGFIELD, MASS

MANUFACTURERS OF

Motor Wagons, Motors, and

Automobile Vehicles of all kinds

"1897" MODEL.

▲ ONE OF THE FIRST AUTOMOBILE ADVERTISEMENTS IN AMERICA, PROMOTING THE 1897 DURYEA. FROM THE PRINTING OF THE DATE IT LOOKS AS IF THIS AD ORIGINALLY APPEARED THE PREVIOUS YEAR, AND WAS MADE TO LAST A FURTHER SEASON BY CHANGING THE 6 TO A 7. THE DAIMLER MOTOR COMPANY, U.S. BRANCH OF THE GERMAN FIRM THAT LATER MADE THE MERCEDES, WAS PRESUMABLY THE DURYEA AGENT FOR THE NEW YORK AREA.

MOTOR VEHICLE MANUFACTURERS' ASSOCIATION

DURYEA MOTOR WAGON CO. FACTORY AT SPRINGFIELD, MASS. MAY 1896

steam engine, cut in half and bored out to the required diameter; the flywheel came from an old lathe; the wheels and seat came from bicycles; and the "horn" was a domestic doorbell screwed to the front. Because of its cycle ancestry, Ford's first car was lighter than those of most of his contemporaries, weighing just over 500 pounds compared with 1,300 for King's, and 700 for the Duryeas'. It had a top speed of 20mph, compared with 5mph for the King. Ford had his car ready on June 4, 1896, but in his enthusiasm to get it finished had failed to consider how it was to get out of his tiny workshop. Finding the door too narrow, he demolished the frame with a pickax, and after removing some bricks was able to manhandle his little machine into Bagley Avenue. It ran around

Detroit for a while (at 2:00 A.M.) and only broke down once, outside the Cadillac Hotel on Washington Boulevard.

Soon Ford felt able to venture outside the city limits, to visit the family farm at Dearborn. Here he ran into the greatest threat to all auto pioneers, the atrocious state of country roads. His particular problem was that the roads were deeply rutted, and as the track of his car was smaller than that of ordinary wagons he was forced to drive with one side of the car in the ruts and the other several inches higher, with the car sharply tilted. This was hardly helpful to the primitive mechanism, let alone the comfort of the driver, his wife, or their three-year-old son Edsel. It has always seemed most unfair that the pioneer cars, which needed

good roads more than any of their successors, had to cope with the worst possible conditions.

By the end of 1896 Ford had sold his first car, or Quadricycle as he called it, for $200, and used the proceeds to help build his second. For this he was also financed by Detroit's Mayor William C. Maybury, and the resulting machine, which was ready by the end of 1897, was a much more sophisticated vehicle than the Quadricycle. The chain drive was now to the center of the rear axle rather than to the offside, and there was proper buggy-type seating (although the modified Quadricycle had this as well). There were stylish mudguards over front and rear wheels, and two headlights. With backing from Maybury and other wealthy Detroiters, the Detroit Automobile Company was organized in July 1899, but although a few more prototypes emerged, no production cars were ever made by the company. Many problems were encountered with inexperienced workmen and inferior quality of components, while one of the partners told a reporter, with delightful candor: "You would be surprised at the amount of detail about an automobile." There was also Ford's grasshopper mind, forever seeking new solutions and jumping to a new model before the one in hand had been perfected. The Detroit Automobile Company was wound up in January 1901, and it was to be another two years before Ford cars were offered in the marketplace.

Meanwhile, in Cleveland, Ohio, a Scottish-born bicycle maker called Alexander Winton (1860–1932) had been enthused by reports of the *Times-Herald* race, even though he did not witness it. He decided that cars should combat the falling sales of two-wheelers, and by October 1896 he announced his first automobile in *The Horseless Age*. It was curious looking, with a short, stubby appearance and a single-cylinder engine mounted between the front and rear seats. The latter faced backwards, an arrangement known in France as the dos-à-dos (back-to-back). The steering tiller also incorporated the speed control, and ahead of it was a dashboard which housed the gas tank. Warning was given by a pedal-operated bell. Weight was over 1,000 pounds, which must have hampered performance, for Winton decided that his next car would be lighter and capable of 30mph.

The actual speed of the second Winton is not

▼ HENRY FORD'S FIRST CAR OF 1896, IN A RECONSTRUCTION OF HIS WORKSHOP AT THE HENRY FORD MUSEUM. WHEN THE CAR WAS COMPLETED, IN JUNE 1896, FORD HAD TO DEMOLISH THE DOORFRAME TO GET IT OUT.

FORD MOTOR COMPANY

known, but from its appearance it does not seem much lighter. It was longer and wider, accommodating three people abreast on both seats, which were still arranged back-to-back. The Winton Motor Carriage Company was incorporated in March 1897, and four cars were completed that year. Winton's chief engineer Leo Melanowski invited Henry Ford for an interview, but Winton was not impressed by the young man from Detroit and did not hire him. By 1898 the company was in production with a single-cylinder two-passenger motor buggy, and the first sale was recorded in March. The purchaser was not a local man, but a 70-year-old Pennsylvania mining engineer who had seen an advertisement for the Winton carriage. He traveled by train to Cleveland and, on being satisfied with his inspection of the car, handed over $1,000 cash. Before the end of the year 22 buggies had been sold, together with eight delivery wagons. One of the buyers was James Ward Packard, whose purchase had far-reaching consequences.

In 1899 more than 100 cars were delivered, which made Alexander Winton by far the largest maker of gasoline vehicles in the United States. The earliest known auto dealership was opened in 1898 by H.W. Koller of Reading, Pennsylvania, to sell Wintons. In fact, after the Duryea brothers ended production at Springfield in 1898 and went their separate ways, there were very few gasoline cars made anywhere until the turn of the century. With steam and electric cars, though, it was a different story.

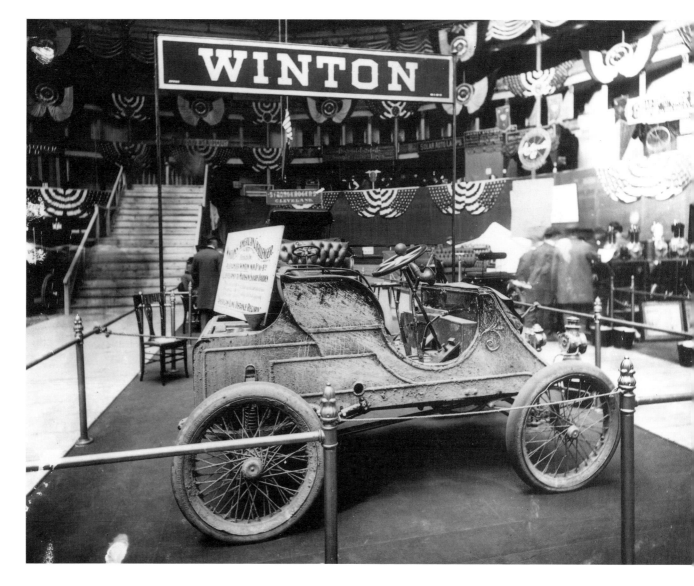

relation to the better known Stanley twins who were just starting up steam car manufacture in nearby Watertown).

The Stanleys, Francis E. and Freelan O., were identical twins born in 1849. They ran a photographic equipment business, first in Lewiston, Maine, and then at Watertown, although they lived in Newton where Frank F. Stanley was making his steam cars. This has caused much confusion ever since, even though Frank F. Stanley's cars were sold under the name McKay. While in Lewiston, they saw a steamer made by Edwin Field, which inspired them to build one of their own. This was in 1888, and it seems that it was a complete failure. Eight years later they saw George Whitney's steam car in Boston and this inspired them to try again.

The light steamer they built was typical of the breed, with a vertical two-cylinder engine and single chain drive. It was completed in 1897, and

NEW ENGLAND STEAMERS

The steam car played a much larger part in the United States than it ever did in Europe, and nearly all the successful makes came from New England. They were totally different from vehicles such as the Oshkosh and Green Bay, which weighed up to 14,000 pounds and used coal fuel (the turn-of-the-century steamers weighed 600–1,000 pounds and were kerosene-fueled). One of the first was built by George Eli Whitney (1862–1963; — no, this isn't a misprint, he really did live to 101), grand nephew of the Eli Whitney who invented the cotton gin. He completed his first car in October 1896, and in the spring of the following year set up the Whitney Motor Wagon Company in Boston. Like so many of the pioneers, Whitney was a tinkerer rather than a dedicated manufacturer; he had built seven cars by the summer of 1898, but they were all different, most with vertical engines, although at least one was horizontal. His designs were subsequently made by Frank F. Stanley of Newton, Massachusetts (no

▲ 1900 MOBILE STEAMER

THE MOBILE, LIKE THE LOCOMOBILE, WAS DEVELOPED FROM THE ORIGINAL STANLEY DESIGN. A VERTICAL TWO-CYLINDER ENGINE DROVE THE REAR AXLE BY SINGLE CHAIN, AND THE FIRE-TUBE BOILER WORKED AT A PRESSURE OF 180 POUNDS/SQUARE INCH. THE WATER TANK HELD 22.5 GALLONS, YET HAD TO BE REFILLED EVERY 20 MILES OR SO. FOR THE MOBILE, MADE IN A FACTORY AT TARRYTOWN, NEW YORK, AND DESIGNED BY THE CELEBRATED ARCHITECT STANFORD WHITE, 1900 WAS THE FIRST YEAR. THIS DOS-À-DOS COST $1,100, BUT THE FRINGED SURREY TOP WAS EXTRA.

OWNERS: MARK AND TOOTSIE ACCOMAZZO (PHOTO NICKY WRIGHT)

by the spring of 1898 they had completed two more, one of which was sold for $600. Later in the year they took one to Boston's Charles River Park, where it won the hill-climbing contest. This involved ascending an 80-foot incline; a Whitney was defeated at 76 feet 8 inches, but the Stanley sailed to the top with little apparent effort. This feat amazed the crowd and resulted in orders for 200 of the little cars within two weeks. It was no easy matter for men whose expertise lay in photographic plates to start making cars in such numbers. Nevertheless, they set about obtaining components for an initial run of 100. In early 1899, before these orders were completed, they were visited by John Brisben Walker (1847–1931), the publisher of *Cosmopolitan* magazine which had sponsored the calamitous New York to Irvington race three years before. He offered to buy the twins out, but they were reluctant to sell because they felt they were overcoming the headaches involved

in quantity production. They decided to ask a ridiculously high price — $250,000 — but to their surprise Walker accepted. Since their investment in the business had been around $20,000, they were not unnaturally delighted, and the sale went through.

To help him raise the purchase price (equivalent to more than $5 million today) Walker secured the backing of asphalt millionaire Amzi Lorenzo Barber (1843–1909). They formed a new company called the Locomobile Company of America in June 1899, and began to make cars of Stanley type in the Watertown factory. Before long the partners quarreled, and Walker left to make a similar design which he called the Mobile at Tarrytown, N.Y. Barber continued with the Locomobile at Watertown, but in 1900 he bought a much larger factory at Bridgeport, Connecticut. This enabled production to rise from 400 in 1899 to 1,500 in 1901 and 2,750 in 1902, when Locomobile

was the largest automobile producer in the country. Mobile was a much smaller operation, and when production ceased at the end of 1903 not more than 600 had been made. Coincidentally, Locomobile also ended steamer production in 1903, going on thenceforth to make gasoline cars, but their total was more than 5,000.

As one would expect, the design of the Stanley/Locomobile/Mobile was very similar. It consisted of a fire-tube boiler working at 180 pounds of pressure per square inch which fed a vertical two-cylinder engine mounted in the center of the tubular frame. Behind the boiler was a 22.5-gallon water tank which occupied the full width of the car, yet only gave a range of about 20 miles before a refill was necessary. Drive was by a single chain from the crankshaft to the center of the rear axle. One of the advantages of the steam engine was that it delivered full power at any speed, so a gearbox was unnecessary. Bodies were mostly

◄ THE LOCOMOBILE WAS MADE TO A STANLEY DESIGN, AND WAS THEREFORE VERY SIMILAR TO THE MOBILE IN SPECIFICATION — AND IN ITS THIRST. BY CONTRAST THE LAST STEAM CARS FROM DOBLE WOULD RUN 1,500 MILES ON A 24-GALLON TANKFUL. ALTHOUGH NOT VERY STRONG, THE LITTLE LOCOMOBILES WERE GOOD VALUE AT $600 IN 1898, AND BY MAY 1902 MORE THAN 4,000 HAD BEEN SOLD. AMONG OVERSEAS CUSTOMERS WAS THE BRITISH WRITER RUDYARD KIPLING.

OWNER: NATIONAL AUTOMOBILE MUSEUM, RENO, NEVADA

(PHOTO NICKY WRIGHT)

▲ A SNOWY MANHATTAN STREET, c.1908, WITH A COLUMBIA ELECTRIC CAB ALONGSIDE A CORBIN GASOLINE
TOURING CAR. THIS DESIGN OF CAB DATED BACK TO THE ELECTROBAT MADE BY MORRIS & SALOM IN 1896;
THEY WERE MANUFACTURED IN THIS REAR-WHEEL-DRIVE FORM FROM 1899 TO 1902.

proportion of steamers from New England must have been around 80 percent. The one prominent make from outside the area was the White from Cleveland, Ohio. This was the product of a sewing machine manufacturer, and although the first model of 1900 looked not unlike a Stanley or Locomobile, it was more sophisticated, with a flash boiler which generated steam much more quickly. A condenser to recycle exhaust steam was added in 1902, and the following year the White took on the appearance of a gasoline car, with its condenser mounted up front and resembling a radiator.

THE SILENT AND ODORLESS ELECTRIC

In many ways battery electric power was the best way to drive an automobile at the turn of the century. It had none of the noise, vibration, or smell of the gasoline car, nor did it need a gearbox whose operation was one of the major challenges to the driver. Admittedly the steamer was also free of gear shifting, but it took up to 45 minutes to start it on a cold morning. No wonder that in 1899 and 1900 electrics outsold all other types of car; the Columbia was the production leader of all U.S. makes.

The history of the Columbia was a complex one, and was tied in with the ambitions of Colonel Albert Augustus Pope (1843–1909), whose aim was to dominate the vehicle industry as Billy Durant was to try to do later. A Civil War veteran, he began bicycle manufacture in 1877, and by 1899 had formed the American Bicycle Company, a trust controlling some 45 manufacturers. He had experimented with a gas-powered tricycle in 1894, but, finding it unsatisfactory, he decided that the future lay with electric vehicles. Unlike Olds and Ford, Pope was a businessman rather than an engineer and had his vehicles built for him by employees. His first electric came in 1896 and by October of that year he began production of a series of light two-seater runabouts which he sold under the name Columbia, also used for his bicycles. For his chief engineer he hired Hiram Percy Maxim, son of the inventor of the machine gun, and in 1898 Maxim came up with a whole range of designs from the runabout to a heavy enclosed brougham. Electric power was selected "for convenience in charging from the ordinary

simple open two-passenger buggy types, although four-passenger versions were offered, and Mobile made a wide range of more expensive types up to a nine-passenger enclosed limousine at $3,000. A two-passenger Locomobile runabout sold for only $750.

The success of the Locomobile led to many imitators, most of whom followed the same basic design. Most manufacturers assembled their cars from bought-out components, which explains the general uniformity. Variations, which on the whole did not sell well, included the shaft-driven Century from Syracuse, N.Y., and the Cotta from Lanark, Illinois, which featured chain drive to all four wheels and four-wheel steering. Variations in

engine design included the V-twin Crouch from New Brighton, Pennsylvania, the three-cylinder shaft-driven Eclipse from Boston, and four cylinders in the Henrietta from New York and the Hood Electronic Safety Steam Vehicle from Danvers, Massachusetts. The latter had magnetic inlet valves operated by three batteries guaranteed for six months. The company itself lasted barely twelve months.

Of the 100 or so makes of American steam car, most of which flourished between 1898 and 1905, 40 were originated in the states of Massachusetts, New Hampshire, New York, and Maine, but as these included nearly all the successful makes, the

worked for Morris & Salom) and Woods in Chicago, but at the turn of the century they were insignificant compared with Columbia.

For obvious reasons, the popularity of electric vehicles was limited to cities, and in the early days many were hired from cab companies rather than bought outright. Wealthy New Yorkers such as Frank Gould and Cornelius Vanderbilt had a cab constantly on call, for which they paid $180 per month. Doctors were also keen users of electric cabs, and one found an ingenious use for his. Wanting to X-ray a broken arm at the patient's home, he was unable to do so because the house was not supplied with electricity. He simply linked up his machine with the battery in his cab and quickly located the fracture.

type of electric light station circuits common to all towns of any size." The range of a middle-sized four-seater surrey was 35 miles between charges, at a speed of 12mph.

Meanwhile two other manufacturers were getting into the electric car act. The Electric Vehicle Company of Elizabethport, New Jersey, headed by Isaac L. Rice, acquired the Electrobat rights from Morris & Salom, and expanded manufacture of the front-drive taxicabs, and New York electrical engineer A.L. Riker began to make a range of vehicles from a two-passenger runabout to heavy trucks. In 1899 financier William Collins Whitney bought out the Electric Vehicle Company with the idea of making 2,000 taxicabs for use in America's major cities. He merged his activities

with Pope's, the idea being that Electric Vehicle would make the cabs and Pope's Columbia Automobile Company the passenger cars, both gasoline and electric. In 1901 the Columbia name was dropped for the company, although cars and cabs continued to be called Columbias. Riker had been working on a gasoline car, but Pope was not interested in this, so Riker offered it to Locomobile, it became the basis of the first gas car from that company and soon ousted the steamers. In 1900 output of electric passenger cars totaled about 1,500, double the number of Locomobile steamers, and to this figure should be added a quantity of cabs and trucks. There were a few other electric car makers, such as Baker in Cleveland (whose founder Walter Baker had

1913 RAMBLER TOURING ▼
OWNER: DAN OBERLE (PHOTO NICKY WRIGHT)

CHAPTER TWO

THE ROAD TO
MASS PRODUCTION

1900 – 1920

"The way to make automobiles is to make one automobile like another,
to make them all alike, to make them come through the factory all alike,
just as one pin is like another pin when it comes from the pin factory."

Henry Ford, 1903

1903 AUTOCAR TONNEAU ▲▼

THE AUTOCAR COMPANY GREW OUT OF A PITTSBURGH, PENNSYLVANIA, FIRM THAT MADE TRICYCLES AND
QUADRICYCLES. IN 1901, FOUNDER LEWIS CLARK SET UP AN AUTOMOBILE FACTORY AT ARDMORE, PENNSYLVANIA,
AND BY 1903 WAS MAKING THE 10hp TWO-CYLINDER CAR SEEN HERE.
THE ONLY BODY STYLE WAS THIS REAR-ENTRANCE TONNEAU, SOON TO GIVE WAY TO THE SIDE-ENTRANCE TONNEAU,
OR TOURING CAR, ONCE WHEELBASES WERE LONG ENOUGH. THE GILLED TUBE RADIATOR MOUNTED BELOW THE HOOD
WAS TYPICAL OF THE PERIOD.

OWNER: AUBURN-CORD-DUESENBERG MUSEUM (PHOTO NICKY WRIGHT)

I N JULY 1899 *McCLURE'S Magazine* published an article extolling the progress that the automobile had made in America over the preceding twelve months. A hundred electric cabs were plying New York, with 200 more on order, a motor ambulance was in operation in Chicago, at least two cities were using self-propelled fire engines, and the Santa Fe railroad had ordered a number of horseless coaches for an Arizona mountain route.

These and other examples were undoubtedly true, but nonetheless even at the turn of the century the impact of the automobile was very small. In 1900 production of passenger automobiles was 4,192, and the total number registered was about 8,000. Manufacture was confined largely to the East Coast, with a few exceptions such as White and Winton in Cleveland, Ohio. Outside the big cities many Americans had never seen a self-propelled vehicle, and the horse and mule reigned supreme. In 1900 it was estimated that the horse population of America numbered some 30 million. There would not be that number of motor vehicles until 1937. To displace the horse from the loyalty of rural Americans was not easy, for the animal was a companion, almost a member of the family, and only the very poorest citizens were without one. The maintenance of horses was easily understood, they reproduced themselves, and they could find their way home if their owner were too tired or intoxicated to do so. Rural communities tended to side with the horse against the automobile, requiring drivers to pull into the side of the road or at least stop and switch off their engine at the approach of a horse.

In order to calm the horse's fears one motorist,

Uriah Smith of Battle Creek, Michigan, made a sculpted, life-size horse's head which he mounted on the dashboard of his car. "It will have all the appearance of a horse and carriage," he wrote to *The Horseless Age* in 1899, "and hence raise no fears in any skittish animal, for the live horse would be thinking of another horse, and before he could discover his error and see that he had been fooled, the strange carriage would be passed, and then it would be too late to grow frantic and fractious." Smith recommended that the horse's head be made hollow, so that it could be used as a gasoline tank.

Less considerate motorists than Mr. Smith aroused great anger among farmers, who sometimes spread tacks and broken glass on the roads or ran strands of rope or barbed wire across them, especially effective at twilight. Automobiles were frequently stoned, and not only by children, while horse whips were used on occasion. To be fair, these incidents were as often as not provoked by the drivers, who killed chickens and dogs with little thought for their owners. An investigator in Iowa counted on one journey (unfortunately we do not know how long it was) 225 dead animals, representing 29 wild and domestic species.

Against this background, the spread of the automobile across America in the first two decades of this century was a remarkable phenomenon. It began in the cities, not only because paved streets were kinder to primitive and low-powered vehicles, but also because the horse was less favored there. In the 1890s New York and Brooklyn had a horse population of some 175,000, and the accumulations of dung posed a serious health problem. Overworked and underfed horses often died in harness and were left by the curbside for several days to add to the pollution.

F IRST STEPS TOWARD MASS PRODUCTION

No industry springs into life without antecedents. The auto industry in America could not have grown in the way that it did without the existence of two established, large-scale businesses, bicycles and carriages. They not only provided the technology on which many early autos were based, but also trained men who subsequently made their name with cars. Colonel Pope's car empire was built on bicycle money, and other well-known names who began their working life with cycles included Alexander Winton, the Duryeas, Thomas B. Jeffery, George N. Pierce, and Erwin R. Thomas. William S. Knudsen, head of General Motors from 1937 to 1940, was a bicycle mechanic, while John N. Willys was a bicycle salesmen.

The best-known name from the carriage and wagon world belonged to the Studebaker brothers, whose business was founded in 1852. By the 1890s it was the largest vehicle builder in the world, with annual sales of over $2 million. Overland, later taken over by Willys, originated as a branch of an Indianapolis buggy maker, while Billy Durant and J. Dallas Dort, both famous for their cars in the 1920s, were partners in a successful carriage business from 1885 to the turn of the century. Other companies that grew from carriage and buggy making included Gardner and Moon.

There were, of course, other apprenticeships that led to auto making. Henry Ford and James Packard were electrical engineers, David Buick was in the plumbing business, International Harvester was well-known in the agricultural equipment field, while the first man to make cars in serious quantities was Ransom Olds, whose father ran a machine shop in Lansing, Michigan. Olds was also a graduate of Lansing Business University, so had the valuable combination of commercial acumen and mechanical skills.

Ransom Eli Olds (1864–1950) was born in Geneva, Ohio, the son of a locksmith of English extraction, Pliny F. Olds. After a spell of farming near Cleveland, the family moved in 1880 to Lansing where Pliny became more ambitious, announcing his new company as practical machinists, manufacturers of steam yachts, steam engines, brass and iron castings. Ransom joined the firm in 1883 and soon bought out his brother's share, becoming a fully fledged partner when he was 21, in 1885. Two years later he built his first vehicle and, given the nature of the family business, it is not surprising that it was a steamer. A three-wheeler with tiller-steered front wheel and seating for two passengers, it does not seem to have been a great success. It was followed by a four-wheeler which was sold to India, some say to a circus, others to a maharajah. The destination really doesn't really matter as the vehicle was lost in

shipwreck. Olds cannot have had much confidence in it, for he said that as a result of the shipwreck "the reputation of the company was saved."

During the 1890s Olds experimented with electric cars before deciding that internal combustion was the motive power of the future. Pliny had retired in 1894, and his son reorganized the firm as the Olds Gas Engine Works. While the money was being brought in from stationary gasoline engines, Ransom Olds tinkered with automobiles. His first was running toward the end of 1896, and in August 1897 he set up a separate company, the Olds Motor Vehicle Company Capitalization was $50,000, with support from Lansing businessmen, but two years later, during which time he had built only five or six cars, Olds set up a new company in Detroit, since he thought that Lansing's population of 2,000 was too small to support a new industry such as he had in mind. In May 1899 the Olds Motor Works came into existence, with nominal capitalization of $350,000, nearly all the money being provided by Samuel L. Smith, a copper and lumber millionaire who had already invested heavily in the Olds Gas Engine

▲ PART OF THE EXTENSIVE OLDSMOBILE WORKS IN 1904, WITH ENGINES AND FRAMES
ALREADY ASSEMBLED. ENGINES CAME FROM LELAND & FAULCONER AT THIS TIME.

OLDSMOBILE HISTORY CENTER, MIRCO DE CET COLLECTION

▲ ONE OF MANY STUNTS PERFORMED TO SHOW THE VERSATILITY
OF THE CURVED DASH WAS CLIMBING THE STEPS OF THE MICHIGAN
STATE CAPITOL.

OLDSMOBILE HISTORY CENTER, MIRCO DE CET COLLECTION

◄ ANOTHER PART OF THE OLDS PLANT AT
LANSING, MICHIGAN, SHOWING CURVED
DASH MODELS ALMOST COMPLETED. THIS
PHOTO WAS TAKEN IN 1905, WHEN OLDS
PRODUCED 6,500 VEHICLES, MORE THAN
ANY OTHER AUTO MAKER IN THE WORLD.

OLDSMOBILE HISTORY CENTER, MIRCO DE CET COLLECTION

Works which was kept entirely separate, just in case the auto business foundered. Olds' stake in the new company was limited to $400.

By the beginning of 1901 the new company had built no more than a dozen cars, and sold even fewer. Little information about them has survived, but they were probably not unlike the 1896/97 models, with 5hp single-cylinder engines slung below the high-built four-passenger carriage-like body, and final drive by double belts. However, a completely new model was in the planning stage when a disastrous fire struck the Detroit plant on March 9, 1901. There were several prototypes in the factory, but there was time to save only one, a light two-passenger runabout. It has been said that because this was the only car saved, Olds had no choice but to concentrate on it, and thus mere chance gave rise to America's first mass-produced automobile, the Curved Dash Olds. It is a good story, but research suggests that the company had decided on that model anyway, and that plans and patterns did survive the fire.

Whatever the story behind it, the Curved Dash Olds was an attractive little car, 98 inches long and weighing 700 pounds. It was powered by a 4½hp single-cylinder engine of 95.5 cubic inches displacement, mounted horizontally under the seat, with a two-speed planetary transmission and final drive by single chain. The front part of the body curved upwards to form the dash, hence the name, while the springs ran from front to rear and formed the side members of the frame. Olds set a price of $650, which remained unchanged through the car's seven-year life. This was a very reasonable figure when compared with competing models, of which there were not many. A Winton cost $1,500, and although it was larger it was still a single-cylinder two-passenger car. Even a Locomobile runabout cost $750, and it was not so simple to operate as the Olds. From the first year, Olds offered extras which included a rear-facing dos-à-dos seat for $25, mudguards for $10 a set, and a folding top which cost $50 in leather and $25 in rubber.

Because of the fire, Olds had to contract out many of his car's components, which gave a boost to several Detroit firms later to become famous in the auto industry. The engines were made for him by Leland & Faulconer (Henry Leland later built the first Cadillac), transmissions by the Dodge brothers, and radiators by the Briscoe brothers. By the end of 1901, Olds had sold 425 of his little runabouts; production jumped to 2,500 in 1902, 4,000 in 1903, 5,508 in 1904, and 6,500 in 1905. The last two years' figures included some larger cars, but the bulk of production was still devoted to the Curved Dash Runabout. Although the rebuilt Detroit factory was continued, Olds moved back to Lansing and operated a larger factory there as well.

This level of production put Olds well in the lead of American auto manufacturers. Once Locomobile gave up its light steamers it was no longer in the race, and indeed Olds overtook Locomobile before this, topping the charts in 1903. Oldsmobile was undisputed leader in 1904 and 1905 as well, but in 1906 sales fell drastically as the

1902 OLDSMOBILE CURVED DASH RUNABOUT ▼

THE CURVED DASH WAS AMERICA'S FIRST QUANTITY-BUILT CAR: MORE THAN 18,000 WERE MADE IN THE SEVEN YEARS 1901 TO 1907. THIS 1902 MODEL HAS WIRE WHEELS, ALTHOUGH WOOD-SPOKED ARTILLERY WHEELS WERE MORE COMMON BY THIS DATE. IN 1905 THE GUS EDWARDS POPULAR SONG, "IN MY MERRY OLDSMOBILE," GAVE THE COMPANY MUCH USEFUL PUBLICITY. THE CURVED DASH WAS MADE UNDER LICENSE IN SEVERAL FOREIGN COUNTRIES, INCLUDING CANADA (AS THE LEROY) AND GERMANY (AS THE POLYMOBIL).

OWNER: CRAWFORD COLLECTION OF THE WESTERN HISTORICAL SOCIETY (PHOTO NICKY WRIGHT)

▲ LINE-UP OF OLDSMOBILES OUTSIDE THEIR MINNEAPOLIS DEALERS, A.F. CHASE & COMPANY. LEFT TO RIGHT: 10hp TONNEAU, CURVED DASH DELIVERY WAGON, 10hp TONNEAU, CURVED DASH RUNABOUT, TONNEAU OF UNKNOWN MAKE. THE OLDS TONNEAU WAS INTRODUCED IN 1904. THE LARGE STATIONARY ENGINE IN THE SHOWROOM WINDOW IS ALSO PROBABLY OF OLDS MAKE.

OLDSMOBILE HISTORY CENTER,
MIRCO DE CET COLLECTION

1910 REO ▶
THE REO MOTOR CAR COMPANY
WAS FORMED WHEN RANSOM OLDS
PARTED FROM HIS COLLEAGUES
IN THE OLDS MOTOR WORKS. BY 1910,
WHEN THIS FIVE-PASSENGER TOURING
WAS MADE, REO WAS THE EIGHTH
LARGEST U.S. AUTO MANUFACTURER,
WITH 6,588 CARS DELIVERED.
OWNER: BOB BENNETT (PHOTO NICKY WRIGHT)

Curved Dash was dropped in favor of more costly cars. This was against Ransom Olds' wishes, but he had left the company at the end of 1904. He was outvoted by the Smith family, who of course owned nearly all the company stock. It is interesting to speculate what might have happened if he had remained in charge. Perhaps Ford would never have become the leading U.S. manufacturer? Instead, Olds found other backers to set him up in a new business which he called Reo Motor Car Company, making a car called the Reo. Similar in general conception to the Curved Dash, but with a small hood at the front, it cost $680 and consistently outsold Oldsmobiles for several years. It was made in Lansing, not far from the Oldsmobile's home. (Although the company name remained Olds Motor Works up to 1943, the cars were known as Oldsmobiles from the early days of the Curved Dash.)

Ransom Olds continued with his new company until 1936, although he went into semi-retirement in the mid-1920s, concentrating on rural subsistence living. He founded a combined agricultural/industrial colony in Florida called Oldsmar, which still exists today. He was also a pioneer in the manufacture of powered lawn mowers, an interest that continued until his death at the age of 86 in 1950.

THE IMPACT OF HENRY FORD

The make which displaced Oldsmobile in 1906 and was to remain at the top of the production league until 1927 was Ford. Credit is always given to the Model T as being the first mass-produced car, and certainly output did not reach massive proportions until the T era, but Ford was making substantial numbers of cars several years before the T's debut in 1908.

We last saw Henry Ford struggling with the Detroit Automobile Company, which was dissolved in January 1901 after hardly any cars had been built. He then turned to racing, with the express aim of beating the Frenchman Henri Fournier, who was achieving great speeds with his 60hp Mors and who was to set a flying mile record of 69.5mph in November 1901. Ford built a massive two-cylinder car with 540-cubic-inch displacement (surely the largest two-cylinder auto engine ever made

▲ THE MASSIVE ENGINE OF FORD'S 999 RACING CAR, EACH CYLINDER OF WHICH DISPLACED 288.83 CUBIC INCHES — THE SAME AS A FORD V8 OF THE 1960s. THE FOUR CYLINDERS WERE CAST IN ONE BLOCK — UNUSUAL FOR THE PERIOD — BUT THE VALVES WERE UNCOVERED, AND THE HUGE CRANKSHAFT WAS ALSO UNPROTECTED FROM THE MUD AND DIRT OF THE ROAD.

FORD MOTOR COMPANY

William Murphy, who had been among the supporters of the Detroit Automobile Company in 1899, but Murphy refused to allow the building of racing cars in company time. Ford said that he was not ready for production yet, so Murphy brought in Henry Leland as a production consultant. Ford was furious and left in March 1902, with $900 compensation and a promise from Murphy that he would not use the Ford name in connection with any car. Murphy was true to his word. The Leland-designed car which he put into production in 1903 was called the Cadillac.

Ford had quarreled with two partners in little over six months and had still earned no money from making or selling cars. Many observers might have forecast that he would fizzle out like countless contemporary tinkerers, warranting no more than a few lines in specialist encyclopedias. However, in 1902 he found a new supporter. In his days with the Edison Illuminating Company, one of his jobs had been to buy coal, and the best merchant to go to was Alexander Young

Malcomson, whose products were marketed as "Hotter Than Sunshine." The two men remained friends, and when Malcomson became bitten by the auto bug he bought a Winton. Hearing that young Ford had beaten Winton, he thought a Ford car might be just what he wanted, and in August 1902 he agreed to provide funds for the manufacture of automobiles. Knowing Ford's doubtful reputation, he kept his involvement quiet at first, but in November agreed to the formation of the Ford & Malcomson Company This became the Ford Motor Company on June 16, 1903, and so it

▼ HENRY FORD (LEFT) ON HIS 999 RACER DURING AN EXHIBITION RUN AT THE GROSSE POINTE HORSE-RACING TRACK IN 1903. ALONGSIDE HIM IS HARRY HARKNESS ON A SIMPLEX. BY THIS DATE FORD HAD ALREADY GIVEN UP RACING, HAVING DECLARED "ONCE IS ENOUGH" AFTER BEATING ALEXANDER WINTON AT GROSSE POINTE IN 1901.

FORD ARCHIVES, MIRCO DE CET COLLECTION

anywhere in the world) in which he beat Alexander Winton over a 25-mile course at Grosse Pointe track in October 1901. He never competed directly against Fournier, although he had plans to go into partnership with the Frenchman in making cars, but in 1904 he took the flying mile record at 91.37mph in a massive four-cylinder car with 1,155.3-cubic-inch displacement, called 999 after the famous New York Central express train. This and a similar car called Arrow had been built in 1902 with financial backing from racing cyclist Tom Cooper. At first, neither Ford nor Cooper drove the monster cars; this they entrusted to another racing cyclist called Barney Oldfield, who had never driven a car of any sort when he first climbed into the seat of 999. He covered 1 mile in 1 minute 1.2 seconds, reducing the time to under 1 minute (59.6 seconds) in June 1903 and going on to a career as one of America's best-known racing drivers. Ford and Cooper parted company in October 1902, and Clara Ford for one was not sorry. "He thinks too much of low down women to suit me," she said.

If Clara was unhappy with Henry's partner, his backers were unhappy with Henry, for they saw no chance of making money from his racing involvement. The Henry Ford Company had been founded in November 1901 with backing from

has remained ever since that day.

The car that Ford put into production as the Model A was similar to the one he had been working on for William Murphy. In appearance it was close to the first Cadillac, the main difference being in the engine, which in the Ford was a horizontally-opposed twin, while Leland's design for the Cadillac was a single-cylinder. Transmission was by two-speed planetary gear and single chain, as on the Curved Dash Olds, Cadillac, and most other American cars of that time. The body had a

single seat for two passengers, but a rear-entrance tonneau giving two additional seats was available for an extra $100 over the basic price of $750. This was more than the Olds, but in the Ford all four passengers faced the same way. Top speed was around 25mph.

The first Ford factory, on Mack Avenue, Detroit, was little more than an assembly plant for the various bought-in components — chassis and engines from the Dodge brothers, bodies from the C.R. Wilson Carriage Company, tires from the Hartford Rubber Company, and wheels from the Prudden Company of Lansing. Profit margin was estimated at $200 on the two-seaters, but only $150 on the four-seaters.

The first sale of a Model A, to Dr. E. Pfennig, a Chicago dentist, took place on July 15, 1903, and by October of 1904 a total of 1,708 cars had been delivered. Toward the end of 1904 a new factory, on Piquette Avenue, came into use, and by April 1905 Ford was making an average of 25 cars a day, with 300 employees. The huge factory sign said "Home of the Celebrated Ford Automobile." By now the Model A had been superseded by the Models B

and C. The C was similar to the A, although different in appearance because the sloping dash had been replaced by a short hood which looked as if it concealed an engine, though in fact it contained a fuel tank and the engine still lived under the front seat. The B was a different matter altogether, a larger and more expensive car with a front-mounted four-cylinder engine of 318 cubic inches and 24hp, with a side-entrance touring body and shaft drive. It cost $2,000 compared with the C's $800, and marked a change in direction which Malcomson favored but Ford did not.

Malcomson reasoned that a higher profit could be made on an expensive car than on a cheap one. Ford clung to the belief that there was a vast market for cars among poorer people, if only the cars could be made cheap enough, and the only answer to this was to make them in larger numbers. The Model B was made only for the 1904 and 1905 seasons and production figures are not known,

although they must have been pretty small. The Malcomson theory had one more airing in the Model K which was even larger, a massive 40hp six of 405 cubic inches on a 114- or 120-inch wheelbase and priced at $2,800. It never sold well, and by 1907 Ford was having to force the car onto dealers by telling them that they must take one Model K for every ten of the popular Model Ns, and by insisting that new dealers took at least one K before they were accepted at all. When even this failed to move the cars, prices were reduced to $1,800 at the end of 1907. Only 584 of the Model Ks were made.

The Model N was a direct ancestor of the T in that it was a four-cylinder car, yet modestly priced at $500 for a two-seater. Its success took Ford from fourth place in the production league in 1905 with 1,599 deliveries, to first place, with 8,729, in 1906. Henry Ford was also changing his manufacturing process. Up to this time "manufacture" was really assembly with components being bought in. Ford was particularly niggled by having to buy from the Dodge brothers because they were profiting from his success twice over, from sales of their components and from the sizable investments they had in the Ford company. In November 1905, therefore, Ford set up the Ford Manufacturing Company to organize the production of engines and transmissions. In fact this work could have been done under the name of the Ford Motor Company but the main purpose of setting up a new company was to exclude Alexander Malcomson. Ford thought that Malcomson's fondness for large cars would lead the company into disaster.

Malcomson was allocated no shares in Ford Manufacturing and responded angrily by setting up a new firm, the Aerocar Company, to make a large air-cooled car priced at $2,800, the same as the Model K Ford. He also retained his holdings in the Ford Motor Company but Henry claimed this was improper as Malcomson would be using his profits from Ford to build up a rival concern. In November 1906, with legal backing, Malcomson was ousted from the Ford Motor Company, although his associate James Couzens remained with Ford. Another important figure close to Ford was Childe Harold Wills, a highly skilled young draftsman who became chief engineer and played a

large part in the development of the Model T.

Once Malcomson was out of the way, Ford quickly reabsorbed Ford Manufacturing into the Ford Motor Company, but he persevered with its aims. If he was to make all the components previously contracted out, he would need greatly increased manufacturing space, so in April 1907 he began work on a new factory at Highland Park six times the size of the one at Piquette Avenue. It was not completed until January 1910, and is still a Ford property today, although used largely for storing machinery rather than manufacturing. Piquette Avenue was sold to Studebaker in 1911.

1911 FORD MODEL T TOURING ▲
THE MODEL T WAS CONSIDERABLY REDESIGNED FOR 1911, WITH NEW FENDERS, WHEELS, AXLES, AND MODIFICATIONS TO THE ENGINE. ITEMS THAT HAD BEEN OPTIONS, SUCH AS HEADLIGHTS AND HORN, BECAME STANDARD EQUIPMENT; INDEED FORD SAID THAT THE COMPANY'S WARRANTY WOULD BECOME VOID IF OTHER ACCESSORIES WERE ADDED, ALTHOUGH IT IS NOT KNOWN IF THIS RULE WAS EVER ENFORCED. CERTAINLY, IN LATER YEARS A VAST INDUSTRY SUPPLYING MODEL T ACCESSORIES GREW UP.

OWNER: GEORGE SANDERS (PHOTO NICKY WRIGHT)

THE MODEL T

The low-priced four-cylinder Model N was joined in 1907 by the Model R, which was essentially the same car, but with additional trimming such as full-length running boards in place of steps, and more brass fittings. These took the price up to $750, and to bridge the gap between the N and the R, Ford brought out the $700 Model S for 1908; with a four-passenger body this also cost $750. These three models kept Ford at the head of the production league, with 14,887 in 1907 and 10,202 in 1908. Ford's nearest rival was Buick, with figures of 4,641 and 8,820 respectively.

During the winter of 1906/07 Henry Ford had a section of the top floor at Piquette Avenue, as yet unused, partitioned off, with a door large enough to get a car through (he hadn't forgotten wielding his pickax in 1896) and a good lock. Here he and a small team which included Wills, a Danish-born woodworker, Charles Sorensen, and a Hungarian-born engineer, Joseph Galamb, worked on the design of the new car which would emerge in the Fall of 1908 as the Model T. In some ways the Model T was evolutionary, using ideas already proved in the Models N, R, and S, in other ways revolutionary, particularly in the ease of servicing the engine. The Model N's engine had four separately cast cylinders and a fixed head; in the T the cylinders were cast in one block and the head was detachable. The crankshaft was made of vanadium steel, which Henry had come across when examining a French racing car in 1905. Much stronger than regular steel, it was made for him by a small steel company in Canton, Ohio, and although the crankshaft looked frail it would withstand twice the actual load given by the engine. The transmission was an improved version of the two forward speed planetary unit used in previous Fords. Ignition was by low-tension magneto incorporated in the flywheel, and another innovation was the left-mounted steering wheel. Although Americans always drove on the right, the majority of cars, including the previous Fords, had right-hand drive. The enormous numbers of Model Ts which soon came onto the roads influenced other makers to follow Ford's lead in this matter. Within ten years only a few high-priced cars such as Pierce-Arrow and Stutz still had steering wheels on the right.

When it was launched in October 1908 the Model T was offered in five body styles, two-passenger coupe and runabout, five-passenger touring, and seven-passenger town car or landaulet. Prices ran from $825 for the runabout to $1,000 for the town car. As one would expect, the open models sold the best, 7,728 tourings and 2,351 runabouts in the first model year. Rarest was the sentry-box-like coupe, of which only 47 were delivered. Most components were Ford-made, apart from tires, which Ford bought from his friend Harvey Firestone, and bodies, which came from a number of suppliers, notably Kelsey and O.J. Beaudette.

Production started slowly, but by the summer of 1909 was running at 100 cars per day. 1909 saw 17,771 cars delivered, and within four years Ford factories were turning out more than ten times this number. The moving assembly line, the key to mass production, was installed at Highland Park in 1913, in which year production rose to 202,667. The following year saw another jump, to 308,162, while

▲ FORD MODEL T STRIPPED TO THE BARE ESSENTIALS. THIS IS THE CAR IN WHICH BERT SCOTT AND JIMMY SMITH WON THE 1909 NEW YORK–SEATTLE RACE, BEATING A $4,500 ACME, A $5,000 SHAWMUT, AND AN IMPORTED ITALA THAT PROBABLY COST MORE STILL. THEIR TIME WAS 22 DAYS AND 55 MINUTES.
FORD MOTOR COMPANY

1909 FORD MODEL T ◄
THE FIRST FULL YEAR OF PRODUCTION FOR THE MODEL T WAS 1909, AND 17,771 WERE DELIVERED IN THE 12 MONTHS. THREE COLORS WERE OFFERED: RED ON THE TOURINGS, GRAY ON THE RUNABOUTS, AND GREEN ON THE TOWN CARS AND LANDAULETS. VARIOUS COLORS WERE AVAILABLE UP TO 1914, AFTER WHICH MODEL Ts WERE SUPPLIED ONLY IN BLACK, ALTHOUGH COLOR WAS TO RETURN IN 1926. THE TWO ACETYLENE GAS HEADLIGHTS ON THIS CAR WERE EXTRAS, AS STANDARD LIGHTING IN 1909 DID NOT EXTEND BEYOND TWO SIDELIGHTS AND ONE TAILLIGHT. THE TOP WAS AN EXTRA AS WELL.
OWNER: CRAWFORD COLLECTION OF THE WESTERN HISTORICAL SOCIETY (PHOTO NICKY WRIGHT)

the figures for 1915 and 1916 were 501,462 and 734,811 respectively.

Henry Ford is sometimes credited with inventing the moving assembly line, but this is not so. Interchangeable parts were used in the assembly of rifles well before the Civil War, and a little later, in the watch and clock industry. Henry, who had planned to mass-produce a watch at one time, is said to have gained his inspiration from the Chicago meat-packing industry, where hog carcasses were brought on overhead trolleys past each worker who would take his cut. Ford's achievement was to adapt the process to the vastly more complicated process of making automobiles.

As production grew the unit price came down, so that by 1915 the touring was down to $440, little

more than half the 1908 figure, for a much better equipped car. It must be admitted that the original Model T was a pretty basic vehicle. Standard equipment consisted of three oil lamps only, two side and one tail. Headlights, windshield, top, horn, bumpers, and speedometer were all extras. By 1915 these were all included in the price, except for bumpers, which were seldom seen on Model Ts. A debit from 1914 onward was that the cars were only available in black. This was because japan black enamel was the only paint that would dry quickly enough to keep up with the assembly line. From 1926 a choice of colors was again provided, thanks to fast-drying Duco lacquer.

The Model T was not the only mass-produced car of its day, but it has passed into folklore as the car that put America on wheels. Certainly no other car aroused such affection, as well as exasperation, among owners. It was the first car owned by most Americans in the first two decades of this century, and even after it went out of production in 1927 it

was bought by many as a "starter car" because of the wide availability and low price of used Ts. Henry Ford came of farming stock and he was particularly pleased that farmers took to the T in such a big way. It was the first car to wean them away from the horse and buggy. "You know," wrote a Georgia farmer's wife to Henry in 1918, "your car lifted us out of the mud. It brought joy into our lives. We loved every rattle of its bones...."

After a slight dip in production during World War I, the Model T surged ahead in the 1920s, topping the million mark each year from 1922 to 1926, and reaching a peak of 1,817,891 in 1923. This was more than four times the number of cars made by Ford's nearest rival, Chevrolet. Prices were down too, with the cheapest two-passenger runabout of 1924 costing a mere $260. Because the car was still pretty basic, an enormous trade in accessories grew up. In the early 1920s the Sears Roebuck catalog offered as many as 5,000 different items for the Model T, fancy lamps, horns, disk wheels, and almost anything that could be bolted or screwed to the car. Some firms offered complete body kits to transform the T's homely appearance, others provided overhead valve conversions to boost its performance. The planetary transmission, widely used and familiar in 1908, was obsolete on every car but the T in the 1920s, and some firms offered conventional three-speed sliding transmissions. The Mayfair Manufacturing Company of Boston bought up used T sedans, tested and replaced parts where necessary, and fitted a sliding transmission and their own style of radiator, selling the result for $485, $175 less than a new 1925 T sedan. Not many people were impressed with this offer, and fewer than ten Mayfairs were sold.

THE SELDEN PATENT

In September 1909, just as the Model T was approaching its first birthday, Judge Charles Merrill Hough of the Circuit Court of Southern New York upheld a patent claim against Ford by the Association of Licensed Automobile Manufacturers (ALAM). This awarded millions of dollars to ALAM in unpaid royalties on every Ford car made since 1903, the year in which the ALAM was set up.

The ALAM arose from the activities of a patent attorney from Rochester, N.Y., called George Baldwin Selden (1846–1932). He had filed a patent in 1879 for an internal combustion motor vehicle, and had gradually updated it as he saw the design of such vehicles changing. His definitive patent was filed in November 1895, and four years later he signed the patent over (for a fee) to a group of Wall Street men headed by William C. Whitney, who acquired the Electric Vehicle Company and allied himself with Colonel Pope. They bought Selden's 1895 patent for $10,000. One may wonder why a maker of electric cars should obtain a patent for gasoline cars, but so long as they held the patent they could enforce it against anyone they liked. Since no one was certain at this point what type of motive power would prove the most popular, they were hedging their bets. Alexander Winton was the first manufacturer to be brought into line, in 1900, and in 1903 the representatives of five other companies, Knox, Locomobile, Oldsmobile, Packard, and Pierce-Arrow formed the ALAM

which agreed the validity of the Selden patent and promised to pay a royalty of 1¼ percent on the price of every car sold. This royalty was to be split, 20 percent to Selden, 40 percent to the Electric Vehicle Company and 40 percent to the ALAM to cover any litigation which might arise.

Up to this time Selden had not made a single car, but in 1903 he had two made to the design he had worked out in 1877, two years before he took out his first patent. They were crude-looking machines, with the two-cycle engines mounted over, and driving, the front axle, which steered on the center pivot system. Henry Cave of Hartford, Connecticut, who built one of them, said that it did not run very well. The other car was made by Selden and his sons, who painted the date 1877 on the side. Surviving photos have led some people to think that the car really was made in 1877, and numerous mugs, beer mats, and other such items have been made illustrating the "1877 Selden."

Membership of the ALAM was not open to everyone, only to those considered to be bona fide manufacturers. In 1903 Henry Ford made inquiries about membership and was told by F. L. Smith, treasurer of Oldsmobile, that he would not be accepted as his company was "a mere assemblage plant." Smith should have known better than to cross swords with as feisty an individual as Ford, or his associates. James Couzens is reported to have said: "Selden can take his patent and go to hell with it." The Ford company resolutely refused to pay any royalties and offered to protect any dealers or users of its cars against prosecution. The battle was on.

In 1907 Selden tried to demonstrate one of his cars to Judge Hough; it required an air compressor to start it and ran no more than 5 yards before spluttering to a standstill, but the judge did not consider that its failure was relevant to the case. In 1909 he rendered his verdict, and so overawed were the auto manufacturers that 30 more joined the ALAM in a matter of weeks. Durant, whose Buick, Cadillac and Oldsmobile companies were longstanding ALAM members, decided to pay up.

Ford was not without supporters, who had formed the American Motor Car Manufacturers' Association. They included Marmon, Reo, Maxwell-Briscoe, Mitchell, and the truck maker Mack, but most of these fell in line with the ALAM

▲ GEORGE B. SELDEN AT THE WHEEL OF THE CRUDE FRONT-DRIVE CAR HE BUILT IN 1903 TO JUSTIFY HIS PATENT. NEITHER IT NOR ITS FELLOW RAN AT ALL WELL, BUT HE USED THEIR EXISTENCE TO EXTRACT MILLIONS OF DOLLARS IN ROYALTIES, UNTIL HE WAS CHALLENGED AT LAW BY HENRY FORD, WHO WAS FINALLY SUCCESSFUL IN 1911.

MOTOR VEHICLE MANUFACTURERS' ASSOCIATION

after the 1909 decision. However, Ford appealed, and on January 9, 1911, Judge Hough's decision was dismissed on the grounds that the Selden patent applied only to two-cycle engines of the Brayton type and those of Ford and nearly all other auto manufacturers used the four-cycle Otto system.

Through his fight against the ALAM Ford became a folk hero, the lone fighter against the large organization, which was ironic as his own company went on to become one of the biggest industrial organizations in the world. But he was for a long time seen as a friend of the common man, and epitomized the distrust felt by the Middle Western country dweller for East Coast big business. He was not a joiner, and never became a member of the National Automobile Chamber of Commerce (NACC), so that up to the end of the 1920s the NACC Handbook, which listed and illustrated a wide variety of cars from companies great and small, never carried a mention of Ford, the greatest of them all.

▲ ONE OF THE MANY FIRMS THAT BILLY DURANT INCORPORATED INTO GENERAL MOTORS WAS THE RELIANCE MOTOR TRUCK COMPANY OF DETROIT. FROM 1912 RELIANCE MODELS SUCH AS THIS CHAIN-DRIVE CAB-OVER TRUCK BORE THE NAME GENERAL MOTORS TRUCK, STARTING A LINE OF GMC TRUCKS THAT LASTED UNTIL THE 1980s AND MERGER WITH THE WHITE RANGE. THIS TRUCK IS CARRYING A LOAD OF TIRES, WHICH WERE FITTED TO NONDETACHABLE RIMS. YOU CHANGED A TIRE IN THOSE DAYS, NOT A WHEEL.

MOTOR VEHICLE MANUFACTURERS' ASSOCIATION

► THE TWO MEN WITHOUT WHOM GENERAL MOTORS WOULD NEVER HAVE COME INTO EXISTENCE: LEFT, THE DEDICATED BUT UNWORLDLY ENGINEER DAVID DUNBAR BUICK (1855–1929); RIGHT, THE DYNAMIC BUT SOMETIMES UNWISE ENTREPRENEUR WILLIAM CRAPO DURANT (1860–1947). BOTH MEN ENDED THEIR LIVES IN HUMBLE JOBS, BUICK AS A RECEPTIONIST, DURANT RUNNING A HAMBURGER JOINT.

MOTOR VEHICLE MANUFACTURERS' ASSOCIATION

B ILLY DURANT AND THE FORMATION OF GENERAL MOTORS

Although Ford certainly dominated American production until the late 1920s, his lead was soon followed by other ambitious men. The most prominent of these was William Crapo Durant (1860–1947), born in Boston but raised in Flint, Michigan. Often described as self-made, Billy Durant did not come from poor stock, for his grandfather William H. Crapo had made a fortune in whaling on the East Coast, then moved west to Michigan where he operated a successful lumber mill. Young Billy worked in the mill until he was 21, then set out on his own in the carriage business, which was a major activity in Flint. He patented a two-wheeled cart, which he sold for $12.50, and in 1885 went into partnership with Josiah Dallas Dort (1861–1925). By the turn of the century they had built up a thriving carriage business; at their peak they made 50,000 carriages a year. Among their employees was future auto maker Charles Nash.

Durant noticed a locally built car with an advanced valve-in-head engine made by Scottish-born David Dunbar Buick (1855–1929). Buick had entered the plumbing business and in the 1890s perfected a technique for applying enamel to cast-iron bathtubs. Today his name is associated only with cars and his major contribution to modern domestic living is forgotten. His plumbing business, Buick and Sherwood, brought him a considerable fortune, but he chose to turn his energies to a new obsession, the automobile. Founded in 1902, the Buick Manufacturing Company made only six cars in 1903 and no more than 37 in 1904 when Billy Durant stepped in, bought a controlling interest, and raised capitalization to $1.5 million.

Durant reorganized production with assembly in a disused Durant-Dort carriage factory at Jackson, Michigan, and manufacture of engines at the Buick factory at Flint and bodies by the Flint Wagon Works. Production jumped to 750 cars in 1905, and to 1,400 in 1906. Manufacture was gradually concentrated in Flint, the Jackson plant being wound down and finally closed in 1912. The 1907 output from Buick was 4,641 cars, which put the make second among U.S. manufacturers, outdone only by Ford.

As Buick prospered under Durant's leadership,

1911 OVERLAND MODEL 55 TOURING ▲

THE WILLYS-OVERLAND COMPANY WAS AMERICA'S THIRD LARGEST AUTO MAKER IN 1911, BEATEN ONLY BY FORD AND BUICK. THIS MODEL 55 WAS PART OF THE 40hp RANGE THAT INCLUDED FIVE STYLES ON A 118-INCH WHEELBASE, FROM THE 55 AT $1,300 TO THE 52 LIMOUSINE AT MORE THAN DOUBLE THE PRICE, $2,750.

OWNER: GEORGE SANDERS (PHOTO NICKY WRIGHT)

there seemed to be less room in the organization for its founder. David Buick was a tinkerer rather than a mass-production man, and he was constantly making suggestions to the engineers, who were mostly Durant men. These met with little sympathy because they would have interrupted the drive toward large-scale manufacture. Buick was also keen on selling his engines to other car makers. Durant was not happy with this either, so in 1908 Buick left the company, with $100,000 as a personal gift from Durant.

The rest of David Buick's story is a sad one. Nothing he touched seemed to go right, from oil and land speculation to the manufacture of carburetors and automobiles. Others made fortunes from oil in the years before World War I, but Buick lost most of what he took out of the Buick Motor Company. Back in Michigan, he tried carburetors with his son Tom, followed by manufacture of a car in Walden, New York. For this he used his other family name, Dunbar, launching the David Dunbar Buick Corporation with a supposed capitalization of $5 million. Nowhere near this figure was ever raised, and only one car was ever made, a roadster powered by a six-cylinder Continental engine. Buick invested the little money he had left in real estate in Florida, but lost this too. In 1927 he took a job as an instructor at the Detroit School of Trades, but he was 72 years old and so frail that he was soon transferred to the reception desk. Outside in the streets countless Buick cars rolled by, but their original creator toiled away unnoticed. David Buick could never afford to retire, and died in 1929.

By then Billy Durant had made and lost two fortunes. He also had a car bearing his own name, but far more important was his organization of General Motors. He had originally hoped to include Maxwell-Briscoe, Ford, and Reo in his empire, but his plan never materialized because of the lack of enthusiasm from Henry Ford, among other reasons. So he used the Buick Company as a base to found General Motors in September 1908, although the only make in it was Buick. On December 28 Oldsmobile was brought into the group, followed by Oakland in May 1909, and

1913 RAMBLER TOURING ▲▼

FOR THE RAMBLER NAME 1913 WAS THE LAST YEAR, FOR 1914 MODELS WERE CALLED JEFFERY FOR THE FAMILY WHO MADE THEM. THIS 42hp FOUR-CYLINDER TOURING WAS CALLED THE CROSS COUNTRY, ALTHOUGH IT WAS HARDLY IN THE JEEP/BRONCO CLASS. PERHAPS THE FACT THAT NED JORDAN WAS GENERAL MANAGER HAD SOMETHING TO DO WITH IT, FOR OTHER RAMBLER MODELS BORE EXOTIC NAMES LIKE VALKYRIE, KNICKERBOCKER, AND COUNTRY CLUB. RAMBLERS WERE UNUSUAL IN 1913 IN HAVING RIGHT-HAND DRIVE. HOWEVER, WHEN THE NAME WAS CHANGED SO WAS THE STEERING WHEEL POSITION. IN 1918 THE JEFFERY BECAME THE NASH.

OWNER: DAN OBERLE (PHOTO NICKY WRIGHT)

1908 BRUSH MODEL B RUNABOUT ▶

THE BRUSH MOTOR CAR COMPANY OF DETROIT WAS ONE OF THE FIRMS MERGED BY BENJAMIN BRISCOE INTO HIS UNITED STATES MOTOR CORPORATION, WHICH HE SAW AS A RIVAL TO GENERAL MOTORS. THE BRUSH WAS THE CHEAPEST CAR IN THE GROUP; THE 6hp SINGLE-CYLINDER RUNABOUT SOLD FOR ONLY $500. IT WAS UNUSUAL IN HAVING SUSPENSION BY COIL SPRINGS ALL ROUND — THE FRONT PAIR ARE CLEARLY VISIBLE HERE. DESIGNER ALANSON P. BRUSH HAD HELPED WITH THE FIRST SINGLE-CYLINDER CADILLAC.

OWNER: NATIONAL AUTOMOBILE MUSEUM, RENO, NAVADA

(PHOTO NICKY WRIGHT)

Cadillac in July. Oakland was eventually replaced by its companion make, Pontiac, so four of the five makes that constitute today's General Motors Corporation were already in the group a year after it was founded. Over the next few years numerous other short-lived companies also became part of General Motors, including Carter, Elmore, Ewing, Marquette, Rainier, Rapid, Reliance, and Welch. Rapid and Reliance were truck makers, and in 1912 evolved into GMC trucks, still being made today. Most of these companies were acquired by issuing General Motors stock, although Cadillac had to be bought for $4.4 million in cash.

The early days of General Motors were by no means easy. Durant wasted a lot of money buying up companies because their patents "might come in useful one day" if design changed. Thus he paid $140,000 for Cartercar because of its friction transmission, and $600,000 for Elmore to secure its two-cycle engine. Neither prospered, and Cartercar was sold in 1915 for only $50,000. Elmore had to be written off completely. Worse still, Durant paid $7 million for the Heany Lamp Company which held a patent on an incandescent light that turned out to be fraudulent, so the whole $7 million went down the drain.

Of the car-making companies, only Cadillac was really profitable by 1910; Buick had been mortgaged to the hilt to provide the purchase price for Cadillac, Oldsmobile sales had declined sharply after the end of the Curved Dash, and Oakland was an untried newcomer. General Motors had to turn to the banks for support, and one of their conditions was that Durant should step down from the presidency of Buick and the vice-presidency of GM. He remained on the board of directors, and a few years later, with the success of Chevrolet, was back in charge.

EXPANSION BY OTHER FIRMS

While Durant was expanding Buick and Ford was embarking on mass production, other makers were contributing cars in the same market. Chief among them were John North Willys, the Studebaker brothers, Thomas Jeffery, and Jonathan D. Maxwell with his partner Benjamin Briscoe.

John North Willys (1873–1935) differed from most contemporary auto men in that he was a dealer before he became a manufacturer. Like many others, he began with bicycles, selling and repairing them in his home town of Canandaigua, New York. He later bought a larger business in Elmira, and at the turn of the century began selling Pierce, Rambler, and Overland automobiles. The Overland was a small car made by the Standard Wheel Company of Indianapolis, one of the largest wheel makers in the country. Willys had seen the car on a visit to Indianapolis in 1905 and had ordered as many as could be made of the 1906 models, a 9hp two-cylinder runabout and a 16hp four-cylinder touring. Overland made 47 cars and Willys took all of them, following this with an order for 500 of the 1907 models.

When no cars arrived and letters went unanswered, an anxious Willys set out for Indianapolis, where he found the Overland company in disarray. No cars were being made, there were parts for only three, and the workforce was rapidly vanishing; those who remained only did so because they had not been paid for several weeks. Willys had $10,000 invested in his order and was determined to see some cars produced, so he borrowed the money to pay off the company's debts and asked his hotel to make no payments until they had enough cash to meet his check to settle the payroll. As the factory premises were inadequate for the production of 500 cars, Willys acquired an enormous circus tent and began making cars there until a new factory could be built.

Thus Willys became, in his own words,

▼ ALTHOUGH NOT IN THE TOP FIVE, COMPANIES SUCH AS HUDSON, HUPMOBILE, AND RAMBLER MADE A SIZABLE CONTRIBUTION TO AMERICA'S AUTOMOBILE OUTPUT IN THE YEARS BEFORE WORLD WAR I. HUDSON BEGAN IN 1909, AND THIS 1911 MODEL 20 FOUR-CYLINDER ROADSTER WAS SIMILAR TO THE FIRM'S INITIAL MODEL.

MOTOR VEHICLE MANUFACTURERS' ASSOCIATION

"manufacturer, president, treasurer, general manager — everything from Lord High Executioner down" of the Overland Company. Output from the circus tent was 465 cars in 1908, all 20/22hp tourings or runabouts with two-speed planetary transmissions. In 1909 he moved to Toledo, Ohio, and changed the company name to Willys-Overland; 4,860 cars were made that year, including models with conventional three-speed transmission as an alternative to the planetary (at $100 extra), and a 45hp six at $2,250 which was called a Willys rather than an Overland. This move upmarket was not continued, and for 1910 all cars were Overlands and none cost more than $1,850. Most were in the $1,000–$1,450 range, and production shot up to 15,598. Willys was now the third largest manufacturer after Ford and Buick. In 1912 the company moved into second place, with 28,572 deliveries, the lowest-priced model being a two-passenger roadster at $850. Willys was to remain in second place until 1918.

In 1913 Willys made an enforced trip to Europe, enforced by his doctor who threatened him with the alternative of a sanatorium if he kept on working so hard. While traveling he met another American, the engineer Charles Yale Knight, who had patented the sleeve-valve engine and had already sold it to European car makers such as Daimler in Britain, Panhard in France, Minerva in Belgium, and Mercedes in Germany. Willys bought up a company which was already making a sleeve-valve car, the Edwards Motor Car Company of New York City, moved production to Elyria, Ohio, and renamed it the Willys-Knight. By the 1920s Willys was making more sleeve-valve engines than all other car makers combined, and continued to produce them up to 1933.

Studebaker was a famous name in American motordom for six decades, yet for some time Studebakers were built by other firms. A history dating back to the middle of the nineteenth century made Studebaker the oldest vehicle-making company in America, its first wagons having been built at South Bend, Indiana, in 1852. The company prospered greatly during the Civil War, and one of the brothers, John Mohler Studebaker, made a separate fortune building wheelbarrows for California gold miners. The first Studebaker automobiles were electrics, made in

1902; they were joined by gasoline cars in 1903. The latter were made for Studebaker by the General Automobile Company of Cleveland and later by the Garford Company of Elyria, Ohio (whose factory was bought by Willys in 1913 for the Willys-Knight).

Garford's production enabled Studebaker to sell 8,142 cars in 1908 (nearly all badged as Studebakers), but they were expensive at $3,750–$4,500, and Studebaker needed a cheaper product in order to compete with Ford and Buick. The answer was the EMF 30, a conventional $1,250 touring put on the market in 1908 by the Everitt-Metzger-Flanders Company of Detroit. The men behind it had plenty of the right experience; Barney Everitt had made a fortune as a body builder, William E. Metzger was a successful salesman who had contributed much to the early success of Cadillac, and Walter E. Flanders had been Henry Ford's production manager. Studebaker contracted to take half of EMF's 1909 production, estimated to be 12,000 cars. The actual figure was 8,132, including 172 made the previous year, but output jumped to 15,598 in 1910 and reached a peak of 28,032 in 1912. Despite good sales, EMF 30s were not without problems, particularly with the rear-axle-mounted gearbox. The initials inevitably gave rise to rude nicknames, such as "Every Morning Fixit" and "Every Mechanical Failure."

In 1909 Everitt and Metzger left the company, and Walter Flanders bought the factory of the defunct Deluxe Company, helped by Studebaker money, to make a smaller car than the EMF, giving it his own name. The Flanders 20 runabout sold for $700 in 1911, only $20 above the price of an equivalent Model T. Walter Flanders remained a Studebaker associate until March 1912, devoting an increasing amount of company time to his own projects, which included an electric car and a four-cylinder motorcycle. This led to a parting of the ways, and for the 1913 season both Flanders and EMF were renamed, the former becoming the Studebaker 25 and the latter the Studebaker 35. The two Detroit factories were kept, as was an EMF plant in Walkerville, Ontario; this began an association with Canada that was to last until after production ceased in the United States, although the last Canadian-made Studebakers were

▲ MAXWELL-BRISCOE BUILT 3,785 CARS IN 1907, THE YEAR WHEN THIS FIVE-PASSENGER TOURING WAS MADE, PUTTING THE COMPANY IN FOURTH PLACE AMONG U.S. MANUFACTURERS. JONATHAN MAXWELL IS AT THE WHEEL, WITH BENJAMIN BRISCOE AT HIS SIDE.
MOTOR VEHICLE MANUFACTURERS' ASSOCIATION

produced in Hamilton rather than Walkerville.

There is no space to mention all the other companies that contributed to the rise of mass production, but Maxwell is a name to remember, if only because it led to the Chrysler empire, the last of the large groups to emerge. The Maxwell-Briscoe Motor Company was built on the familiar combination of one man's technical skills combined with another man's money. Jonathan D. Maxwell (1864–1928) had been with the Apperson brothers when they built their first car for Elwood Haynes, and later worked for Olds before designing a single-cylinder car for the Northern Manufacturing Company of Detroit. His partner at Northern was Charles King, who had helped Henry Ford to build his first prototype, but he and Maxwell did not get on, so the latter found a new partner in Benjamin Briscoe (1869–1945), a successful maker of sheet metal goods who had got into the auto business by

HUPMOBILE WAS A SUCCESSFUL MEDIUM-SIZED MANUFACTURER FOR MANY YEARS. THIS WAS ROBERT HUPP'S FIRST MODEL, A TWO-PASSENGER RUNABOUT WITH GAS TANK MOUNTED BEHIND THE SEAT. KNOWN AS MODEL 20, IT HAD A 16.9hp FOUR-CYLINDER ENGINE, AND SOLD FOR $750. FOR A CAR IN THAT PRICE RANGE IT WAS UNUSUAL IN HAVING A SLIDING GEAR TRANSMISSION AND MAGNETO IGNITION. MOST OF ITS RIVALS STILL HAD PLANETARY TRANSMISSION AND BATTERY IGNITION.

OWNER: CRAWFORD COLLECTION OF WESTERN HISTORICAL SOCIETY (PHOTO NICKY WRIGHT)

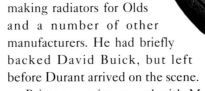

making radiators for Olds and a number of other manufacturers. He had briefly backed David Buick, but left before Durant arrived on the scene.

Briscoe was impressed with Maxwell's ability and in 1904 set up Maxwell-Briscoe, renting the Tarrytown, N.Y., plant which John Brisben Walker had used for making Mobile steamers. Although Briscoe raised the money, more than two-thirds of it came from the financial house of J.P. Morgan in New York. The first Maxwell-Briscoe was a two-passenger runabout with a horizontally opposed two-cylinder engine of square dimensions (4 x 4 inches). Only ten cars were made in 1904, but two years later this had burgeoned to nearly 2,200; putting Maxwell into fifth place. Third place arrived in 1909 with 9,460 deliveries; Maxwell-Briscoe generally managed to remain in the top six up to 1920.

In 1906 Briscoe, feeling insecure in a rented factory, started to construct a large new plant at

New Castle, Indiana, which was not completed until 1909. He also bought premises at Pawtucket, Rhode Island, and Auburn, N.Y., all of which contributed to the output of about 20,000 Maxwells in 1910. Their super-salesman Cadwallader Washburn Kelsey (1880–1970) promoted them by making short films showing the cars in police chases, driving up the steps of churches and other public buildings, and showing them in nickelodeons. He also supported long-distance trials such as the Glidden Tours, which Maxwell won outright in 1911 and 1912. It was a Maxwell that Alice Huyler Ramsey and her three lady companions drove across the continent in 1909, earning more press coverage than all Kelsey's other activities combined.

Unfortunately, in 1910 Briscoe, using his company as the base, organized a rival to General Motors which he called the United States Motor Corporation, for which he acquired the car-producing companies of Brush, Columbia, Courier, and Stoddard-Dayton, among others. The new group was unwieldy from the start, with seven marque names, 52 models, and 18 factories, and soon found itself in a similar position to British Leyland Motor Corporation in the early 1970s. However, Briscoe had no government to bail him out, and the group collapsed in 1912. He later made cars under his own name, while Maxwell, having the soundest of the United States Motor Corporation's companies, saw control pass to Walter Flanders, one of the partners in Everitt-Mitzger-Flanders. Maxwell left, but he must have derived some satisfaction from knowing that Flanders retained the Maxwell name, as a good selling point. The four-cylinder Maxwells were now being made at New Castle and in the former Stoddard-Dayton plant at Dayton, Ohio, while the six-cylinder 50-6 model was made in the Flanders plant in Detroit. The six was soon dropped, and Maxwell concentrated on a low-price 25hp four selling for $750. Sales jumped to 75,000 by 1917, but dropped after World War I when the company was combined with Chalmers, the maker of a more expensive six-cylinder car. Maxwell-Chalmers came under the control of Walter P. Chrysler in November 1921, and for 1926 the Maxwell four was renamed the Chrysler 58, having the same engine with Chrysler styling. The same basic car, with important improvements such as four-wheel hydraulic brakes, was renamed Plymouth for the 1929 season.

Another empire that rose and fell was that of Colonel Albert Pope. In addition to the Columbia electrics described earlier, he bought up another electric car maker, Waverley of Indianapolis, and built four makes of gasoline car, the Pope-Hartford, Pope-Robinson, Pope-Toledo, and Pope-Tribune. The latter, located at Hagerstown, Maryland, in a plant managed by the Colonel's son Harold, was a low-priced single-cylinder runabout initially, although prices rose with the introduction of four-cylinder cars to a peak of $2,750 in 1908, the Pope-Tribune's last year. Other marques in the empire were costlier, in particular the massive Pope-Toledo, which reached a peak of $6,000 for a 50hp limousine in 1907. The unwieldy Pope group was

already in difficulties when the Colonel died in August 1909: Pope-Hartford went into receivership, Pope-Waverley was sold and the product renamed Waverley, Pope-Toledo closed, and Pope-Tribune had already gone. The Hartford business continued until 1914 under the Colonel's brother George, when it, too, closed down.

CHEVROLET AND DODGE

By 1920 the major U.S. makes were the same as they are today; Ford had the biggest market share, followed by Dodge, Chevrolet, and Buick. The rise of two new names represented almost the last successful intrusion of fresh blood into the established Detroit hierarchy: Chrysler was the first intruder in the 1920s, building on the base of Maxwell-Chalmers and later acquiring Dodge, and Kaiser-Frazer came to prominence after World War II, but the latter, "the last onslaught on Detroit," failed after ten years.

In their early years Chevrolet and Dodge built much the same sort of cars, but their histories were different. Louis Chevrolet was new to the auto industry when he planned his first car in 1910, although he was already well known as a racing driver, while the Dodge brothers had been prominent suppliers to the industry since the turn of the century, first to Olds and then to Ford. Indeed as far as components were concerned, the early Fords had more Dodge than Ford in them, being largely assembled machines.

The Chevrolet brothers, Gaston, Arthur, and Louis, were Swiss-born but lived in France before emigrating to Canada and thence to the United States around 1900. Louis was the mechanically minded one, having invented a pump for extracting wine from barrels when the family lived in the Beaune region of France, and later worked for the New York De Dion Bouton importer and the fellow Swiss vehicle maker, William Walter. From 1908 he raced cars for Buick, which brought him to the attention of Billy Durant. In 1910 Durant was out of a job, having been eased out of General Motors, and on the lookout for a new opportunity. It is not certain whether Chevrolet had begun work on a car

design before Durant approached him, or whether the idea was Billy's from the start. Anyway, Chevrolet was soon planning a car, and as he had little engineering training he sought the assistance of Etienne Planche, a Frenchman he had met at the Walter company who had designed a car for Walter which eventually evolved into the Mercer.

Although Chevrolet and Planche had promised a "French-type light car," the vehicle they came up with was more typically American and by no means light. Launched late in 1911, the Chevrolet Classic Six had a T-head six-cylinder engine whose displacement of 299 cubic inches was larger than that of any other Chevrolet until 1958. Its wheelbase was 120 inches, as long as any Chevrolet ever made, and Durant could not juggle the price below $2,250. The Classic Six was clearly not the car to rebuild his career with, so he also brought out a smaller four called the Little, not for its size but for William H. Little, his former production manager at Buick. This sold for $690, closer to Durant's ideal, but it did not sell very well, perhaps because the name was unappealing, but also because it was not very well made. Durant himself remarked that it would be "driven to its death in less than 25,000 miles."

Between early 1912 and its discontinuance in May 1913, the Little sold about 3,500 units, including a six at $1,250, less than the Chevrolet Classic Six, which managed nearly 9,000 sales between the summer of 1912 and the end of the 1914 season. It was then replaced by a smaller L-head six, but much more important was the new Chevrolet four, the Series H. This was somewhat larger than the Little, with a 104-inch wheelbase against 90 inches for the earlier car, and an overhead valve engine. It did not please Louis Chevrolet who, for all his European ancestry, favored a larger, American-style car.

There was also the matter of his smoking habits. Durant had suggested that cigars were more appropriate than cheap cigarettes now that Chevrolet was a motor industry executive, and he particularly objected to the way Louis constantly had a cigarette hanging on his lower lip. This was too much for Louis; he is reported to have exploded: "I sold you my car and I sold you my name, but I'm not going to sell myself to you." This was the final flashpoint reflecting deep

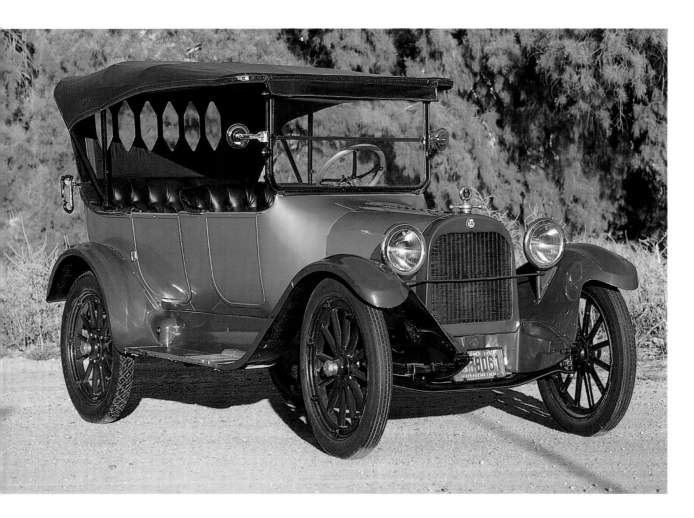

1918 DODGE TOURING ◄ ►

DODGES OF THIS PERIOD COULD BE IDENTIFIED BY
THE SIX VERTICAL WINDOWS IN THE REAR OF THE TOP,
ALSO SEEN ON TWO-PASSENGER ROADSTERS. THE
RUGGED FOUR-CYLINDER DODGE WAS A LEADING STAFF
CAR FOR THE U.S. ARMY. THE TYPE WAS USED BY
GENERAL JOHN PERSHING IN THE MEXICAN CAMPAIGNS
OF 1916 AGAINST PANCHO VILLA; THE FIRST
MECHANIZED CAVALRY CHARGE WAS LED BY AN
UNKNOWN YOUNG OFFICER, LT. GEORGE S. PATTON,
IN A DODGE. THE SAME CAR WAS THEN USED BY
PERSHING DURING WORLD WAR I IN EUROPE, WHERE
HE WAS CHAUFFEURED BY CAPT. EDDIE RICKENBACKER,
LATER TO MAKE HIS OWN CARS.

OWNER: DICK TRAVERS (PHOTOS NICKY WRIGHT)

without electric lights and starter you will make a mistake." This was a dig at Ford, which still had to be hand-cranked, and whose side- and tail-lights were lit by kerosene.

To build the 490 in the numbers planned, Durant had to find more factory space, so he began by buying up the former Maxwell plant at Tarrytown, N.Y. (still a GM plant today), and followed this by obtaining manufacturing space from his former carriage-building friend Russell Gardner at St. Louis and Norman de Vaux in Oakland, California. He wanted a Canadian plant as well and talked the McLaughlins, who were already making Buicks for him in their carriage works at Oshawa, Ontario, into giving up carriages in favor of Chevrolets.

The 490 took Chevrolet into the big league very rapidly; in 1915, only 13,292 cars were made, but in the following year production shot up to 62,898, putting the company into sixth place. By 1919 this had become second place, with 123,371 cars sold. From 1922, Chevrolet was in second place behind Ford, a position it held until it overtook Ford in 1927. With the profits accruing from Chevrolet, Durant was able to buy back into General Motors. And aided by explosives makers E. I. duPont he regained control of the company he had started and lost on the seventh anniversary of its founding, September 16, 1915. The Chevrolet Motors Company now owned the General Motors Company, which in 1918 assumed its present title of the General Motors Corporation.

disagreement, and Chevrolet left the company in 1914. He later built successful racing cars under the name Frontenac, which won the Indianapolis 500 in 1920 and 1921. He never made the money he could have done with Durant, and died in obscurity in 1941. He always said that he was prouder of his Indy winners than of all the millions of cars that bore his name, which is understandable, as he had nothing to do with their design. His partner Etienne Planche joined Durant's erstwhile partner J. Dallas Dort, for whom he designed a four-cylinder car not unlike the Chevrolet, although it was never so successful.

The Series H was continued for the 1915 season, priced at a modest $750 for a roadster. There was also a de luxe model called the Amesbury Special, with more attractive lines, one-piece windshield with wiper, and rumble seat with its own windshield. The Amesbury Special was mostly delivered in white and cost $985 or, with optional Houk wire wheels, $1,110. The other models were

a two-passenger roadster called the Royal Mail and a five-passenger touring called the Baby Grand. The Series H engine, designed by Arthur Mason and made by the Durant-owned Mason Motor Company, was a 170.9-cubic-inch four whose dimensions remained unchanged until fours were discontinued in 1928. This was the basis for the car with which Durant planned to meet Henry Ford head on, the 490. Announced in December 1914 but not put into production until the summer of 1915, the 490 was named for the price of a Model T touring, and this was to be the Chevrolet's price too. Six weeks after the 490 went on sale, Henry reduced the T to $440 and Durant was soon forced to up the price of his car to $550, although this included electric lighting and starting. He managed to have it both ways by claiming that the basic price was still $490, but adding in the brochure: "We strongly recommend the purchase of the Model 490 with electric lighting and starting equipment, as no car is complete today without it. If you buy a car

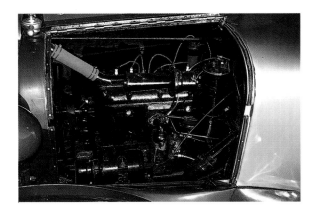

Durant's triumph was not to last long, however, for he overextended the corporation's finances in 1919, as he had done earlier, by rash purchases, notably of the Samson Tractor Company of Stockton, California. This purchase was clear evidence of Durant's ambition to challenge Henry Ford all along the line. He had a successful car in the Chevrolet 490, but the Samson was a failure. Durant bought the rights to the Samson Sieve Grip tractor and put it into production in a large plant at Janesville, Wisconsin, but the $1,750 tractor was no competition for the $750 Fordson. It was hastily replaced by the Model M, which sold for $650 and was better equipped than the Fordson. This might have been the basis for a successful business, but Durant spoiled it all by buying up the rights to the Dandy motor cultivator, which he sold under the name Iron Horse. This was a curious machine with steering by reins rather than wheel, and belt-and-pulley transmission with independent clutch control for the pair of wheels on each side of the tractor. Even at $450 it did not sell, and the small profits made on the Model M were eaten up by the losses on the Iron Horse. Durant's judgment was once again called into question by his partners, particularly Walter Chrysler, who resigned over the tractor affair, and GM's vice-president, Alfred P. Sloan. Durant's personal finances were shaky, due to stock market losses in the 1920 slump, and a convenient solution to both problems was for Durant to sell his 2.5 million GM shares to pay off his debts. His place as president of General Motors was taken by Pierre S. duPont, but Billy was by no means finished. He was soon back with fresh supporters in Durant Motors Inc. but that story belongs to the next chapter.

THE DODGE STORY

They were born four years apart, but they looked as alike as twins and were seldom separated. The Dodge brothers, John and Horace, grew up in a little wooden cottage in a poor district of Niles, Michigan, and left school early to help their father and uncle run a small machine shop. It made little money, and John earned extra by driving a cow to pasture twice a day for 50 cents a week.

Both brothers were gifted mechanically, Horace probably more than John, and after various spells of employment in Detroit and across the border in Windsor, Ontario, they set up in business on their own account in 1901. The Dodge Brothers Machine Shop on Beaubien Street, Detroit, turned its hand to any machining jobs, but soon most of its business was being done with the Olds Motor Works. At first Dodge Brothers supplied engines, then transmissions. In 1903 the company began to deliver 8hp two-cylinder engines to Henry Ford, and was soon making engines, transmissions, and axles for him. The contract was worth $5,000 a month, with the brothers also receiving 50 Ford shares each; this alone was sufficient to make them millionaires ten years later. The company continued to supply Ford for some time, making the engines of the Models B and K. Even after Ford built his Highland Park plant he continued to obtain some supplies from the company. This state of affairs lasted until the summer of 1914, but by then the Dodge brothers were ready to launch a car of their own.

In many ways the Dodge Four was a grown-up version of Ford's Model T. Its engine was larger, at 212.3 cubic inches, and gave 35bhp to the Ford's 20bhp, and the transmission was a three-speed sliding one, although with a distinctive gearshift pattern, the reverse of the normal. The 12-volt electrical system was unusual in a low-priced car, but the most radical feature was the all-steel welded body developed in Philadelphia by Edward Budd. The Dodge brothers did not understand wood, and a steel body seemed the logical way to go. Being a little apprehensive about the all-welded construction that was Budd's pride, "they added rivets here and there, just in case," recalled employee Ralph Vail.

Announced in November 1914, the Dodge Four touring cost $785 and was an immediate sensation,

thanks to the well-established reputation of the brothers. No new make could have had a better start. Some 22,000 firms applied for dealerships before the car was even launched. Production in the last six weeks of 1914 was 249 cars, but by the end of 1915 45,000 had been made, putting Dodge in third place behind Ford and Willys-Overland. By 1920 Dodge was second, the highest position it ever reached, with 141,000 sales. Design did not change greatly during the company's first six years: however, a two-passenger roadster was added in 1915 and a center-door sedan for 1916. More significant was the company's first all-steel four-door sedan, new in 1919.

For the Dodge family 1920 was a sad year. While on a visit to New York for the Auto Show in January, Horace contracted pneumonia and very nearly died. Although the doctors offered little hope, John encouraged him to keep fighting and just as Horace rallied, John himself also caught pneumonia and died on January 14. The brothers had always been very close and Horace never got over John's death. He struggled through the year, and went to Florida for his usual winter vacation, where he died on December 10, officially of cirrhosis of the liver, but many people said of a broken heart. He was a great music lover and supporter of the Detroit Symphony Orchestra, which turned out *in toto* for his funeral and later gave a concert in his honor. Both brothers died very wealthy, leaving more than $20 million apiece. Inheritance taxes of $900,000 were the highest ever paid in Michigan history. Their widows remarried and lived a long time; John's widow Matilda died in 1967, aged 83, and Horace's widow Anna lived three years longer, dying at the age of 103. Thanks to their inheritances, careful investments, and wealthy second husbands, Matilda and Anna were among the richest women in the world.

1913 CADILLAC 30 TOURING ▼

OWNER: AALHOLM MUSEUM, DENMARK (PHOTO AALHOLM MUSEUM)

CHAPTER THREE

LUXURY AND UNORTHODOXY

1900 – 1920

"Price is secondary. We build always the highest
attainable quality, and the price is fixed
by the production cost."

Packard advertisement, 1915

▲ GENERAL VIEW OF THE 1915 NEW YORK SHOW; THE WINTON, BUICK, HAYNES, AND FRANKLIN STANDS ARE VISIBLE. COMPARED WITH TODAY'S SHOWS ONLY A LITTLE SPACE WAS ALLOTTED TO EACH MAKE, BUT THEN THERE WERE MANY, MANY MORE AUTO BUILDERS TO FIT IN!

MOTOR VEHICLE MANUFACTURERS' ASSOCIATION

WHILE THE LIKES OF FORD and Durant were putting America on wheels, another group of engineers set about catering to the wishes of the rich. They did not make their mark straightaway, and often started with modestly priced small cars, while the limited market for expensive machines was mostly filled by foreign imports. In the first few years of the century the wealthy American who wanted the best in private transportation bought a French-built Panhard or C.G.V., or a German-made Mercedes, but from 1905 onward he had a growing choice of home-built luxury cars. By coincidence, three of the best began with P. The Packard, Peerless, and Pierce-Arrow have become known as the "three Ps" of American motordom.

THE THREE Ps AND THEIR RIVALS
In 1898 an Ohio electrical engineer named James Ward Packard (1863–1928) bought the twelfth Winton car to be made. Like many early motorists he was not entirely satisfied with his purchase and took it back for adjustments, with some suggestions about how it could be improved. The irascible Alexander Winton, who by then had made more than 20 cars, was not pleased to be told his job by a man who had made none. No one knows exactly what the two men said to each other, but the story that has gone down in history is derived from the account by journalist Hugh Dolnar, written in 1901. He wrote: "Mr. Winton...replied...to the effect that the Winton

1910 HAYNES TOURING ◄▲

ELWOOD HAYNES PARTED COMPANY WITH THE APPERSON BROTHERS IN 1902 AND SET UP A RIVAL FACTORY IN THE SAME TOWN, KOKOMO, INDIANA. IN 1910, WHEN THIS MODEL 20 FOUR-CYLINDER TOURING WAS MADE, HAYNES PRODUCTS WERE CONVENTIONAL CARS BUILT IN TOURING AND ROADSTER FORMS. HAYNES WAS LATER TO MAKE A PIONEER V12. PRODUCTION ENDED IN 1925.

OWNER: TOM BARRETT (PHOTO NICKY WRIGHT)

wagon as it stood was the ripened and perfected product of many years of lofty thought, aided by mechanical skill of the highest grade, and could not be improved in any detail, and that if Mr. Packard wanted any of his own cats and dogs worked into a wagon, he had better build it himself, as he, Winton, would not stultify himself by any departure whatever from his own incontestably superior productions."

It is said that, following this outburst, Packard promptly went off and built himself a car. He had been thinking about automobiles since 1893, and before the Winton he had bought a De Dion Bouton tricycle. However, he did set to work on his own car in 1899, aided by his brother William Doud Packard and two former Winton men, George L. Weiss and William A. Hatcher. The first Packard left the workshops of the New York & Ohio Company in November 1899, and by the end of the year it had been followed by four more. They were quite typical of their time, relatively light two-passenger buggies with single-cylinder engines, two-speed planetary transmission, chain drive, and tiller steering. They did have one advanced feature, though: an H-pattern gearshift.

Only one of the 1899 Packards, called the Model A, was sold, the others being retained for experimental purposes. The Model B of 1900 was generally similar, but it had an automatic spark advance and a foot throttle. There was also a dual warning system, a normal hand-operated bulb horn

and a pedal-operated chime. Production was 49 cars, of which two were bought by William D. Rockefeller at the New York Auto Show in November 1900. These were the first of many Packards bought by the Rockefeller family. In 1901 Packard built 81 model Cs, whose chief improvement over previous designs was a steering wheel which replaced the tiller. Whereas the Model B could carry four passengers with a dos-à-dos seat, the Model C was offered with four forward-facing seats in addition to the dos-à-dos. All body styles were priced at a uniform $1,500.

The Model C was shown at the 1901 New York Show, and seen by a railroad and banking magnate from Detroit, Henry Bourne Joy (1864–1936). He and a friend were admiring a Packard outside the show when a fire engine went by. The Packard's owner gave the crank handle one turn, starting the motor immediately, and set off in hot pursuit of the fire engine. Joy was so impressed that he contacted the Packards and decided to invest in the business. This enabled them to expand and move from Ohio to Detroit in 1903. Without the intervention of Henry Joy, the Packard might never have become the world-renowned make that it did, for William Packard did not favor a move to multicylinders. "More than one cylinder in a Packard would be like two tails on a cat — you just don't need it." However, Joy thought otherwise and therefore hired a French engineer, Charles Schmidt, to design a four-cylinder for 1903.

Schmidt's first design was the Model K, a large 24hp car with four-speed sliding transmission and shaft drive. Expensive to manufacture, it had to be priced at an enormous $7,300, but still lost money for the company. Only 34 were made, and the K was hastily replaced by the smaller Model L. This was still a four-cylinder shaft-drive car, but with a three-speed transmission, and the price was a more reasonable $3,000. The longer wheelbase Model N came in 1905 and was the first Packard to be offered with closed bodywork, a brougham or limousine at $4,100 and $4,600 respectively. Packard was now set to become one of America's leading quality automobiles.

Peerless and Pierce-Arrow had quite similar backgrounds. Both were making bicycles in the 1890s, following such diverse productions as clothes wringers (Peerless) and bird cages (Pierce, hence the nickname "Fierce Sparrow"). Peerless was made in Cleveland and Pierce in Buffalo, and both entered the car world with small buggies powered by single-cylinder De Dion Bouton engines. What is more, both companies called their little cars Motorettes.

Larger machines soon followed, twin cylinders from Peerless in 1902 and Pierce in 1903, and by 1904 they had joined Packard in making four-cylinder cars. Pierce's was named the Great Arrow (the marque name Pierce-Arrow was not adopted until 1909); it was quite like a Mercedes in appearance, and had a 24/28hp T-head engine and shaft drive. The price for a touring was $4,000, and for 1905 there were three closed models on a longer wheelbase at $5,000. Peerless manufactured three four-cylinder cars in 1904, from $4,000 to $6,000,

beating both Packard and Pierce by having closed models that year.

The similarity of year-by-year changes is hardly surprising, for every manufacturer followed his rivals closely, workers moved from one factory to another, and there was undoubtedly a degree of industrial espionage. Each year wheelbases grew longer and bodies more elaborate, with electrically lit interiors, flower vases, and even hand washbasins. Packard had its own body-building department, as did most other American companies, in contrast to European luxury car makers such as Rolls-Royce, who supplied only chassis for specialist coachbuilders to work on. However, coachbuilders flourished in America as well, and being specialists were often in advance of the auto makers in their ideas. Most of the coachbuilders in the pre-1920 era were horse carriage makers, and some of the best known were Brewster of Long

Island City, whose history dated back to 1810, Cunningham of Rochester, New York, who began making complete cars in 1908, Judkins of Merrimac, Massachusetts, and Quinby of Newark, New Jersey.

The next major mechanical development to hit the auto industry was the six-cylinder engine. This had appeared in Europe on the Dutch Spyker of 1902 (which also offered four-wheel drive), and on the better-known British Napier of 1904, and the first in the United States appeared on the 1906 Franklin Type H 30hp. The six was promoted as giving a smoother-running engine, there being more explosions per revolution, an argument later used to justify eights, twelves, and sixteens. The overlapping power impulses gave better low-speed torque, which reduced the need for gear shifting. This was undoubtedly true, but on the debit side six-cylinder crankshafts were generally lighter in build and their

greater length made them subject to torsional stresses that led to fractures and total destruction of the engine. The solution was to mount an extra flywheel at the front of the crankshaft; this was proposed by the English engineer Frederick Lanchester and marketed in the United States as the Warner Crankshaft Damper. The Franklin adopted it in late 1905.

Following the Franklin's lead, numerous other American companies launched sixes; Ford with the Model K and Stevens-Duryea in 1906, Chadwick, Pierce-Arrow, and Stearns in 1907, Lozier, Oldsmobile, Peerless Thomas, and Winton in 1908. Packard ignored the trend longer than most and did not make a six until the 1912 season.

Some of these early sixes were monstrous cars. The Stearns 45/90hp had a displacement of 795 cubic inches and an engine so long that the rear pair of cylinders projected into the driving compartment. Prices ranged from $6,250 for a touring roadster to $7,500 for a limousine. The Oldsmobile Limited, made from 1910 to 1912, was one of the most impressive American cars

1911 ALCO FOUR-PASSENGER SPEEDSTER ◀ ▶

THE AMERICAN LOCOMOTIVE COMPANY WAS ONE OF THE COUNTRY'S LARGEST BUILDERS OF STEAM LOCOMOTIVES, WITH EIGHT PLANTS IN THE EASTERN STATES. IN 1905 AUTOMOBILE MANUFACTURE BEGAN IN THE PROVIDENCE, RHODE ISLAND, PLANT, USING THE FRENCH BERLIET AS A MODEL. UP TO 1909 THE CARS WERE KNOWN AS AMERICAN BERLIETS, THEN ALCOS. THEY WERE HIGH-QUALITY, HIGH-PRICED VEHICLES WITH HUGE ENGINES: 453 CUBIC INCHES IN THIS 40hp FOUR, AND 579 CUBIC INCHES IN THE 60hp SIX. ALCO BOASTED THAT IT TOOK A YEAR AND SEVEN MONTHS TO BUILD A SINGLE CAR.

OWNER: DUKE DAVENPORT (PHOTO NICKY WRIGHT)

A 1911 ADVERTISEMENT FOR THE ENORMOUS AND POWERFUL OLDSMOBILE LIMITED. THE CLAIM THAT IT COULD SOAR UP INCLINES IN HIGH GEAR WITH SEVEN PASSENGERS ABOARD WAS NO EXAGGERATION.

MIRCO DE CET COLLECTION

1903 PIERCE MOTORETTE ▶

PIERCE AND RIVAL PEERLESS BOTH BEGAN WITH SMALL CARS POWERED BY FRENCH-BUILT DE DION BOUTON ENGINES. AFTER STARTING WITH A 2¾hp UNIT, PIERCE WENT UP TO 3½hp IN 1902, AND TO 5hp AND 6hp IN 1903 WHEN THIS MOTORETTE WAS BUILT. BY THEN GEORGE PIERCE WAS MAKING HIS OWN ENGINES WITH SEVERAL IMPROVEMENTS OVER THE FRENCH DESIGN. THIS IS THE FOLDING FRONT SEAT MODEL SIMILAR TO THE ONE IN WHICH GEORGE'S SON, PERCY PIERCE, WON HIS CLASS IN THE NEW YORK–PITTSBURGH ENDURANCE TEST IN OCTOBER 1903.

OWNER: GEORGE SANDERS (PHOTO NICKY WRIGHT)

ever built, with 42-inch wheels and an engine displacement of 706 cubic inches. Passengers needed two steps to climb into the Limited, which looked deceptively low because of its enormous wheels (other Oldsmobiles had 36- or 38-inch wheels, while the Model T's were only 30 inches). The Limited was made for three seasons, 1910–1912, prices starting at $4,600 for a 1910 runabout and rising to $6,300 for a 1912 limousine. Total production was only 825, but Oldsmobile was at a low ebb anyway, output of all models being only 4,175 for the three years.

At the same time that Oldsmobile was making the Limited, over in Buffalo Pierce-Arrow had introduced the mighty 66, which vied with the Peerless for the largest engine of any production American car. With a displacement of 824 cubic inches, it exceeded even the famed Bugatti Royale (778 cubic inches), while the short-lived Fageol of 1917/18, often claimed as America's largest car, had the same displacement as the 66, although it was more expensive. The 66 was the largest of three Pierce-Arrow sixes, all of which had pair-cast T-head engines. Pierce-Arrows were among the

highest-quality American cars, and were much favored by conservative East Coast buyers who wanted the best without ostentation. The 66 was introduced in 1910, although it did not reach its full size of 824 cubic inches until 1912, while the longest wheelbase of 147½ inches did not arrive until 1913. The car was made up to 1918, production reaching a total of a very respectable 1,071 units.

Features of the big Pierce-Arrows included compressed air starters and a power air pump driven from the transmission, for pumping up tires. Prices ran from around $4,000 for the "small" Model UU to over $7,000 for a Model 66 vestibule suburban, which was a limousine with raised rear doors to allow ladies with fancy hats to enter without too much bending. Custom-built models were even more costly; Pierce-Arrow president George Birge had a special touring landau on the 66-QQ chassis, with running boards enlarged to contain storage compartments, a sliding drawer under the rear seat, and a fold-out washbasin supplied with running water from a pressurized tank under the body. This car cost $8,250, and two others were subsequently made, one of them for the cereal magnate Charles W. Post.

Locomobile also made big and expensive sixes, starting in 1911 with the 522-cubic-inch Model 48.

The engine was a T-head, like the Pierce-Arrow's, and Locomobile persisted with this layout up to the end of production in 1929, when it had long been abandoned by all other manufacturers in favor of the L-head. Indeed the 48 itself was still made in 1929, but with power upped from 48 to 103bhp and modern features such as balloon tires and four-wheel brakes. Late in 1914 Locomobile set up a custom body department headed by Frank de Causse, who later worked for Franklin. This turned out some very handsome and advanced coachwork, and Locomobiles were found in the garages of many famous names such as William Carnegie, Lawrence Copley Thaw, and Willie K. Vanderbilt. In 1916 de Causse designed a dual cowl phaeton for Rodman Wanamaker, the first of its kind, subsequently cataloged as the Sportif. Fittings and metal work for Locomobile bodies were designed by Tiffany and interiors were planned by the well-known actress and interior decorator Elsie de Wolf. In 1918 General John "Black Jack" Pershing had two 48s built for his use in France, with sloping Vee windshield, narrow body to reduce wind resistance, and dual rear tires. Ordinary 48s were also used by the U.S. Army in France, but it was found that at top speed (80mph) the vertical windshield had a tendency to crack, hence Pershing's request for a Vee-shaped one.

V 8s AND V12s

By 1914 the six-cylinder engine was commonplace on medium-priced cars such as Buick, Chalmers, and Studebaker. But for still greater smoothness eight cylinders were needed, and in order not to have too long a crankshaft a Vee layout was preferable to an in-line one (in-line eights became very popular and fashionable in the 1920s when crankshaft strengths were greater).

The first V8 engine had been made in 1903 by the Frenchman Clément Ader, but it was little more than four V-twins coupled together. In America Buffum had offered a V8 touring in 1906 and Hewitt had one in 1907, but few if any were sold. Another French make, De Dion Bouton, was the first to commercialize the V8 engine, from 1910 onward, but the honor for the first successful large-

1913 CADILLAC ROADSTER ◄ ▲
THE 1913 CADILLACS CONTINUED THE DELCO INTEGRATED ELECTRIC LIGHTING AND STARTING SYSTEM INTRODUCED IN 1912, AND ALSO HAD LARGER ENGINES WITH POWER UPPED FROM 40bhp TO 50bhp, AND WHEELBASES WERE EXTENDED BY 4 INCHES TO 120 INCHES. APPEARANCE WAS IMPROVED WHEN A CURVED COWL REPLACED THE STRAIGHT DASH. THE SLOGAN "STANDARD OF THE WORLD" WAS USED FOR THE FIRST TIME IN 1913.

OWNER: NATIONAL AUTOMOBILE MUSEUM, RENO, NEVADA

(PHOTO NICKY WRIGHT)

1920 PACKARD TWIN SIX 3-35 LIMOUSINE ▶

THE WORLD'S FIRST QUANTITY-PRODUCED AUTOMOBILE
WITH A V12 ENGINE, THE PACKARD TWIN SIX WAS
IN ITS SIXTH SEASON BY 1920. THE MAIN IMPROVEMENT
THAT YEAR WAS THE FUELIZER: A SPARK PLUG IN THE
INTAKE MANIFOLD, WHICH HELPED TO VAPORIZE THE
GASOLINE. EIGHT BODY STYLES WERE OFFERED — THIS
LIMOUSINE WAS THE SECOND MOST EXPENSIVE
OF THEM AT $7,900. IN 1921 THE CAR THAT
WARREN G. HARDING RODE IN TO HIS INAUGURATION AS
PRESIDENT WAS A PACKARD TWIN SIX. THIS WAS
THE FIRST TIME THAT AN AUTOMOBILE HAD REPLACED
A HORSE-DRAWN CARRIAGE FOR THIS EVENT.

OWNER: NATIONAL AUTOMOBILE MUSEUM, RENO, NEVADA

(PHOTO NICKY WRIGHT)

1915 CADILLAC V8 TOURING ▲

THE WORLD'S FIRST SUCCESSFUL QUANTITY-BUILT V8,
THE CADILLAC TYPE 51 WAS LAUNCHED IN SEPTEMBER
1914 IN NINE BODY STYLES, OF WHICH THE FIVE- AND
SEVEN-PASSENGER TOURING CARS WERE THE LOWEST
PRICED AT $1,975. BEFORE THE CADILLAC, THE FEW V8s
MADE HAD BEEN VERY EXPENSIVE AND OF DOUBTFUL
RELIABILITY. CADILLAC'S ENGINEER D. McCALL WHITE
GAVE THE WORLD A DEPENDABLE, SMOOTH, AND
POWERFUL UNIT THAT WAS COPIED BY MANY OTHER
FIRMS, AND BECAME THE STANDARD LAYOUT FOR
AMERICAN ENGINES AFTER WORLD WAR II.

OWNER: CRAWFORD COLLECTION OF THE WESTERN HISTORICAL SOCIETY

(PHOTO NICKY WRIGHT)

scale production V8 goes to Cadillac.

In 1914 Cadillac did not hold the prestige position among American automobiles that it enjoyed in later years. Rather Cadillacs were well-respected four-cylinder cars in the upper-middle price bracket, selling for $1,975 to $3,250, around half the asking price for the larger Pierce-Arrows and Locomobiles. In 1912 Cadillac had set a lead with the introduction of a combined electric lighting and starting set. This was largely the work of Charles F. Kettering of the Dayton Engineering Laboratories Company (later Delco), but the V8 engine was designed by Cadillac's own D. McCall White, a Scottish-born engineer whose previous appointments had been with Daimler and Napier in England.

The two banks of cylinders were mounted at 90° to each other and had a displacement of 314 cubic inches. They were in cast-iron blocks of four on an aluminum crankcase. Maximum output was 70bhp at 2,400rpm, but in 1916 this went up to 77bhp at 2,600rpm, and in the 1920s the V8 was advertised as giving 80+bhp. This was a great improvement over the 40bhp given by the larger 365.8-cubic-inch four-cylinder engine. As on the four, the V8 engine drove through a three-speed transmission, but the driver was now on the left, with a central gear lever, although right-hand drives could still be had as an option. The V8's wheelbase was 2 inches longer than its predecessor's, but the car's appearance was virtually the same — the same body styles were offered at almost the same prices. This made the V8 remarkable value. The four was dropped for 1915, not to be reintroduced for another 67 years.

The Cadillac V8 was announced in September 1914 and seems to have taken the industry by surprise. Rivals were quick to criticize it, and to counter such criticism Cadillac's advertising agency came up with one of the most famous advertising slogans in history, "The Penalty of Leadership." Cadillac sold 13,002 cars in the 1915 model year, and 18,004 for 1916. Imitations came initially not from the big manufacturers who made their own engines, but from proprietary engine builders such as Ferro, Herschell-Spillman, Massnick-Phipps, Northway, and Perkins, who began to offer V8s that enabled many smaller car makers to get in on the act. For 1916 Detroiter and Remington offered V8s (by Perkins and Massnick-Phipps respectively), and by 1918 at least 20 American car makers were listing V8s, from the $1,050 Homer-Laughlin to the 566-cubic-inch nine-passenger RiChard listed at $8,000. Cadillac's engines were made by the GM-owned Northway company, which also supplied V8s to Oldsmobile from 1915 and, perhaps surprisingly, sold them to companies outside the GM fold, such as Cole of Indianapolis and Jackson of Jackson, Michigan. The discreet luxury car maker Cunningham of Rochester, N.Y., used its own 442-cubic-inch V8 from 1917, while the equally discreet Daniels, which carried its name nowhere on the car, only the letter D on the hubcaps, used a Herschell-Spillman V8 from 1915 to 1919, then made its own.

The V8 was followed with remarkable speed by the V12. In May 1915 Packard announced the Twin Six, which had been under development for nearly two years, designed by Jesse Vincent, who had come from Hudson three years earlier. The two banks of six cylinders were mounted at a narrower angle than in the V8 Cadillac, at 60°. Displacement was 424.1 cubic inches and output 88bhp at 2,600rpm. The Twin Six engine weighed 400 pounds less than the previous Packard six, yet torque was 100 percent better, and 50 percent better than it would have been had he used a V8, said Vincent.

The Packard Six was continued to September 1915 to allow Twin Six production to build up, but thereafter the new model took over and was the sole Packard until the 1921 season. For such a sophisticated car it was remarkably cheap. In 1916 the lowest-priced model was the touring on the shorter of two wheelbases, which sold for $2,750, while the most expensive was a long-wheelbase imperial limousine at $4,650. In its first season the Twin Six sold 3,606 units, slightly fewer than for all models the previous year, but the 1917 season saw nearly 9,000 sold, and 9,586 in 1918/19. By the end of Twin Six production in 1923, sales reached over

30,900. Twin Sixes were very popular in Latin America, where Packard agencies were set up for the first time in Buenos Aires and Rio de Janeiro.

As with Cadillac's V8, so Packard's Twin Six encouraged imitators. National of Indianapolis launched its Highway Twelve just after Packard. In 1916 the proprietary engine maker Weidely brought out a 390-cubic-inch V12 which enabled several small firms to offer the prestige of a twelve, something they could never have done if they had had to make their own engines. The HAL from Cleveland, Pathfinder from Indianapolis, and Singer from Mount Vernon, New York, were all twelves. However, none of them had much success, and by 1921 Packard was almost the only purveyor of twelve-cylinder automobiles.

▲ THE NATIONAL WAS A RESPECTED MAKE THAT FLOURISHED IN INDIANAPOLIS FROM 1900 TO 1924. THIS IS A 1913 SERIES V FOUR-CYLINDER TOURING, WHICH SOLD FOR $3,000. FOR 1915 NATIONAL WENT OVER TO SIXES, AND THEN THE FOLLOWING YEAR INTRODUCED ITS V12 HIGHWAY TWELVE.

MOTOR VEHICLE MANUFACTURERS' ASSOCIATION

ONE OF THE GREATEST GIFTS OF THE AUTOMOBILE TO
THE AMERICAN PEOPLE WAS THE FREEDOM OF THE
COUNTRYSIDE, ESPECIALLY ENJOYABLE IN THE DAYS
BEFORE THERE WERE TOO MANY TOURISTS. PICNICS
WERE POPULAR, AS THESE PHOTOS SHOW.

▲ THE CAR HERE IS A 1911 ABBOTT-DETROIT.

▶ A c.1914 PICTURE WHERE, NOT SURPRISINGLY,
MOST OF THE CARS ARE FORD MODEL Ts.

MOTOR VEHICLE MANUFACTURERS' ASSOCIATION

◀ TIRE CHANGING WAS PROBABLY THE EARLY
MOTORIST'S GREATEST PROBLEM. BURSTS
OCCURRED FREQUENTLY BECAUSE OF
INFERIOR RUBBER AND ALSO THE VARIETY
OF OBJECTS LITTERING THE ROADS,
SUCH AS STONES AND HORSESHOE NAILS.
TIRES HAD TO BE LEVERED OFF THE RIMS,
AS DETACHABLE RIMS DID NOT COME IN
UNTIL AROUND 1910, AND DETACHABLE
WHEELS EVEN LATER.
MOTOR VEHICLE MANUFACTURERS' ASSOCIATION

◀▼ BEFORE THE DAYS OF DRIVE-IN
FORECOURTS, GASOLINE WAS
SUPPLIED TO CARS STANDING AT THE
CURBSIDE BY OVERHEAD PIPE.
MORE CONVENTIONAL DELIVERY OF
GASOLINE, NEW YORK, c.1920.
MOTOR VEHICLE MANUFACTURERS' ASSOCIATION

▲ "G & J TIRE DOES NOT BURST" SAID THE 1910
ADVERTISEMENT, BUT THIS INNER TUBE HAD BALLOONED
TO AN ALARMING SIZE.
MOTOR VEHICLE MANUFACTURERS' ASSOCIATION

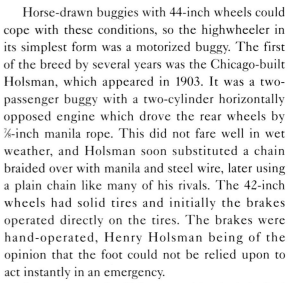

1909 SEARS HIGH-WHEEL BUGGY ◄▲
THE SEARS ROEBUCK CATALOG WAS SECOND ONLY TO
THE BIBLE IN MANY AMERICAN HOMES, AND FROM 1908
TO 1912 YOU COULD ORDER AN AUTOMOBILE FROM IT.
THE SEARS HIGHWHEELER (CATALOG NUMBER 21R333)
WAS TYPICAL OF ITS KIND, WITH 10hp HORIZONTAL
TWIN ENGINE, FRICTION TRANSMISSION, AND DOUBLE
CHAIN DRIVE. UP TO THE END OF 1909 THE BUGGIES
WERE MADE FOR SEARS BY COLONEL WILLIAM H.
McCURDY AT EVANSVILLE, INDIANA, BUT AFTER THAT
SEARS OPENED ITS OWN PLANT IN CHICAGO. ABOUT
3,500 SEARS WERE MADE BETWEEN 1908 AND 1912.
OWNER: CRAWFORD COLLECTION OF THE WESTERN HISTORICAL SOCIETY
(PHOTO NICKY WRIGHT)

HIGHWHEELERS, CYCLECARS AND ODDITIES

By about 1905 automobile design had settled down
to a general pattern of front-mounted vertical
water-cooled engines, driving through planetary or
sliding gear transmission to a bevel gear rear axle.
There were, of course, exceptions, such as the air-
cooled Franklin and cars defined as highwheelers
and cyclecars, and a few machines that were
downright weird.

The highwheeler, as historian Beverly Rae
Kimes has observed, may or
may not have been a practical
answer to a crying need, but it
was definitely as American as
the Fourth of July. It was born
just after the turn of the
century in response to the
appalling state of country roads. As a correspondent
from Montana wrote in *The Horseless Age*: "All roads
have ruts at each side varying from two to fifteen
inches deep. To run a car with a nine inch
clearance over these roads in daylight is
exasperating, and it is practically impossible to run
after dark."

Horse-drawn buggies with 44-inch wheels could
cope with these conditions, so the highwheeler in
its simplest form was a motorized buggy. The first
of the breed by several years was the Chicago-built
Holsman, which appeared in 1903. It was a two-
passenger buggy with a two-cylinder horizontally
opposed engine which drove the rear wheels by
⅞-inch manila rope. This did not fare well in wet
weather, and Holsman soon substituted a chain
braided over with manila and steel wire, later using
a plain chain like many of his rivals. The 42-inch
wheels had solid tires and initially the brakes
operated directly on the tires. The brakes were
hand-operated, Henry Holsman being of the
opinion that the foot could not be relied upon to
act instantly in an emergency.

In many ways the Holsman and its rivals looked
at least ten years behind the times with their
spidery wheels, lack of fenders, and piano box
bodies perched on full elliptic springs. Many of the
companies making them were in the buggy trade,
and it showed in their appearance. The Holsman
company had increased its factory space sixfold by
1906, and was working night shifts to keep up with
demand. This spurred others to get in on the
lucrative field, and in the next few years nearly 100
makers offered highwheelers. Chicago was the
center of production; apart from the Holsman, it
was home to the International Harvester Company,
makers of the I.H.C., and to the Sears, offered from
1908 to 1912 in Sears Roebuck's famous catalog. A
Sears owner probably spoke for many when he
wrote to the company: "It beats a horse bad as it
don't eat when I ain't working it, and it stands
without hitching, and best of all it don't get scared
at automobiles."

St. Louis had a number of
well-known makes such as the
A.B.C. and Success, while
Auburn, Indiana, was home to
the Kiblinger, McIntyre, and
Zimmerman, and Cincinnati to
the Schacht. Most highwheelers came from the
Midwest, although exceptions included the Kearns
from Beavertown, Pennsylvania, and the White
Star from Atlanta, Georgia. North of the border the
Tudhope Carriage Company of Orillia, Ontario,
made a highwheeler using the McIntyre engine.
Highwheelers appealed particularly to farmers, but

1913 IMP CYCLECAR ◄

THE IMP, BUILT AT AUBURN, INDIANA, LOOKED A TYPICAL CYCLECAR, BUT IT HAD A NUMBER OF UNUSUAL FEATURES. THESE INCLUDED WHEELS MOUNTED ON THE ENDS OF TRANSVERSE SPRINGS, WHICH DID AWAY WITH AXLES, AND STARTING FROM THE DRIVER'S SEAT. THIS WAS EFFECTED BY INSERTING A CRANK IN THE CENTER OF THE STEERING COLUMN, WHICH CONNECTED WITH A RATCHET ON THE CRANKSHAFT. THE AIR-COOLED V-TWIN ENGINE GAVE 15bhp, AND DROVE VIA FRICTION TRANSMISSION AND LONG BELTS TO THE REAR WHEELS.

OWNER: AUBURN-CORD-DUESENBERG MUSEUM (PHOTO NICKY WRIGHT)

1908 ZIMMERMAN HIGH-WHEEL BUGGY ◄▼

THE ZIMMERMAN MANUFACTURING COMPANY OF AUBURN, INDIANA, WAS ONE OF MANY HORSE BUGGY-BUILDING FIRMS THAT TURNED TO MOTOR POWER. THIS EXAMPLE FROM THE FIRST YEAR OF PRODUCTION HAD A 14hp TWO-CYLINDER AIR-COOLED ENGINE AND CHAIN DRIVE. NOTE THE DOUBLE-LEAVED TRANSVERSE FRONT SPRING. THE COMPANY LATER OFFERED STANDARD FOUR-CYLINDER CARS, WHICH WERE BUILT FOR ZIMMERMAN BY THE AUBURN AUTOMOBILE COMPANY. THESE WERE MADE UP TO 1914; THE LAST ZIMMERMAN WAS A SIX, BUILT FROM 1913 TO 1915.

were not exclusively country vehicles. In 1907 there were nearly 100 Holsmans operating in Chicago, and of these 75 percent were owned by physicians.

After about six years highwheelers fell victim to progress. They were very slow, 25mph being a good top speed, and offered little in the way of weather protection, although Holsman did make a closed model called the coupelette. Cheaper than most cars initially, they were soon undercut by the Model T, which was also pretty good at coping with bad roads. Better sometimes, for the highwheeler's narrow solid tires would break through the frozen crust to the mud below while wider pneumatic tires stayed on top. By 1913 practically all the highwheelers had gone. I.H.C. and Schacht turned to trucks, McIntyre to cyclecars, and most of the others gave up altogether.

If the highwheeler was uniquely American, the next craze to hit the industry was an import from Europe: the cyclecar. This was a light two-passenger auto using many motorcycle components in its specification, which emerged in France in 1910 and spawned a large number of makes there and in Britain over the next ten years. The fashion did not hit America until 1913, but when it did, it hit hard.

Between the summer of 1913 and the end of 1915 at least 215 ambitious individuals or companies tried to build cyclecars, although probably not more than 30 ever got as far as serious production. They were widespread geographically, from Laconia, New Hampshire (Laconia), to Seattle, Washington (Tilikum), while Detroit had at least nine by November 1913.

As in Europe, none of the big car makers turned to the cyclecar. A lone Ford cyclecar, resembling a scaled-down Model T, did show up in front of Detroit's Pontchartrain Hotel, but this was Henry's ruse to deter a possible threat to the T. He reasoned that if the smaller makers thought that Ford was going to enter the cyclecar market they would give up.

In January 1914 the American Cyclecar Manufacturers' Association was founded, defining the cyclecar as a four-wheeled vehicle with an engine displacement of not more than 71 cubic inches. A consequence of this was that cyclecars were almost all two-passenger cars, although

1904 ORIENT BUCKBOARD ▲
BILLED AS "THE CHEAPEST AUTOMOBILE IN THE WORLD — EVERYBODY SHOULD HAVE ONE," THE ORIENT BUCKBOARD WAS BUILT BY THE WALTHAM MANUFACTURING COMPANY OF WALTHAM, MASSACHUSETTS, AND COST ONLY $375 IN 1903. RIDING ON AN 80-INCH WHEELBASE, IT HAD A 4hp SINGLE-CYLINDER ENGINE AND NO SPRINGS, AS THE FLEXING OF THE WOODEN SLATS THAT FORMED THE CHASSIS WAS CONSIDERED SUFFICIENT SUSPENSION. EVIDENTLY CUSTOMERS THOUGHT OTHERWISE, FOR THIS 1904 MODEL HAS FULLY ELLIPTIC SPRINGS AT THE FRONT. BUCKBOARDS WERE BUILT THROUGH THE 1907 SEASON.
OWNER: CRAWFORD COLLECTION OF THE WESTERN HISTORICAL SOCIETY (PHOTO NICKY WRIGHT)

designers differed as to whether the passengers should sit side by side, staggered, or in line one behind the other. If the latter, should the driver be in front or behind? The driver-behind solution was favored by the makers of the Automobilette, Davis, Greyhound, and one or two others, and was practical so long as the passenger in front was not fatter or taller than the driver.

Cyclecar engines were mostly V-twins, with their crankshafts mounted transversely so that they could drive a belt transmission to a pulley on the back wheel. The engines were usually under a hood, but the Detroit-built Cricket carried its engine beside the driver on the running board.

This had the advantage of needing a shorter belt, but against this the weight distribution must have been distinctly odd, while the driver had to scramble over a hot engine or enter from the passenger side. Throttles were usually hand-controlled, as on a motorcycle.

One of the cyclecar's advantages was its size, in particular the tread, which seldom exceeded 36 inches. This meant that it could be driven through the garden gate, up the path, and garaged beneath the porch. For those who did not have porches, a simple garage could be fashioned from rough lumber by almost anyone, and did not need to be more than 4½ feet high, 3½ feet wide, and 9 feet

1915 METZ ROADSTER ▶

CHARLES METZ HAD BEEN AN IMPORTANT PRODUCER OF
BICYCLES IN THE 1890s, AND IN 1898 MADE AMERICA'S
FIRST MOTORCYCLE. IN 1909 HE BEGAN TO OFFER CARS
UNDER THE METZ PLAN, WHEREBY 14 PACKAGES OF
PARTS WERE SOLD IN STAGES TO SUIT THE CUSTOMER'S
WALLET AND THE TIME HE THOUGHT HE WOULD TAKE
TO ASSEMBLE THE CAR. ALTHOUGH METZ WAS NOT THE
FIRST TO OFFER A KIT CAR, HIS FINANCING WAS
CERTAINLY UNUSUAL. IN 1911 HE BEGAN TO PRODUCE
COMPLETE CARS AND BY 1915, WHEN THIS ROADSTER
WAS MADE, THE KITS WERE NO LONGER AVAILABLE. THIS
CAR HAD A 22hp FOUR-CYLINDER ENGINE, FRICTION
TRANSMISSION, AND CHAIN FINAL DRIVE. METZ'S BEST
YEAR WAS 1915, WITH 7,200 CARS DELIVERED.

OWNER: GEORGE SANDERS (PHOTO NICKY WRIGHT)

1912 INTERNATIONAL HARVESTER ▲

INTERNATIONAL MADE HIGH-WHEEL PASSENGER CARS FROM 1907 TO 1911, AND TRUCKS UP TO 1916.
THIS 1912 MOTOR TRUCK HAD A HORIZONTALLY OPPOSED TWO-CYLINDER ENGINE GIVING 18-20hp, AND
COULD BE FITTED WITH "SUNDAY-GO-TO-MEETIN'" SEATS IN THE LOAD-CARRYING SPACE.

OWNER: CRAWFORD COLLECTION OF THE WESTERN HISTORICAL SOCIETY (PHOTO NICKY WRIGHT)

long. Another advantage, initially, was its price, which ran from just under $300 for the simplest machines and seldom exceeded $400. In 1913 the cheapest Model T was $525.

There was boundless optimism among cyclecar manufacturers and dealers. Charles Coey of Chicago, who had begun manufacture of his Coey Bear as a sideline to his full-size Flyers, said: "We believe that the 1,125,000 horse-drawn buggies that were sold in 1913 will all be supplanted by two-passenger light cars." The nation's first female cyclecar dealer, 21-year-old Anna Sheeley of Passaic, New Jersey, expected to sell 500 cyclecars in southern New Jersey alone in 1914, and added "...there is no limit apparently to the number of cars I can sell."

At least three magazines sprang up in 1913 to cater for the new craze, *Cyclecar Age* (New York), *The American Cyclecar* (Chicago), and *Cyclecar and Motorette*. However in 1914 *Cyclecar Age* changed its name to *Light Car Age*, and *The American Cyclecar* to *Carette*, reflecting a growing disillusion with the cyclecar concept. The little cars were just too flimsy in their design, and when this was coupled with sometimes bad workmanship and harsh usage, they did not offer what the American motorist expected. Transmissions were a particular weakness, for the long belts slipped, stretched, and sometimes broke, and friction drives became increasingly useless in wet weather, so that the slightest hill brought the vehicle to a standstill. Tops were either nonexistent or hopeless at

keeping out driving rain. And by 1915 even their low price had ceased to be an advantage, for Henry Ford had lowered the price of a Model T two-passenger roadster to $440. The cyclecar makers couldn't afford to reduce their prices. It cost only an extra $40 to buy a full-sized car with a four-cylinder engine, shaft transmission, and proper weather protection, and all the benefits of an established reputation and nationwide servicing facilities.

The demise of the cyclecar was as rapid as its birth; by the end of 1915 the breed was just about extinct, as were the magazines that had promoted it. The spidery belt-drive tandem-seated models went first, while cars like the Trumbull, which had a four-cylinder engine and sliding gear transmission, lasted into 1915. The Trumbull might have survived longer if its founder Isaac Trumbull, together with 20 cars, had not gone to the bottom of the Atlantic when the liner *Lusitania* was sunk by a German torpedo in May 1915.

Given their flimsy construction, it is not surprising that the survival rate of cyclecars was very low, much lower than that of larger cars made in the same era. Nothing is left of most of the 200-odd makes beyond a few photographs.

Apart from highwheelers and cyclecars, there were other automobiles which differed from the norm. Strange though these may seem today, one must remember that in the early days there was no

tradition of car design, nothing except a certain degree of common sense, to keep their makers on the straight and narrow.

Take motive power, for example. Gasoline, steam, and electricity sufficed for most car makers, but a few were lured by compressed air stored in large cylinders at pressures up to 3,000 pounds per square inch and admitted to the working cylinders through a pressure regulating gauge giving a constant 100 pounds per square inch. The expanded air drove pistons in the same way as hot air in a steam engine. The idea was first proposed by MacKenzie and MacArthur of New Haven, Connecticut, in 1895, although it is not certain if they ever built a running vehicle. In 1896 a six-seater carriage called the Pneumatic, built by the American Wheelock Engine Company of Worcester, Massachusetts, definitely took to the road, reaching 15mph at the low engine speed of 350rpm. In the Pneumatic, the expansion of air was aided by hot water stored in a separate tank, presumably very well lagged so that it kept hot for a reasonable length of time. Limited range was the main drawback of the compressed air engine, whose proposers tended to be visionaries who imagined a vast network of storage facilities with their attendant compressing plants. Six companies proposed or built compressed-air cars between 1895 and 1900, all in the states of New York, Connecticut, or Massachusetts, but none went into production.

A variation on compressed air was liquid air, whose evaporation produced the compressing force for the engine. This seems to have been even less practical than compressed air, and the much touted Liquid Air Power & Automobile Company of New York and Boston was a stock promotion fraud which may never have built a car at all. More modest was the Tripler Liquid Air Company, also of New York City, which built at least one car that still exists today. The company claimed that the liquid air could be stored safely for up to ten days, but the car's prospects were doomed by the scandal surrounding the other company. Both ventures had collapsed by 1901.

Kerosene-powered cars were not unknown in the early days, but none came stranger than the Brooklyn-built Tuck of 1904. In this the oil was admitted to the cylinder without being vaporized, and there was no explosion. One wonders how any motive power was developed, but the maker claimed that high torque was developed at low speed, so there was no need for gears. There was no reverse either; when the driver wanted to back up he just reversed the direction of the engine, although to do so he had to stop the motor and pull a lever which "shifted the cams in such a manner that the direction of rotation was changed." An easily impressed reporter said that the Tuck was "full of very novel ideas, of which much is expected," but it not surprising that no more was heard of it.

Another kerosene-driven car from a later era was the Ingram Hatch, made in a former steam laundry on Staten Island in 1917. It was exceptional for what it lacked rather than otherwise. It was advertised as having "no clutch, no radiator, no magneto, no gearshift, no water system, no central controlled shaft, no carburetor, no water jackets, no timers, no selective transmission, no need for gasoline." What did it have, one wonders? It had an air-cooled four-cylinder engine with friction transmission from which twin shafts took power to each half of the rear

axle. So the boasted "no central shaft" was replaced by two shafts, more complication rather than less! The most unusual feature of the Ingram Hatch was its wheel design, which consisted of heart-shaped springs in place of spokes, with compressed-air cushions between them to reduce road shock. With all this there was no need for pneumatic tires, so these were made of leather and steel in sections that could be replaced if they became worn, rather than changing whole tires. Alas, no one seemed to take Joseph Ingram or William Hatch very seriously, and only one car was made.

Most designers were content with three or four wheels, but cars were made with five, six, or eight. The best-known five-wheeler was the Smith Flyer, also sold under the names Briggs & Stratton and Auto Red Bug. First marketed in 1917, it was a very simple buckboard with four cycle-type wheels at each corner and six wooden slats for a frame. There were no springs, as the slats were thought to be sufficiently flexible to provide a reasonably comfortable ride. Power came from a 2½hp single-cylinder engine mounted on a wheel which was let down onto the road behind the buckboard. The engine was started first, and care had to taken with the throttle; too little and the engine stalled, too much and you burned all the tread off the tire! Still, the buckboard was quite popular, and several hundred were sold at around $200 each. From 1924

to 1930 they were made by a firm in New Jersey that offered electrically-powered models as well; these used a 12-volt battery and motor employed in Dodge cars, which drove directly to the rear axle, so there was no need for the fifth wheel.

Another, more obscure, five-wheeler was the Chicago-built Glover of 1902, which had a traction drum in the middle of the frame, with face plates of soft steel between two disks. Chain-driven from a four-cylinder engine, the drum was spring-loaded to keep contact with the ground and was said to enable the car to pull two heavy coal wagons, one with its brakes locked. Glover also built a steam-powered version in which the drum could be filled with hot water from the boiler to melt snow in winter!

The six- and eight-wheelers were built by Milton O. Reeves of Columbus, Indiana, who took his inspiration from a Pullman railroad coach, believing that more wheels equaled greater comfort. His Octo-Auto of 1911 was converted from an Overland touring, with two pairs of wheels at each end. Wheelbase was 180 inches and overall length 248 inches. The first rear axle was powered, and steering was on all eight wheels, the front pair of axles turning in the normal direction, the rear pair in the opposite direction, as in today's Honda Prelude and Mazda 626. Reeves quoted a price of $3,200 for his Octo-Auto, but received no orders, and in 1912 decided to think a little smaller. He made two Sexto-Autos, the first the Octo-Auto with only one front axle, the second based on a Stutz. For this he asked $5,000, doubtless because of the greater price of the base car (a standard Overland 40 touring cost $1,300, a Stutz $2,250).

You would think that there would be little disagreement over where to place the wheels on a four-wheeled car, but at least two designers arranged them in a diamond pattern, one each at front and back and one on each side. In 1907 Thomas Vandergrift's Autocycle emerged from its Philadelphia workshop. Powered by an air-cooled 6hp twin driving the rear wheel by belt, it had two normal-sized wheels front and back, and two smaller ones on either side, almost like the stabilizers on a child's bike. With a very small turning circle (three of the four wheels steered), a 45mph top speed, and a $400 price tag, the Autocycle seemed an attractive proposition, but production lasted only one year.

1905 STANLEY ROADSTER ▲ ▶
BY 1905 STANLEY HAD ADOPTED THE
CHARACTERISTIC ROUNDED HOOD,
UNDER WHICH LURKED THE BOILER.
THE HORIZONTAL TWO-CYLINDER ENGINE
WAS LOCATED AHEAD OF THE REAR AXLE,
WHICH IT DROVE DIRECTLY WITHOUT ANY
NEED FOR VARIABLE GEARS.
OWNER: CRAWFORD COLLECTION OF THE WESTERN
HISTORICAL SOCIETY (PHOTO NICKY WRIGHT)

On similar lines was the Serpentina roadster made in New York City in 1915 by Claudius Mezzacasa. This was more streamlined than the Autocycle, almost torpedo-shaped, and the wheels were of equal size, those at the front and rear steering in opposite directions, whereas on the Autocycle the front and center pair steered, the rear wheel being fixed. *Scientific American* reported: "A traffic policeman at Columbus Circle did not trust his eyes when the car showed up for the first time. The driver swung the steering wheel round just as the car reached the policeman, and it performed a pirouette of the most amazing swiftness. Before the surprised policeman could

open his mouth, it had darted off in a right-handed direction — after having described an arc of 450 degrees." Sadly, no more were made than of the Autocycle, possibly only Mezzacasa's prototype.

S TEAM AND ELECTRICITY

Although they were to become marginal by the 1920s, steam- and electric-powered cars were a significant part of the automotive scene in the first two decades of the century. Particularly in the northeastern United States steam was dominant at the turn of the century; more than 50 percent of all cars registered in the state of New York in 1902 were steam-powered. But Locomobile's changeover to gasoline at the end of the 1903 season marked a sharp downturn, and during the next two years many smaller makes followed suit or went out of business altogether. Only two significant makes carried on, Stanley and White.

The Stanley had been redesigned in 1902 to avoid infringing the patents which the brothers had

granted to A. L. Barber of Locomobile and J. B. Walker of Mobile. The engine was now horizontal and geared directly to the rear axle, a layout which Stanley maintained until the last one left the factory in 1927. In 1905 the frontal boiler was covered under a rounded hood. This became the marque's characteristic feature until 1915, when a Vee-shaped dummy radiator was substituted. It acted as a condenser to reduce the exhaust steam to water for re-use, a feature seen on many steamers ten years earlier, but the cautious Stanley twins were never in a hurry to adopt other people's ideas. They retained wooden frames until 1915, long after most other American car makers, with the exception of Franklin, had gone over to steel.

For their price, Stanleys gave excellent performance, something appreciated by the Boston police department as early as 1903 when it bought several of the folding front seat models. The

1902 WHITE STANHOPE ▲

ALTHOUGH THE WHITE LOOKED SIMILAR TO THE STANLEY AT THIS TIME, IT WAS A MORE ADVANCED DESIGN, WITH SEMIFLASH BOILER. THIS MUST BE AN EARLY 1902 MODEL, FOR THAT YEAR BROUGHT THE INTRODUCTION OF THE FRONT-MOUNTED CONDENSER, WHICH LOOKED LIKE A RADIATOR AND RECYCLED THE EXHAUST STEAM. IN 1903 WHITES LOST THEIR BUGGY LOOK, FOR THEY NOW HAD HOODS LIKE A GASOLINE CAR.

OWNER: CRAWFORD COLLECTION OF THE WESTERN HISTORICAL SOCIETY
(PHOTO NICKY WRIGHT)

1913 BAKER ELECTRIC VICTORIA ▲▶

BY 1913 THE TYPICAL ELECTRIC CAR WAS A CLOSED COUPE, BUT BAKER STILL OFFERED THIS OPEN TWO-PASSENGER VICTORIA. IT IS UNMISTAKABLY AN ELECTRIC, BUT SOME BAKERS HAD LONG HOODS GIVING THEM THE APPEARANCE OF GASOLINE CARS. TOP SPEED WAS NOT MORE THAN 25mph, ALTHOUGH IN 1902 WALTER BAKER COVERED A MILE IN 47 SECONDS (EQUAL TO 76.6mph) IN HIS STREAMLINED ELECTRIC TORPEDO. SADLY, HE CRASHED INTO THE CROWD AT THE END OF THE RUN, KILLING TWO SPECTATORS.

OWNER: CRAWFORD COLLECTION OF THE WESTERN HISTORICAL SOCIETY
(PHOTO NICKY WRIGHT)

Newton fire department bought them as well. In 1906 the company brought out a range of roadsters, in 10, 20, and 30hp sizes, the latter capable of 68mph yet costing only $1,800. The 10hp roadster was priced at only $850. The 20hp, selling for $1,350, went by the charming name of Gentleman's Speedy Roadster. Some Stanleys were faster still. F. E. Stanley was once driving an experimental model on a straight road near Boston when he was stopped by a policeman who, although he was a friend, said he would have to book him because he was going so fast. When the case came up in court, the officer said the car was doing nearly 60mph, to which Stanley pleaded "not guilty." When the judge asked how this could be in face of the evidence, Stanley replied: "I plead not guilty to going 60mph. When I passed the officer my speedometer showed I was going 87mph." He was fined $5 and all the Boston papers carried the story.

In 1906 a streamlined Stanley racecar called the Beetle took the unofficial Land Speed Record at 127.66mph at Daytona Beach in Florida. This was the company's peak period, although production was no higher than 700 cars per year. As time passed the Stanley Steamer grew heavier, more complicated, and more expensive in an attempt to keep up with gasoline cars. A particular blow was the arrival of Cadillac's self-starter in 1914, for this was a system both easy and quick. The Stanley took up to 45 minutes to start on a cold morning, but before 1914 it could at least boast that this involved no muscular cranking. Stanley never took to the flash boiler, which gave quicker starting, but did introduce electric lighting in 1913.

By the end of World War I prices ranged from $3,425 to $5,100, above those of Cadillac, and sales dwindled year by year.

The White is not as well remembered as the Stanley, although more Whites were made in the years 1900–1910, after which the company went over to gasoline. Whites were more sophisticated than Stanleys, with condensers from 1902 and flash boilers, or steam generators as the company preferred to call them, from 1903. By 1905 Whites had a water feed controlled by the driver, and a clutch which allowed the engine to run and operate the pumps while the car was stationary. Previously, when the car was not moving, the pumps had to be operated by hand. Although more expensive than Stanleys, Whites sold better, reaching 1,534 deliveries in 1906 and totaling 9,122 over their ten-year lifetime, compared with 5,122 Stanleys sold in the same period. Whites were the first official White House cars, President William Howard Taft using one from 1909. His predecessor Theodore Roosevelt had been the first U.S. president to drive a car, also a White steamer, in Puerto Rico in 1906. In 1910 White made 1,208 steamers and 1,200 gasoline cars, and that was that for the steamers. Gas cars were made up to 1918, after which White concentrated on trucks, still making them today, under Volvo ownership. Steam had a final flowering in the California-built Doble, but that belongs to the next chapter.

The electric car was proportionally more important than the steamer, and was a familar feature of city life, particularly between about 1906 and 1916. Columbia led the field in the early days, and was then joined by Baker and Rauch & Lang from Cleveland (merged in 1915) and Detroit, which became the best-known makers of electric cars, with 1,500 sales in 1910 and a peak of 4,669 in 1914. There were also about 20 other electrics of some importance, such as Argo, Borland, Chicago (which sold a car to the Pope in 1915), Fritchle, Milburn, Ohio, and Woods. The electric car's appeal was

▲ 1904 POPE-WAVERLEY ELECTRIC RUNABOUT WITH TWO FASHIONABLY DRESSED LADIES, TYPICAL USERS OF SUCH CARS. WITHIN A FEW YEARS, MOST ELECTRICS WERE CLOSED COUPES, NICKNAMED "MOBILE CHINA CLOSETS."
MOTOR VEHICLE MANUFACTURERS' ASSOCIATION

to women, who appreciated its silence and ease of driving, and who found hand-cranking undignified at best and often physically impossible. Most electrics were closed broughams, sometimes nicknamed "mobile china closets" because of their tall, angular lines and generous areas of glass all round. With her electric brougham, the American matron could go shopping and pay social calls independent of husband or chauffeur, fully protected from the weather. What she could not do was to travel more than about 50 miles a day, or venture beyond the city's paved roads, but then on the whole she didn't want to.

The importance of the electric car is shown in a photograph taken outside the Detroit Athletic Club in about 1914, when the members threw open the club for their wives' inspection. There are about 35 cars visible in the photo, and all but three are electrics. This preponderance did not last for long. By 1920 the electric was definitely on the wane. The advent of the self-starter had something

1911 RAUCH & LANG ELECTRIC COUPE ▲
RAUCH & LANG WERE AMONG THE BETTER-KNOWN MAKERS OF ELECTRIC CARS, AND BEGAN AS CARRIAGE BUILDERS
IN CLEVELAND IN 1884. ELECTRIC POWER WAS ADDED IN 1905, AND BY 1911 THE COMPANY WAS MAKING SIX DIFFERENT
DESIGNS ON 77- OR 85-INCH WHEELBASES. THIS COUPE, ALMOST AS TALL AS IT IS LONG, WAS TYPICAL OF ELECTRICS
AT THIS TIME. IN 1915 RAUCH & LANG MERGED WITH BAKER, ANOTHER CLEVELAND ELECTRIC VEHICLE MAKER.
OWNERS: MARK AND TOOTSIE ACCOMAZZO (PHOTO NICKY WRIGHT)

to do with it, but also the public's expectations had risen. In 1914 a top speed of 20mph and a limited range seemed acceptable, but not so six years later, when improved roads made out-of-town journeys more possible. The electric car always had a "lady image," but by the 1920s this had become an "old lady image." Younger women went for a Dodge or Chevrolet coupe, or, if sufficiently sporting, for a Jordan Playboy. In 1921, out of 9 million passenger cars registered in the United States, only 18,184 were electric. There were more Auburns or Peerlesses, not particularly well-known makes, than all the electrics put together. Ten years later the number of electrics was so insignificant that it did not feature in statistics.

THE FRONTIERS OPEN UP

Ever since the 1895 *Chicago Times-Herald* race, autombile enthusiasts had been pushing back the frontiers imposed on their vehicles. By the turn of the century town-to-town endurance runs of several hundred miles were becoming common. In 1901, the 380-mile New York to Buffalo run involved some 50 cars, and soon roadside touring signs were being set up on popular routes such as New York to Boston or Philadelphia. Also in 1901, 21-year-old Roy Chapin achieved fame when he drove a Curved Dash Olds from Detroit to New York for the Auto Show, taking 7½ days for the trip. On his arrival he was so muddy that the doorman of the Waldorf Astoria where Ransom Olds was staying turned him away. Chapin later became president of Hudson. However, the real challenge was the crossing of the continent, coast to coast, and although there were several attempts, no one succeeded until the summer of 1903.

Horatio Nelson Jackson was a 31-year-old Vermont doctor who accepted a $50 wager that he could not drive across the continent. He bought a Winton, and with a hired driver, Sewell Crocker, and camping equipment, picks, and shovels, set off from San Francisco on May 23. He also took a rifle and pistols, just in case of hostilities, and a fishing rod to help with food along the way. In Wyoming the pair rescued a bulldog from a fight and, given the name Bud, he became part of the crew for the

▼ "REFUELING STOP" FOR A DETROIT ELECTRIC COUPE. THE 40-CELL BATTERIES WERE HOUSED UNDER THE HOOD AND AT THE REAR. IN A COMPANY-SPONSORED TEST A DETROIT ELECTRIC RAN 211 MILES ON A SINGLE CHARGE, ALTHOUGH 80 MILES WAS THE GENERALLY ADVERTISED FIGURE.
U.S. LIBRARY OF CONGRESS

▲ ELECTRIC CARS WERE GENERALLY USED IN CITIES, BUT THIS DETROIT WENT ON A PROMOTIONAL TRIP FROM SEATTLE TO MOUNT RAINIER AROUND 1915.
U.S. LIBRARY OF CONGRESS

▲ THE LITTLE CURVED DASH OLDSMOBILE IN WHICH L. L. WHITMAN (LEFT) AND EUGENE HAMMOND CROSSED THE CONTINENT, PAUSING IN DETROIT, WHICH THEY REACHED IN 60 DAYS FROM SAN FRANCISCO. ALTHOUGH THEY TOOK LONGER TO REACH NEW YORK THAN THE JACKSON/CROCKER OR FETCH/KRARUP TEAMS, THEIR CAR WAS CHEAPER AND SMALLER, WITH ONLY ONE CYLINDER.
OLDSMOBILE HISTORY CENTER

▶ A PAUSE FOR WHEEL ADJUSTMENTS DURING THE NEW YORK TO ST. LOUIS TOUR IN JULY 1904. THE CAR IS AN OLDSMOBILE LIGHT TONNEAU, THE FIRST OLDS TO HAVE A STEERING WHEEL IN PLACE OF A TILLER.
MOTOR VEHICLE MANUFACTURERS' ASSOCIATION

rest of that pioneering car journey.

Jackson's worst enemies were not hostile animals or humans, but punctures and mud. The car constantly bogged down in Idaho, and in Wyoming Jackson and Crocker frequently resorted to block and tackle to get out of sand dunes and river beds. Reactions to their passing varied from intense curiosity to sheer terror. One young man who heard of their arrival in his state rode 70 miles across the prairie just to look at an automobile. "I have seen lots of pictures of them," he said, "but this is the first real live one I ever saw."

Jackson and Crocker reached New York after 64 days, and were promptly followed by others. Indeed, before they had even arrived, Tom Fetch and Marius Krarup set out from San Francisco in a single-cylinder Packard, making the journey in 61 days. Krarup was editor of *The Automobile*, which ensured plenty of publicity. The next to cross were L.L. Whitman and Eugene Hammond, who drove a little Curved Dash, again from San Francisco to New York, in 73 days. Two years later, two Curved Dash models called Old Scout (the Whitman-Hammond car) and Old Steady took part in an East–West jaunt, from New York to Portland, Oregon, making the 3,890-mile trek in only 44 days.

All these journeys were accomplished by men, but in 1909 22-year-old Alice Huyler Ramsey decided that women ought to be able to do just as well. She used a four-cylinder Maxwell Model DA touring her husband had bought her when her horse bolted (after being frightened by a car). She had less than a year's driving experience when she set out with three female companions, none of whom could drive, from New York on June 9. The trip to San Francisco took 53 days, of which 13 were needed to traverse Iowa, in whose notorious gumbo (black heavy clay) horses had been known to drown. Gumbo could add 250-300 pounds of extra weight on each wheel. In Wyoming and Utah they found that heavy rains had washed out some roads to a depth of 12 feet. Often the roads were no more than wagon or horse trails, and some ran across private ranches where the travelers had to open and close gates as they went.

The appalling state of American country roads was highlighted by journeys such as that of Alice Huyler Ramsey, and gradually improvements were made. The first rural mile of concrete pavement in

the United States was laid in Wayne County, Michigan, in July 1909, and a Federal Road Act was passed in July 1916 authorizing the establishment of a nationwide system of interstate highways. Even before that conditions had become easier. In 1916 Amanda Preuss was unimpressed with the current women's record of 43 days held by movie star Anita King. "Gracious," she said "I can beat that and never half try." Driving an Oldsmobile V8 roadster, she went from San Francisco to New York in 11 days, 5 hours 45 minutes. This was little more than a fifth of Alice Ramsey's time, and although her car was undoubtedly faster, most of the credit must have been due to better roads. The outright record in 1916 was 7½ days, set by Erwin "Cannonball" Baker in a Cadillac V8.

The earliest long-distance American motorist,

who gave his name to a series of tours still commemorated today, was Charles Jasper Glidden (1857–1927), a Bostonian telephone magnate who at one time controlled one sixth of the Bell Telephone Company. Retiring a wealthy man at age 43, he looked for something to do with the rest of his life, and decided to travel the world by automobile. He began in 1901 with a British Napier, and over the next eight years covered 46,528 miles in 39 countries. Where roads were unsuitable, he fixed flanged wheels to his Napier and drove on the railroad tracks, scheduled as a regular train and carrying flags and a whistle.

In 1904 Glidden promoted a reliability run from New York to St. Louis, and the next year organized the first Glidden Tour. Covering 870 miles from New York to Bretton Woods, New Hampshire, and back, 34 cars made the journey, their drivers including such luminaries as Ransom Olds in a Reo, Percy Pierce in a Pierce Great Arrow, and Walter White in one of his steamers. On the whole they were well received, although a Manchester, New Hampshire, newspaper disapproved of their speed: "Concord to here, 18 miles, in forty minutes. Have they any right to do such a thing?"

One who clearly thought they had no such right was a judge from Worcester, Massachusetts, who said: "If these people want to race, let them go elsewhere. If they want to come to Massachusetts, they must behave themselves and obey the law." Despite the fact that it was not a race, he fined six drivers $15 each.

The Glidden Tours were held annually through 1913, reaching a maximum length of 2,636 miles in 1909. They were revived after World War II to cater for the growing number of antique car enthusiasts who wanted to give their cars some good exercise.

There were countless other automobile tours and record attempts, but mention must be made of the New York to Paris Race of 1908, jointly sponsored by *The New York Times* and *Le Matin*. Six cars set off from Times Square on February 12, crossing the American continent to San Francisco, where they were shipped to Alaska and then again to Japan and to the Russian port of Vladivostok. After that, it was land all the way to Paris, the total journey being 13,341 miles. The winner was George Schuster driving a Buffalo-built Thomas Flyer, who took 169 days. The next finisher, a German Protos, reached Paris 16 days later. All the contestants agreed that the winter roads of upstate New York were worse than anything Siberia or Eastern Europe could offer. In some Western states they took to the railroad tracks, but not as Glidden did with flanged wheels; they just bumped along over the sleepers because even this was better than an almost nonexistent road. As a result of Schuster's victory, sales of Thomas cars jumped by 27 percent and Schuster (who died in 1972, aged 99) became a national celebrity. His car still survives as one of the most valuable exhibits in Harrah's Collection at Reno.

▲ THE ITALIAN-BUILT ZÜST CAR IN CHICAGO DURING THE 1908 NEW YORK–PARIS RACE. THE DRIVER IS POET/JOURNALIST ANTONIO SCARFOGLIO. THE CARS LEFT NEW YORK'S TIMES SQUARE ON FEBRUARY 12, AND THE WINNING THOMAS FLYER DID NOT REACH PARIS UNTIL JULY 30.
MOTOR VEHICLE MANUFACTURERS' ASSOCIATION

◄►THREE PHOTOS SHOWING THE TERRIBLE ROAD CONDITIONS ENCOUNTERED ALL OVER THE UNITED STATES IN THE EARLY YEARS OF THE 20TH CENTURY. ROADS LIKE THESE WERE AN ADDITIONAL BURDEN TO DRIVERS WHOSE CARS FREQUENTLY BOILED OR SUFFERED BROKEN TRANSMISSIONS. NOT THAT TODAY'S MODELS WOULD DO ANY BETTER IN THESE CONDITIONS — APART, THAT IS, FROM FOUR-WHEEL-DRIVE CHEVROLET BLAZERS OR FORD BRONCOS.
MOTOR VEHICLE MANUFACTURERS' ASSOCIATION

1930 FORD MODEL A COUPE DE LUXE ▼
OWNER: JIM RANSOM (PHOTO NICKY WRIGHT)

CHAPTER FOUR

THE GREAT BOOM
ON WHEELS

1920 – 1929

"You can't ride to town in a bathtub."
Indiana farmer's wife, 1925

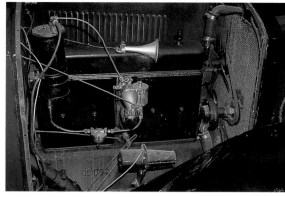

1920 CLEVELAND ROADSTER ◄▲
PRODUCED FROM 1919 TO 1926, THE CLEVELAND WAS A
SMALLER COMPANION MAKE TO THE CHANDLER, BUILT
IN A SEPARATE FACTORY AND SELLING FOR AROUND
$500 LESS. THIS ROADSTER WAS ONE OF FOUR BODY
STYLES OFFERED IN 1920, AND HAD A CONVENTIONAL
L-HEAD SIX-CYLINDER ENGINE. PRICES RAN FROM $1,385
FOR THE ROADSTER AND TOURER TO $2,195 FOR A FOUR-
PASSENGER COUPE OR FIVE-PASSENGER SEDAN
OWNER: CRAWFORD COLLECTION OF THE WESTERN HISTORICAL SOCIETY
(PHOTO NICKY WRIGHT)

THE 1 MILLION MARK IN U.S. passenger car production was passed for the first time in 1916, slightly exceeded in 1917, then after a dip caused by the war reached nearly 2 million (1,905,560) in 1920. The market seemed to be expanding without limit, and in 1929 even these figures were dwarfed by a record 4,455,178 sales. Over the same nine years, registrations of cars rose from 8,132,000 to 23,121,000. No decade since has seen such an increase, nor is it likely ever to be repeated. In the 1920s and 1930s car ownership passed from being the pleasure of a minority, albeit a substantial minority, to one of the majority of Americans. By 1930 there was one car for every 1.3 households, compared with one for 44 households 20 years before.

This phenomenal growth was partly due to higher living standards, but also to the high value that Americans put on car ownership. They were prepared to make sacrifices on other purchases such as clothing. In 1923 *The Chicago Evening Post* reported that retailers blamed the automobile for the slump in the clothing trade. "We'd rather do without clothes than give up the car," one mother of nine children said, while another remarked, "We don't have no fancy clothes when we have the car to pay for." A survey made in Muncie, Indiana, in 1925 revealed that 21 out of 26 car-owning homes surveyed had no bathtubs with running water. When a farmer's wife was asked why they chose a car in preference to indoor plumbing, she replied: "You can't ride to town in a bathtub."

JOCKEYING FOR POSITION
The manufacturers catering to this booming demand were mostly the same as in the previous decade: Ford well ahead, followed by Chevrolet, Willys-Overland, Dodge, and Buick. The numbers were swelled for a while by Billy Durant's Durant and Star, and by Hudson's low-priced Essex, which arrived in 1919. There were also numerous smaller manufacturers, although few in the low-priced field.

Ford dominated the field in the first half of the 1920s, selling more than four times as many cars as its nearest rival, Chevrolet, between 1922 and 1926. Sales came so easily that Ford did not bother to advertise nationally between 1917 and 1923, although local dealers still did so. Prices reached an all-time low in 1923, when a two-passenger runabout cost $260 and a five-passenger touring cost $290. The closest that Chevrolet could get to these prices was $490 and $495 respectively.

By 1926, although Ford was still outselling Chevrolet, the gap was closing, and the Model T

"FROM COUNTRY COUSIN TO COUNTRY CLUB" — THE
MODEL A TOOK FORD FROM FARMER'S FRIEND INTO
THE WORLD OF STYLE. MOVIE STARS AND POLITICIANS
FAVORED IT IN A WAY THEY NEVER DID THE T,
ALTHOUGH MECHANICALLY IT WAS NOT A VERY
REMARKABLE CAR. THE 1930 MODELS HAD LARGER
TIRES ON SMALLER SHEELS, RESULTING IN A DISTINCTLY
LOWER LOOK. AT $550 THIS DE LUXE COUPE COST
$50 MORE THAN THE STANDARD VERSION.

OWNER: JIM RANSOM (PHOTO NICKY WRIGHT)

was selling largely on its low price. With rising
prosperity and expectations, this was not enough.
Wire wheels and balloon tires became available in
1925 and a range of colors in 1926, thanks to quick-
drying Duco lacquer, but still the T was ripe for
replacement. This was clear to everyone but Henry
Ford, who in his homespun way thought that
getting from one place to another was all that
should be expected of a car. He blamed falling
sales on indolent dealers and alienated them so
much that a number changed franchises in
favor of General Motors. His son's

brother-in-law and vice-president Ernest Kanzler
was strongly in favor of a six-cylinder car to replace
the T, but Ford distrusted sixes after the failure of
the Model K. He considered an X-8 engine, but it
was too radical and too heavy, so, after the departure
of Kanzler in August 1926, work went ahead on the
design of a conventional four-cylinder car.

The last Model T officially left the Highland
Park factory on May 27, 1927, although production
actually continued through June. Engine
manufacture lasted much longer; you could still
buy a new Model T engine in August 1941. Today,
old models are seldom discontinued until their
replacements are well into production, but this was
not Henry's way. The T's successor, the Model A,
was not launched until December 1927, and in the
meantime 60,000 men were thrown out of work in
Detroit alone, across the nation 23 assembly plants
were shut down, and dealers had to survive by
selling spare parts.

It is a tribute to the public's faith in the Ford
name that so many people held back from buying a
new car until they saw what the Model A
would be like, and also that so many dealers
remained loyal for the six
months when they had
no new cars to sell. The A
was launched
in Detroit,
New York,

and other cities on December 2, 1927, to greater
acclaim than any other new car. In New York
crowds began gathering at three in the morning
outside the Broadway showroom, and in Cleveland
mounted police had to be called out to control the
crowds. Dallas newspapers described it as the
greatest event there since the signing of the
Armistice. In less than a week 25 million people
had looked at the A, and by Christmas nearly half a
million firm orders had been taken, even though
there were virtually no cars available for a test
drive. So scarce were the new cars that they were
driven around the country, stopping for no more
than a few hours' display in each city before
speeding on to the next.

The car that aroused everyone's excitement was
not really very remarkable. It had a four-cylinder L-
head engine of slightly larger displacement than
the T, with 200.5 against 176.7 cubic inches, but
output was doubled from 20 to 40bhp. Weights
were 20–25 percent up on the equivalent T
models, but the extra power gave a 65mph top
speed, better than many more costly cars. Henry

1931 FORD MODEL A
CONVERTIBLE SEDAN ▶
THIS BODY STYLE WAS NEW TO THE MODEL A
RANGE FOR 1931, AND ONLY 4,864 WERE MADE.
IT WAS ONE OF THE RAREST OF ALL MODEL A
STYLES, ONLY BEATEN BY THE TAXICAB (4,850) AND
THE TOWN CAR (1,065). AT $640 IT WAS THE MOST
EXPENSIVE OF THE 1931 MODELS.

OWNER: GILMORE CAR MUSEUM, KALAMAZOO, MICHIGAN

(PHOTO NICKY WRIGHT)

▲ EVEN AT THE BEGINNING OF THE 1920s THE AUTOMOBILE DOMINATED THE STREETS OF LARGE CITIES.
THIS NEW YORK PHOTO WAS TAKEN ON 42nd STREET WITH BRYANT PARK ON THE RIGHT. CLOSED CARS
PREDOMINATE, ALTHOUGH THEY WERE IN THE MINORITY IN THE NATION AS A WHOLE. THE FEW
HORSE-DRAWN VEHICLES ARE ALL TRUCKS; THE HORSE SURVIVED IN COMMERCIAL TRANSPORTATION
AFTER IT HAD DISAPPEARED FROM PRIVATE USE.

MOTOR VEHICLE MANUFACTURERS' ASSOCIATION

THE FIRST TRAFFIC CONTROL LIGHT IN AMERICA — AND PROBABLY IN THE WORLD — APPEARED IN CLEVELAND, OHIO, ON AUGUST 5, 1914. THE FIRST TRAFFIC LIGHT WITH RED, AMBER, AND GREEN CAME INTO USE IN NEW YORK IN 1918.

TWO EARLY EXAMPLES OF MECHANICAL TRAFFIC CONTROL ARE SHOWN HERE.

▲ A FAIRLY COMPLEX SYSTEM IS SEEN HERE; IT HAS THE COP IN AN ELEVATED POSITION AND GIVES INSTRUCTIONS TO PEDESTRIANS. IT DATES FROM THE EARLY 1920s.

▶ DETROIT'S FIRST ELECTRIC STOP LIGHT, INSTALLED IN 1914.

MOTOR VEHICLE MANUFACTURERS' ASSOCIATION

did not favor a conventional sliding gear transmission, largely because he did not want to be thought imitative, but the wishes of his son Edsel and others prevailed, and the A had a three-speed system modeled on that of the luxury Lincoln which Ford was making. Also inherited from Lincoln were the hydraulic shock absorbers, while safety glass in the windshield was a first in a low-priced car. The transverse leaf suspension was unchanged from the T; indeed no Ford had conventional lateral springs until 1948.

In styling the A bore some resemblance to the Lincoln, although its short wheelbase prevented it from being really elegant. Body options were similar to those on the T, with the addition of a taxicab and panel delivery van. Prices were higher,

1,310,147 As, and later years, hit by the Depression, recorded fewer Model A station wagons (a total of 11,317 in four seasons). Still, the station wagon did better than the town car, which notched up only 1,065 sales over the same period, and was the ancestor of countless station wagons in years to come made not only by Ford, but by most other U.S. manufacturers.

Ford biographer Robert Lacey couldn't have put it better when he wrote that with the unveiling of the A, the Ford swung overnight from country cousin to country club. Gone were the countless jokes about the Lizzie. Its scarcity alone gave the A considerable cachet in its early years. Few celebrities had been willing to be photographed alongside a Model T, but Douglas Fairbanks gave Mary Pickford a Model A coupe for Christmas, and both were happy to appear with the car. Other Hollywood figures who bought As included Cecil B. de Mille, Lon Chaney, Wallace Beery, and Louis B. Mayer. In Washington, Senator James Couzens requested that he receive the first A to be delivered in the capital. President-to-be Franklin D. Roosevelt recorded his pride on operating a Model A, and across the ocean Prince Nicholas of Rumania took delivery of the first A in his country.

The Model A was phased out over the winter of 1931/32. Henry Ford announced the indefinite shutdown of production in August 1931, and there were no 1932 models, but in fact the last A was not delivered until April 1932. Total production was 3,837,503, of which about 900,000 are thought to survive today. On the surface, the A would seem to have been a success, but the balance sheets showed a different story. It was not the fault of the car, but the disastrous and unnecessary halt in

1924 CHEVROLET ▲▼

SUPERIOR SERIES F WAS THE DESIGNATION FOR 1924 CHEVROLETS, WHICH WERE MADE
IN SIX BODY STYLES ON A SINGLE 103-INCH WHEELBASE. BETTER EQUIPPED THAN
THE RIVAL FORD MODEL T, THE CHEVROLET INCLUDED AN ELECTRIC STARTER AS STANDARD EQUIPMENT,
ALSO AN AMMETER AND ELECTRIC HORN. CLOSED MODELS HAD A WINDSHIELD WIPER.

OWNER: DICK TRAVERS (PHOTO NICKY WRIGHT)

from $460 for the four-passenger touring, now called a phaeton, to $600 for the taxi. For 1929 the range was extended from 9 to 18 models, including bodies by Briggs and Murphy as well as Ford, and two new styles, a station wagon at $650 and a town car at $1,200. The latter was something of a folly, and few were made, although after the Depression there was a short-lived vogue for expensive town car bodies on Ford chassis. The station wagon was another matter, however; this style had been offered on the T, often rebodying chassis which had lasted longer than the original bodies, but the 1929 Model A was the first to be a listed style. It took some time to find a niche in the market; 1929 calendar year sales were 4,954 out of a total of

production in 1927 which led to a loss of $30 million over the year. The halt was unnecessary because the A was made at Ford's vast new River Rouge plant, whereas the T had been made at Highland Park, so an overlap would have been perfectly feasible. The 1928 year saw losses up to $250 million. The assembly line was moving so slowly that Ford was losing more than $300 per car. In the same period General Motors and Chrysler were making record profits, largely due to management being delegated rather than concentrated in the hands of one strong-willed 65-year-old. Because of the changeover, Ford inevitably lost the lead to Chevrolet in 1927, and was 254,000 units behind in 1928 too. Although the company regained first position in 1929 and 1930, thereafter it came second to Chevrolet in almost every year to the present.

Chevrolet began the 1920s badly, in the wake of Billy Durant's sudden departure from GM. While Ford doubled its sales in 1921 to nearly 1 million, Chevrolet's halved to just under 62,000. Alfred P. Sloan (1875–1966) was executive vice-president of GM after the end of the Durant regime, becoming president in 1923. He realized that Chevrolet could never compete head-on with Ford, but his strategy was to take a slice off the top of the Ford market and cater to those who wanted to trade up to something a bit more stylish and better equipped than a Model T. Had Ford sales not been so good, one could say that it was a weakness of Henry Ford that his customers had nothing to move up to. This gap was not plugged until the arrival of the Edsel-inspired Mercury for 1939. Sloan, of course, had a whole range of cars carefully priced for a particular market; above Chevrolet came Oakland, then Oldsmobile, Buick, and finally Cadillac.

The cheap Chevrolet in 1922 was still the 490, priced from $510 for a two-passenger roadster to $875 for a four-door sedan. Comparable Ford prices were $269 to $725. For 1923 the 490 was renamed the Superior, with some improvements. There was also a short-lived air-cooled model called the Copper-Cooled Chevrolet. This had a 135-cubic-inch engine with square dimensions (3½ x 3½ inches) cooled by the copper fins that gave it its name. It looked much like the Superior, sharing the same wheelbase and most of the same body styles, although the Copper-Cooled range had an

additional coach. The engine was supposed to be simpler and cheaper to make than the Superior's, but this was not reflected in the price, which was $200 more. The main problem was pre-ignition, which got worse with higher temperatures, and a fan that did not give even cooling over the whole engine. The engine was in fact a complete failure; of the 739 cars made, 239 were scrapped before leaving the factory, 300 were assigned to dealers, and only about 100 went to the public. Chevrolet recalled them all in the summer of 1923, although one Bostonian refused to give his back, and this survives today, together with one other bought by Henry Ford to see if there was anything worth copying. There wasn't.

The Superior Series K of 1925 had many improvements, including a stronger crankshaft, enclosed and automatically lubricated rocker arms, dry plate disk clutch in place of cone, stiffer chassis frame, and, most important, a new banjo-type rear axle which eliminated the "Chevrolet hum" that was something of a joke about the previous models. Chevrolet was the first low-priced car to adopt the new Duco fast-drying paint. Unlike the Ford, still available in any color so long as it was black, Chevrolet cars did not include that hue in their color schemes at all.

The Chevrolet fours were continued through the 1928 season with little change apart from being named Capitols for 1927 and Nationals for 1928, when they gained four-wheel brakes and an extra 4

inches of wheelbase. Former Ford executive William S. Knudsen headed Chevrolet during these years of revival. Apart from the improvements in the Chevrolet and the obsolescence of the Model T, one of GM's most valuable weapons was a low-interest flexible instalment plan. Henry Ford refused to sell on credit, claiming that it damaged the traditional thrift on which he believed America had been built. In fact, Henry's principles, wise though they may seem in retrospect, were increasingly out of step with the business practices of the 1920s. Although he may never have heard of "built-in obsolescence," Alfred Sloan believed it was important for new models to create a certain amount of dissatisfaction with the old ones. To Ford it seemed ridiculous that a 1923 model should be rejected because it did not look like a 1924. "We want the man who buys one of our products never to have to buy another," he said. This was not a little naive when he was turning out 1.8 million cars per year, many of which must have been replacements for older Fords.

Chevrolet obviously outsold Ford in 1927, the figures being 1,749,998 to 356,188, and triumphed in 1928 too, when the Model A was up and running. To counter the A, Chevrolet launched a brand-new six-cylinder engine to go into the 1928 107-inch chassis. It had overhead valves like the previous fours, and the 195-cubic-inch displacement gave 46bhp at 2,400rpm. The pistons were of cast iron, giving rise to the nickname "Cast Iron Wonder;" an

1926 CHEVROLET SUPERIOR SERIES V LANDAU COUPE ▲
CHEVROLETS FOR 1926 WERE LITTLE CHANGED FROM THE PREVIOUS YEAR,
BUT COULD BE DISTINGUISHED BY THE TIE BAR BETWEEN THE HEADLIGHTS.
THE BUMPERS WERE AN EXTRA, AS WAS A SPARE TIRE. THE DISK WHEELS SEEN
HERE WERE STANDARD, WOOD SPOKES BEING AN OPTIONAL EXTRA.
OWNERS: DAN AND CAROL HANSEN (PHOTO NICKY WRIGHT)

alternative name was "Stove Bolt Six," from the slotted head bolts similar to those used to hold the pipes on domestic stoves.

The company's advertising slogan for the car was "A Six for the price of a Four," which was somewhat optimistic. It all depended on what four you were looking at. Both the previous Chevrolet and the Ford Model A were somewhat cheaper model for model, but the newly introduced Plymouth Four was between $20 and $100 more expensive. The 1928 Chevrolet Four had been the National series, so the 1929 Six was the International, possibly in reference to its styling, which owed something to Harley Earl's La Salle, which in turn took its inspiration from the French Hispano-Suiza. The 1930 models were called Universal, the 1931s Independence, and the 1932s Confederate, after which the name Master was adopted, lasting until 1942.

The 1931 Independence series had subtly improved styling and an extra 2 inches of wheelbase, making them the best-looking Chevrolets yet, and definitely more expensive-looking than the Model A. Yet expensive they were not; the roadster was $475, less than the fours had ever been, and even the luxurious-looking five-passenger Landau Phaeton was only $650. Prices were lower still in 1932, very close to Ford's, but that was the year in which Ford brought out its V8 engine, giving a considerable performance advantage over Chevrolet. However, it was not enough to give Ford the lead again, and Chevrolet topped a very depressed market, with 306,716 sales to Ford's 232,125. The Depression bottomed out in 1932: sales throughout the industry were less than 25 percent of what they had been in 1929.

From 1928 there was a third challenger in the low-priced field, Walter Chrysler's Plymouth. Its ancestry could be traced back to the Maxwell Four, which was restyled and reissued as the Chrysler 58 in 1926. Two years later, with styling updated to parallel that of the six-cylinder Chryslers, the design was launched under the name Plymouth. This was the name of a popular twine used by farmers. As they were an important market for any low-priced car, Walter Chrysler chose this name, although Chrysler's PR department also made much of the connection with Plymouth Rock and the Pilgrim Fathers. The name was said to "typify

the endurance and strength, the rugged honesty and enterprise, the determination of achievement and the freedom from old limitations of that Pilgrim Band who were the first American colonists." Dealers were dressed up as Pilgrim Fathers, while the car was touted as America's lowest-priced full-size car, implying that the Ford and Chevrolet were mere compacts.

The Plymouth did have several advantages over its rivals, including four-wheel hydraulic brakes, full-pressure engine lubrication, and alloy pistons. Prices were not all that much higher, at $655–$745, and sales to the end of the first model year (February 4, 1929) were an encouraging 66,097.

To meet demand, a new factory was put up on Lynch Road, Detroit, over the winter of 1928/29. Assembly workers were making cars while the building went up around them. Heating was provided by a steam locomotive parked on a spur track nearby, and four crews of building workers were involved, two working outward from the middle and one from each end toward the middle. Completion took only three months. In 1931 Plymouth built 106,259 cars, displacing Buick from third place, a position it retained until the mid-1950s. An important factor in Plymouth's rapid rise was the dealer network, which Walter Chrysler had quickly expanded when he acquired Dodge in 1928. His existing network selling his more expensive Chryslers would not have been adequate for a popularly priced car like the Plymouth. And since mid-1928 he had another marque in his empire, the low-/medium-priced six-cylinder De Soto.

Plymouth went over to a six for 1933, but the original Model PC was unpopular. It looked no larger than the four which it succeeded. Interestingly, Ford did not suffer the same market resistance with its V8, which was externally identical with the four-cylinder Model B, yet easily outsold the four. After Plymouth had given its six an extra 5 inches of wheelbase and a good dollop of restyling, sales improved. The 190-cubic-inch L-head engine was enlarged over the years, but in its basic form it was still available in a Plymouth in 1959, and lasted into the 1960s in Dodge trucks.

Another newcomer, from the beginning of the 1920s, and one that made a significant contribution to growing production figures, was the Essex. This was Hudson's attempt to enter the low-price field to counter the dominance of the large manufacturers (Ford, General Motors, Dodge), which Hudson's secretary-treasurer Roscoe B. Jackson deplored. A separate company, Essex Motors, was set up, and a former Studebaker factory in Detroit was leased for a production start in February 1918. But the growing needs of war production put paid to this and only 92 Essexes were built in the whole year; 1919 was a different story, though, with 21,879 delivered, more than the 18,175 output from the parent Hudson company.

The Essex is said to have been named for the English county and because the name hinted at six cylinders, but in fact it was an F-head four (inlet valves in the cylinder head, exhaust valves at the side). Displacement was 180 cubic inches and output 55bhp, which gave the car sparkling

1925 HUDSON SUPER SIX BROUGHAM ▲▶
HUDSON WAS A LEADING BUILDER OF CLOSED CARS IN THE 1920s, AND THE TWO-DOOR, FOUR-WINDOW COACH WAS A POPULAR STYLE FIRST SEEN IN 1922. STYLING WAS CHANGED IN MIDSEASON 1925, WITH PILLARS BECOMING THINNER AND A CURVE TO THE LOWER EDGE OF THE WINDSHIELD — AS ON THIS FOUR-DOOR BROUGHAM, A NEW STYLE FOR 1925. THE BODY WAS BUILT FOR HUDSON BY BIDDLE & SMART. IT SOLD FOR $1,595, REDUCED TO $1,450 IN OCTOBER.
OWNER: CHRISTOPHER G. FOSTER (PHOTO NICK GEORGANO)

performance. From the start the makers entered various record-breaking attempts, such as a world long-distance endurance record of 3,037 miles in 50 hours at the Cincinnati Speedway. Also in 1919 a stock touring car covered 1,061 miles of snowy Iowa roads in 24 hours. And in 1920 four Essex tourings crossed the continent, two from East to West and two in the opposite direction. The first to arrive in New York took only 4 days, 14 hours 43 minutes.

Body styles of the 1919 Essex were a two-passenger roadster at $1,595, a five-passenger touring at $1,395, and a five-passenger sedan at $2,250. For 1922 Essex caused a sensation by offering a two-door coach sedan, nicknamed "a crackerbox on a raft," at $1,495. By the beginning of the year this had been reduced to $1,345, and a few months later to $1,245, only $200 more than the open touring car. The coach sedan was not a beauty; it used the same two-door, five-passenger body designed for the longer-wheelbase Hudson and this did not transfer very well to the 17-inches-

shorter Essex. Nevertheless its significance was not lost on rivals. Alfred Sloan wrote later that the introduction of the Essex coach was "an event which was to profoundly influence the fortunes of Pontiac, Chevrolet, and the Model T."

By the end of the 1924 season, closed models were accounting for 90 percent of Hudson-Essex production. A year later, when the coach had been redesigned with better proportions, its price of $765 was the same as the open touring and for 1926, $100 less than the open car. A new four-door sedan was the same price as the touring. Rivals such as Chevrolet and Ford were still asking up to $200 more for their closed models, and Essex was in the forefront of the trend which led to nearly 90 percent of cars sold in America in 1929 being closed models. Ten years earlier, little more than 10 percent had been closed.

Essex replaced the F-head four by a smaller L-head six in 1925, which made for smoother running but less performance. No longer would Essexes set

coast-to-coast records or storm up Pikes Peak (as they did again in the 1930s), but the public liked the sixes, and in 1928 bought 229,887 Essexes, a record for the make.

Essex and Hudson closed bodies, important though they were in terms of production, were conventional in construction, with pressed steel panels over a wooden frame. Dodge, on the other hand, brought out the world's first all-steel four-door sedan in 1919, with bodywork by the Budd Manufacturing Company of Philadelphia. Luxuriously equipped with velvet mohair upholstery and wire wheels, it cost $1,900, but by 1927 Dodge had the price down to $895, which was maintained even after the car went over to six cylinders in 1928.

Ford built its first all-steel sedan body in 1923. General Motors was slower to abandon traditional methods, not giving up on the composite body until 1937, despite the much vaunted Turret Top on the 1935 LaSalle, which was simply a one-piece steel roof over a composite frame.

Two other companies that competed in the low-price field in the 1920s were Willys-Overland and Durant. John North Willys entered the postwar era riding high, in second place behind Ford in 1918. However, 1919 saw a disastrous strike which might never have happened had Willys been on the spot at Toledo, but he was away in New York where he had made his home to suit his other interests, which included the National Committee on War Camp Recreation. It seems that the labor unions chose the Willys plant as a test case for their demands on the closed shop, increased pay, and a shorter working week. The plant was big, but not as big as those of the giants of Detroit, and it would have been a foolhardy union leader who challenged Henry Ford. Willys' deputy, Clarence Earl, refused to meet any of the unions' demands or even to negotiate, and when the work force walked out in the spring of 1919 he called in non-union labor. Riots ensued, and an auxiliary police force was called in, with the result that two workers were shot dead and 70 others injured. Toledo's mayor said that the city was powerless to protect the factory, and the State Governor placed the area under martial law. Earl closed the factory, and it did not resume full production until just before Christmas. In the circumstances, it is surprising that the company managed to make as many cars as

it did — 80,853 for the year — but finances were badly damaged. Willys owed $18 million to the banks and $14 million to suppliers.

The Chase National Bank's condition for extending its loan to Willys was that a manager should be brought in, and the man chosen was Walter Chrysler. His price for reorganizing Willys was a free hand to do as he wished and a salary of $1 million a year, a record at the time. One of his first acts was to halve Willys' salary of $150,000, which possibly led Willys to sell his $200,000 Pasadena home to Chrysler in April 1921. Chrysler stayed at Willys-Overland for two years and when he left the company was in much better shape. As well as his record salary, Chrysler took away with him the designs of a new six-cylinder car which was to have been built in Willys' New Jersey plant. He was so confident that he took a full-page advertisement in the January 1921 Show Number of *MoTor* announcing that his new Chrysler Six would be available for delivery in July. However, the plant closed before production could begin, and was acquired by Durant. The deal included Chrysler's prototype, so what would have been a Chrysler Six emerged as the Flint. Chrysler then went to work on a modified version which appeared three years later.

The mainstay of production at Toledo was the Overland Four, intended as competition for the

Model T. But the problems of 1919 meant that the price could not be brought below $945, which was not much competition at all. However, the price came steadily down over the next five years and in 1924 was only $495 for a touring or roadster. Sales soared from 48,016 in 1921 to 215,000 in 1925. In the fall of 1926 came the Overland Four's successor, the Whippet, often listed as a marque in its own right. John Willys was a frequent traveler in Europe and hankered after building a European-type small car. On one of his trips he acquired several French and British examples, and set his chief engineer A. J. Baker to test and disassemble them. He found them underpowered and too narrow for American rural roads, but some of their features found their way into the Whippet, particularly the small-bore/long-stroke cylinder dimensions which suited taxation in some foreign markets such as Britain. The radiator styling was reminiscent of the Fiat 501, and overall lines were a great improvement on the Overland Four. Other improvements included pressure lubrication, pump cooling instead of thermo-syphon, and four-wheel brakes.

With a displacement of only 134 cubic inches, the Whippet had the smallest engine of any American car, yet its 30bhp gave it good performance. The advertised top speed was 55mph, but the car was a good deal faster than that. Unfortunately its nippy ways tempted owners to

1925 STEARNS-KNIGHT MODEL 6-C TOURING ◄▼
THE CLEVELAND-BASED F .B. STEARNS COMPANY WAS THE
FIRST IN AMERICA TO TAKE UP THE KNIGHT SLEEVE-VALVE
ENGINE, AND USED THIS DESIGN
EXCLUSIVELY FROM 1911 TO THE END
IN 1929. FOUR- AND SIX-CYLINDER
CARS WERE MADE IN 1925,
WHEN THIS TOURING SOLD
FOR $1,875. IN DECEMBER
THAT YEAR JOHN NORTH
WILLYS BOUGHT STEARNS,
MAKING IT THE MOST
EXPENSIVE OF HIS
SLEEVE-VALVE RANGE.
OWNER; WOLFGANG H. GAWOR
(PHOTO NICK GEORGANO)

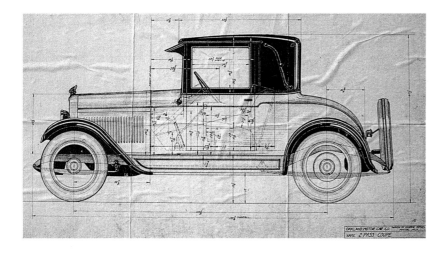

1926 PONTIAC TWO-PASSENGER COUPE ▲ ▼ ▶
THE PONTIAC WAS CREATED BY GM PRESIDENT ALFRED P. SLOAN UNDER HIS POLICY
"A CAR FOR EVERY PURSE," AND WAS INTENDED TO FILL THE GAP BETWEEN THE
$525 CHEVROLET ROADSTER AND THE $890 OLDSMOBILE. BUILT BY GM'S OAKLAND
DIVISION, THE PONTIAC USED MANY CHEVROLET CHASSIS COMPONENTS, BUT HAD
A NEW SHORT-STROKE SIX-CYLINDER ENGINE. THIS WAS DESIGNED BY HENRY M.
CRANE, WHO HAD MADE THE LUXURY CRANE-SIMPLEX TEN YEARS BEFORE. IN OVERALL CHARGE OF PONTIAC
ENGINEERING WAS BENJAMIN ANIBAL. THE CAR WAS NAMED FOR ITS HOME CITY OF PONTIAC, MICHIGAN, WHICH IN
TURN TOOK ITS NAME FROM AN INDIAN CHIEF, HENCE THE PROMINENCE OF THE CHIEF'S HEAD IN PONTIAC MASCOTS.
THIS COUPE IS THE VERY FIRST PONTIAC BUILT, COMPLETED ON DECEMBER 28, 1925. LIKE THE TWO-DOOR COACH,
WHICH WAS THE ONLY OTHER STYLE FOR 1926, IT WAS PRICED AT $825.

PONTIAC DIVISION, GENERAL MOTORS

abuse it, and the long-stroke engine was not happy with sustained high speeds. The Ford Model A was slower, but it could be driven flat out all day, which the Whippet most definitely could not. At $625 for a two-door coach sedan, it undercut all its competitors apart from Ford, and in 1928 a cabriolet was down to $545, just $5 less than the equivalent Model A.

For 1927 the Whippet Four was joined by a six on a slightly longer wheelbase. In 1928 the Whippets took fourth place in the industry, with 197,910 sales, and they were fourth again in 1929. They were discontinued after 1931, with a total of 545,890 having been made. The four-cylinder engine was continued in the small Willys of the 1930s, and after extensive reworking by Barney Roos, which raised power from 30 to 61bhp, it went into the World War II Jeep.

In January 1921, less than a month after being ousted from General Motors for the second time, Billy Durant formed Durant Motors Inc. with funds of $7 million contributed by 67 individuals who had faith in the man who had built up and twice headed GM. Having supervised the making of countless cars bearing other people's names, Durant at last had one of his own, the Durant Four Model A. It was a conventional car with a 35bhp overhead valve engine made by Continental, and had a 109-inch wheelbase with three body styles — touring, coupe, and sedan — priced from $890 to $1,365. His General Motors experience led him to favor a simultaneous attack on the market in several price brackets, so in 1922 he brought out a smaller, Ford-challenging car called the Star, as well as a six-cylinder Ansted-powered Durant selling for about double the price of the four. He also acquired the prestigious Locomobile to challenge the very top-price cars.

The Star was the most important Durant Motors car in terms of sales, finding about 130,000 buyers in 1923. It was a conventional and simple car, with a 130.4-cubic-engine by Continental, giving a modest 33bhp, and a three-speed transmission separate from the engine, a feature common to all Durant's cars but very unusual at that time in America. The basic price of $348 for a five-passenger touring did not include a self-starter or demountable rims; these became available on the 1923 models, when the price had gone up to $443. A significant model for 1923 was an open-sided station wagon, the first to be offered complete by an American manufacturer. The Star's main plant was at Elizabeth, New Jersey, but it was also made at Lansing, Michigan, Oakland, California, and Toronto in Canada.

The Star was made up to the end of the 1928 season, being offered in six-cylinder form in 1926 and 1927, and more than 1 million were made. In the mid-1920s Durant's companies were taking practically all of Continental's engine output. He then launched two new makes, the Flint and the Princeton. The Flint was designed by the triumvirate responsible for the first Chrysler —

Carl Breer, Owen Skelton, Fred Zeder — and there were many similarities between the two. It had originally been planned as a Willys, but when Willys vacated the Elizabeth, New Jersey, plant, the prototype left behind was revamped as the Flint. Meanwhile the three engineers had left with Walter Chrysler to work on a further improved version which became the Chrysler 70 in 1924. The Flint was a medium-sized six-cylinder car selling in the $1,195–$2,085 bracket, remarkable for its four-wheel hydraulic brakes, also a leading feature of the first Chrysler. A rival to the six-cylinder Buick,

the Flint sold about 24,000 units in five seasons, 1923–1927.

To fill the gap between the Flint and the Locomobile, which sold for upward of $7,600, Durant created a new marque, the Princeton, which he regarded as his Cadillac. Announced in 1923, it was powered by a six-cylinder Ansted engine, had wheelbases of 128 or 132 inches, and was to come in six body styles at prices from $2,485 to $3,675. Several prototypes were made in Durant's Muncie, Indiana, plant, and then it was announced that production would begin in the Locomobile plant at Bridgeport, Connecticut, in 1924. However, the idea got lost somewhere between Muncie and Bridgeport, and the Princeton never went on the market.

The Durant lasted longer than any of the Billy's other makes, but it, too, died in the wake of the Depression, by which time the Flint factory had been sold to General Motors and the Long Island City factory to Ford. In fact Durant had closed more than half his factories before the stock market crash, but even so the company was dealt a deadly blow. Durant put $90 million of his own money into Durant Motors, only to see it all evaporate with the drastic decline in sales for every make of car; 1930 sales were 20,900, and in 1931 only 7,270 Durants found buyers. There were 1932 models, but they were only revamped 1931s and hardly any were sold. The Canadian factory, which sold cars under the name Frontenac, lasted a year longer.

In 1936 Billy Durant filed for personal bankruptcy; his debts were $914,000 and his assets only the clothes he stood up in, which he valued at $250. In his last years he ran a bowling alley and a restaurant. One unpleasant-sounding car dealer used to take customers and salesmen there so that he could show off by ordering a hamburger from the man who founded General Motors. In 1942 a stroke rendered Durant an invalid. His wife Catherine had to sell her jewelry piece by piece, and they were virtually penniless when the 85-year-old Durant died in July 1947. Unlike David Buick or Louis Chevrolet, who also died in poverty, he didn't even have a flourishing make of car to be remembered by.

1924 CHRYSLER MODEL B PHAETON ▼

ENGINEERED BY CARL BREER, OWEN SKELTON, AND FRED ZEDER, THE FIRST CHRYSLER WAS AN UP-TO-DATE CAR WITH SIX-CYLINDER HIGH-COMPRESSION ENGINE (4.7:1 WHEN THE INDUSTRY NORM WAS 4.0:1), ALUMINUM PISTONS, AND VIBRATION DAMPER. ITS 68bhp GAVE IT A TOP SPEED OF 70mph, ONLY 5mph SLOWER THAN THE PACKARD EIGHT. SUCH SPEEDS WERE CURBED BY HYDRAULIC BRAKES ON ALL FOUR WHEELS. THE CHRYSLER 70 WAS INTRODUCED IN JANUARY 1924 IN NINE BODY STYLES, FROM A FOUR-DOOR TOURING AT $1,335 TO A TOWN CAR AT $3,735. THIS PHAETON WAS A BETTER-EQUIPPED VERSION OF THE TOURING, AND COST $1,395.

OWNER: NATIONAL AUTOMOBILE MUSEUM. RENO, NEVADA (PHOTO NICKY WRIGHT)

SURVIVAL OF THE FITTEST

In 1922 nearly 200 domestic makes of car were competing for the attention of the American motorist, as well as a number of imports, mostly in the luxury field. In 1929 the figure was down to 47, and a decade later to 22. The process continued after World War II, although the number of makes has been swelled from time to time by small sports cars and latterly by kit cars and neo-classics. Statistically, however, the numbers of the latter have been unimportant. Significant marques or makes were down to 16 in 1960 and 13 in 1992, although to the latter one must add the U.S. plants of the Japanese Honda, Mazda, Nissan, and Toyota companies.

The 1920s saw by far the greatest mortality, for which there were several reasons. Chief among them was the need for greater capital investment to keep up with technical trends, and this was simply unavailable to smaller firms. Added to this was the reduced unit cost which resulted from mass production, itself only made possible by heavy investment in machinery. One mistaken design could be fatal, as for example, the "drunken Mitchell."

Mitchell Motors Company was a well-respected firm in Racine, Wisconsin, dating from 1903 as car builders, although as wagon makers Mitchell went back to 1834. In the first decade of the century Mitchell was making around 6,000 cars per year, raising this to 10,000 in the years 1917 to 1919. For 1920 Mitchells were restyled by sloping the radiator backward, presumably to give some idea of streamlining. Unfortunately the windshield remained uncompromisingly vertical, and the contrast between the two made the radiator seem to be leaning at a drunken angle, hence the uncomplimentary nickname. Mitchell did some hasty redesigning for the 1921 season, but the damage had been done; lost customers could not be regained by a conventional though not particularly good-looking car, and sales dropped to about 3,500 in 1921 and 1922.

As well as financing the redesign, Mitchell spent a lot of money on publicity stunts, such as a 1-million-mile test put up by 109 cars, but it was all to no avail. Only 100 cars were made in the first few months of 1923 and in May Mitchell filed for bankruptcy, with assets of $3.7 million and debts of $3.9 million. Among the assets were finished and unfinished automobiles, and raw materials, worth $1.6 million, and the factory. This was sold to Nash and used for the manufacture of the Ajax. Thus passed from the industry a name, wrote *Automobile Topics*, "that was once familiar to everyone, and a concern that in the early days was a real factor in the business." As well as Mitchell, another 49 makes closed their doors in 1923, including some that had hardly started, such as the Ace, Detroit Steamer, Rotary, and Strattan, and more or less well-known names like Biddle, Chalmers and Dorris. In 1924 a further 36 makes disappeared, including the long-established Crow-Elkhart, Paterson, Premier, and Winton.

Technical progress spelled the downfall of a number of the smaller firms. Most could cope with self-starters and electric lighting, because these were bought from outside suppliers and did not necessitate a redesign of the car. Both were practically universal by 1920. Front-wheel brakes were another matter; their first appearance on an American car was on the high-priced Duesenberg straight-8 of 1920, and in 1923/4 there was a surge in their popularity, so that no self-respecting manufacturer in anything but the lowest price bracket could afford to be without them. But they were not cheap, for tires, steering, front axles, springs, and shock absorbers all had to be redesigned. Among those whose end was hastened by the incorporation of four-wheel brakes were Premier from Indianapolis and the two formerly joined Kokomo makes, Apperson and Haynes. All three were out of business by 1926, as were other respected makes with production of several thousand cars a year, such as Cole, Dort, King, and Stephens.

Some manufacturers who were prominent in other fields decided to abandon the automobile market when the going got too tough. One was the J.I. Case Company, which had been famous for agricultural equipment since 1842 and which introduced a medium-sized car in 1910. Sales began to fall after 1923, for the Continental-powered Case

1920 ROAMER ROADSTER ◄▲

THE ROAMER WAS A GOOD-LOOKING ASSEMBLED CAR FROM KALAMAZOO, MICHIGAN, WHICH SOLD QUITE WELL IN THE EARLY 1920s, THEN GRADUALLY DECLINED UNTIL ITS DEMISE IN 1929. MOST ROAMERS HAD SIX-CYLINDER CONTINENTAL ENGINES, BUT COULD BE HAD WITH THE MORE POWERFUL 80bhp ROCHESTER-DUESENBERG FOUR. THIS MODEL D-4-75 ROADSTER COST $4,375, WHICH WAS $1,000 MORE THAN THE SAME CAR WITH THE 54bhp CONTINENTAL SIX. ROAMER WAS ROCHESTER'S BEST CUSTOMER, TAKING BETWEEN 800 AND 1,000 ENGINES FROM THE FALL OF 1917 TO 1925, POSSIBLY A YEAR OR TWO LATER. THE ROAMER RADIATOR WAS AN UNASHAMED COPY OF THE ROLLS-ROYCE, BUT NEITHER THE BRITISH FIRM NOR ITS SPRINGFIELD, MASSACHUSETTS, BRANCH TOOK ANY ACTION.

OWNER: GILMORE CAR MUSEUM, KALAMAZOO, MICHIGAN (PHOTO NICKY WRIGHT)

Another factor which led to reduced variety among American cars was a growing conformity, a reluctance to step out of line and appear eccentric. After 1929 this was coupled with a reluctance to flaunt one's wealth, even if one still had it. A victim of these trends was the speedster, a type of car which had its origins before World War I.

The first speedsters, otherwise called roadsters, runabouts, or raceabouts, were made on stock chassis using unmodified engines with light two- or three-passenger bodies. It was a simple matter for a dealer to put a light body on a stock touring chassis and enter it in local hill climbs and races to boost sales. If the car was successful, the makers would be told and, if it made economic sense, a roadster would find its way into the next year's catalog. Although Maxwell was not thought of as a sporting make, a few 22hp roadsters were built by branch dealers to compete in 1909 events; as they did well, a two-passenger Sportsman roadster was listed for 1910. Finished in pearl gray, it had a large exterior gas tank and spare tires behind, while the seats were tilted to give a rakish look. Sportsman models won their class at two important hill climbs in 1910: Giant's Despair at Wilkes Barre, Pennsylvania, and Sunset at Ossining, New York.

Numerous other makers listed sporting models in the years 1910–1914, including Apperson, Kissel, Marion, National, Overland, Peerless, and Thomas. Better known than any of these were the Mercer Raceabout and Stutz Bearcat. The Mercer Type 35 appeared in 1910, with a Beaver T-head four of 299 cubic inches. Initial models were a touring, toy tonneau, and speedster, the last a not particularly sporting car. The immortal Raceabout came for the 1911 model year and was the idea of Washington A. Roebling II, son of Mercer's founder C.G. Roebling. It was engineered by Finlay Robertson Porter, who later made his own cars under the names F.R.P. and Porter. The engine was not large, but thanks to high gearing and low weight a top speed of 75mph was possible. The body was classically simple; two bucket seats with a bolster gas tank behind them, and behind that a small tool box and two spare tires. There were neither doors or windshield, the latter being replaced by a circular monocle attached to the steering column. It cannot have been much use as weather protection,

six was not sufficiently different from many rivals and was more expensive than the Buick. It was becoming a drag on the balance sheet and Case could only have reduced the price by increasing production at the expense of its traditional products such as tractors, so after 1927 the Case car was no more.

Another factor which killed off some of the smaller firms was the improved distribution of the larger ones. The South's most prominent make was the Anderson from Rock Hill, South Carolina, made from 1916 to 1925 with the slogan "A Little Higher in Price, BUT Made in Dixie," which appealed to local pride. It was a pretty good car, although like many it used a number of bought out components, particularly its Continental engine. Anderson did sell outside its own territory, but most customers were fairly local. Once makes like Buick and Oldsmobile set up dealerships in Rock Hill and many other Southern towns the competition became too great, and Anderson closed down. The few other Southern makes, such as Hanson from Atlanta, Georgia, and the Climber from Little Rock, Arkansas, never tried to sell north of the Mason-Dixon line.

Improved communications meant that cars could be delivered from the manufacturing centers to all parts of the country, usually by railroad, although if the distances were not too great they could be driven. Haulaway trucks came into use from the early 1930s. In areas really remote from Detroit, such as the West Coast, assembly plants were set up by Ford, General Motors, and Durant. This was another blow to local manufacturers. Over the years automobiles have been built in all 49 mainland states, but many had disappeared before 1920. Probably the peak at any one time was reached in 1909, when 290 different makes were being built in 145 cities in 24 states. By 1923, 23 states were still home to 164 auto makes (excluding assembly plants), but by 1929 the figure was down to 9 states and 47 makes.

but drivers normally wore goggles anyway.

Compared with its rivals, the Mercer Raceabout had a rather delicate appearance, which was complemented by fine handling. "The Mercer is the Steinway of the automobile world," ran a 1914 advertisement. "It is possible to thread a needle while traveling 60mph." Its great rival, the Stutz Bearcat, was an altogether more rugged and heavier vehicle, although its 390-cubic-inch engine gave about the same power, 60bhp. Harry C. Stutz entered the first car he built in the 1911 Indianapolis 500, finishing eleventh out of 40 starters. From this he coined the slogan "The Car that Made Good in a Day," which might seem a bit of hype, but the Stutz did have the smallest engine in the race, and had it not been hampered by many tire changes would undoubtedly have finished higher.

Several weeks after the race, Stutz formed the Ideal Car Company to make replicas of the race car. These were characterized by a three-speed transmission in the rear axle. Touring, coupe, and roadster models were offered, and the most sporting was called the Bearcat. The name may have been chosen in response to Marion's Bobcat, a similar type of roadster. The Stutz Bearcat sold for $2,000, some $500 less than the Mercer, and even with the optional six-cylinder engine the price was only $2,125. The roadster with doors was continued, but it was the stark, doorless Bearcat that grabbed all the attention and triggered off

intense rivalry with Mercer owners. "There's no car worser than a Mercer," they chorused, which brought forth the response "You have to be nuts to drive a Stutz." There really wasn't much to choose between the cars, which achieved countless amateur successes in hill climbs and races, although the Mercer was more fragile. Some social snobbery may have been involved; the Mercer was an East Coast make from Trenton, New Jersey, backed by blue-blooded families like the Roeblings, while Harry Stutz was a Middle Western farm boy turned mechanic.

The T-head Mercer Raceabout did not last long. In 1912 Washington Roebling II lost his life in the *Titanic* disaster, and Finlay Robertson Porter left Mercer two years later. His place was taken by Erik Delling, who designed a new line called the 22–70. This had an L-head four engine. A roadster was still in the range, but it had a proper windshield, bench seat, and enclosed coachwork with doors. Although quite popular, these "softer" Mercer raceabouts lacked the charisma of the original. For 1923 they acquired a six-cylinder valve-in-head engine by Rochester, but production ended in 1925, when Mercer went out of business. The Stutz Bearcat was also made into the early 1920s, and then the name was revived in 1932 for a very small series of short-wheelbase versions of

1912 STUTZ BEARCAT ◀▼

THE FAMOUS BEARCAT SPEEDSTER WAS PART OF THE STUTZ RANGE FROM THE FIRM'S FIRST PRODUCTION YEAR, AND WAS AVAILABLE WITH FOUR- AND SIX-CYLINDER ENGINES. THEY WERE NO MORE EXPENSIVE THAN TOURING STUTZES. IN 1912 STUTZ ENTERED 30 RACES AND WON 25 OF THEM. BEARCATS WERE HEAVY TO HANDLE. HOWEVER, THE STORY THAT HARRY STUTZ MADE THE CLUTCH SPRINGS SO STIFF THAT A WOMAN COULD NOT OPERATE THEM IS PROBABLY APOCRYPHAL.

OWNER: AUBURN-CORD-DUESENBERG MUSEUM (PHOTO NICKY WRIGHT)

the DV-32 Dual Valve straight-8.

Stutz and Mercer had a number of rivals in the 1920s, for there was quite a fashion for speedsters, from makes such as Biddle, Jordan, Kissel, Marmon, and Paige, as well as the lesser-known Argonne, Noma, Richelieu, and ReVere. The Biddle was an assembled car, but a high-quality one of handsome appearance thanks to its Mercedes-type pointed radiator and high-grade coachwork. Among a variety of listed bodies was a rakish roadster styled by a young Maryland girl, Miriam Warren Hubbard. Tired of Mercers and Stutzes which, she said, were always going wrong, she took Biddle up on its offer to build a car for anyone, and designed a roadster with Vee-shaped headlight glass to match the radiator, separate fenders and running boards, and no top.

Miriam's roadster was subsequently repeated for several clients. Biddles were offered with either Buda or Rochester-Duesenberg engines, the former giving 48bhp, the latter up to 100bhp in race tune. One would imagine that the roadsters would have had the more powerful engine, but one cannot be sure. Like other roadsters, Biddles were not performance automobiles; their function was to look

1920 MERCER SERIES 5 ▼▶

THE MERCER 35J RACEABOUT GAVE WAY TO ERIK DELLING'S 22-70 DESIGN IN 1915. THIS SERIES 5 OF 1920 WAS A DESCENDANT, WITH DOORS AND A WINDSHIELD IN PLACE OF THE 35's MONOCLE. IT WAS 17 INCHES SHORTER THAN THE TOURING MERCERS, ON A 115-INCH WHEELBASE, AND COST $4,200.

OWNER: CRAWFORD COLLECTION OF THE WESTERN HISTORICAL SOCIETY

(PHOTO NICKY WRIGHT)

stylish and sporty, to complement their owners whose sports might be golf, polo, or deepsea fishing.

The Biddle was expensive, up to $3,750 for an Ormond two-passenger roadster in 1921, but more modestly priced and better known roadsters were made by Jordan and Kissel. Ned Jordan has become more famous for his advertisements than his cars, with the immortal "Somewhere West of Laramie," "A Golden Girl from Somewhere," "A Million Miles from Dull Care," and "I Think She Came from a Land of Fire." All these featured the Jordan Playboy, a typical roadster with a rumble seat, powered by a six-cylinder Continental engine, which was launched in 1919, three years after the first Jordan appeared. Claimed top speed was 65mph, although the British magazine *The Autocar* could not get more than 50.7mph (they must have had an off-tune model). Its price was $2,550.

The Playboy (named from J.M. Synge's *Playboy of the Western World*) was not a particularly distinguished car, and was only one of a wide range of Jordan styles, yet it is the model with which the make is always associated, even more so than Bearcat is with Stutz. Advertising must have made a big difference: "Some day in June, when happy hours abound, a wonderful girl and a wonderful boy will leave their friends in a shower of rice, and start to roam....Give them a Jordan Playboy, the blue sky overhead and the green turf flying by, and a thousand miles of open road." Only Ned Jordan wrote copy like that.

Jordan got the Playboy's price down to $1,750 in 1924, and the following year the name went onto an eight-cylinder roadster, also Continental-powered. By now it was less sporty-looking, no different from many other two-passenger open cars with rumble seats.

Kissel's speedster was called the Gold Bug and was developed from a line of custom bodies on Kissel chassis designed and sold by New York distributor Conover T. Silver (who also built bodies on Apperson and Willys chassis). Launched in 1919, the Gold Bug had a doorless two-passenger body with an auxiliary seat which could be pulled out, with its accompanying foot rest, like a drawer from the side of the body. One would have been pretty daring to occupy this seat at any speed, but this was all part of the speedster's devil-may-care image. Historian Keith Marvin thinks that these seats were soon curtailed legally because of the horrific possibilities of a side-swipe accident. The 1922 Paige Daytona 6–66 roadster also featured such a seat, and had a 66bhp Continental six engine

1920 APPERSON EIGHT SPORTSTER ▼▶

THE PIONEER INDIANA MAKE, APPERSON,
FEATURED A V8 ENGINE FROM 1916 TO 1925,
WHEN APPERSON WENT OVER TO A LYCOMING-BUILT
STRAIGHT-8. THIS SPORTSTER HAS THE DISK WHEELS
POPULAR AT THE TIME, ALTHOUGH APPERSONS
WERE MADE WITH ARTILLERY OR WIRE WHEELS
AS WELL. IT WAS ONE OF NINE BODY STYLES
OFFERED IN 1920, AND SOLD FOR $2,950.
OWNER: AUBURN-CORD-DUESENBERG MUSEUM (PHOTO NICKY WRIGHT)

giving an 80mph top speed. For 1923 the Paige was better equipped, with two side-mounted spare wheels, front and rear bumpers, a power-operated windshield wiper, and an eight-day clock, cigar lighter, and rear-view mirror. All this for only $2,400, or $1,000 less than in 1922. The price was probably too low, for the Daytona was withdrawn after only 56 had been made in two seasons.

After the middle of the 1920s speedsters had mostly disappeared or become tamer, but the end of the decade saw a final flowering of the breed. The most striking was the Auburn, product of an Indiana firm which had been on the point of extinction in 1924 when Errett Lobban Cord joined the company. A whiz kid several decades before the phrase was coined, Cord had, by his own confession, made and lost three fortunes before he was 21. He had been a highly successful salesman for Moon cars in Chicago when he came to Auburn as general manager. He added some nickel plating and gave new paint jobs to the countless unsold Auburns he found there, and before the end of the year most of them had found customers.

In 1925 he hired a new designer, J.M. Crawford, ordered a consignment of Lycoming straight-8 engines, and launched a new line of Auburns as the 8–53 and 8–88. With stylish bodies and two-tone color schemes, the new Auburns sold very well. Cord sent his cars record-breaking, and in 1928 launched an A1 Leamy-designed speedster with Vee-windshield, pointed tail body, and an engine that gave 115bhp thanks to alloy pistons and connecting rods, larger valves, and a high-lift camshaft. All Auburns that year had hydraulic

brakes. A V12 joined the Auburn range for 1932. There was also a speedster which sold for the low price of $1,145 (the cheapest V-12 was the coupe at $975, the only twelve-cylinder car to sell for under $1,000). The Depression was not the best time to market exotic cars like the Auburn speedsters, and sales dropped alarmingly after 1931. Auburn ceased to make cars after 1936, but not before creating a final speedster, the low-slung supercharged 851 of 1935 styled by Gordon Buehrig. The Schwitzer-Cummins supercharger boosted the output of the

1936 AUBURN 654 SEDAN AND 852 PHAETON ▲▶▼
TWO LATE MODEL AUBURNS, A SIX-CYLINDER SEDAN AND EIGHT-CYLINDER PHAETON. LIKE THE V12s, BOTH
WERE AVAILABLE WITH STANDARD TRANSMISSION OR WITH CUSTOM DUAL RATIO REAR AXLE. THE EIGHTS
COULD BE HAD IN SUPER CHARGED FORM, LIKE THIS PHAETON. THESE MODELS WERE USED BY THE INDIANA
STATE POLICE, EARNING GOOD PUBLICITY FOR A LOCAL MAKE. HOWEVER, 1936 WAS AUBURN'S LAST YEAR,
WITH ONLY 1,848 CARS OF ALL TYPES DELIVERED.
OWNER: AUBURN-CORD-DUESENBERG MUSEUM (PHOTO NICKY WRIGHT)

274-cubic-inch Lycoming straight-8 from 115 to
150bhp, and all cars sold bore a plaque to certify
that they had exceeded 100mph. About 500 were
sold, at $2,245. Auburn lost money on each one,
but they were intended as bait to lure customers
into the showrooms to buy the regular six- and
eight-cylinder sedans. Sales rose by 20 percent
between 1934 and 1935, but this was not enough to
save the Auburn, which went down with the other
marques of Cord's empire, the Cord and the
Duesenberg.

There were other short-lived speedsters at the
end of the 1920s, including the straight-8 twin-
camshaft Stutz Black Hawk, the Packard Model
734 with 384-cubic-inch engine, also a straight-8,
and the duPont Model G. This was the speedster
version of a wide range of duPonts, all powered by
Continental straight-8 engines, and was very
expensive at $5,335.

HIGH NOON OF THE LUXURY CAR

The 1920s were the peak years for cars at the
top of the price scale, and for the fortunate few
with upward of $5,000 to spend on an
automobile, there was a wide choice.
The more conservative East Coast rich
tended to favor traditional makes
such as Locomobile, Pierce-Arrow,
Cunningham, and Rolls-Royce (made
in Springfield, Massachusetts, from
1921), while the more flamboyant oil-
rich and Hollywood families chose
exotica like the Daniels,
McFarlan, and the Doble
Steamer, and at the end of
the decade the Model J
Duesenberg. Imported
luxury cars were also seen
in growing numbers, from
Minerva, Hispano-Suiza,
Isotta-Fraschini, Mercedes-
Benz, and Renault. This era
was also the great heyday

of the American custom coachbuilder.

Many of the buyers of luxury cars, whether they
were Wall Street bankers or Boston dowagers, were
more interested in comfort and exclusiveness than
in the latest technical innovations, which accounts
for the conservatism of some of their cars.
Locomobile, in particular, continued the monster
T-head Model 48 through 1929 with little change to
the specification, apart from a gradual updating of
body styling. In December 1923 front-wheel brakes
were announced as an option, at an extra cost of
$350 on new cars and at $450 on cars which the
owner returned to the factory. This was perhaps not
exorbitant when compared with an overall price of
up to $13,000, but for the same money the owner's
cook could buy a Model T and have enough change
for a year's gasoline.

In 1923 production of the
Model 48 was only two chassis
per day, and by 1929 probably
not more than one per week.
Prices were $9,600–$12,500 in
this its last year. Locomobile
was bought by Billy Durant in
1922, and four years
later he brought
out another
luxury model,
as well as
cheaper sixes
and eights.
The new
luxury car
was called
the Model
90 and had an

L-head monobloc six engine only a little smaller than the 525-cubic-inch 48. Wheelbase was 4 inches shorter at 138 inches, and prices were considerably lower, at $5,500–$7,500.

Pierce-Arrow entered the 1920s with designs similar to the Locomobile, big, slow-turning T-head sixes of 414 and 524 cubic inches, called the 38 and 48 respectively. They were among the last American cars to go over to left-hand drive with centrally mounted gearshift and parking brake. This move was resisted by P-A's chief engineer David Fergusson, who had tried a left-hand drive conversion back in 1911, when most other manufacturers were making the change. It has been said that Pierce-Arrow preferred right-hand drive as the chauffeur could leap onto the sidewalk and open the door for the passengers. However, this was probably a useful side effect of conservatism rather than the cause of it. In 1911 Fergusson's impressions of the left-hand drive car were not

favorable, and the change was not made until 1921, the year that Fergusson retired from Pierce-Arrow.

Other top grade manufacturers who stuck to six cylinders included Stevens-Duryea, Winton, and Rolls-Royce. The first made old-fashioned designs with pair-cast cylinders at prices up to $10,000. These sold to the same clientele as the

Locomobile, although in smaller numbers. Winton continued their sixes up to 1924. Rolls-Royce had been represented in the United States since 1906. A prominent early customer was Mrs. John Jacob Astor, so much the leader of New York society that if she grew tired of a performance at the Metropolitan Opera and left during the intermission everyone else left too and the cast sang to an empty house. She was not so slavishly followed in the matter of automobiles, however, and Rolls-Royce's New York dealer failed to meet his promise to order 50 cars in 1908. Little more was heard of Rolls-Royce in America until after World War I.

In 1919 Rolls-Royce's director Claude Johnson decided that the United States was potentially the firm's best market (he was worried about socialist legislation in Britain), but that import duties would make the price too high. Manufacture in the United States was the answer, so a factory was acquired at

1933 AUBURN 8-105 ▲▶
BOAT-TAIL SPEEDSTER
THE BOAT-TAIL SPEEDSTER WAS THE MOST STRIKING STYLE IN THE AUBURN LINE, FROM ITS INTRODUCTION IN 1928 TO THE FINAL 852 OF 1936. IN 1933 THE DESIGN WAS AVAILABLE ON BOTH EIGHT- AND TWELVE-CYLINDER MODELS, WHICH COULD BE HAD WITH THE COLUMBIA DUAL RATIO AXLE. THIS 8-105 COST $1,345.
OWNER: DUKE DAVENPORT
(PHOTO NICKY WRIGHT)

Springfield, Massachusetts, which began to turn out Silver Ghosts at first identical to the British ones. Like them, they were supplied in chassis form only, although Rolls-Royce-designed bodies were made for them by prestigious coachbuilders, including Merrimac of Merrimac, Massachusetts, Biddle & Smart of Amesbury, Massachusetts, and Willoughby of Utica, New York.

In 1923 Rolls-Royce of America set up its own bodywork department at Springfield and no longer farmed the work out, although there were always special requests for custom bodies. Even the regular coachwork made the Springfield Silver Ghost more expensive than any other American-built car. In November 1924 prices ranged from $12,930 for a Pall Mall five-passenger touring to $15,880 for a Mayfair full cabriolet. Custom work by such firms as Brewster, Brunn, Derham, or Locke could cost several thousand dollars more, while the ultimate was probably reached by the town car built by Waterhouse for Harry Orndorff of Providence, Rhode Island.

The Phantom I delivered to Mr. Orndorff in 1926 was only the fifth of this model to be made at Springfield. After five years of use, its owner returned it to the works asking for the chassis to be lengthened from 146½ to 160 inches to accommodate the body he had in mind. This was built by Waterhouse, a lesser-known coachbuilder formed to make bodies for duPont. The floor was decorated with oriental rugs, and the seats were duplicates of the owner's favorite armchairs, with winter and summer covers. Like many cars of the period, the Phantom had two spare wheels mounted on the running board; the one on the right-hand side contained not a wheel but a two-octave chime which Mr. Orndorff could operate by a keyboard located ahead of the front passenger seat. The total cost of this Phantom was in excess of $30,000. Unfortunately the additional weight on one side caused springing problems, and the car had to be returned to Springfield several times before an ideal ride was obtained.

The 1925 season prices quoted above were a considerable increase on those of the previous year, mainly because Rolls-Royce went over to left-hand drive that year, necessitating a redesign not only of the axle and steering controls but also of the exhaust manifold. A number of right-hand drive

1929 ROLLS-ROYCE PHANTOM 1 ASCOT PHAETON ▲

THE ASCOT WAS ONE OF SEVERAL BODY STYLES MADE FOR ROLLS-ROYCE OF AMERICA BY BREWSTER. THEY ALL TENDED TO HAVE VERY ENGLISH NAMES SUCH AS ASCOT, DERBY, PICCADILLY, PALL MALL, AND NEWMARKET, ALTHOUGH A FRENCH TOUCH WAS GIVEN BY THE TROUVILLE TOWN CAR. PRICES WERE VERY HIGH; THE ASCOT COST $17,250, AND A HIBBERD & DARRIN CONVERTIBLE SEDAN SET THE CUSTOMER BACK $19,665. A TOTAL OF 25 ASCOTS WERE MADE, ALL ON THE 144¾-INCH WHEELBASE.

OWNER: GILMORE CAR MUSEUM, KALAMAZOO, MICHIGAN (PHOTO NICKY WRIGHT)

cars were traded in for the new models and proved difficult to resell, since the less well-off who might have bought a used Rolls-Royce were unlikely to have chauffeurs and were therefore less happy with right-hand drive. Rolls-Royce Inc. was able to move some of the remaining right-hand drive stock by selling them in Argentina and Uruguay, both of which still favored driving on the left.

Prices went up again when the Phantom I was introduced late in 1926. Although not a very different car apart from the larger engine with overhead valves, expensive retooling was needed, so Phantom prices ran from $17,840 for a Derby four-passenger touring to $19,965 for a Trouville

town car. Sales dropped from the 325–365 per year which the Silver Ghost had enjoyed between 1923 and 1926 to 275 in 1928 and 251 in 1929. The Phantom II introduced in 1929 would have cost even more in retooling, at which point Rolls-Royce of America gave up its manufacturing rights. The Phantom I was assembled for six more years, from parts on hand, and 116 Phantom II chassis were imported from England. They were equipped with left-hand steering and most carried bodies by Brewster, which had become a Rolls-Royce subsidiary in 1926.

Customers for the American Rolls-Royce ranged right across the social spectrum and the continent,

from prominent East Coast families such as the Carnegies, Guggenheims, Rockefellers, and Vanderbilts to many Hollywood personalities, including Jackie Coogan, Pola Negri, Gloria Swanson, Tom Mix, Al Jolson, Clara Bow, Zeppo Marx, and Daryl Zanuck. The celebrated New York hostess Mrs. E.T. Stotesbury had several. It was at her Pennsylvania mansion, Whitemarsh Hall, that

Henry Ford murmured to his wife in the entrance hall: "It's instructive to see how the rich live."

Ex-president Woodrow Wilson had a Silver Ghost Oxford seven-passenger touring in 1923, although the official White House cars remained Pierce-Arrows into the 1930s. Among foreign rulers, owners of American Rolls-Royces included General Morales of Cuba (1926 Oxford touring) and

Poland's Marshal Pitsudski, who had a 1931 Phantom II with a 28-gallon gas tank and two horns, "very loud" and "loudest possible."

Other lesser known luxury cars which vied with the aforementioned included the McFarlan, Phianna, and Porter. The McFarlan from Connersville, Indiana, had the largest engine in any production American car of the 1920s. This was a

AUBURN'S V12 WAS CONSIDERABLY LOWER IN PRICE
THAN ANY OTHER TWELVE-CYLINDERED CAR, AND
THE COMPANY MANAGED TO GET ONE MODEL,
THE 1932 STANDARD COUPE, BELOW THE $1,000 MARK
AT $975. THIS TWO-DOOR SEDAN WAS KNOWN
AS THE BROUGHAM. THE "A" IN THE DESIGNATION
INDICATES THE HIGHER-PRICED CUSTOM RANGE,
WHICH INCLUDED THE DUAL-RATIO REAR AXLE
GIVING SIX FORWARD SPEEDS.

OWNERS: GARY AND SHARON VICK (PHOTO NICKY WRIGHT)

572-cubic-inch T-head six made under license from Teetor-Hartley, who had designed it for use in Maxim fire engines. In fact, the Maxim company of Middleboro, Massachusetts, acted as New England distributors for McFarlan automobiles. The engine was called the TV for Twin Valve (four valves per cylinder), a design that became common for high-performance engines in the 1980s. It developed 120bhp, a record for American engines in 1920.

The TV was a massive car standing more than 6 feet high in sedan form, and on a wheelbase of 140 inches. Up to 1925 Disteel disk wheels were usually featured, although wood-spoked or wire were available and were more common in the later 1920s. In 1921, 11 body styles were available, from a two-passenger roadster at $6,300 to the Knickerbocker cabriolet at $9,000. This spectacular vehicle was a town car with an open front for the chauffeur and a folding roof at the rear. For 1923 it became even more distinctive, with small fenders hugging the front wheels, no running board, but a smaller step plate for the driver and a slightly larger one for the rear-seat passengers. Carriage-type side lamps were mounted just ahead of the rear doors, and there were dummy landau irons behind the windows. Since they were dummies the car was no longer properly a cabriolet and for 1924 it was renamed the town car. The well-known antique car collector Cameron Peck offered one for sale in 1949, describing it as "like nothing so much as a Moorish castle on wheels" and "the largest possible motor car in the worst possible taste." He was asking only $500, including delivery to railroad, but this was not so much a reflection of his opinions of the car as of the generally low prices of old cars at that time.

McFarlan made its own bodies, and few of the

custom firms built on the TV chassis. The 1922 New York Salon did reveal a Brooks-Ostruk town car priced at $11,650, but the most remarkable body of all was exhibited by McFarlan at the 1923 Chicago Show. This had a Knickerbocker cabriolet body, but the radiator shell (one of the largest in the business), hubs, rims, door handles, and other exterior metal work, even the bumpers and canisters for the Gruss air springs, were all gold-plated. It was apparently built as a speculative venture, not specially ordered, and carried a price tag of $25,000. Unsold for six months, it was eventually bought by a lady from an oil-rich

Oklahoma family, although whether she paid the full price is not known. Other well-known McFarlan owners included heavyweight boxing champion Jack Dempsey and bandleader Paul Whiteman, who toured England in his TV and found it was too large for many small roads. Movie star Dorothy Dalton was photographed in a McFarlan, but whether she owned it or just posed for the picture we do not know. McFarlan built a smaller single-valve six from 1924 and a Lycoming-powered straight-8 from 1926, but these were cheaper and less glamorous than the mighty TV. All production ended in 1928.

The Phianna and Porter were unusual among expensive cars in having four-cylinder engines. The former began life in Newark, New Jersey, in 1917, descended from the S.G.V. and named for the daughters of one of the promoters, Phyllis and Anna. Few were made under the original ownership, but in 1919 the car was relaunched by a young enthusiast, Miles Harold Carpenter, who set up a new factory at Long Island City. He retained the four-cylinder engine with an interesting modification in the form of a laminated walnut and ash fan, the work of airplane propeller designer Fred Charavey. The wheelbase was lengthened by

1932 WILLYS-OVERLAND 6-90 ROADSTER ▲

WILLYS BUILT FOUR SERIES IN 1932, ON TWO WHEELBASES. TWO USED POPPET-VALVE ENGINES IN SIX- AND EIGHT-CYLINDER MODELS, AND TWO HAD SIX-CYLINDER KNIGHT SLEEVE-VALVE ENGINES. THIS IS A 6-90 POPPET-VALVE SIX ROADSTER WHICH SOLD FOR A MODEST $515. THERE WAS NO KNIGHT-ENGINED ROADSTER, BUT IN STYLES WHERE BOTH ENGINES WERE USED, SUCH AS SEDANS AND COUPES, THE SLEEVE-VALVE MODELS COST OVER $300 MORE. OF 26,710 CARS SOLD BY WILLYS IN 1932, ONLY 3,265 WERE WILLYS-KNIGHTS.

OWNER; GEORGE SANDERS (PHOTO NICKY WRIGHT)

The Porter had some similarities with the Phianna in that it was also a high-priced four-cylinder luxury car that had evolved out of a previous make, in this case the F.R.P. But if Miles Carpenter was an unknown, not so the Porter's designer, Finlay Robertson Porter, the man responsible for the famous Mercer Type 35. The Porter had a large four-cylinder engine made by the American & British Mfg Corporation of Bridgeport, Connecticut, which developed 120–125bhp, possibly putting it ahead of the McFarlan. The finest custom bodies by such firms as Brewster, Demarest, and Fleetwood were mounted on a whopping 142-inch wheelbase, and prices were in excess of $10,000. Only 36 were sold, between 1919 and 1922.

While the traditional luxury car makers stuck to six cylinders, there was a considerable vogue for eights, not only the V8s that had been popular since Cadillac launched the fashion in 1914, but also for in-line or straight-8s. Of the V8 adherents, Cadillac remained faithful throughout the 1920s, and indeed up to the present day, supplementing them with V12s and V16s in the 1930s. Peerless adopted a V8 for 1916 and through 1928, going over to a straight-8 and a cheaper six for its last few years. Other firms favoring the V8 included the luxury car makers Cunningham and Daniels, who made their own, the mid-priced Apperson and King, which also featured home-built engines, and Cole, which bought from Northway. Most of these firms went out of business by the middle of the decade, although Cunningham carried on in a small way, eventually concentrating on hearses, which had been a mainstay of production for the company from the beginning. Cunningham's final fling was a Ford V8-powered town car in the mid-1930s.

An important newcomer to the luxury car market was the Lincoln, made initially by Henry M. Leland and his son Wilfred, who walked out of Cadillac in 1917 after harsh words with Billy Durant. With America's entry into World War I threatening, the first products of the new Lincoln Motor Company were Liberty airplane engines, of which 6,500 were made. Once the war was over they had to find some way of keeping their large plant and 6,000 payroll occupied. With their background, it was hardly surprising that they turned again to automobiles.

10 inches to 125 inches, and custom-built coachwork was available at prices from $6,000 for a standard brougham to $11,500 for a limousine. These prices were way up in Locomobile country, and most buyers expected at least six cylinders for this kind of money.

Few Phiannas were made, probably not more than 300, although customers included R.B. Horne, president of Canadian Pacific, the president of Brazil, and Bainbridge Colby, secretary of state in President Wilson's government. When four meat tycoons, Messrs. Armour, Benjamin, Curahy, and

Swift, were discussing cars, it turned out that all of them were Phianna owners. Carpenter remembered delivering one Phianna to a splendid mansion at Irvington-on-the-Hudson where a party was in progress, and being surprised to find that the customer and all her guests were blacks. In a gathering of some 80 people, he was the only white man present. He was happy to do business with a black client, in contrast to the members of the Imported Car Association, who had an unwritten agreement that they would not sell their cars to black people.

Announced in September 1920, the Lincoln V8 was not unlike the Cadillac, except that the angle between the cylinder banks was 60° rather than the more usual 90°. This gave an uneven firing sequence alternating between 60° and 120° of crankshaft revolution. Leland's aim was to damp out the harmonic vibration periods which troubled earlier V8 engines. Both engines had side valves in an L-head. Displacement and output were 358 cubic inches and 81bhp, compared with the Cadillac's 314 cubic inches and 60bhp. This gave a good performance, a top speed of 80mph with a touring body. Prices ran from $4,300 to $6,600 for standard bodies built by the American Body Company of Buffalo, or the Anderson Electric Car Company, which had made Detroit Electric cars until the latter were hived off to a subsidiary. Custom bodies by Brunn or Judkins were considerably more expensive. Cadillac prices ran from $3,740 to $5,690 at this time.

The name of Leland carried so much weight that $6.5 million of stock was subscribed in one day and over 1,000 orders were received before the first Lincoln rolled from the plant. Unfortunately a number of these were canceled when buyers saw the cars; the engineering and performance were acceptable, but the body styling seemed uninspired, even old-fashioned. Today Lincolns do not seem too bad when compared with other 1920 cars, but the public had been led to expect something exceptional from a new make with the Leland reputation. Added to this, there was a recession at the end of 1920, which resulted in a disappointing first year for Lincoln, with 3,407 cars sold to the end of 1921 instead of an anticipated total of 6,000.

A heavy tax bill forced Lincoln into receivership in November 1921 and in February 1922 the company was put up for sale. The only bid came from Henry Ford, with an offer of $8 million, which was accepted. Clara Ford was a friend of Wilfred Leland's wife, and she said, in one of her very few public statements: "If Detroit will stand by and see the Lelands and their men who put money into that concern lose everything they've got and not lift a hand to help them, there's something wrong with our public spirit." Edsel Ford added his bit: "It would be a shame, a blot on the good name of the whole community, if Detroit

1937 LASALLE SEDAN ▲◄
ALTHOUGH NOT VERY DIFFERENT IN APPEARANCE FROM THE 1936 CARS, THE 1937 LASALLES WERE NOW MORE LIKE JUNIOR CADILLACS THAN THEY HAD BEEN, WITH THE SAME 322-CUBIC-INCH V8 THAT WAS USED IN CADILLAC'S SERIES 60. BOTH CARS NOW HAD A HYPOID REAR AXLE. THERE WERE FIVE BODY STYLES, INCLUDING FOR THE FIRST TIME A CONVERTIBLE SEDAN. THIS FOUR-DOOR SEDAN COST $1,145. FOR LASALLE 1937 WAS THE BEST YEAR, WITH 32,005 CARS DELIVERED.
OWNER: WALLY HERMAN (PHOTO NICKY WRIGHT)

than spectacular during the 1920s. The aluminum pistons introduced under the Ford regime boosted power to 90bhp, and the 1923 cars were better-looking thanks to the option of wire wheels and a longer wheelbase of 136 inches. This was standardized from 1924 and remained unchanged until 1931, when it went up to 145 inches. Apart from wealthy customers at home and abroad, Lincolns were favored by the members of the Detroit Police Flying Squad, who chose them after testing 11 other makes. They needed fast cars in the 1920s to apprehend the rum runners who brought their merchandise from Canada to supply the countless bootleggers and speakeasies of the Prohibition era. Police Lincolns were equipped with front-wheel brakes from 1924, although regular customers didn't get these until the 1927 season. Other features available on police vehicles included bullet-resistant glass and gun racks in the rear compartment.

Lincoln production rose satisfactorily. In 1922 5,767 cars were delivered, 255 of them Leland-built, the rest built by Ford. By 1926 the figure was 8,858, the highest until the introduction of the lower-priced Zephyr in the 1930s. These figures were small compared with those achieved by Cadillac, which sold 27,340 cars in 1926, but were ahead of the really expensive Locomobile and Pierce-Arrow.

Cadillac had a good decade, with one model of V8 until 1927, when it was joined by the smaller companion make, LaSalle. Named for the French explorer René Robert Cavalier de la Salle, who claimed Louisiana for his king, Louis XIV, in 1682,

let the Leland company go to ruin."

Henry's community spirit was not so evident. He had been approached by the Lelands in June 1921, when he could have helped with a loan, but this would not have given him full control. By waiting until Leland was forced into receivership he got a potentially valuable company at a bargain price. After a few months, during which Henry Leland celebrated his 79th birthday, the Lelands were so discouraged by the interference of Ford men that they offered to buy back their company for what Ford had paid, plus interest. "Mr. Leland," Ford replied, "I wouldn't sell the Lincoln plant for five hundred million dollars."

Ford promised to spend at least two hours a day with Henry Leland, sorting out any problems that might arise, but he never saw the Lelands again. In June 1922 an emissary from Ford requested the departure of Wilfred Leland, and not unnaturally his father resigned the same day. Lincoln Motor

Company was now wholly Henry Ford's, although styling and promotion became the special responsibility of Edsel.

Few changes were evident at first, and indeed most 1922 Lincolns carried the word "Lincoln, Leland built" on their radiators. The 151 dealers whom the Lelands had commissioned were soon replaced by Ford dealers, which extended Lincoln sales to such countries as Cuba, China, and Japan. Edsel engaged Herman Brunn of the famous Buffalo coachbuilding company to design a new range of bodies and these were adopted on a semi-custom basis on late 1922 and 1923 Lincolns, although the styles with fewer trimmings were made by the American Body Company. A wide range of open and closed styles by Judkins was also available. Prices ran from $3,800 for a standard seven-passenger touring to $7,200 for a Brunn town car version.

Development of the Lincoln was gradual rather

the make was intended to fill a gap between the highest-priced Buick ($1,995) and the lowest-priced Cadillac ($2,995). Successful competitors in this field included the Packard Single Six and Chrysler Imperial. The 303-cubic-inch LaSalle engine was more efficient than the Cadillac's, with a smaller stroke/bore ratio, 1.58:1 compared with 1.64:1. The right cylinder bank was 1⅜ inch forward of the left, making it possible to fit the rods side by side on the crankpins. Output was a respectable 75bhp, only 5bhp less than from the 314.5-cubic-inch Cadillac. The LaSalle cylinder layout was adopted in Cadillac engines from 1928 onward.

Probably the most striking aspect of the new LaSalle was its appearance. It was the first car to be styled by Harley Earl, who had worked for the Don Lee coachbuilding company in Los Angeles. Indeed it was the car that led to the setting up of an Art & Colour Section (later redesignated Styling) at GM. Earl modeled his car on the French Hispano-Suiza, at that time the ultimate in chic and luxury, but a very small seller in the United States thanks to prices in the $10,750–$19,500 region. The French car's influence was particularly strong in the radiator shape, winged radiator emblem, and the badge tie-bar between the headlights. Dual color schemes were offered on all 11 body types, eight of them on a 125-inch wheelbase, 7 inches shorter than the shortest Cadillac, and three on a 134-inch chassis. Prices ran from $2,495 for a short-wheelbase phaeton to $2,920 for a long-wheelbase seven-passenger Imperial Sedan. For 1928 a line of custom bodies by Fleetwood took the highest prices up to $4,900. At the same time, Cadillac was offering 50 different variations of body and chassis, with 500 color combinations. In the years 1927 and 1928, LaSalle accounted for more than half of the Cadillac Division's registrations, 26,807 out of 47,136.

LaSalle V8s were built until the end of the 1933 season, after which they were replaced by an Oldsmobile straight-8. From 1931, they were the same engines as in the Cadillac, yet they were at least $500 lower in price. An important technical development common to both makes was the synchromesh transmission, new for 1929. This was a world first for General Motors, although at the time few people realized that within ten years synchromesh transmission would be almost

universal and double-declutching would become as obsolete as hand-cranking. There was no synchromesh on first gear, though.

The V12 layout, so popular in the first decade of the century, survived only in Packard's Twin Six, and then only to 1923, until there was a revival around 1930. The only exception was the gloriously extravagant Heine-Velox, the work of German-born piano maker Gustav Otto Heine (1868–1959). He had built a few cars in San Francisco until his plant was destroyed in the 1906 earthquake, then returned to pianos until 1921, when he announced a massive car on a 148-inch wheelbase, powered by a 389.5-cubic-inch Weidely V12 engine. The car bristled with unusual features, including hydraulic brakes on all four wheels, thought to be a first for the U.S. industry, with a five-gallon reserve tank for the hydraulic system, which could be adjusted

to refill either the front or rear brakes, or both at once. The windows pivoted instead of sliding, and the body was fastened to the side of the frame rather than the top, giving greater rigidity and a lower center of gravity. All bodywork was carried out by the Heine-Velox Engineering Company in its San Francisco workshops. The headlights were mounted on top of the fenders, rather in the manner of the Pierce-Arrow.

Heine announced prices from $17,000 to $25,000 for his car, but he never sold any. Five were built, a sporting victoria, three sedans, and an unfinished limousine. At least one purchaser, a Hollywood actor, had his check returned to him with a message from Heine scribbled across it: "We do not accept charity." One or two cars he gave away, the others he kept. At the time of his death in 1959 two remained, a sedan and the unfinished limousine, and they are still in storage in California.

A popular layout which appeared for the first time in the 1920s was the straight-8 or eight in line. The design was pioneered by the Italian Isotta-Fraschini company in 1919, and their cars were particularly popular in the United States, where about 450 were sold between 1920 and 1932. Who made America's first straight-8 has been a subject of dispute for some time. The claim has been argued between the two Duesenberg brothers of Indianapolis and Cloyd Y. Kenworthy of

Mishawaka, Indiana. Both announced their cars at the end of 1920, but the Duesenbergs had theirs on show at the New York Automobile Salon in mid-November, while the Kenworthy was not announced until December. By the acid test of subsequent success in the market place, the Duesenbergs won hands down, for few, if any, of the $5,550 Kenworthy Line-O-Eights were sold, while the Duesenberg Model A was made into 1926, to be followed by one of the most glamorous cars America has ever seen.

The Duesenberg brothers, Fred and Augie, made their name with racing cars, first under the Mason name from 1912 to 1913 and then under their own name. The Model A touring on which they worked during 1920 was their first road-going car, and employed a 260-cubic-inch straight-8 engine with a single overhead camshaft. It also had hydraulic brakes on all four wheels, a feature shared coincidentally with the Kenworthy and with the V12 Heine-Velox. Beautifully built, the Model A was far from cheap, prices running from $6,500 for a five-passenger touring to $8,800 for a town car. The first cars did not reach customers until 1922, and about 600 were made up to 1926 when Errett Lobban Cord bought the company.

Cord, who had already revitalized Auburn, saw the Duesenberg as a step into the top ranks of American motordom, but the Model A was not the car to take that step. He therefore gave the Duesenbergs a free hand to develop a car that could hold its head up among the finest that America or the rest of the world could make. While an interim design similar to the A and called the Model X was listed for 1927 (only about a dozen

were made), Fred worked on the new car. This was launched at the New York Salon on December 1, 1928. Called the Model J, it had a straight-8 engine of 420-cubic-inch displacement, with not one overhead camshaft but two, a layout hitherto only seen on racing cars and a few low-production European sports cars. Output was claimed to be 265bhp at 4,250rpm, and while this has been disputed and was almost certainly the gross figure without taking into account losses through the transmission, it was still more than double that of any other contemporary car. The massive French-built V12 Hispano-Suiza, which appeared two years later and had a 575-cubic-inch engine, gave only 220bhp, while the next most powerful American car was the Cadillac V16, which gave 175bhp when it was introduced in 1930.

The Model J was inevitably very expensive, but this was probably a bonus to Cord rather than a disappointment. He was aiming unashamedly at the ostentatious rich, the "if you've got it, flaunt it" crowd, of which there were many in pre-Depression America. Chassis price was $8,500, to which the buyer had to add anything from $2,500 to $8,000 for the body. Bodies varied from those offered by Duesenberg under the name La Grande, although they were built by other firms, to custom designs from America's finest coachbuilders. In fact few bare chassis left the factory, and most of these went to Europe. The

usual pattern was for the customer to choose a body from the wide range of designs on show in the Duesenberg styling department, which worked in close cooperation with the coachbuilders. Head of styling from 1929 to 1931 was Gordon Buehrig, later to design the Model 810 Cord. He preferred to supervise what would be appearing on a Duesenberg chassis rather than give the coachbuilder a free hand to do as he or the customer liked. Thus many Duesenberg bodies seem similar, although few were absolutely identical.

The most popular coachbuilding firm, who bodied probably 150 of the 470 Model Js, was Murphy of Pasadena, best known for its convertible sedans and Beverly sedans. Others whose work was regularly seen on Model J chassis included Brunn, Derham, Holbrook, Judkins, Locke, Rollston, Weymann, and Willoughby. Bohman & Schwartz built some original bodies, but were best-known for updating bodies in mid-1930s style, seldom improving on the original, but this is what customers wanted. One of the most unusual Bohman & Schwartz bodies was built on a chassis specially lengthened from an already long 153½ inches to 178 inches. Known as the Throne Car for its raised rear seats, it was built for the popular 1930s evangelist, Father Divine, and is said to have cost $25,000.

Duesenberg owners were not all so flamboyant

as Father Divine, but most were very different from the conservative owners of Locomobiles and Pierce-Arrows. Relatively few Duesenbergs were sold on the East Coast, although one went to New York's mayor Jimmy Walker. Hollywood was particularly fertile ground for Duesenberg dealers: buyers included Marion Davies, Mae West, Greta Garbo, Gary Cooper, and Clark Gable, also newspaper tycoon William Randolph Hearst. Cooper and Gable had the only two short-chassis SSJ two-passenger sports cars made. Another Duesenberg owner was Cliff Durant, son of Billy, who had a 1931 Murphy boat-tail roadster which he sold to oil magnate J. Paul Getty in 1932. Getty kept it for eight years, then traded it in for a new Mercury! The car was later owned by novelist John O'Hara. Foreign owners of Duesenbergs included the Kings of Italy and Spain, Queen Marie of Yugoslovia, Prince Nicholas of Rumania, and the Holkar of Indore. Most of these cars had European bodies, such as the sedan by Franay of Paris for Queen Marie, and the Holkar's two-passenger roadster (on a long wheelbase) by Gurney Nutting of London.

In July 1932, about three weeks after an auto accident from which he was thought to be recovering well, Fred Duesenberg died of pneumonia. His last design was a centrifugal supercharger which boosted output to a claimed 320bhp. This had already gone onto some cars, which bore the designation SJ. The first was

delivered in May 1932, the last in October 1935. Mostly built on the shorter of the two standard wheelbases (142½ inches), the SJ chassis cost $8,000 in 1934 and $10,000 in 1935. An SJ convertible coupe reached 129mph at Indianapolis. Only about 36 SJs were made out of a total generally thought to be 470 Model Js, although some were converted to supercharged form after they left the factory. The last Duesenberg chassis was made in 1937, although the last car to be completed was not delivered to its owner, a German artist called Rudolph Bauer, until early in 1940. Bauer planned to have his car bodied in Germany by Erdmann & Rossi, then thought

better of it, deciding to make his home in the United States and not in the Third Reich. The commission was given to Rollson, as Rollston became in 1939, who built a fully convertible town car with wheel-hugging fenders and a sloping chromed grille quite unlike that of a regular Duesenberg.

The next important straight-8 after Duesenberg came from Packard, who replaced its Twin Six in June 1923 by the Single Eight. This had a 357.9-cubic-inch engine with nine main bearing crankshaft, side valves in an L-head and aluminum crankcase. It developed 84bhp, which rose to 160bhp by 1940, with a slightly smaller engine of

FOR 1932 CHRYSLER'S IMPERIAL RANGE WAS DIVIDED INTO TWO SERIES, THE CH ON A 135-INCH WHEELBASE, AND THE CL ON 146 INCHES. BOTH USED THE 384.8-CUBIC-INCH 135bhp STRAIGHT-8 ENGINE INTRODUCED IN 1931, AND FEATURED DOUBLE DROP FRAMES, AND FOUR-SPEED TRANSMISSIONS WITH FREE WHEELING. THE CH WAS MADE IN LARGER NUMBERS: 1,402 TO THE 220 OF THE CL. THIS FIVE-PASSENGER SEDAN WAS THE MOST POPULAR STYLE, WITH 1,002 DELIVERED.

OWNER: DUKE DAVENPORT (PHOTO NICKY WRIGHT)

and light body, speeds of over 100mph. Four bodies were cataloged in the 734 series, a two-passenger runabout, four-passenger phaeton, victoria, and sedan. Only 113 were made, and the model was not repeated for 1931.

The fashion for straight-8s spread rapidly in the late 1920s, as medium-priced cars like Chandler and Marmon adopted them, and smaller manufacturers like Jordan, Kissel, and Roamer got in on the act thanks to straight-8 engines available from proprietary firms Continental and Lycoming. In 1929, 18 U.S. manufacturers were making straight-8s, and the following decade saw even more from famous firms such as Dodge and Hudson (1930), Buick and Chrysler (1931), Oldsmobile (1932), and Pontiac (1933). The last named were the lowest-priced straight-8s ever made, costing $585–$695.

THE LAST PUFF OF STEAM

One of America's finest and rarest luxury cars, the Doble, had only four cylinders, and these were steam-powered. Abner Doble (1895–1961) built his first steamer while still in high school, and while studying at the Massachusetts Institute of Technology he naturally visited the Stanley plant. The conservative attitudes of the Stanley twins left him quite unimpressed, and in 1914, with the help of his brothers and a family fortune founded on mining tools, he built his first car of which records survive. It had a condenser which consumed all exhaust steam, and a two-cylinder double-acting engine.

Doble built five of these Model As at Waltham, Massachusetts, then moved to Detroit where a few

all cast-iron contruction. Like the Duesenberg, it had four-wheel brakes, although these were not hydraulically operated until 1937.

The Packard Eight (the title Single Eight was dropped after the first year) came on two wheelbases, 136 and 143 inches, and was known as the 136 and 143 in its first year, 236 and 243 in its second year, and so on up to the 1931 season, which was the eighth series. After that, wheelbases no longer figured in the model name, although Packard Eights were known by Series rather than year right up to the 26th Series of 1953. Prices were

a little lower than those of the Twin Six, and production was much higher, more than 11,000 in 1924 and 43,000 in 1928. These were remarkable figures for a car in the Packard's price bracket, giving Packard a lead over Cadillac-LaSalle sales in most years through the late 1920s and early 1930s. When Packard brought out a low-priced Eight in 1935 the lead became still greater.

The rarest and most valued by collectors of Packard Eights were the Series 734 Speedsters of 1930. These had a modified De Luxe Eight engine giving up to 145bhp and, with a 3.3:1 rear axle ratio more were made under the name Doble-Detroit, but it was not until 1924 that he made his masterpiece, the Model E, for which a new factory at Emeryville, California, was built. No expense was spared in incorporating the latest technology and the finest components. The Model E had a four-cylinder engine delivering 125bhp, a very efficient condenser which gave a range of 1,500 miles on one 24-gallon tankful of water (Stanleys still had to take on fresh water every 150–250 miles), and a flash boiler which gave a working head of steam in just over 1 minute. In one test, a Doble was left in the street where the temperature was just on freezing; operating pressure was reached in 23 seconds after switching on, and 41 seconds later the car moved off with a load of four passengers. The Model E's acceleration was quite remarkable, 0–40mph in 8 seconds, while a stripped chassis went to 75mph in 10 seconds.

The Doble Model E rode on a 142-inch wheelbase and was offered with a choice of eight body styles, all of which were built by Murphy of Pasadena. Prices ran from $8,000 to $11,200, which put the Doble up against Locomobile and Rolls-Royce, or expensive imports such as Hispano-Suiza and Isotta-Fraschini. It could outperform all these and the only gasoline car Abner Doble feared was the Lincoln; even then a Doble on full throttle could get away from one.

Abner Doble's customer list was a distinguished one, including Joseph Schenk, Norma Talmadge, Howard Hughes, and the Maharajah of Bharatpur, who had a shooting brake body built by Hooper of London and used his car for tiger hunting. One California couple, the H.W. Hostetters, had two Dobles, a seven-passenger touring for him and a town car for her. Unfortunately, although distinguished, the list was also very small, for not enough wealthy people

appreciated the Doble's refinement and performance. The Doble company was also badly hit by fraudulent stock manipulations of which Abner Doble, busy in his workshops, was unaware until it was too late. Not more than a dozen Model Es were made, and even fewer of the improved Model F.

Apart from the Doble, steam was practically dead by the end of the 1920s. More steam cars were made in Canada than in the States, for the Brooks company of Stratford, Ontario, built about 180 steam sedans, many of which saw service as taxicabs in Stratford and Toronto. Stanley struggled on with occasional improvements, rising prices, and declining sales until 1927. There was a short flurry of activity in 1922/23, with several new makes such as American, Bryan, Crossland, Delling, Detroit, Gearless, and MacDonald, but only prototypes were built, and most of MacDonald's business was in converting gasoline cars to steam, not that there were many customers who wanted such a service.

GOLDEN AGE OF THE COACHBUILDER

The 1920s saw the finest flowering of the coachbuilder's craft, with many innovative designs that later found their way onto mass-production cars, and at least 20 firms of the highest quality plying their craft. There were basically three groups of quality coachbuilders: those who had started their work in the nineteenth century with horse-drawn vehicles, of which the best-known were Brewster, Derham, Healey, Judkins, and Quinby; those who began in the early years of the twentieth century, staffed by craftsman from the first group (Brunn, Holbrook, Locke, Willoughby); and companies set up later specifically to make automobile bodies (Bohman & Schwartz, Fleetwood, LeBaron, Murphy, Rollston).

Brewster of Long Island City was the oldest established American coachbuilder, founded in 1810 and known throughout the nineteenth century as "Carriage Builders to American Gentlemen," but Quinby dated to 1834, Judkins to 1857, Biddle & Smart to 1870, and Derham to

1884. Most of these firms began to make automobile bodies in the period 1900–1910, although Brewster's first body was made for an 1896 Barrett & Perret electric car. At first the coachbuilders worked on any chassis that was submitted to them, but in some cases they later became associated with a particular make, Brewster with Rolls-Royce, Biddle & Smart with Hudson, Fleetwood with Cadillac, or Murphy with Duesenberg, and so on. Brewster was bought by Rolls-Royce in 1926 and Fleetwood by General Motors in 1925, although this did not prevent them from working on other chassis for a while.

The coachbuilding era is often thought of as a time when rich individuals went to a firm with their own ideas, which the craftsmen would put into reality. There were certainly some examples of this, but more often than not the customer did not know what he or she really wanted, so coachbuilders had pattern books from which a design could be chosen, with an almost limitless range of detailed accessories. Sometimes designs were initiated by dealers; in 1916 the New York

Packard dealer asked the major custom body builders of the Northeast to submit designs, 24 of which were incorporated in a custom body sales catalog. Those by Derham were a six-passenger limousine and a landaulet brougham, the latter with silver-plated accessories and pleated broadcloth upholstery priced at $5,800. Packard became one of Derham's best customers, although the two were not officially linked, and Derham work was also seen on Cadillac, Chrysler, Duesenberg, Franklin, Lincoln, Minerva, Rolls-Royce, and Stutz, among other chassis.

Not all coachbuilders' designs were home-grown. Locomobile had its own styling studios from 1914 commissioning bodies from Demarest and others, while Duesenberg's styling chief Gordon Buehrig penned such classics as the four-passenger Tourster made by Derham and Murphy's Beverly sport sedan. The latter was strictly a four-passenger car, with a narrow rear compartment that seated two people separated by an armchair division which could be removed when "more intimate seating arrangements were desired."

1929 DUESENBERG MODEL J DUAL-COWL PHAETON ▲▼
THE DUAL-COWL PHAETON WAS ONE OF THE MOST POPULAR BODY STYLES ON THE DUESENBERG MODEL J,
AND WAS MADE BY DERHAM, LEBARON, MURPHY, AND UNION BODY (LA GRANDE), AMONG OTHERS.
THIS MURPHY BODY WAS DESIGNED BY MAURICE SCHWARTZ WHO FORMED BOHMAN & SCHWARTZ
WITH FELLOW MURPHY EMPLOYEE CHRISTIAN BOHMAN. ALTHOUGH TO A SIMILAR BASIC DESIGN,
INDIVIDUAL MURPHY PHAETONS DIFFERED IN MANY DETAILS: SOME, FOR EXAMPLE, HAD NO EXTERNAL DOOR
HANDLES. THEY WERE MADE ON BOTH SHORT- AND LONG-WHEELBASE CHASSIS.
OWNER: GILMORE CAR MUSEUM, KALAMAZOO, MICHIGAN (PHOTO NICKY WRIGHT)

Other features included a lighted instrument panel for rear-seat passengers, a built-in radio, and a bar.

Even genuine custom bodies built for particular owners often had as much input from the coachbuilder as from the customer. One of the most striking was the enormous touring car built for comedian Roscoe "Fatty" Arbuckle by the Don Lee Studios of Los Angeles in 1919. For his chassis he chose a car already obsolete, the Pierce-Arrow 66 on its longest wheelbase of 147½ inches. Don Lee's chief stylist was Harley Earl, who later became head of General Motors' Art & Colour section, and this was the third custom car he had designed for Fatty Arbuckle. The Pierce-Arrow identity was completely disguised under a body that flowed in a straight horizontal line from radiator to windshield, while the dipped belt line from behind the windshield to the rear made the car seem lower than it was. Gone were the Pierce-Arrow frog headlights, replaced by huge drum-shaped lights, while the radiator was restyled to incorporate a badge featuring the actor's initials. Only the A pierced by an arrow atop the radiator cap gave a clue to the make of car. The estimated cost of this body was $28,000, with the chassis

adding another $6,000. It was Arbuckle's last custom job from Don Lee Studios, for in 1921 he was implicated in the death of an obscure film starlet and tried for murder. Although acquitted (at a cost of $785,000), he never sought publicity again.

The Don Lee Studios, or Don Lee Coach & Body Works as the company was also called, came into being when Cadillac distributor Don Lee took over the Earl Automobile Works, started by Harley Earl's father. The firm was an interesting one in that it grew up alongside the Hollywood movie business and flourished largely through orders from the movie world. Earl's first customized Cadillacs appeared around 1917, but before that the works had built carriages to be used in films, from Roman chariots to Napoleonic coaches. One of Harley's first designs was a four-passenger sport touring on a Marmon 34 chassis, built at a cost of $7,000 for a New York banker. *The Los Angeles Times* made much of the fact that a New Yorker should go to the extra expense of ordering a body from California, when he had the cream of America's coachbuilders almost on his doorstep.

Another early Harley Earl creation was a dual-cowl phaeton on a Pierce-Arrow built in 1919 for oil millionaire E.L. Doheny. The car was a gift to his wife, and along with the car went a chauffeur. Shortly afterward car, chauffeur, and Mrs. Doheny vanished from the family home, so perhaps Mr. Doheny would have been better off with a Model T that he drove himself.

In 1919 and 1920 the Don Lee Studios built about 300 custom bodies, mostly on Cadillac chassis, but some on Packard, Locomobile, and Crane-Simplex chassis as well. These were generally flamboyant, in keeping with their owners, which included movie stars Mary Miles Minter, Anne May, Tom Mix and Blanche Sweet, Mary Pickford's brother Jack, and movie directors Cecil B. de Mille and Henry Lehrman. Bodies tended to feature step plates instead of running boards, and innovative three-piece windshields.

As the years passed, the Don Lee Studios turned to longer runs rather than individual bodies, and it was an order for 100 Cadillac chassis in 1925 that brought Harley Earl to the attention of GM's boss Alfred Sloan. Earl was hired to design the LaSalle, and in June 1927 he left Los Angeles to head the newly formed Art & Colour Section. Don

1932 CHRYSLER CUSTOM IMPERIAL CL CONVERTIBLE COUPE BY LEBARON ▲ ▶
THE IMPERIAL CL WAS A NEW MODEL FOR 1932, AND WAS ONE OF THE FINEST CHRYSLERS
EVER MADE. IT RODE ON A 146-INCH WHEELBASE, AND USED THE 135bhp 384.8-CUBIC-INCH
STRAIGHT-8 ENGINE, WHICH ALSO POWERED THE SMALLER IMPERIAL CH. ONLY 375 WERE MADE
IN 1932 AND 1933. LEBARON BUILT CONVERTIBLE COUPES, CONVERTIBLE SEDANS,
AND LIMOUSINES ON THE CL TO SPECIAL ORDER, SO THEY WERE NOT IDENTICAL. ONLY
28 OF THESE CONVERTIBLES WERE DELIVERED IN 1932.

OWNER: DUKE DAVENPORT (PHOTO NICKY WRIGHT)

Lee Studios closed down shortly afterward.

Another West Coast coachbuilder was the Walter M. Murphy Company of Pasadena, which began in 1921 with stylish phaetons on Lincoln chassis, at a time when standard Lincolns were homely and old-fashioned. One Murphy phaeton was bought by Douglas Fairbanks. Like Don Lee, Murphy soon had many customers from the movie colony as well as among industrial chiefs and older Californian land-owning families. An early Murphy roadster had a curved glass windshield, something very difficult and expensive to fabricate at that time (Don Lee thought this too expensive and settled for three-piece windshields). Murphy built nearly all the bodies on the Doble Series E steam car chassis, and also worked on Packard, Mercedes-Benz, Minerva, and later on Duesenberg and Cord chassis. Much of Murphy's work was by in-house designers George McQuerry Jr., Franklin Hershey, and Frank Spring, although, as we have seen, the company was also willing to work to the designs of outsider Gordon Buehrig. Murphy built more bodies on Duesenberg chassis than on any other, but by no means all were Buehrig's designs. Also built were some beautiful Hershey-styled dual-cowl phaetons and town cars on the front-drive Cord L-29 chassis, although the bulk of L-29s carried standard bodywork built for Cord by his associate company, the Union City Body Company.

Like many coachbuilders, Murphy was badly hit by the Depression, and closed its doors in 1932 after building the sedan body for the prototype Peerless V16. Two Murphy employees, Christian Bohman and Maurice Schwartz, managed to bid on work on two cars which were still in the workshops, one of them for Gary Cooper. Moving some machinery to new premises, they started a custom body plant which continued until after World War II. Most of their work was in updating earlier coachwork, particularly on Duesenbergs, and converting cars for invalid use. However, they made a few original designs, including Father Divine's Throne Car and a streamlined town car for Ethel V. Mars of the Mars candy bar family on a 1936 Duesenberg J. They also built the body for Rust Heinz's extraordinary Phantom Corsair coupe on a Cord 810 chassis, which he might have put into production at $12,500 had he not died in an auto accident in 1939. Bohman and Schwartz parted in 1947, but both continued to work independently. Maurice Schwartz lived long enough to end his days (in 1961) working on classic car restoration, especially for Harrah's Automobile Collection.

Generally, coachbuilders left hoods and grilles alone, for these were features that gave distinction

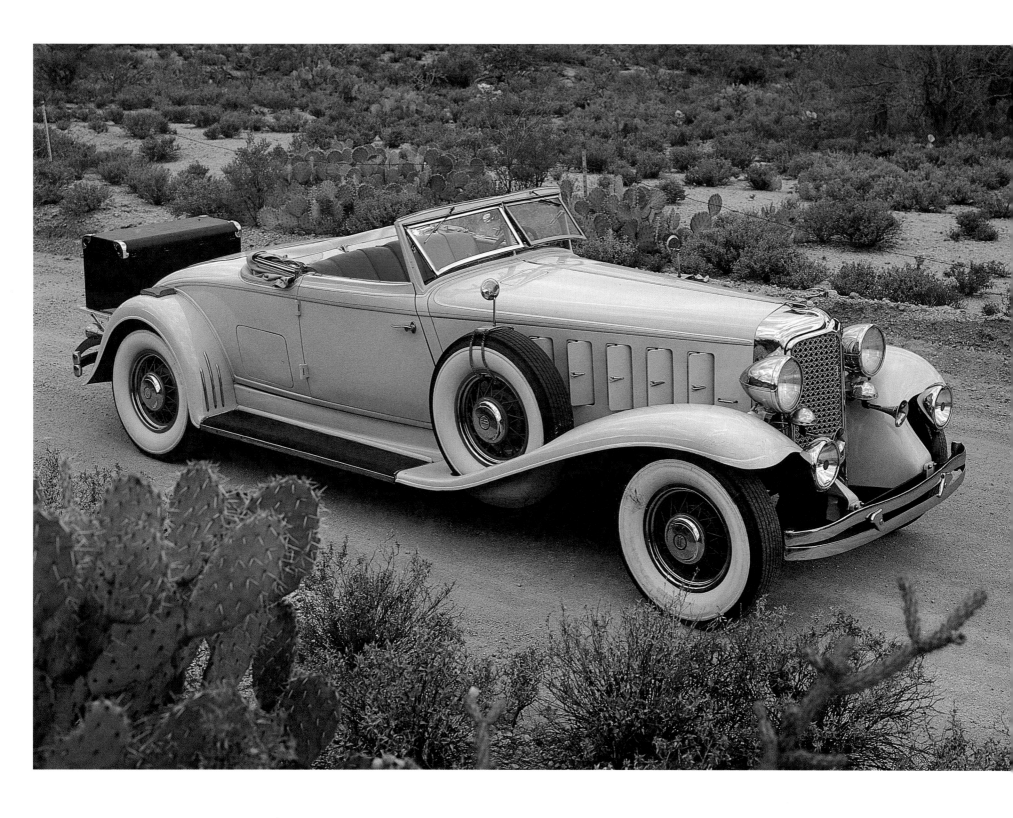

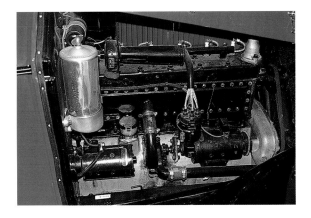

to the whole vehicle when they identified such quality marques as Rolls-Royce, Packard, Lincoln, and so on. However, there were exceptions, such as Arbuckle's Pierce-Arrow, a Packard dressed up to look like a Rolls-Royce by Don Lee in 1924, and a series of disguised Cadillacs marketed by Inglis M. Uppercu of New York in the mid-1920s. These were made for Uppercu by a little-known New England coachbuilder, Hollander & Morrill of Amesbury, Massachusetts. In the 1930s Bohman & Schwartz updated the classic vertical Duesenberg radiator with various styles of sloping grille for customers who wanted to be in fashion, in one case even using a stock 1936 Buick grille.

An appropriate setting for the exhibition of custom-bodied cars was provided by the Automobile Salon, first held in New York's Hotel Commodore in 1921. This was a very different affair from the National Automobile Show at the Field Artillery Armory, which was open to anyone who could afford the entrance charge and showed run-of-the-mill cars like Chevrolet and Maxwell. The Salon was only open to selected car manufacturers, importers, and coachbuilders, admission was by invitation only, and formal dress was expected of visitors. High-pressure salesmanship was severely frowned upon, although of course the purpose of the Salon was to sell cars. Among coachbuilders who were regular attenders were Brewster, Brunn, Derham, Judkins, Holbrook LeBaron, Locke, Rollston, and Willoughby, with Murphy exhibiting at the West Coast equivalents at the Biltmore, Los Angeles, and Palace, San Francisco. Salons were also held in Chicago at the

Drake Hotel. Some firms built cars especially for the shows, without being sure of orders. One of the more extreme examples was the English Coaching Brougham which Judkins showed on a Lincoln chassis at the Commodore in 1927. Styled after the eighteenth-century Concord coaches, it featured carriage lamps, rooftop luggage rails, and a wicker trunk. It didn't sell at the Salon, but after touring the other shows it was bought by movie actress Ethel Jackson.

The Depression spelled the end of the exclusive salons whose deliberately elitist image did not sit well with bread lines, soup kitchens, and the New Deal. The last New York Salon was held at the Park Lane Hotel in 1933, and by then the numbers of coachbuilders had been drastically reduced. Holbrook, LeBaron, Locke, Murphy, Willoughby, and many others had gone, Brewster was about to turn to quality bodies on Ford V8 chassis, and by the outbreak of World War II most of the others were out of business.

1927 PIERCE-ARROW SERIES 80 ◄▲
THE SERIES 80 WAS A SMALLER AND LOWER-PRICED PIERCE-ARROW INTRODUCED FOR 1924. BETTER SUITED TO THE OWNER-DRIVER THAN PREVIOUS PIERCES, IT HAD A 289-CUBIC-INCH L-HEAD ENGINE DEVELOPING 70bhp. IN 1927 IT WAS OFFERED IN 13 BODY STYLES, AT PRICES FROM $2,895 FOR THIS ROADSTER TO $4,045 FOR A SEVEN-PASSENGER ENCLOSED LIMOUSINE. THESE PRICES WERE WELL BELOW THOSE FOR THE LARGER MODEL 36, WHICH COULD COST AS MUCH AS $7,500.

OWNER: GEORGE SANDERS   (PHOTO NICKY WRIGHT)

1927 FRANKLIN 11-B SEDAN ◄▼

IN 1925 FRANKLINS WERE COMPLETELY RESTYLED, AND ALTHOUGH STILL AIR-COOLED, LOOKED MUCH MORE LIKE CONVENTIONAL AUTOMOBILES. THE BODY STYLIST WAS J. FRANK DE CAUSSE (1879–1928), WHO HAD FORMERLY WORKED FOR LOCOMOBILE. THIS 1927 EXAMPLE WAS KNOWN AS THE SEMICOLLAPSIBLE CUSTOM SPORT SEDAN; OTHER COACHBUILDERS MIGHT HAVE CALLED IT A LANDAULET ON ACCOUNT OF THE FOLDING REAR PORTION OF THE TOP. ITS PRICE WAS $3,150.

OWNER: DAVID BODWELL (PHOTO NICKY WRIGHT)

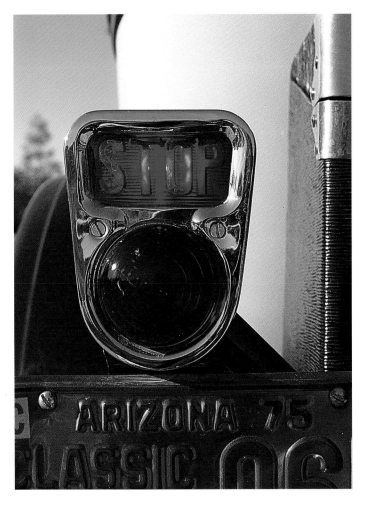

1934 PACKARD CONVERTIBLE COUPE ▼
OWNER: AUBURN-CORD-DUESENBERG MUSEUM (PHOTO NICKY WRIGHT)

CHAPTER FIVE

DEPRESSION AND RECOVERY

1929 – 1942

"Buy an automobile, and help restore prosperity."
President Herbert Hoover, 1932

1934 PONTIAC EIGHT SEDAN ▶ ▼

PONTIAC BROKE NEW GROUND IN LAUNCHING THIS STRAIGHT-8 FOR 1933. GIVING 77bhp FROM 223.4 CUBIC INCHES, THIS POWER UNIT WAS SMOOTH, QUIET, AND ECONOMICAL, AND WAS LESS EXPENSIVE TO MAKE THAN THE V8s USED IN THE 1932 PONTIACS. STYLING WAS NEW AND UP-TO-THE-MINUTE AS WELL; CHIEF DESIGNER FRANKLIN QUICK HERSHEY ADAPTED CHEVROLET MASTER BODY STAMPINGS TO A STRETCHED CHEVY FRAME, AND ADDED GRAHAM-LIKE SKIRTED FENDERS. FOR 1934 WHEELBASES WENT UP BY 2¼ INCHES AND POWER TO 84bhp, BUT THERE WERE NO MAJOR CHANGES. AT $805 THIS TOURING SEDAN WITH TRUNK WAS THE MOST EXPENSIVE 1934 PONTIAC.

OWNER: DICK GINTHER

(PHOTO NICKY WRIGHT)

HISTORY SELDOM FALLS into such neat categories as the turn of the decade.at the end of 1929. The year saw a boom in American business generally, and the auto industry registered a record 4,455,178 passenger cars, not to be equaled for another 20 years. The crash which wiped billions of dollars off the value of shares came toward the end of the year and had little immediate effect on production. But 1930 was another story, with sales down to 2,787,456. The depth of the Depression was reached in 1932, with only 1,103,557 sales, the worst figure since the war year of 1918. After that matters slowly improved, with 1,560,599 in 1933. By 1937 sales had recovered to a healthy 3,929,203. There was a short recession in 1938, with motor vehicle production down 48.2 percent on the previous year, probably caused by fears of war in Europe. This sent jitters through the stock market, and with memories of 1929 very fresh, people preferred to save their money rather than spend it on automobiles. However, the industry soon bounced back. The last year of peace, 1941, saw the second best year's production since 1929, with 3,779,682 passenger cars made and total vehicle production reaching 4,840,502. Several milestones were celebrated in 1941: the 4 millionth Plymouth, 5 millionth Dodge, and 29 millionth Ford.

The auto industry was undecided how to face the Depression. Income was reduced, so there was not the money to spend on new models, yet there was a desperate need to pry out of the public the few remaining dollars it had, if the factories were to keep open at all. There were widespread lay-offs, with Ford almost halving its payroll between 1929 and 1932, from 101,069 to 56,277. For a while Henry Ford tried to keep his work force occupied with non-automotive jobs such as moving and reconstructing the historic buildings at Greenfield Village, and building America's first airport hotel, the Dearborn Inn. He also raised wages to $7.00 a day minimum in 1931 to increase spending power, "spending one's way out of the Depression," as President Franklin Roosevelt was to urge a few years later. However, even Ford couldn't keep this up in the face of declining income; the daily wage was quietly reduced to $6.00 at the end of 1931, and a year later it was only $4.00.

Of the Big Three mass producers, Chevrolet already had a new model in the Six introduced in 1929, Plymouth carried on with its existing models, although it brought out the considerably modified PA for 1932, with "Floating Power" engine mounting and "Free Wheel" drive, and Ford had a brand new engine in the V8 of 1932.

Henry Ford had planned his V8 in 1929, possibly earlier. Certainly in that year he made his ideas public, telling his engineering assistant Fred Thomas: "We're going from a four to an eight because Chevrolet is going to a six." A lot of Ford's ideas came from a determination to be different, from espousing the V8 to avoiding items like hydraulic brakes and longitudinal springs just because they were the norm with other manufacturers. The V8 was launched in March 1932, having a 221-cubic-inch displacement L-head engine, with cylinders set at 90°, giving 65bhp. This was the best specific output of 16 cars in the low and medium price range, and soon earned the Ford V8 an excellent reputation for performance. The roadster, in particular, was a favorite with young enthusiasts, and in later years became the foundation stone of the hot rod movement.

The V8 was built alongside the four-cylinder Model B, a developed version of the A. Externally there was no difference between the two, apart from the V8 emblem on the tie-bar between the headlights, and the hubcaps, which were lettered Ford on the B rather than V8. Body styles were identical, and the price difference was only $50 right across the range. Most people thought it was $50 well spent. The Model B managed to attract 261,055 buyers in the three seasons 1932 to 1934 out of a total of 1,186,175 Ford sales. After 1934 the

1936 FORD V8 COUPE ▲▼

FOR THE FORD V8, 1936 WAS THE FIFTH SEASON AND THAT YEAR'S CARS WERE KNOWN AS MODEL 68s. THEY WERE SLIGHTLY RESTYLED COMPARED WITH THE 1935 MODEL 48s, WITH NEW GRILLES, AND THEIR WHEELS WERE OF PRESSED STEEL RATHER THAN WIRE. THERE WERE TWO SERIES, STANDARD AND DE LUXE, THE LATTER BEING IDENTIFIED BY CHROME TRIM AROUND THE GRILLE AS ON THIS FIVE-WINDOW COUPE. IT WAS PRICED AT $555, WHICH WAS $45 MORE THAN THE STANDARD COUPE.

OWNER: CURLY PHILLIPS (PHOTO NICKY WRIGHT)

1932 CHEVROLET ROADSTER ▲▶

THE SIX-CYLINDER CHEVROLET WAS IN ITS FOURTH YEAR IN 1932, AND MODELS WERE KNOWN AS THE CONFEDERATE
SERIES BA. FOURTEEN BODY STYLES WERE OFFERED, THE SAME NUMBER AS FORD. THIS ROADSTER WAS THE LOWEST
PRICED AT $445. THE YEAR MARKED THE BOTTOM OF THE DEPRESSION, AND CHEVROLET SOLD ONLY 306,716 CARS, BUT
STILL BEAT FORD BY MORE THAN 74,000.

OWNER: HUBERT FRIEND (PHOTO NICKY WRIGHT)

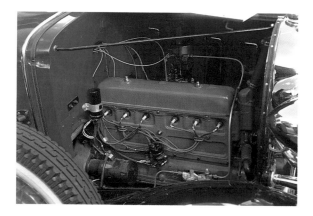

four-cylinder engine was no longer available in passenger cars, although it was continued in light trucks and some foreign Fords until World War II.

The first V8 engines were less than perfect, particularly in their terrible thirst for oil due to leaking piston rings. However, this was put right on later examples, and the 221-cubic-inch V8 enjoyed a long career, powering Ford automobiles up to 1946 when it was enlarged to 239 cubic inches, giving it another eight years of life. Overhead valves were featured from 1954. The flathead V8

was also used in trucks (both sides had them in World War II, since the German Ford factory made V8 engines as well as the British and American), gun carriers, boats, and airplanes.

The Ford V8 was the first low-priced eight-cylinder engine, and it was a long time before the competition caught up. Chevrolet and Plymouth did not offer one until 1955, and in the 1930s the next lowest priced eight was the $585 Pontiac straight-8. V8 engines were, in fact, rare in the 1930s, being offered only by Oakland up to 1931, Cunningham in very small numbers to 1936, Cadillac and LaSalle, and Cord in the 810/812 made in relatively small numbers from 1936 through 1937. Straight-8s, on the other hand, were offered by 28 U.S. car makers, including well-known firms such as Buick, Chrysler, Nash, Oldsmobile, Packard, Pontiac, and Studebaker, who made this layout through most or all of the decade.

Despite having a performance and image advantage over its rivals, Ford struggled to match Chevrolet in sales, and in fact only beat its rival once, in 1935 with 942,439 units sold to Chevrolet's

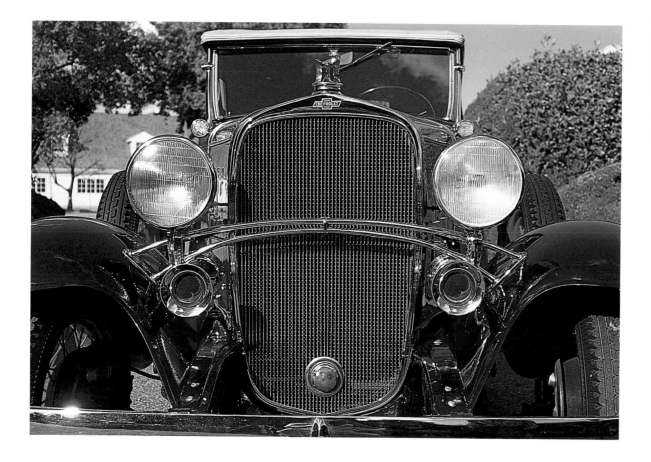

793,437. Indeed from 1936 Ford was third behind GM and Chrysler in overall sales, but at that time GM had six makes and Chrysler four, to Ford's two. These hardly spanned the market, with Ford at one end and Lincoln at the other, and it was to remedy this that Mercury was introduced as a new make for 1939.

Ford made some improvements during the 1930s. Styling was fully up to date and arguably the best of the low-priced three. Hydraulic brakes finally arrived on 1939 models, and a steering column gear change was introduced for 1940. However, springing remained the transverse leaves inherited from the Model T ("We use transverse springs for the same reason we use round wheels," said Henry, "because we have found nothing better for the purpose"). The Ford V8 certainly outperformed Chevrolet and Plymouth, but this was perhaps more appreciated overseas. British motor journals published road tests with acceleration times and maximum speeds, something their U.S. equivalents did not do at that time. Europeans were impressed by Ford victories in the 1936 and 1938 Monte Carlo Rallies, but these meant little to the average buyer in Topeka, Kansas. Ford's performance was appreciated by high school and college kids, but they seldom bought new. Others who enthused over the 85+mph top speed were Bonnie Parker and Clyde Barrow, whose bullet-

1933 BUICK SERIES 90 TOURING SEDAN ◀▲
THE SERIES 90 WAS THE LARGEST BUICK OF THE 1930s, AND INDEED ONE OF THE LARGEST OF ANY AMERICAN CARS, WITH A 138-INCH WHEELBASE AND A WEIGHT OF UP TO 4,780 POUNDS. WITH JUMP SEATS, THIS SEDAN ACCOMMODATED SEVEN PASSENGERS FOR A COST OF $1,955. THERE WAS ALSO A LIMOUSINE AT $2,055. ONLY 890 WERE BUILT FOR DOMESTIC SALES, AND 12 FOR EXPORT.

OWNER: BOB DEBOW (PHOTO NICKY WRIGHT)

ridden car started first time after the fatal shoot-out in the pine hills of north Louisiana; and John Dillinger, branded Public Enemy Number One in 1934, who wrote to Henry Ford saying: "Hello Old Pal, you have a wonderful car. It's a treat to drive one." Franklin Roosevelt drove a Ford V8, and so did Charles Lindbergh and many movie stars, but the public still bought more Chevrolets.

There were other reasons for Ford's slippage in the sales charts. Henry had little time for advertising, remembering the days when the Model T sold itself and there was no national advertising at all. Ford did advertise in the 1930s,

but Henry would not sanction a large budget. "Don't exaggerate, the truth is big enough," he said, and "There are some things we refuse to do to sell a car." His political attitudes did not help either. His strong anti-union position and the employment of strong-arm man Harry Bennett and his thugs to deal with union organizers must have alienated some liberal-minded buyers. More serious was his anti-Semitism, which surfaced in his journal *The Detroit Independent* during World War I. Although the articles were discontinued in 1921 and *The Independent* closed down in 1927, the animosity lasted a long time. Ford's erstwhile friend Rabbi Leo Franklin returned the Model T that Henry gave him, and Jewish sales lost to other makes were not easily won back.

Chevrolet and Plymouth had a number of advantages over Ford in design. In place of Ford's transverse leaf springs Chevrolet had, from 1934, independent front suspension by Dubonnet coils, the much-touted "Knee Action," and, for those who distrusted this newfangled engineering, conventional longitudinal semi-elliptics could be had up to 1940, old-fashioned but still better than Ford's suspension — except over plowed fields. Plymouth tried independent front suspension briefly in 1934, then dropped it until 1939, but both Ford's rivals had hydraulic brakes, Plymouth from 1931 and Chevrolet from 1936. This was a distinct safety argument, and customers tended to ask what was the point of Ford's faster cars if they couldn't stop as well as their slower rivals. Not that they were much slower; a 1937 Chevrolet Master Six sedan was tested (by a British magazine) at 78mph, against 87mph for a Ford V8. Hydraulic brakes finally came to Ford for 1939.

MIDDLE-PRICED CARS AND THE DECLINE OF THE INDEPENDENTS

Above the low-priced three a variety of automobiles was on offer in the 1930s, from independent manufacturers as well as Detroit's big guns, GM and Chrysler. Ford was weak in that it lacked anything between the top V8 at $750 and the cheapest Lincoln V12 at $4,200, although the introduction of the Lincoln Zephyr at $1,275–$1,320 went some way to plugging the gap, and market coverage was further extended with the arrival of the Mercury for 1939.

Many people have questioned why the Mercury did not appear before it did, but it was Edsel Ford's idea and he had a hard time persuading his father to allow him that much independence. He had contributed a lot to the styling side, particularly of Lincolns, but the Mercury was a marketing venture, although it looked pretty good as well. Introduced on October 8, 1938, a month before the 1939 model Fords, the Mercury bore a close family resemblance to them, although it was 4 inches longer in wheelbase and proportionally wider and heavier. Its engine was a Ford V8 enlarged to 239.4

cubic inches and 95bhp, and a good power-to-weight ratio gave a top speed of 93mph. Although it bridged the gap between the Ford and the Lincoln Zephyr, the Mercury was much closer to a Ford, being $165 more than the Ford as a four-door sedan and $430 less than the Zephyr.

The Mercury was aimed at the section of the market occupied by the Dodge De Luxe, Pontiac De Luxe Eight, and Studebaker Commander, and with first season sales of 70,835 was clearly a success. By 1941 Ford was able to claim: "It's made 150,000 owners change cars." Sales before the production line shut down in January 1942 totaled about 275,000. Mercurys were also built in foreign countries such as Brazil, where production continued throughout the war years, and Rumania, where production ceased in 1940.

General Motors' offerings were carefully graded, with an increasing interchangeability of engines and bodies toward the end of the decade. Above Chevrolet came Pontiac, which introduced a six in 1935 to complement its straight-8. The 80bhp six was priced from $615–$745 in the Standard series and from $675–$795 in the De Luxe series, overlapping Chevrolet's $465–$675, and at the other end the Pontiac straight-8 at $730–$860.

Pontiac sixes and eights were continued up to 1942, as were Oldsmobiles, although the latter were in a higher price bracket ($800–$970 in 1935). For the extra money, Oldsmobile owners got technical advances before other GM customers, including steel-spoke wheels in 1933, hydraulic brakes in 1934, a semi-automatic transmission in 1938, and fully automatic HydraMatic in 1940. Buick made

1938 OLDSMOBILE L-38 CONVERTIBLE ▲

OLDSMOBILE OFFERED SIX- AND EIGHT-CYLINDER ENGINES IN 1938, ON TWO WHEELBASES, WITH SLIGHTLY DIFFERENT GRILLES TO DISTINGUISH THE F-38 SIXES FROM THE L-38 EIGHTS. THIS L-38 CONVERTIBLE WAS A RARE MODEL, WITH ONLY 407 DELIVERED, OF WHICH 30 WENT FOR EXPORT. IT WAS THE COSTLIEST OLDS OF THE YEAR, AT $1,163. A RADIO ADDED $53 FOR A STANDARD UNIT, $66.50 FOR A DE LUXE.

(PHOTO NICKY WRIGHT)

only eights from 1931 onward, but in several sizes and qualities of trim. Four different engines were used in 1935, from 233 cubic inches and 93bhp in the Series 40 to 345 cubic inches and 116bhp in the Series 90. The Series 40 had a short-stroke engine introduced in 1934; combined with bodies of Chevrolet size and Buick styling, it gave excellent performance. Priced from $855–$925, the Series 40 helped Buick to almost double its production in 1934 to 78,757; by 1939 the company was in fourth position overall, with 321,219 sales. The Series 90, or Limited as it was called from 1936, was a really large car on a 140-inch wheelbase, priced at up to $2,453 for a seven-passenger limousine in 1937/38.

Despite their upper middle class image ("The Doctor's Friend" they were often called), Buicks shot to royal fame in 1936 when England's King Edward VIII ordered two Canadian-built Limited limousines. One of them conveyed his bride-to-be Mrs. Simpson on her "escape" to France later in the year. After he became Duke of Windsor, he ordered two more Buicks, in 1938 and 1939. His brother, the Duke of Kent, also liked Buicks.

From the mid-1930s onward there was a definite General Motors style of body, hardly surprising as all bodies were made by Fisher. One couldn't fail to identify a GM sedan from the rear, though it might not be so easy to say if it were a Buick, Oldsmobile, or Pontiac. The A-body four-door sedan and coupe were used in 1940 by Chevrolet and the lower-priced Pontiacs and Oldsmobiles, while the 1939 B-body sedan was seen on the 1940 Buick Century, Oldsmobile 60, and Pontiac De Luxe. A new and more modern style for 1940 was the C-body, inspired by the 1938 Cadillac 60 Special. A low and sleek-looking four-door, four-window sedan, the C-body was available on the Buick Series 50 Super and Series 70 Roadmaster, Cadillac Series 62, LaSalle Special, Oldsmobile 90, and Pontiac Torpedo Eight. There

1939 CADILLAC SERIES 75 CONVERTIBLE ◀▼

CADILLACS WERE CONSIDERABLY RESTYLED FOR 1939, WITH WATERFALL GRILLES DIVIDED BY A POINTED PROW. THE SERIES 75 WAS THE TOP OF THE RANGE, APART FROM THE VERY LIMITED PRODUCTION SIXTEEN. ALL 75s HAD FLEETWOOD BODIES, AND WERE MADE IN RELATIVELY SMALL NUMBERS. ONLY 27 OF THIS TWO-DOOR CONVERTIBLE WERE BUILT. IT SEATED TWO IN COMFORT, WITH TWO FOLDING OPERA SEATS IN THE REAR. ITS PRICE WAS $3,380.

OWNER: ED OBERHAUS (PHOTO NICKY WRIGHT)

were also C-bodied coupes and convertibles in all five marques. 1941 saw a continuation of the C Series and also a new B Series with fastback sedans and coupes on Buick, Cadillac, Oldsmobile, and Pontiac chassis.

Chrysler Corporation had two marques between its low-priced Plymouth and Chrysler itself, which offered models between the upper-middle and upper price brackets. These were De Soto and Dodge. De Soto had been created in 1928, the same year as Plymouth, to catch the Pontiac market. Actually the cheaper Dodges were hardly more expensive, but Walter Chrysler had planned the De Soto before he bought Dodge. Indeed there is a theory that he announced the De Soto in order to alarm the bankers of Dillon Read, who owned

Dodge, into thinking that they could not compete and had better sell to Chrysler, which is what they did, in fact.

Whatever the rationale behind De Soto, Chrysler was stuck with it, and in fact the make sold very well to start with, although from the Depression onward sales never matched those of Dodge. Both makes were offered with straight-8 engines from 1930 through 1932, and the Dodge Eight was continued for 1933. De Soto was unfortunately saddled with an Airflow model (companion to Chrysler's larger car with similar styling) from 1934 through 1936. In De Soto guise it sold even more poorly than the Chrysler, only 25,737 in three seasons, against Chrysler's 31,850 in four seasons. The conventionally styled De Sotos

from 1936 onward sold better, but they were now in a higher price bracket than Dodge, and this was reflected in sales of less than a third of Dodge's. By 1939 De Sotos and Dodges were very similar in appearance, although the former had a slightly larger engine, 228.1 cubic inches and 93bhp compared with 217.8 cubic inches and 87bhp. The De Soto was 2 inches longer in wheelbase and around $100 more expensive than equivalent models. As well as standard models, both De Soto and Dodge (and Chrysler) included in their 1939 range a limited production Custom Club Coupe by the Hayes Body Company. As well as having different lines from the regular coupes, the car featured a radio, heater, overdrive, and de luxe wheel covers. It cost $1,055 in the Dodge range and $1,145 in the De Soto, and sold in very small numbers, 363 Dodges and 264 De Sotos. The Chrysler version, available with an eight-cylinder engine as well as the six, sold 497 units.

The 1930s saw Detroit's Big Three extend their grip on automobile sales. At the beginning of the decade they were in a strong position, with 75 percent of the market, leaving the remaining 25 percent to be contested by 27 makes, several of which disappeared within a year or two. By 1939 the Big Three accounted for 90 percent of sales, and only five makes of any importance remained to squabble over the rest of the market.

Setting aside the midget and luxury car makers, the independents of the 1930s fell into three categories. The largest, numerically, consisted of makers which failed within a year or two; then came those which staggered through to the middle or end of the decade, such as Auburn, Reo, Graham, and Hupmobile; then came those which survived into the postwar era, like Hudson, Nash, Packard, Studebaker, and Willys.

The Depression is often blamed for the decimation among car makers, but most casualties of the 1930s were doomed anyway. They included medium-sized companies like Chandler, Elcar, Jordan, and Kissel, which kept afloat with sales of anything from 10,000 to 20,000 units a year in the 1920s, but unit costs were high because so many components were bought in from outside suppliers. Who wanted a 1931 Jordan Eight coupe at $2,495 when he could have a Buick of the same size and quality, with better servicing facilities, for $1,765? Durant was much larger than Jordan and Kissel, but even before the Depression he was in trouble, and a planned new empire, to include Chandler, Gardner, Hupmobile, Jordan, Moon, and Peerless, came to nothing.

Makes that might have survived had there been no depression included Graham and Hupmobile.

1936 HUPMOBILE D 618 SEDAN ▼▶

THE FAILING HUPMOBILE COMPANY INTRODUCED AERODYNAMIC STYLING BY RAYMOND LOEWY ON THE 1934 MODELS, AND THIS RARE 1936 SEDAN IS A DIRECT DESCENDANT, WITH A LITTLE ADDED CHROME TO THE GRILLE. IT HAS A 101bhp SIX-CYLINDER ENGINE, BUT THE HUPP COMPANY ALSO OFFERED A 120bhp EIGHT FOR 1936. ONLY 1,556 OF ANY HUPMOBILES WERE MADE IN 1936, AND THERE WERE NO 1937 MODELS. THE FACTORY REOPENED FOR 1938 TO MAKE A NEW LINE OF SIXES AND EIGHTS WITH THE SAME ENGINES AS BEFORE, BUT EVEN FEWER WERE BUILT.

OWNER: AUBURN-CORD-DUESENBERG MUSEUM

(PHOTO NICKY WRIGHT)

The former started in 1928 as Graham-Paige, founded by the three Graham brothers who had made trucks for Dodge and who took over the Paige-Detroit Motor Car Company. Sales in the first year were 73,195, a record for a new make, and in 1929 the company had 2,270 distributors worldwide. Production that year topped 77,000, a figure never reached subsequently. The Depression forced sales down to 12,967 in 1932, the year in which Graham introduced the Blue Streak series, the first production cars to be fitted with full-skirted fenders. Bodies were styled by Amos Northup of Murray; with sloping radiator grilles, they were a

year in advance of other U.S. makes, yet sales were only 10,967. By 1935 the Graham brothers had lost their styling lead — they did not have the capital for major redesigns — and for 1936 they shared Hayes-built bodies with Reo, another make on the way out.

The Grahams had made sixes and eights, but only the former from 1936 onward. Their only distinction was the supercharger offered from 1934. The 1938 models had completely fresh styling, with a forward-sloping grille which gave rise to the nickname "Sharknose," although the makers called it "Spirit of Motion." Other features were square headlights faired into the fenders, skirts over the rear wheels, and concealed door hinges. It was said that the public either loved or intensely disliked the car. Unfortunately there seemed to be more of the latter, or perhaps too few were ready to pay out money for a new car, for 1938 saw a marked dip in car sales nationwide. The Sharknose sold only 4,139 in 1938 and 3,876 in 1939, when Joe Graham put in $560,000 from his personal fortune to keep the company afloat.

The Sharknose was still offered in 1940, but only about 1,000 found buyers. Graham was now trying a new solution to the company's problems. A joint venture was set up with another ailing firm, Hupmobile, to combine the body dies from the Cord 810 with the six-cylinder Continental engine used in the Sharknose. In contrast to the Cord, the engine drove the rear wheels. The Graham version was called the Hollywood and the Hupmobile the Skylark, and both were built in the Graham factory. Only 859 Hollywoods and 319 Skylarks were made, and by September 1940 it was all over. Some Hollywoods and Skylarks were sold as 1941 models,

and a few were assembled as late as 1946, after the factory officially belonged to Kaiser-Frazer.

Hupmobile was one of the more substantial independents, with sales of 65,862 cars and profits of more than $8.75 million in 1928. The company's history in the 1930s was much more checkered, with poorly accepted aerodynamic sedans in 1934, abortive plans for a merger with Willys, and closure of the factory between December 1935 and July 1937. Much of Hupmobile's trouble was due to Archie M. Andrews, an entrepreneur who had been involved in the front-drive Ruxton car of 1929/30, manufacture of which contributed to the downfall of both Kissel and Moon. For 1938 Hupmobile introduced a conventional four-door sedan with six-

or eight-cylinder engines, but there was only one body style, whereas rivals were offering at least four. The company made 3,483 of the 1938/39 sedans, of which only 397 had eight-cylinder engines, then joined with Graham in the Skylark/Hollywood venture.

Of the more successful independents, Hudson and Studebaker had much wider market coverage than Graham or Hupmobile, with sub-marques to reach a lower price bracket. Hudson's was the Essex, which gave way to the Terraplane, while Studebaker's was the Erskine, made from 1927 through 1930. Not a great success, the Erskine was about the size of the Model A Ford, yet sold for over $500 more. Granted, it was a higher-quality product, but Studebaker was not the first or the last company to learn that the quality small car does not appeal to American buyers. It tried again in 1932 with the Rockne, named for famed Notre Dame University football coach Knute Rockne, who had been hired by Studebaker as head of sales promotion, but died in an air crash in the spring of 1931. The Rockne came in two sizes of six-cylinder engine, giving 66 or 72bhp, and two wheelbases, 110 and 114 inches. Prices were lower than the Erskine, at $585–$795, but the car faced stiff competition from the new Ford V8, lower in price and with two extra cylinders. Total Rockne production was 23,201 in two seasons.

At the end of the decade Studebaker brought out another small car, the Champion, but this was priced low as well, around $50 less than a De Luxe Chevrolet. Price and excellent fuel economy of 20–22mpg earned the Champion many friends, and it accounted for well over half of all Studebaker's sales in the years 1939 through 1941.

Hudson's Terraplane was appreciably cheaper than its big sister, even in eight-cylinder form, but it was also a hot performer, for it followed the formula of a powerful engine in a light, short chassis. In its first season, 1932, the Terraplane was a model of Essex, with a more powerful engine of 70bhp in a 106-inch wheelbase. At $425 the roadster was $35 cheaper than the Ford V8, yet its performance was by no means inferior. For 1933 the Essex part of the name was dropped, and Hudson put its 94bhp straight-8 engine into a 113-inch Terraplane frame as an additional model to the six. Terraplanes soon acquired the nickname "Hill Busters" on account of their prowess on hill climbs all over the country. They took many records at Pikes Peak and also set speed and endurance records at Daytona Beach. The Terraplane Eight engine was used by Englishman Reid Railton for his first Railton sports cars of 1933, although he subsequently turned to the slightly larger Hudson Eight.

The Terraplane lost something of its performance image in 1934 when the eight was no

1936 HUDSON DE LUXE EIGHT SEDAN ◀
ALL HUDSONS AND TERRAPLANES WERE COMPLETELY RESTYLED FOR 1936, WITH NARROW GRILLES AND MORE ROUNDED BODIES. MECHANICALLY, THE MOST IMPORTANT INNOVATION WAS THAT OF HYDRAULIC BRAKES, ALTHOUGH A BACK-UP CABLE-OPERATED SYSTEM OPERATED ON THE REAR WHEELS IN CASE OF HYDRAULIC FAILURE. HUDSON EIGHTS CAME IN TWO SERIES, DE LUXE AND CUSTOM, EACH WITH TWO WHEELBASES OF 120 OR 127 INCHES. DIFFERENCES IN TRIM ACCOUNTED FOR AROUND $90–$100 VARIATION IN PRICE. THIS DE LUXE EIGHT SEDAN COST $855.

OWNER: NATIONAL AUTOMOBILE MUSEUM, RENO, NEVADA

(PHOTO NICKY WRIGHT)

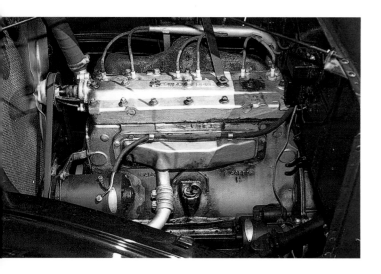

longer made, becoming a lower-priced model of Hudson, with the same body styles and the 116-inch wheelbase of the shortest Hudson. The marque was dropped for the 1938 season, becoming a model of Hudson, and for 1939 the name disappeared altogether. Hudson's small model for 1938 was the 112, named for its wheelbase. It was made in 16 different models, eight bodies in Standard and De Luxe forms, and used an 83bhp six-cylinder engine of 173-cubic-inch displacement. Styling was similar to the larger Hudsons, but the hood opened from the rear. The 112 gained useful publicity when a convertible was chosen as the Pace Car for the Indianapolis 500 Mile race. This was the only year in which a Hudson received this honor. The 112 was made for a further season, with different styling from the larger Hudsons, but for 1940 it gave way to the Series 40 Six with an extra inch on the wheelbase and the same grille as other Hudsons.

LUXURY CARS IN A DEPRESSION ERA

It is ironical that some of the finest American cars of any age were made during the depths of the Depression. They had, of course, been planned several years before 1929, and it is a sobering thought that if the Depression had struck, say, in 1927, we might never have had such glorious machines as the Cadillac V12 and V16, Lincoln or Packard V12s, or the Marmon 16.

Cadillac was first in the field with a V16 engine, developed by a team led by Ernest W. Seaholm, who had been with Cadillac since 1913 and had therefore been in on the birth of the V8. Most of the detail work on the V16 was by former Marmon engineer Owen Nacker, who worked full-time on the project for four years. The cylinder banks were angled at a narrow 45° and had overhead valves with hydraulic valve silencers. Displacement was 452 cubic inches and output 165bhp, which made it America's second most powerful car, after the Model J Duesenberg.

The Cadillac V16, or Model 452 as it was named for its displacement, was launched at the New York Automobile Show in January 1930, although only one car was ready. This was an Imperial Landaulette by Fleetwood, of which only four were ever made. Its price does not seem

to have been recorded, but is likely to have been at least as much as the $7,350 asked for a four-door Imperial Cabriolet, also by Fleetwood. As production got underway during 1930, a vast choice of 54 semi-custom bodies was offered, all by Fleetwood, a GM-owned coachbuilder who built only on Cadillacs from 1933. Prices ran from $5,350 for a two-passenger roadster with two-passenger rumble seat to $9,700 for a five/seven-passenger four-door Town Brougham. Among the 452 range was a limited production series called the Madam X models, after a popular stage play. These had a number of styling features, including a flat windshield sloped at 18°, with very thin pillars. The 452 was also supplied in chassis form for full custom bodies, which were made by Murphy and Waterhouse in the United States, Saoutchik in France, and Pininfarina in Italy.

The V16 Cadillac sold well in its first year, with more than 2,800 finding customers; 1931 was much less encouraging, with only 364 sales, and fewer than 300 in 1932. This was partly due to the deepening Depression, but also to inroads made by rival twelve-cylinder cars from Lincoln, Packard, and Pierce-Arrow, as well as Cadillac's own V12. Introduced for 1931, this was essentially a V16 with four fewer cylinders and a displacement of 368 cubic inches. It was in no way inferior in smoothness, and with 135bhp its performance was almost as good. With prices between $800 and $2,200 lower, no wonder the V12 took sales from the larger car. It would have done

1934 TERRAPLANE KU DE LUXE SIX COUPE ▲▶
HUDSON'S TERRAPLANE WAS MADE ONLY AS A SIX IN 1934, SO WAS LESS OF A PERFORMER THAN IN PREVIOUS YEARS. STYLING WAS NEW, AND CLOSELY FOLLOWED THAT OF HUDSON. THE 116-INCH WHEELBASE WAS SHARED WITH THE SMALLEST HUDSON. THIS TWO-PASSENGER COUPE COST $600.

OWNER: IRA GAMBLE (PHOTO NICKY WRIGHT)

so even without the onset of the Depression.

In 1933 Cadillac and LaSalle were freshly styled, with Vee radiator grilles and skirted fenders. But it was a rock bottom year for sales, with only 6,655 from all four lines, LaSalle and Cadillac V8s, Cadillac V12s and V16s. At the beginning of the year Cadillac announced that only 400 V16s would be made, but in fact the year's total did not exceed 126. Even fewer were made in later years, 60 in 1934, 50 in 1935, and 52 in 1936. Of the latter, 49 were complete cars from a greatly reduced Fleetwood range, and three were chassis supplied to outside coachbuilders; 49 were delivered in 1937. From 1938 through 1940 a new V16 with a short-stroke, side-valve engine was built. This was slightly smaller, at 431 cubic inches, but power was equal to the old V16 at 185bhp. The new engine looked very different, though, for the cylinders were splayed out at a shallow 135°, giving almost the appearance of a horizontally opposed unit.

The new V16, known as the Series 90, took the industry by surprise when it was launched in the fall of 1937. With sales of the previous model so low, people wondered how GM hoped to sell any more in a market where other multicylinder cars like Lincoln and Packard's V12 were floundering. Pierce-Arrow was on the verge of going out of business. The Series 90, which looked like a larger V8 and was offered with twelve Fleetwood body styles, sold 315 units in the 1938 model year, but only 138 in 1939 and 61 in 1940. With such a limited run, it was not worth updating the styling, with the result that the 1940 Series 90 looked distinctly old-fashioned next to the sleek V8s. A few chassis were supplied to outside coachbuilders, including Derham, and two gigantic convertible sedans were built by Fleetwood on a 165-inch wheelbase for the White House. They were used by secret service staff rather than by President Roosevelt, who rode in Lincolns, and survived into the Truman era when they were repowered with V8 engines.

The only other production V16 was the pet project of Colonel Howard C. Marmon (1876–1943). Although work started on the design

1937 CADILLAC SERIES 37-85 V12 FORMAL SEDAN ▲▶
THE V12 AND V6 CADILLACS ENDED THEIR RUN IN 1937, ALTHOUGH A NEW SIXTEEN
WITH FLATTER ENGINE WAS TO APPEAR FOR 1938. SIX FLEETWOOD STYLES WERE OFFERED
ON THE V12 CHASSIS: SEDANS, CONVERTIBLE SEDANS, LIMOUSINES, AND TOWN CARS.
THIS FORMAL SEDAN, STYLE 7509F, SOLD FOR $4,195. THE LARGE TRUNK AT THE REAR
IS AN OPTIONAL EXTRA.
OWNER: DUKE DAVENPORT (PHOTO NICKY WRIGHT)

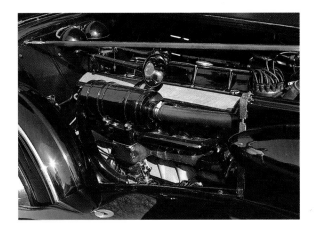

in 1926, it was not revealed to the public until November 1930, eleven months after Cadillac's V16. Known as the 16 or Sixteen, never as a V16, the Marmon was similar to the Cadillac in being an overhead valve unit with cylinders at 45°, but was larger at 490.87 cubic inches and 200bhp. The block, crankcase, intake manifold, oil pan, cylinder heads, and flywheel housing were all in light alloy, making for an exceptionally light engine and a power/weight ratio of 4.65 pounds per horsepower. The 6:1 compression ratio was the highest in the U.S. industry at that time.

Bodywork on the Marmon Sixteen was designed by Walter Dorwin Teague and built for Marmon by LeBaron. Each of the eight styles was attractive to look at, complemented by the sloping Vee radiator grille which gave a lower look than Cadillac's, but they were built to a price and did not have the quality of some other LeBaron work. Many people think that the Sixteen was priced too low, for the 1931 models were $5,200–$5,470, less than a V16 Cadillac, and by 1933 the price of a Marmon Sixteen sedan or coupe was down to $4,825. This price cutting was a desperate measure to help flagging sales, and Marmon cannot have made any profit at this figure. Only 390 Sixteens were sold in three

1936 CADILLAC SERIES 90 V16 LIMOUSINE ◄▼
THE YEAR 1936 WAS ALMOST THE LAST FOR THE FIRST GENERATION V16 CADILLAC, AND ONLY 52 WERE MADE. HALF OF THEM WERE LIMOUSINES, THE BALANCE BEING MADE UP OF CONVERTIBLE SEDANS, AND VARIOUS CUSTOM TOWN CARS, MOSTLY BY FLEETWOOD OR BRUNN. THE SAME 452-CUBIC-INCH ENGINE WAS USED AS IN THE FIRST V16s OF 1930, BUT THE WHEELBASE WAS NOW A WHOPPING 154 INCHES. THIS FLEETWOOD LIMOUSINE COST $7,750.
OWNER: TOM BARRATT (PHOTO NICKY WRIGHT)

seasons, and manufacture ceased altogether at the end of 1933. Marmon undoubtedly suffered badly from being a year later on the market than Cadillac, for while 1930 may not have the best of years to launch a new luxury car, 1931 was worse. Cadillac sold only 790 V16s in the same three-year period, out of total V16 sales of 4,403.

One other sixteen-cylinder car was planned in the early 1930s, but never reached the market place. This was the Peerless, of which just one prototype was built, with a 464-cubic-inch 170bhp engine and aluminum sedan body by Murphy on a 145-inch wheelbase. The car was enthusiastically promoted by James Bohannon, who came to Peerless from Marmon in 1929, but there is no hard evidence that he brought more than the general

idea with him. The same applies to Owen Nacker and the V16 Cadillac, for he was more of a consultant than a regular Marmon employee.

The V12 layout was offered by five manufacturers during the 1930s, Auburn, Franklin, Lincoln, Packard, and Pierce-Arrow, in addition to Cadillac already mentioned. The Auburn was the lowest-priced V12 ever made. At prices from $975 to $1,275 in 1932, it was not in the same price range as other V12s at all. It was also the only V12 of that era to have an engine bought from outside, although "outside" was perhaps not strictly accurate as engine maker Lycoming was part of the Cord empire, as was Auburn. The 390-cubic-inch engine gave 160bhp, which propelled the handsome two-passenger roadsters at over 100mph,

Herbert Franklin and his engineers Glen Shoemaker, Ed Marks, and Carl Doman, it was to have had the new V12 engine in an extended Franklin frame, with bodies by Dietrich in traditional Franklin styling. In 1929 Herbert Franklin borrowed $5 million from a bank, the first time he had done so. When the Depression struck, the bank put in one of its men, Edwin McEwan, to supervise all Franklin operations. Although four prototypes of the car as conceived by Franklin and his engineers had already been built, and two of them had been exhibited at the New York Automobile Show, McEwan ordered a complete redesign in the interests of cost cutting. The engine was about the only thing that was not altered, for the frame was made much heavier (the traditional light and flexible Franklin frame was undoubtedly expensive to make), the full elliptic springs were replaced by semi-elliptics, and the wheelbase was extended from 137 to 144 inches. This made the whole car heavier by about 1,200 pounds. The handsome Dietrich bodies were replaced by LeBaron-designed two-door club brougham and four-door sedan bodies, which Franklin expert Thomas Hubbard thinks may have been designed for Lincoln and rejected by Edsel or Henry Ford.

Despite McEwan's cost cutting, the Franklin V12 was priced from $3,885 to $4,185, too much for the depressed state of the market. For 1934, prices were reduced by $1,000 across the range, but this did not help. Only 200 V12s were made, and Franklin went out of business by the end of 1934. The four prototypes were sold off to private customers, an unusual step, for companies generally destroy prototypes, considering them inferior to production models. However, as Franklin clearly thought the prototypes were superior, perhaps it is not so surprising. None of them is known to have survived, but Thomas Hubbard has built a "Franklin that never was but should have been" by installing a V12 engine in a 1932 chassis clothed with a particularly lovely four-passenger phaeton body styled after a Merrimac design.

Lincoln, Packard, and Pierce-Arrow all launched their V12s for the 1932 season. The engines were all massive L-head units, displacements being 447.9 cubic inches for the Lincoln KB, 445.5 for the Packard Twin Six, and 398 or 429 for the Pierce-Arrow. Quoted output was

1932 FRANKLIN SEDAN ▲▼

THE FRANKLIN COMPANY WAS NEAR THE END OF THE ROAD IN 1932, BUT BROUGHT OUT A NEW MODEL, THE AIRMAN LINE. THESE CARS USED THE SAME SIX-CYLINDER AIR-COOLED ENGINE AS THEIR PREDECESSORS, BUT HAD NEW BODIES IN NINE STYLES. THIS FOUR-DOOR SEDAN COST $2,345. FRANKLIN BUILT ONLY 1,577 CARS IN 1932, AND WENT OUT OF BUSINESS TWO YEARS LATER.

OWNERS: MARK AND TOOTSIE ACCOMAZZO (PHOTO NICKY WRIGHT)

and the five-passenger sedans and phaetons at 90+mph. There were effectively six forward speeds, thanks to the Columbia Two-speed Axle with which all Auburns were offered. The Auburn V12 was on the market for three seasons, 1932/34, but did not sell particularly well, probably not more than 2,000 or 3,000 out of total Auburn sales of 17,276 during those years.

Even rarer was the Franklin V12, whose engine was slightly larger than the Auburn's at 414 cubic inches, but gave 10 fewer bhp and was, like all Franklin units, air-cooled. It was launched for the 1933 season, but had been under development since 1927 and had undergone radical changes when the design was quite advanced. As conceived by

150bhp for the Lincoln and Pierce-Arrow, and 160bhp for the Packard. These were all large cars, with wheelbases between 142 and 147 inches and weighing up to 6,000 pounds. Like Cadillac, they were available with standard bodies and semi-custom styles, and also as bare chassis for individual custom work. Among the favored coachbuilders for Lincoln were Brunn, Dietrich, Judkins, and Murphy, and for Packard, Dietrich and LeBaron. Pierce-Arrow mostly made its own coachwork, although individual custom designs by Brunn, LeBaron, Rollston, and others were seen.

In price the twelves were fairly similar, starting at $3,450 for the lowest-priced smaller Pierce-Arrow and $3,895 for the Packard standard touring. Lincolns were more expensive, with nothing under $4,300. Upper prices depended on coachwork, but even the semi-customs ran to nearly $8,000. In 1933 Pierce-Arrow announced a very special model, the streamlined Silver Arrow fastback sedan. Priced

at $10,000, it was the most expensive American-built car that year, with the exception of the Duesenberg. Only five were made, of which four survive. In 1934 a much less radical fastback two-door coupe was made, also called Silver Arrow. It was available on the eight-cylinder chassis as well as the twelve, and cost only $3,295, but by then all prices had been sharply reduced.

In happier times all three cars might have sold to their makers' satisfaction, but 1932 was the bottom of the Depression, and only 1,623 Lincoln V12s, 549 Packards, and 447 Pierce-Arrows found buyers that year. Prices were dropped accordingly for 1933, a Lincoln sedan costing $3,200, a Packard $3,860, and a Pierce $2,975. All three had smaller and lower-priced lines to back them up, Lincoln the KA 381.7-cubic-inch V12, Packard two lines of straight-8, and Pierce one straight-8. However, all of these were still costly cars, conceived in the expansive pre-Depression years. What was needed was a model in

the upper-middle bracket to sell in numbers hitherto unknown to these luxury car builders. By 1936 Lincoln and Packard came up with such cars; Pierce-Arrow lacked the resources and perhaps the will to do so, and went under in 1938.

The luxury Lincoln and Packard twelves were continued up to 1939, but in diminishing numbers. Only 446 Packard Twelves were made in their last model year, and 139 Lincolns in the calendar year 1939. The cars which took over from them were very different in design and appearance, yet both were logical for the firms that made them. They were the conservative-looking Packard 120 and the advanced, streamlined Lincoln Zephyr V12.

Packard's 120 was introduced in January 1935, selling at $980 for a two-passenger business coupe. Other models were into four figures but only just, with the top price five-passenger club sedan costing $1,085. The 120s, which had a 120-inch wheelbase, were just over half the price of any Packard made

1933 FRANKLIN SERIES 17-B V12 CLUB BROUGHAM ◄

TWO BODY STYLES WERE OFFERED ON THE FRANKLIN V12 CHASSIS, THIS TWO-DOOR CLUB BROUGHAM AND A FOUR-DOOR SEDAN, ALTHOUGH THE LATTER WAS ALSO AVAILABLE AS A LIMOUSINE. THEY WERE DESIGNED BY LEBARON, AND IT IS THOUGHT THEY MAY HAVE BEEN PLANNED FOR LINCOLN. THESE CARS WERE EXPENSIVE AT $3,885 TO $4,185 AND IN ORDER TO IMPROVE SALES, PRICES WERE CUT BY $1,000 ACROSS THE RANGE FOR 1934. THIS CANNOT HAVE HELPED COMPANY PROFITS, AND THE BANKS FORECLOSED ON FRANKLIN AT THE END OF 1934.

OWNER: NATIONAL AUTOMOBILE MUSEUM, RENO, NEVADA

(PHOTO NICKY WRIGHT)

1936 PACKARD V12 MODEL 1407 DIETRICH CONVERTIBLE VICTORIA ▶
PACKARD RETURNED TO THE 12-CYLINDER FIELD FOR 1932. FOR THIS SEASON THE CARS WERE KNOWN BY THE TRADITIONAL NAME, TWIN SIX, BUT THEREAFTER THEY WERE SIMPLY CALLED THE PACKARD TWELVE. BY 1936 OUTPUT WAS 175bhp FROM 473.3 CUBIC INCHES. THE 1936 MODEL CARS WERE THE 14th SERIES, AND 07 INDICATES THE MIDDLE OF THE THREE WHEELBASES AVAILABLE, AT 139.25 INCHES. DIETRICH WAS ONE OF THE FAVORITE BUILDERS OF SEMICUSTOM COACHWORK FOR PACKARD. THE FIRM WAS THE CUSTOM BODY SUBSIDIARY OF THE MURRAY CORPORATION; STYLING WAS BY RAYMOND DIETRICH WHO HAD BEEN LURED AWAY FROM LEBARON.
OWNER: GILMORE CAR MUSEUM, KALAMAZOO, MICHIGAN
(PHOTO NICKY WRIGHT)

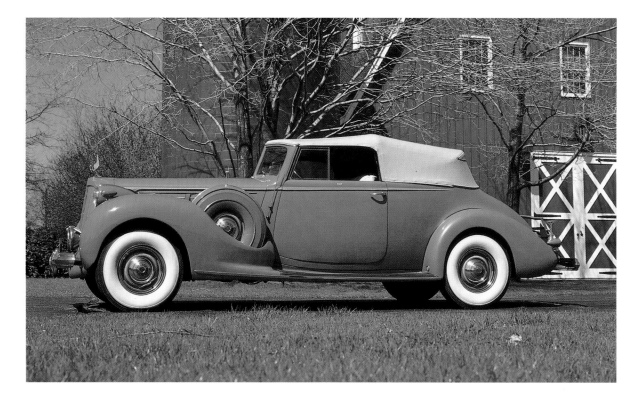

1932 PIERCE-ARROW MODEL 53 V12 LIMOUSINE ▼
PIERCE-ARROW BUILT TWO SIZES OF V12 IN 1932; THIS IS THE SMALLER TYPE 53 WITH 140bhp FROM A CAPACITY OF 429 CUBIC INCHES. THE PIERCE COMPANY HAD ITS OWN BODY SHOP, AND A LARGE PROPORTION OF THE CARS WERE DELIVERED COMPLETE. ALL-STEEL BODIES HAD REPLACED HAND-BUILT WOOD-AND-ALUMINUM ONES IN 1929.
OWNER: ED OBERHAUS (PHOTO NICKY WRIGHT)

up to then, but still a quality product, with a straight-8 engine designed by ex-Pontiac engineer G.T. Christopher. This displaced 256 cubic inches and gave 110bhp. In 1936 power went up to 120bhp, a double reason for the name. The 120 also incorporated two innovations that would not be seen on larger Packards for a few years, independent front suspension and hydraulic brakes.

In its first season the 120 sold 24,995 units, out of total Packard production of 31,889, and in the succeeding years the lower-priced Packard accounted for an increasing proportion of the firm's output. The 1937 season saw a six-cylinder companion to the 120, with basically the same engine minus two cylinders on a 115-inch wheelbase. The interior was less expensive, but very similar in appearance. Designated the 115, it sold from $795 for a business coupe to $1,295 for a station wagon, Packard's first example of this body style.

The 1937 Packard sales breakdown was 30,050 115s, 50,100 120s, 5,793 Senior Eights, and 1,300 Twelves. However, these expensive cars occupied 50 percent of the work force for only 8.8 percent of cars built. Profit margins, if any, must have been much tighter than on lower-priced models. This, combined with the continuing poor market for luxury cars, led Packard management to

manner of the Czech Tatra, but not even a prototype was made in this form. The design attracted the attention of Edsel Ford, and the first two prototypes were tested with Ford V8 engines before any definite plans were made to build the car as a Lincoln. An advanced feature that got carried over into the production models was the integral body/chassis construction.

Before the Zephyr went into production, the front end was restyled by Ford's Bob Gregorie to give it a strong resemblance to a 1937 Ford, then a year away. Tjaarda's proposed all-independent suspension gave way to Ford's traditional transverse leaves, and the engine, although a V12, was much closer to Ford than Lincoln, having many interchangeable parts with the V8 as well as the same stroke. Its displacement was 267.3 cubic inches and it developed 110bhp.

The Zephyr was priced to compete directly with Cadillac's LaSalle, and was about $200 more

1935 LINCOLN K V12 SEVEN-PASSENGER TOURING ▼
THE BIG V12 LINCOLNS WERE RESTYLED FOR 1935, WITH BULLET-SHAPED HEADLIGHTS, CLOSE-MESH GRILLES, AND LONGER HOODS WITH THERMOSTATICALLY CONTROLLED HORIZONTAL SHUTTERS. ONLY 1,400 WERE MADE, BUT EVEN SO THEY EXCEEDED THE COMBINED PRODUCTION OF RIVAL V12 MAKERS, CADILLAC, PACKARD, AND PIERCE-ARROW. THIS CAR IS REPUTED TO HAVE BEEN USED BY PRESIDENT ROOSEVELT; HE CERTAINLY USED SIMILAR CARS. LINCOLNS HAVE LONG BEEN FAVORITE WHITE HOUSE TRANSPORTATION.

OWNER: TOM BARRATT (PHOTO NICKY WRIGHT)

discontinue the big 384-cubic-inch Senior Eight after 1936, although the smaller 320-cubic-inch model was continued, giving way to the 356-cubic-inch Super Eight 160 and 180 for the 1940 season. These were closer to the 120 in appearance, especially the short-wheelbase models, and in price. The lowest-priced 160 cost $1,524 and the top price 120 cost $1,573. The big seller was now the six, designated the 110, which notched up 62,300 units compared with 28,138 of the 120s and only 7,562 Senior Packards.

The last prewar Packards were the Clippers, introduced in mid-1941 in the 120 series only, although for 1942 they were available with the six-cylinder and Super Eight 160 engines as well. Until the Clipper, Packard styling was behind other American makes, but it drew ahead, with wide, low, fastback bodies, fenders faired into the front doors, and rear wheel covers. Many rivals were not so modern-looking until their 1949 models.

Lincoln's answer to the Packard 120 was about as different as could be imagined. Named Zephyr after the streamlined train, Burlington Zephyr, which captured the nation's imagination in 1934, it had a highly streamlined body designed by John Tjaarda of the Briggs Body Corporation. Tjaarda planned his body for a rear-located engine, in the

1940 PACKARD DARRIN CONVERTIBLE VICTORIA ◄

PROMOTED AS THE "GLAMOUR CAR OF THE YEAR," THIS SPORTY-LOOKING OPEN FOUR-SEATER WAS STYLED BY HOWARD "DUTCH" DARRIN, AND BUILT IN LIMITED NUMBERS AS PART OF THE CUSTOM SUPER EIGHT SERIES. DARRIN ALSO DESIGNED A SPORTS SEDAN AND CONVERTIBLE SEDAN, BUT THE VICTORIAS ATTRACTED THE MOST ATTENTION. BODIES WERE BUILT IN A SPECIAL PLANT AT CONNERSVILLE, INDIANA, FOR 1940, THEN IN PACKARD'S DETROIT BODY PLANT FOR 1941 AND 1942. THE 1940 DARRIN VICTORIA COST $4,570: MORE THAN TWICE THE PRICE OF A REGULAR SEDAN.

OWNER: DUKE DAVENPORT (PHOTO NICKY WRIGHT)

1934 PACKARD CONVERTIBLE COUPE ▼►

THE 1934 PACKARDS WERE THE 11th SERIES, AND WERE LAUNCHED ON AUGUST 21, 1933. THERE WERE NO DRAMATIC IMPROVEMENTS OVER THE 10th SERIES, BUT MANY DETAIL CHANGES WERE INCLUDED, SUCH AS AN OIL TEMPERATURE REGULATOR, AND FACTORY-INSTALLED RADIO WHICH NECESSITATED A LARGER, HEAVY-DUTY GENERATOR. THIS CONVERTIBLE COUPE IS A SERIES 1100 EIGHT ON THE 129½-INCH WHEELBASE, AND SOLD FOR $2,580. THE "FLYING LADY" RADIATOR ORNAMENT WAS A $10.00 EXTRA; THE TRADITIONAL PACKARD CORMORANT COST $20.00.

OWNER: AUBURN-CORD-DUESENBERG MUSEUM (PHOTO NICKY WRIGHT)

expensive than the Packard 120. A two-door sedan cost $1,275 and a four-door $1,320. Buyers got a lot of car for their money. Apart from the prestige of twelve cylinders, the body was roomier than the competition, top speed was 90mph, and 0–50mph acceleration took only 10 seconds. Fuel consumption was not at all bad, at 19mpg. The Zephyr sold very well, 14,994 in its first season, 1935/36, which was ten times the figure for the senior Lincolns, and far more than any previously achieved by Lincoln. For the 1937 season a two-door coupe was added to the range, and production rose to 29,997. A further extension of the range came in 1938 with a four-door convertible, while small grilles on either side of the prow set a new styling fashion.

After the demise of the big K Series Lincoln, the small V12 became the sole Lincoln model; displacement was raised to 292 cubic inches (120bhp) for 1940 and to 306 cubic inches (130bhp) for 1942. The car became a lot heavier (the 1942 models weighed 580 pounds more than the original 1936 Zephyr) and more expensive, 1942 prices running from $1,748 for a two-door coupe to $2,274 for a convertible. But the model that attracted most attention, although not so many sales, was the Continental, launched for the 1940 season.

Although always overshadowed by his father,

1939 PACKARD 1700 SIX AND 1703 SUPER EIGHT SEDANS ◀▲
PACKARD OFFERED A WIDE RANGE FOR 1939, FROM THE 100bhp SIX
TO THE 175bhp TWELVE, NOW IN ITS LAST YEAR. THE 1700 SERIES SIX
WAS THE MARQUE'S BEST-SELLER, WITH 24,350 DELIVERED IN SIX BODY STYLES.
THIS SEDAN WAS THE MOST POPULAR OF THESE AND SOLD FOR ONLY $995.
THE 1703 WAS OTHERWISE KNOWN AS THE SUPER EIGHT, AND WAS ALSO
MADE IN SIX MODELS, PRICED FROM $1,650 FOR A CLUB COUPE TO $2,294
FOR A LIMOUSINE ON A LONGER WHEELBASE. PRODUCTION FOR THE
1939 MODEL YEAR WAS 3,962 CARS.

OWNERS: 1700 JOHN BALL; 1703 ROSS ARMIJO (PHOTOS NICKY WRIGHT)

THE ZEPHYR WAS IN ITS FIFTH SEASON IN 1940 WHEN
IT RECEIVED A RESTYLED BODY AND MORE POWERFUL
ENGINE. THE FOUR-DOOR CONVERTIBLE SEDAN WAS NO
LONGER LISTED, BUT THERE WERE SIX STANDARD BODIES
OFFERED. THIS SEDAN WAS BY FAR THE MOST POPULAR
OF THEM WITH 15,764 MADE, OUT OF A TOTAL OF 21,642
ZEPHYRS. IN ADDITION, FOUR MODELS EACH OF
LIMOUSINE AND TOWN CAR WERE MADE, TOGETHER
WITH 404 CONTINENTAL COUPES.

LINCOLN MERCURY DIVISION, FORD MOTOR COMPANY

Edsel Ford was the driving force behind several cars of the 1930s, the Lincoln Zephyr, the Mercury, and the Lincoln Continental. But whereas the first two were quantity-produced cars, the Continental was a pet project of Edsel's, originally a special model for his personal use. It was styled by his friend and colleague Bob Gregorie, using a 1939 Zephyr as the starting point and retaining its front end, hood, and fenders, although the latter were lengthened by 12 inches. At the rear Gregorie gave a squared-off chunkier trunk with, at Edsel's request, an externally mounted spare wheel. While the car was under construction, Edsel paid daily visits to the studio, although he was on vacation in Florida when it was completed. The car was delivered to him there in March 1939, and the reaction of his friends was so enthusiastic that about 200 of them placed orders before it was established that there would even be a production Continental.

For the 1940 season the Continental four-passenger convertible, known as the cabriolet to emphasize its continental connections, was added to the Lincoln range. The production model did not differ greatly from Edsel's personal car, except that the rear end was somewhat bulkier. The hood was 3 inches lower and 7 inches longer than the standard Lincoln Zephyr. The cabriolet was introduced with the other Zephyrs in October 1939, and was joined in the spring of 1940 by a two-door coupe. Only 404 Continentals were made in the 1940 model year, 350 cabriolets and 54 coupes. These were minute figures when compared with the total of 22,046 Lincolns made that year.

The Continental sold on its styling and image, for its performance was no better than that of the regular Lincoln Zephyr. There were hardly any modifications to the V12 engine, and the cabriolet weighed about the same as the Zephyr convertible. Suspension was by the good old Ford transverse leaf system, which dated back to the Model T. Continental buyers paid a hefty premium for their stylish cars, $2,840 for the 1940 cabriolet, while the Zephyr convertible cost a mere $1,770.

The 1941 Lincolns were offered in three series, the Zephyrs in five body styles, the two Continentals, and two Lincoln Customs. These had wheelbases lengthened by 13 inches, and were made only as a seven-passenger sedan or limousine. Very small changes were made to the Continentals, of which the obvious identifying features were push-button doors in place of handles. In 1941 the coupe outsold the cabriolet by 850 to 400. The 1942 Lincolns carried heavier and less attractive grilles; few were made because of the war, only 6,547 altogether, of which 336 were Continentals and 113 Customs.

1940 LINCOLN CONTINENTAL CONVERTIBLE ◀▲
DERIVED FROM A PROTOTYPE BUILT FOR EDSEL FORD
IN 1939, THE CONTINENTAL COMBINED ZEPHYR
MECHANICAL COMPONENTS WITH AN INSPIRED BODY
DESIGN THAT EARNED THE MODEL CLASSIC STATUS
IN LATER YEARS. ENGINE CHANGES WERE CONFINED
TO A SIDE-MOUNTED AIR CLEANER (BECAUSE OF THE
LOWER HOOD) AND POLISHED ALUMINUM HEADS AND
MANIFOLDS. AT $2,840 THE 1940 CABRIOLET ILLUSTRATED
COST 60% MORE THAN A ZEPHYR CONVERTIBLE, AND
ONLY 350 WERE SOLD. THE 1941 CONTINENTALS HAD
PUSH-BUTTON DOOR HANDLES.

OWNER: GILMORE CAR MUSEUM, KALAMAZOO, MICHIGAN

(PHOTO NICKY WRIGHT)

TWILIGHT OF THE COACHBUILDER

From a high point in 1930 the prewar decade saw a sad decline in the number of coachbuilders, mirrored by a similar trend in other countries. The prestigious New York Salons, which were for coachbuilders as much as chassis makers, ended in 1933, by which time many of top names such as Holbrook, Locke, Murphy, and Waterhouse, had gone out of business. The survivors tended to be linked with chassis makers building small series of bodies, such as Brunn, Judkins, and Willoughby with Lincoln, LeBaron with Chrysler, and LeBaron and Darrin with Packard.

Two coachbuilders built small series on Ford V8 chassis, marketing the cars under their own names. These were Brewster and Cunningham. The Brewsters were the more distinctive, with their heart-shaped grilles and cutaway fenders, while Cunningham used standard Ford grilles and fenders. Brewsters were made under the direction of John S. Inskip, whose philosophy was that the

chassis could be replaced from time to time, while the owner retained his craftsman-built Brewster body. How many people actually did this is not known, but there were doubtless some engine transplants. The first Brewster of 1934 was a town car priced at $3,500, but the following year additional body styles were offered, a four-passenger convertible, a limousine, and a "coupelet," which was no more than a two-passenger convertible with rumble seat. All carried the same price tag of $3,500, which made the limousine and town car better value, as there was much more craftsmanship in their bodies, particularly in their interiors. About 120 Brewsters were made in three seasons, 1934/36. At least one body was transferred to a 1940 Buick 90 Limited chassis and used for many years by Mr. J. Whitney of the New York Stock Exchange.

Between 100 and 150 Cunninghams were made, and only in the years 1935 and 1936. Costing less than the Brewster, at $2,600 for a town car, the

Cunningham was an elegant-looking vehicle whose formal coachwork blended quite well with the Ford V8 front end, hood, and fenders. Cunningham discontinued its large cars, powered by an own-make V8 engine, in 1933, and its coachwork department concentrated on Ford-powered cars plus a few ambulances and hearses on Packard chassis. Car making ceased in 1936, although the company remained in business in other fields.

The number of true custom bodies shrank drastically as the 1930s progressed. Among them were the antique-looking town car with vertical body lines and artillery wheels built by Derham on a 1938 Packard Super Eight chassis. More typical

1940 CHRYSLER NEWPORT DUAL-COWL PHAETON ◀▲
ONE OF TWO DESIGNS OF SHOW CAR BUILT FOR CHRYSLER BY LEBARON, THE NEWPORT HAD AN ALUMINUM BODY WITH DUAL COCKPITS AND SEPARATE WINDSHIELDS, PUSH-BUTTON DOORS, AND CONCEALED HEADLIGHTS. A NEWPORT WAS THE OFFICIAL PACEMAKER FOR THE 1941 INDIANAPOLIS 500 MILE RACE, THE FIRST TIME A NONPRODUCTION CAR HAD BEEN CHOSEN FOR THIS ROLE. THIS PARTICULAR CAR WAS BOUGHT BY MILLIONAIRE PLAYBOY HENRY J. TOPPING, WHO SUBSTITUTED A CADILLAC ENGINE AND TRANSMISSION. HE ALSO PERSONALIZED THE CAR BY HAVING HIS NAME CAST IN THE HUBCAPS AND VALVE COVERS, AND ADDING HIS INITIALS TO THE GRILLE. HE WAS MARRIED TO FILM STAR LANA TURNER, HENCE THE LANA LICENSE PLATES.

OWNER: NATIONAL AUTOMOBILE MUSEUM, RENO, NAVADA
(PHOTO NICKY WRIGHT)

Chrysler Thunderbolt — THE CAR OF THE FUTURE

THE CHRYSLER THUNDERBOLT
(ADDITIONAL PICTURES SHOWN UNDER THE THUNDERBOLT PICTURE)

Here is the Thunderbolt, reproduced in four colors, exactly as it will appear on your Chrysler Calendars. The Car of the Future has an irresistible appeal that makes it an outstanding calendar illustration—commanding attention all year long.

CHRYSLER *Thunderbolt* THE CAR OF THE FUTURE

1940 CHRYSLER THUNDERBOLT
CONVERTIBLE ◄▼
NAMED FOR GEORGE EYSTON'S LAND SPEED
RECORD CAR OF 1937, THE THUNDERBOLT WAS
THE MORE STREAMLINED OF CHRYSLER'S
TWO CONCEPT CARS. STYLED IN TEN DAYS
BY ALEX TREMULIS, IT HAD A FULL-WIDTH
BODY WITH SEATING FOR THREE ABREAST,
CONCEALED HEADLIGHTS, AND A RETRACTABLE
HARDTOP THAT WAS NOT TO SEE PRODUCTION
UNTIL THE FORD SKYLINER OF 1957. ALTHOUGH
MADE FOR CHRYSLER BY LEBARON,
THE NEWPORT AND THUNDERBOLT WERE NOT
DESIGNED BY THE COACHBUILDERS.
TREMULIS AND NEWPORT STYLIST RALPH ROBERTS
BOTH WORKED FOR BRIGGS AT THE TIME.
CHRYSLER CORPORATION, MIRCO DE CET COLLECTION

was the customizing of production bodies, adding closed rear panels for greater formality, removing the front part of the top to make a town car, or opening the rear to give a landaulette style. This was done by LeBaron on Chrysler Imperials from 1936 through 1938 and by Derham on Cadillac, Chrysler, and Packard up to 1942. More individual designs from LeBaron were the Newport parade phaeton and Thunderbolt convertible on Chrysler chassis in 1940. These anticipated the show cars of the postwar years in that they were built for the Chrysler Corporation to display around the nation. The Newports were striking enough, with their dual cockpits and windshields for both cockpits, but the Thunderbolts were the more advanced of the two designs. With all-enveloping aluminum bodies with wheels skirted front and rear, they still looked modern in 1960. Six were made of each design; four Newports and two Thunderbolts are known to exist today.

Favorite coachbuilders on the K Series Lincoln chassis were Brunn, Judkins, LeBaron, and Willoughby. Most were semi-custom designs. The Brunn brougham had a town car front and the Judkins berline was really a six-window sedan, but these were made in very small numbers, just 13 broughams and 11 berlines. The breakdown of 1938 Model K chassis figures tells an interesting story: 227 complete cars were made with Lincoln bodywork, 199 chassis were sent to the four coachbuilders just mentioned for cataloged semi-custom work, and 7 went for full custom work. Some of the last-named went to professional bodybuilders (ambulances and hearses). In 1939 only 97 standard bodies were made, 34 semi-customs and seven full customs, although the coachbuilders for the latter have not been traced. In addition, there was one extra-long 160-inch wheelbase chassis bodied by Brunn as a parade car for President Roosevelt. Known as the Sunshine Special, it was fitted with an updated grille in 1942 and accompanied the President to the famous conferences at Casablanca, Teheran, and Yalta. It also went with President Truman to the 1945 Potsdam Conference.

The demise of the Lincoln K at the end of the 1939 season spelled the end for Judkins and Willoughby, who built no more custom bodies. Brunn tried to keep going with a series of semi-custom landaulettes and town cars on the Buick Limited chassis, but Cadillac saw these as a threat to Fleetwood custom bodies and convinced GM to veto their manufacture. Four styles were proposed on 1941 chassis, and at least one of each was built. Brunn closed its doors at the end of 1941.

Packard provided chassis for some striking coachwork by Darrin, LeBaron, and Rollston. All were semicustoms cataloged from 1939 through 1942. The best known was the Darrin convertible victoria, a sporty-looking two-door four-passenger convertible with cutaway doors available on the Super Eight 180 chassis for $4,570 in 1940, and $4,595 in 1941 and 1942. Darrin also did a five-passenger sport sedan with lower lines than the regular sedans at $6,300, and Rollston an all-weather town car at $4,574. These semi-customs were expensive when compared with the regular 180 five-passenger sedan at $2,243.

The only coachbuilder to survive the war and continue with its traditional work was Derham, which built the prototype of Gordon Buehrig's futuristic Tasco coupe on a Mercury chassis in 1948, and customized a number of Cadillacs and Chryslers into the mid-1950s. Among customers for the modified Cadillac 75 were Pope Pius XII and the Sultan of Kuwait. Derham continued to produce sales catalogs up to 1957, but its last important piece of work was a convertible on the 1956 Lincoln Continental Mark II, which was delivered to Mrs. William Clay Ford. Like Bohman & Schwartz, Derham got into classic car restoration toward the end of its life. The author visited the premises in 1970, and among the interesting cars receiving attention were a 1941 Lincoln Continental, the Tasco coupe, and the only example of the French-built Pedroso twin-cam straight-8 of the 1920s. When Enos Derham died in 1974, the Derham Body Company closed down, ending 164 years of distinguished American coachbuilding.

LITTLE CARS THAT COULDN'T

After the Ford Model A had been laid to rest, and setting aside such ephemerals as the Littlemac from Muscatine, Iowa, of which no more than 12 were made, only three cars with less than six cylinders were offered by American makers in the 1930s. These were the American Austin/Bantam, Crosley, and Willys Four. The last was not a true baby car, having a 134.2-cubic-inch 48bhp engine derived from that used in the Whippet. Known as the 77 from 1933 through 1936 it was restyled for 1937 in the contemporary rounded fashion, and received hydraulic brakes for 1939, when power was raised to 62bhp and the old name of Overland was revived, just for one year. The car sold mainly on its economy and price, being just $200 cheaper than the cheapest Chevrolet in 1939. Willys was near the bottom of the production league, but nevertheless sold 76,803 cars in 1937, and between 25,000 and nearly 29,000 in the years 1939–41. The engine achieved its greatest fame in the Jeeps made by Willys and Ford during World War II.

The American Austin was an attempt to give the nation a taste of European-style motoring three decades before there was really any demand for it. The Austin Seven was small even by British standards, and was regarded with amused affection in its own country, although it sold very well, about 300,000 between 1923 and 1939. The same 45-

cubic-inch four-cylinder engine and 75-inch wheelbase were used for the American version, but the bodies were something else. Styled by Alexis de Saknoffsky and built by Hayes, they had dual color schemes, disk wheels, and on the roadster a curved color panel which cheekily aped that of the Model J Duesenberg. The cars looked larger than their actual length of 122 inches. The original 1930 models were priced from $445 for a roadster to $550 for a de luxe coupe. Unfortunately Ford

Model A prices that year started at $435, and buyers got a lot more than they did from American Austins. Admittedly fuel consumption was lower at 40mpg, but gasoline costs were not a significant factor at that time. The Austin factory was located at Butler, Pennsylvania, in the plant of the Standard Steel Car Company, maker of the Standard V8 car from 1916 through 1923.

The American Austin had plenty of novelty value, but failed to make a hit with the average

Main Street buyer. Showbusiness folk like Buster Keaton, Marion Davies, Laurel and Hardy, and Al Jolson bought them, and so did Ernest Hemingway. A fleet of Austins appeared in the Will Rogers movie *A Connecticut Yankee in King Arthur's Court*, and Austins became a stock-in-trade of radio skits and vaudeville acts. "Tell me, do you get into that car, or do you put it on?", was a favorite joke. More Austins went to California than to any other state, but overall sales for 1930 were only 8,858, a bitter disappointment to the promoters, who had spoken of 100,000 or more. 1931 was even worse, with only 1,279 cars sold and more than 1,500 unfinished cars in the factory, with no buyers in prospect.

The American Austin story might have ended there, but for super-salesman Roy Evans who had handled 80 percent of sales. He took the unfinished cars, had them completed outside the factory, and sold them in Florida for $295 each. He then assumed control of the company and built 4,726 units in 1933, including pick ups and delivery vans. The latter were very popular as mobile billboards, their small size and cute appearance attracting more attention than larger vans. Prices were as low as $275 for a business coupe, and bodies were now made in Butler instead of by Hayes at Grand Rapids, Michigan. Only 1,057 vehicles were delivered in 1934 and after that there was a three-year gap before Evans reorganized as the American Bantam Car Company.

The new car was called American Bantam, or simply Bantam (*never* Austin Bantam), and featured fresh styling by de Saknoffsky, who, aware of the precarious finances, gave his services for $300, which represented simply his expenses. The cars featured Vee grilles, and rear wheel covers on the open models, which included a convertible (for 1940) as well as a roadster, and for 1939 a station wagon. Under the hood the engine was modified by race car wizard Harry A. Miller; shortage of money prevented him from doing all he wanted, but a redesigned manifold was sufficient to avoid paying the $10 per car royalty to the Austin Motor Company Ltd. Later, displacement went up to 50 cubic inches and power to 22bhp.

Despite glamorous names like Riviera and Hollywood, the Bantams did not sell very well, about 2,000 in 1938, 1,225 in 1939, and 800 in 1940. Production ended in June 1940, although a 1941 catalog was issued. By then the company was concentrating on the four-wheel-drive army vehicle that would be immortalized as the Jeep.

America's other small car was the Crosley, made in Cincinnati by Powel Crosley (1886–1961), who was 53 years old when he launched the third automobile of his career. His previous efforts were the Marathon Six of 1909 and the DeCross cyclecar of 1913, but his fame and fortune came from making radios and refrigerators. In 1922 he was said

to have been the largest radio manufacturer in the world, while his Shelvadoor refrigerator was the first to have shelves in the doors. In 1934 he became president and owner of the Cincinnati Redlegs baseball team.

Crosley's third attempt at automobile manufacture, and the only one that achieved any success, was planned as early as 1934, but the first car did not appear until April 1939, when it was launched at the Indianapolis Motor Speedway. Smaller than the Bantam, at 120 inches overall, it seated four passengers in the convertible sedan form and sold for $350. Compared with the Bantam, it seemed rather crude, with a two-cylinder air-cooled engine made by the Waukesha Motor Company and derived from an orchard-spraying unit. Seats were simple tube frames covered in stretched fabric, and the windshield wiper was hand-operated. By 1942 an automatic wiper was offered. Top speed was 50mph, although the makers advised 40mph as a more suitable limit for touring. Although 2 inches shorter than the Bantam, the Crosley was roomier, doubtless to suit the 6-foot 4-inch frame of its creator. Another large man, Erwin "Cannonball" Baker, drove a Crosley from Cincinnati to Los Angeles to New York to

Chicago in the summer of 1940, averaging 50.4mpg for 6,517.3 miles. His costs for both gasoline and oil from Cincinnati to Los Angeles were only $9.41.

Crosleys were sold through department stores and other outlets handling Powel's radios and refrigerators. Sales in the first year were quite encouraging, at 2,017 between June and December, but serious problems with breaking driveshafts reduced 1940 sales to 422 units. After redesign by Paul Klotsch, the 1941 models sold 2,289 and the 1942 models 1,029. A $450 station wagon joined the range in 1940, while panel deliveries and pickups were also made. Crosley was to achieve greater fame after World War II with small four-cylinder cars.

1939 CROSLEY CONVERTIBLE SEDAN ◄▲►

THE LITTLE CROSLEY WAS LAUNCHED ON APRIL 29, 1939, ONE DAY AFTER POWEL CROSLEY'S CINCINNATI REDLEGS ROUTED THE CHICAGO CUBS IN THE FIRST OF SEVERAL WINS. MORE OF A LATTER-DAY CYCLECAR THAN A FORERUNNER OF THE SUBCOMPACTS, THE CROSLEY'S FLAT-TWIN ENGINE GAVE 15bhp FROM 38.87 CUBIC INCHES, AND COULD PROPEL THE LITTLE CAR AT UP TO 50mph. BRAKES WERE CABLE OPERATED, AND THERE WERE NO UNIVERSAL JOINTS IN THE DRIVESHAFT. ANY NECESSARY DEFLECTIONS WERE SUPPOSED TO BE HANDLED BY FLEXING OF THE RUBBER-MOUNTED ENGINE.

OWNER: AUBURN-CORD-DUESENBERG MUSEUM (PHOTO NICKY WRIGHT)

THE DECADE OF STYLING AND CONVENIENCE

Although the 1930s saw the introduction of several important mechanical features, such as GM's "Knee Action" independent front suspension and "Turret Top" steel bodies, the main impact of the decade was in styling and convenience features for driver and passengers.

No decade has brought more changes in styling than the 1930s. At the beginning cars were not so different in appearance from those of the 1920s: radiators, windshields, and rear ends were vertical, headlights separate, fenders unskirted. Wheels mostly had wire or pressed steel "artillery" spokes. By 1940 the radiator had disappeared behind a stylish grille, windshields were sloping two-piece units, and sedan backs were sloping and rounded. Fenders acquired skirts around 1932–34, and by 1942 were beginning to be faired into the doors on Buicks and Packard Clippers, anticipating the straight-through lines of postwar cars. Wheels had steel disks with large hubcaps, not too different from those of today.

For their general progress in styling, three cars stood out, the Lincoln Zephyr already described, the Chrysler Airflow, and the Cord 810. The Chrysler was the most significant, since it combined advanced engineering with an ambitious market coverage, and showed auto makers that being ahead of the times could be as dangerous as lagging behind. Chief designer Carl Breer said that he was inspired to study aerodynamics as early as 1927, when cars were just "big boxes with little boxes up front." He noted that aircraft followed the shape of birds in their lines, and asked pioneer aviator Orville Wright to set up a small wind tunnel in which streamlined shapes could be tested. This was followed by a larger tunnel at Chrysler's Highland Park research center. Several prototypes were made, some runners, others merely wooden mock-ups. One had a rear-mounted straight-8 engine but was hopelessly tail heavy, and others had three-abreast seating with central steering, a design which Chrysler never put in production, although the French Panhard company did so a few years later.

The first running Airflow prototype, the Trifon Special, took to the road in December 1932, and the Airflow was shown to the public in January 1934. Its revolutionary appearance was matched by

1934 CHRYSLER AIRFLOW COUPE ▲
1935 CHRYSLER AIRFLOW C-1 SEDAN ▶
AFTER THE POOR RECEPTION OF THE 1934 AIRFLOWS, CHRYSLER'S STYLIST OLIVER CLARK REDESIGNED THE FRONT END TO GIVE IT A PRONOUNCED PROW IN PLACE OF 1934'S WATERFALL GRILLE. YOU COULD EVEN BUY A NEW HOOD TO UPDATE YOUR 1934 AIRFLOW. RESTYLING DID NOT HELP SALES, HOWEVER, WHICH WERE LOWER THAN IN 1934.

OWNERS: STEVE AND EVELYN BENN (PHOTO NICKY WRIGHT)

its engineering, for underneath the waterfall grille, recessed headlights, and rounded sedan back was unitary construction of chassis and body, with a light, cage-like steel girder network carrying the body panels. Unlike most contemporary American cars, no wood whatsoever was used in the construction. Seating for six passengers was within the wheelbase, which necessitated mounting the engine further forward than was usual, about one third of the block being ahead of the front axle, and tilting it rearward at 5°. Access to the trunk was by lifting the rear seat backs, an innovation for the time. Transmission included Borg-Warner's automatic overdrive, the first use of this on an American car. At speeds above 40mph, when the driver lifted his foot from the gas pedal, overdrive was automatically engaged; below 25mph, it dropped back to underdrive.

The engines were the least innovative aspects of the Airflow, being standard Chrysler eights, the 299-cubic-inch in the CU, 323.5-cubic-inch in the

Imperial CV and CX, and 384.8-cubic-inch in the Imperial CW. This last one was the largest and heaviest car ever built by Chrysler, riding on a 146-inch wheelbase and weighing in at up to 5,900 pounds. Only 67 were built, prices being up to $5,145 for the Custom Limousine. By contrast, the cheapest Chrysler Airflow cost only $1,345, and there was an even lower-priced Airflow in the De Soto line, with a 241.5-cubic-inch six-cylinder engine, at $995. The most popular body style was a six-window sedan, but there was also a four-window town sedan and a two-door coupe. The Airflow was never offered in convertible or roadster form.

Although the Airflow was announced at the New York Automobile Show in January 1934, cars did not reach customers until April, which gave rivals, especially General Motors, ample time to spread disparaging rumors. As Carl Breer put it: "We had a lot of fallacies to combat, and no cars to combat them with." When the cars did get into customers' hands, complaints poured in, mostly

arising from faulty building. One owner suffered the engine breaking loose from the frame at 80mph. Probably the first 3,000 Airflows suffered from construction problems, and by the time these had been rectified the damage had been done to the car's reputation. Chrysler kept two conventional cars in the 1934 range, the six-cylinder CA and CB, and these easily outsold the Airflows; of 36,929 Chryslers that year, only 11,292 were Airflows. De Soto had no conventional line for 1934 and sold 13,940 Airflows.

It has been suggested that if Chrysler had had no conventional cars to siphon off sales, the streamlined Airflows might have done better, but it is equally possible that customers would have bought other makes instead. At least the conventional Chryslers kept the company in profit during the Airflow years, while the Airflow car never earned a cent for its makers. For 1935 Walter Chrysler hired Ray Dietrich to style a new line of conventional cars. Called Airstreams, these were

available in six- and eight-cylinder forms, thus eating into the Airflow's market, although the most expensive Airstream undercut the cheapest Airflow by $10. The Airflow was also restyled, giving it a prow which made the front seem less radical. In retrospect, this may have been unwise, since it spoiled the pure waterfall grille which was one of the Airflow's attractions. It certainly did not help sales, which were only 7,751 out of a Chrysler total of 38,533. The front end underwent further modifications in 1936 and 1937, but to no avail; sales were 6,276 and 4,600 respectively, and the Airflow was quietly dropped in August 1937.

The Cord 810 rivaled the Airflow in innovative styling, and has been described as perhaps the most instantly recognizable of all American cars. After the demise of the front-driven straight-8 Cord L-29 in 1932, Errett Lobban Cord's name was absent from cars, although he was still making Auburns and Duesenbergs. Gordon Buehrig was retained as stylist for the group, dividing his time between the marques as Cord decided. In 1934 Cord planned to make a cheaper Duesenberg and asked Buehrig to produce a design. It was radically different from anything seen before, with a "coffin nose" hood and

horizontal louvers, headlights that disappeared into the fenders, no running boards, and a fastback sedan body. It was intended to have rear-wheel drive, and the prototype was built on an Auburn chassis.

Before the mock-up was completed Buehrig was moved to Auburn, where he designed the 851 speedster. When he returned to the Duesenberg project a year later, he found that it was to have front drive and to be called a Cord. He revised his drawings somewhat, with a lower four-window sedan in place of the original six-window design, but otherwise the appearance of the 1935 Cord was

1929 CORD L-29 SEDAN ◄▲

THE FIRST CAR TO BEAR THE NAME OF ERRETT LOBBAN CORD WAS THE L-29, NAMED FOR THE YEAR
OF ITS INTRODUCTION. ITS MOST STRIKING FEATURE WAS DRIVE TO THE FRONT WHEELS, WHICH HAD
BEEN SEEN ONLY ON A FEW EXPERIMENTAL ROAD CARS AND ON INDIANAPOLIS RACERS. INDEED,
RACE CAR ENGINEERS HARRY MILLER AND CORNELIUS VAN RANST WERE CONSULTANTS TO THE L-29
PROJECT. IT WAS POWERED BY A 125bhp STRAIGHT-8 LYCOMING ENGINE, AND WAS PRICED
FROM $3,095 to $3,295; BUT THESE PRICES WERE LOWERED FOR 1930. PRODUCTION CEASED
ON DECEMBER 31, 1931, WITH JUST OVER 5,000 CARS MADE.

OWNER: AUBURN-CORD-DUESENBERG MUSEUM (PHOTO NICKY WRIGHT)

very similar to that of the 1934 baby Duesenberg. The Cord was powered by a 288.6-cubic-inch 125bhp V-8 Lycoming engine designed to Cord's specification, Lycoming being part of his empire. It drove the front wheels through a four-speed transmission, with steering column gear selector and shifting by depression of the clutch.

Called the Model 810, the new Cord was launched at the New York and Los Angeles Shows in November 1935. The rules of the Automobile Manufacturers' Association insisted on at least 100 cars being completed before the shows opened, and the Cord company had a struggle to build these in time. In fact, they were not runners, for the transmissions could not be completed. Their appearance scored a big hit with the public, and they were voted best-looking cars at the New York Show. The Packard 120 was voted second, while the other streamlined cars of the era, Lincoln Zephyr and Chrysler Airflow, were sixth and ninth

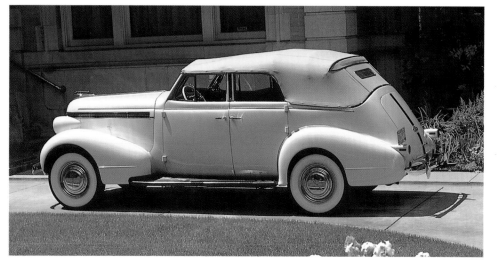

◄◄► TWO EXAMPLES OF THE RELATIVELY RARE FOUR-DOOR OPEN CARS THAT HAD THEIR LAST FLING IN THE 1930s. THE STYLE WAS OFFERED IN 1937 AND 1938 ONLY, IN BOTH THE SIX- AND EIGHT-CYLINDER PONTIAC LINES. THIS IS A 1937 DE LUXE EIGHT, WHICH AT $1,235 WAS THE MOST EXPENSIVE PONTIAC THAT YEAR. FEW WERE MADE, AND ONLY FIVE ARE KNOWN TO SURVIVE, THREE SIXES AND TWO EIGHTS. BUICK'S VERSION WAS KNOWN AS THE PHAETON, AND WAS AVAILABLE IN THE SPECIAL, CENTURY, AND ROADMASTER LINES. THIS IS A 1939 CENTURY MODEL 61-C, OF WHICH ONLY 249 WERE BUILT FOR DOMESTIC SALES, AND 20 FOR EXPORT.
PONTIAC OWNER: DICK CHOLER; BUICK OWNER: BOB DEBOW
(PHOTOS NICKY WRIGHT)

respectively. People were less enthusiastic about their prices, only 0.9 percent believing that the Cords offered best value for money, which is understandable, for they were priced from $1,995 for a Westchester sedan to $2,195 for a two-door phaeton, well above Buick or any but the top Chryslers, and $300 above the lowest-priced Cadillac V8.

But the Model 810 was a specialty car, not to be compared with the products of the Big Three. With its low lines (a height of 60 inches for the sedan and 58 inches for the convertibles made it the lowest full-sized American car) and striking appearance, it was a car for the individualist. Unfortunately individualists are often impatient, and many orders were canceled between the end of 1935 and the spring of 1936 when the production models were at last ready. Those who had placed firm orders got Cords for Christmas, but they were bronze models in 1/32 scale! The first production cars were troublesome, particularly in the transmission department, where they tended to shift back to neutral without warning. Even when they were working well, the semi-automatic gearshift was slower than a normal stick shift. This was a drawback on a car sold at least partly on its performance. Top speed was 92mph, or over 100mph with the supercharger offered on 1937 Cords, but acceleration through the gears was not so remarkable; rest to 60mph took 20.1 seconds (unsupercharged), an achievement that could be beaten by a Ford V8.

Model 810 output for 1936 was 1,174, a further 1,146 being made between January and August 1937. The supercharged Model 812 was an addition to the 1937 range, but prices were well up, $2,445–$2,645 for the 810 and $2,960–$3,060 for the 812s, which had longer wheelbases as well as superchargers. The Cords were the last cars of Errett Lobban's empire, but they will never be forgotten. In 1951 the New York Museum of Modern Art recognized the design as one of the ten finest examples of industrial styling of all time. With the Auburn speedster, the Cord was one of the first cars to be made in replica form; two companies offered convertible replicas powered by Chevrolet Corvair, Ford, and Chrysler V8 engines between 1964 and 1970.

▲ TWO CONVERTIBLES IN CHRYSLER'S AIRSTREAM EIGHT RANGE FOR 1936. ALTHOUGH THEY WERE CERTAINLY HANDSOME CARS, THEY WERE NOT AS LONG AND SLEEK AS THE ARTIST HAS MADE THEM OUT TO BE IN THIS DUMMY ADVERTISEMENT. BOTH WERE RARE MODELS: THE CONVERTIBLE ACCOUNTED FOR ONLY 240 SALES, THE CONVERTIBLE SEDAN FOR 362. CONVERTIBLE CHRYSLERS HAD ONE-PIECE WINDSHIELDS; THE CLOSED MODELS USED TWO-PIECE DESIGNS.

CHRYSLER ARCHIVES, MIRCO DE CET COLLECTION

BODY STYLES — GOOD-BYE AND HELLO

The 1930s saw the disappearance of one body style and the emergence of a new one that has continued in popularity to the present day. The departure was the four-door open car, the arrival was the station wagon.

Open four-door bodies for five passengers were the norm at the beginning of the 1920s, but had become a minority taste a decade later. During the 1930s many manufacturers offered sophisticated versions of the old touring. Generally known as convertible sedans or phaetons, these had much improved weather protection, with wind-up windows. They were also often the most expensive in their ranges, which gave them an air of luxury and chic, whereas the touring had been lower priced than the sedan.

Ford offered a convertible sedan from 1935 through 1940, but not Chevrolet. The other GM divisions did, Buick from 1932 through 1941, Cadillac from 1929 through 1941, LaSalle from 1937 through 1940, Oldsmobile from 1940 through 1941, and Pontiac from 1937 through 1938. As an example, the 1941 Oldsmobile 98 phaeton cost $1,575, compared with $1,135 for the equivalent sedan, and sold only 119 units, against 22,081 sedans and total Olds output of 270,040 for the 1941 model year.

All the Chrysler divisions offered four-door convertibles, although Plymouth's convertible sedan was only available for the 1939 season, Chrysler's last. Among the independents, convertible sedans could be had from Hupmobile, Nash, Packard, and Studebaker, but never from Hudson, Graham, or Reo. The style was dead by 1942, and the only postwar offerings were from Frazer (1949–1951) and Lincoln (1961–1967).

Station wagons were also small-production, expensive vehicles but unlike convertible sedans they became more numerous during the 1930s. Nevertheless they did not come into their own until well after World War II. Right up to the outbreak of war, they were generally regarded as commercial vehicles, and were sold along with vans and pickups.

The first station wagon bodies were built by the Stoughton Wagon Company of Stoughton, Wisconsin, on Model T chassis from 1919 and on the Star from 1923. The latter was the first dealer-available woody, costing $610, but the number made was very small. Although they were not cataloged models until 1929, there were plenty of station wagon bodies on Ford chassis, mostly used by farmers, who were large-scale Ford customers. In 1929 a Model A station wagon was cataloged at $695, $170 more than a sedan, but only 5,251 were made out of a total 1,507,132 Fords built that year. The bodies were by Briggs from wood supplied by the Mengel company of Louisville, Kentucky. After 1937 the wood came from Ford's own forests at Iron Mountain in northern Michigan. Yet output remained small. In fact the original 1929 figure was not matched until 1938, when 6,012 were built, by then on the V8 chassis.

Nearly all station wagon bodies were supplied from outside in the 1930s; General Motors bought from Hercules or Ionia, Dodge from Cantrell, Plymouth from the U.S. Body & Forging Company, Packard from Cantrell and Hercules, and Willys from Mifflinburg. The numbers involved were not important enough to warrant production by the car makers themselves and, besides, the wooden construction was quite alien to firms now working largely if not entirely in steel. Only after the war, when the "woody" became a steel pressing with mock wood panels, were they made in house.

At first the station wagon went by various names such as "depot hack," "suburban," "beach wagon," or "carryall," and was used by farmers, explorers, film studios, and hotels rather than by ordinary families. Yet, by the end of the decade it was becoming more widely accepted; the author

remembers riding to school in Baltimore in a 1941 Plymouth station wagon which carried about nine kids. Apart from Cadillac, De Soto, Lincoln, and Nash, all the U.S. makers offered a woody in their range. After the war De Soto and Nash also joined the woody brigade.

COMFORT AND CONVENIENCE

It was not only in styling that the 1930s saw a revolution, but also in comfort and convenience for driver and passengers. The car of 1940 had many of the features taken for granted today, including heating and air conditioning, push-button radios, windshield washers and two-speed wipers, power-operated tops, and automatic transmissions. Air conditioning was first offered by Nash in 1938, while another heavily promoted feature of the company was a front seat that could be folded to make a comfortable double bed, offered from 1936 onward. In fact, Nash was not first with this, for Billy Durant made it an option in 1931, although there were few takers.

Car radios were first offered commercially by the Philadelphia Storage Battery Corporation in 1927 under the name Philco Transitone. Radios

were offered as regular production options by Cadillac and Pontiac in 1930, by Plymouth in 1931, by Chrysler, Dodge, and Studebaker in 1932, by Oldsmobile in 1933, and by Buick, Hudson, and Packard in 1934. In 1935 it was estimated that there were more than 1 million radio-equipped cars in the United States. By 1940 radios were available in all cars except the most basic, and push-button tuning was coming into widespread use. Pontiac offered a radio that could be removed from the car for picnics.

The power-operated top (by vacuum cylinders located behind the front seat) was pioneered not on a high-priced car but on the $895 1939 Plymouth De Luxe convertible coupe. It was later seen on 1940 De Sotos, while the 1941 Lincoln Continental and 1942 Oldsmobile featured a power top operated by dual electric motors. Power-operated windows were first seen as an option on 1941 Chrysler Crown Imperials, although some custom-bodied limousines had electric divisions between chauffeur and passenger compartments several years earlier. The industry's first power-adjusted front seats were introduced on the 1941 Lincoln Custom sedan.

Transmissions underwent some tremendous

A 1942 FORD SUPER DE LUXE STATION WAGON, TYPICAL OF THE ERA WHEN A "WOODY" REALLY HAD QUITE A LOT OF WOOD IN ITS CONSTRUCTION. THE SUPER DE LUXE WAS THE TOP LINE FORD V8 AND INCLUDED AN ELECTRIC CLOCK, LEFT FRONT DOOR ARMRESTS, AND SEQUOIA GRAIN INSTRUMENT PANEL, FEATURES NOT FOUND IN THE DE LUXE LINE.

FORD MOTOR COMPANY

41-9000

THE AMERICAN AUTOMOBILE: A CENTENARY 1893–1993

improvements during the last prewar decade. In 1930 not all cars had synchromesh, although this became universal during the next few years. Most gearboxes had three speeds, although there was a short-lived vogue for four among the more expensive cars in the early 1930s. This was a tribute to the "more is better" philosophy rather than a serious improvement, for the big, powerful Stutzes, Packards, and Pierce-Arrows were precisely the cars that did not need the extra ratio, having enough power and flexibility to cope with three speeds. Also, the average American driver did not want to be constantly gear-shifting, as his European counterpart, with a small, high-revving engine, was obliged to do. Nevertheless 15 makers offered four-speed transmission between 1929 and 1933, including Chrysler, Packard, Pierce-Arrow, and Stutz, as well as small firms on their last legs such as Elcar, Jordan, Kissel, and Windsor. The arrival of automatic overdrive, on the 1934 Chrysler Airflow giving an extra-high ratio without using the gearstick, marked the end of the ordinary four-speed transmission until the 1960s.

Chrysler's Warner overdrive, mounted behind the transmission, was adopted by Ford in 1948 and by GM in 1955, but earlier Fords had an alternative, the Columbia two-speed axle, which gave alternative ratios of 4.11:1 or 2.94:1. This effectively gave six forward speeds, although it was normally only used in high gear. Operation was by depressing the clutch, which actuated a vacuum-powered shift mechanism. The two-speed axle was an option costing around $100, offered on Fords between 1934 and 1948, and also on Auburns and the Franklin V12 in the early 1930s.

Another short-lived device was the freewheel, introduced by Studebaker in 1930 and within two years adopted by nearly all makers except Buick and Ford. It consisted of a small overriding clutch in the transmission which disengaged the drive, enabling the car to coast as a bicycle would.

Advantages were lower gas consumption and less wear and tear, but against these advantages, the brakes had to work harder in the absence of engine braking, which could be dangerous on long downhill stretches where the driver was most likely to freewheel. Also, the unstressed engines had a tendency to die. By 1935 freewheeling was just about obsolete.

The first steps toward automatic transmission were made by Reo with its Self-Shifter of 1933. This had two ranges, Hi and Lo, each with two speeds; shifting within each range was automatic, but between Lo and Hi shifting was manual. Acceleration in Hi was distinctly leisurely, so both ratios had to be used, and indeed it was necessary to double declutch for a rapid change. Even though the Self-Shifter was relatively cheap, adding only $80 to the cost of a Flying Cloud sedan, it did not prove popular and was dropped after 1935. Coincidentally or not, this was the year when Hudson introduced its Electric Hand, a preselector in which speeds were selected by a small lever extending from the steering column, and actuated when the clutch pedal was dipped. Shifting was by vacuum, electrically actuated. The Electric Hand was standard on Hudson Custom Eights, and a $20 option on others, less than half the cost of a Zenith radio ($44). In 1939 it gave way to a Selective Automatic Shift which, the makers claimed, allowed one to drive without ever needing to use the clutch pedal, although one was present.

True two-pedal automatic transmission did not arrive until 1940, when Oldsmobile introduced the famous HydraMatic Drive as a $75 option. GM had made a step in the same direction with its dual-range semi-automatic transmission of 1937, available on Oldsmobiles and Buicks. This was similar to the Reo Self-Shifter, although changes from one range to the other could be made without using the clutch. Use of the clutch was still necessary for starting from a standstill, though. The system was developed by Earl A. Thompson, and was offered first by the Oldsmobile Division because of the forward thinking of Olds' general manager Charles L. McCuen. The Automatic Safety Transmission, as it was called, was manufactured by Buick and was offered on Oldsmobiles from June 1937 through September 1939, and by Buick from the fall of 1937, for the

1938 season only. The cost was $80, but very few customers (probably fewer than 7 percent of all Oldsmobile and Buick buyers) chose it during the years it was on offer.

The semi-automatic had the same planetary gearsets controlled by a centrifugal governor as HydraMatic, but lacked the latter's fluid torque converter, hence the need for a clutch. When the fluid coupling, which consisted of two vaned rotors in an oil-filled enclosure with no mechanical link between them, was combined with the planetary gearsets, a proper two-pedal system became possible. Oldsmobile launched this in September 1939 on its 1940 models, and demand soon outstripped supply. Production of HydraMatics was woefully low in 1940, probably because Olds remembered the poor demand for the semi-automatic transmission; but, encouraged by public response, output was stepped up and by the beginning of the 1942 season, about 45 percent of Oldsmobiles were equipped with HydraMatic. It was also offered on 1941 and 1942 Cadillacs. The early HydraMatics were by no means trouble-free, suffering from rough and erratic shifting and a relatively short life. However, they were greatly improved during World War II, being used in armored cars, gun carriages, tanks, and in snowmobiles. As a result, GM entered the postwar era with a much better transmission, with a life of 30,000–50,000 miles between overhauls.

OWNER: CARL W. REID (PHOTO NICKY WRIGHT)

CHAPTER SIX

THE AMERICAN AUTOMOBILE TRIUMPHANT

1945 – 1970

"To the average American, our present car and its size represent an outward symbol of prestige and well-being."

Ford Division report, 1951

W ORLD WAR II HAD A MUCH greater effect on the American auto industry than World War I. Whereas automobiles continued to be turned out during 1917 and 1918, in February 1942 all passenger car production came to an end. In fact, a very limited number of cars were delivered later, as statistics show production of 139 passenger cars in 1943 and 610 in 1944, doubtless all for military or government use. The 1943 figure included 69 Hudsons, which were the last of the reserve of 1942 models. During 1941 the industry was already gearing up for war production, and in the following four years turned out an enormous quantity of material. Approximately 92 percent of scout cars and carriers, 87 percent of bombs, and 75 percent of aircraft engines were produced by the auto and truck industries.

This is not the place to list all these achievements, but among the more remarkable was Ford's production of 8,675 B-24 Liberator bombers at a specially built plant at Willow Run, near Ypsilanti, Michigan, and 57,585 Pratt & Whitney R-2800 radial engines at the River Rouge plant. Ford also built 277,896 Jeeps, nearly 50 percent of the total, and all amphibious Jeeps. Lincoln's

Detroit plant built 25,332 500bhp 32-valve twin-cam engines which powered the majority of Sherman tanks and tank-destroyers. Buick built 2,507 Hellcat tank-destroyers powered by Continental engines, and over 3 million cylinder heads for Pratt & Whitney aircraft engines. Hudson was particularly involved with aircraft, making components for B-26 Marauder bombers, P-38 Lightning fighter-bombers, and P-39 Airacobra fighters. Studebaker's specialty was vehicles, including 197,678 trucks, mostly 6 x 4 and 6 x 6, and 25,124 Weasel amphibious troop carriers.

◄ CAR-HUNGRY AMERICANS HAD A CHANCE TO SEE THE FIRST POSTWAR CARS AT THE CHICAGO AUTO SHOW HELD IN SEPTEMBER 1945. THE OLDSMOBILES SEEN HERE WERE ANNOUNCED IN JULY, ALTHOUGH PRODUCTION DID NOT GET UNDER WAY UNTIL OCTOBER. THE FASTBACK STYLING IN THE FOREGROUND, AVAILABLE ON THE MORE EXPENSIVE OLDSMOBILES IN 1942, WAS EXTENDED TO ALL MODELS FOR 1946.
OLDSMOBILE HISTORICAL CENTER

Passenger car manufacture was sanctioned on July 1, 1945. Ford was first to take advantage of this, starting its production lines on July 3 and remaining the only supplier of new cars for some time. General Motors did not start up until October and then in November was hit by a 113-day strike by the United Auto Workers Union, which saw the emergence of Walter Reuther as America's foremost labor chief. Chrysler, fearing that the strike would spread and reluctant to set the lines rolling until it could be sure of continuous production, restarted even later. Only 322 Chryslers were made by the end of the year, together with 947 De Sotos, 770 Plymouths, and 420 Dodges. The independents did better, Nash starting up in September for a year's production of 6,148, Hudson on August 30 (4,735), and Packard on October 19 (2,722). Nash, in fact, was in third position for 1945, behind Ford and Chevrolet.

The year of 1946 was difficult, with strikes and shortages of materials keeping output lower than hoped for. There was no window glass in January and again in September, while March saw a

STUDEBAKER INTRODUCED NEW BODIES THROUGH THE
RANGE FOR 1953, OF WHICH THE STARLIGHT COUPES
WERE THE MOST ATTRACTIVE. DESIGNED BY ROBERT E.
BOURKE OF THE LOEWY STUDIOS, THEIR POPULARITY
WAS EMBARRASSING FOR STUDEBAKER, WHO HAD
ENVISAGED THAT SEDANS WOULD OUTSELL COUPES
BY AROUND FOUR TO ONE, WHEREAS DEMAND WAS
ALMOST PRECISELY THE OPPOSITE. THIS STARLIGHT
COUPE SOLD FOR $1,995.

OWNER: NATIONAL AUTOMOBILE MUSEUM, RENO, NEVADA

(PHOTO NICKY WRIGHT)

shortage of door locks. Then in June hood locks disappeared, and by October there were plenty of locks but no doors. Strikes among component makers were particularly damaging because they hit production of all makes. However, by the end of the year a guaranteed minimum wage and a 40-hour week were agreed upon, and industrial disputes became fewer. Passenger car output in 1946 was 2,148,699, lower than in any year since depression-hit 1938. In 1947 and 1948 it was well over the 3 million mark, and in 1949 beat all previous records, with 5,119,466 cars made.

The pent-up demand for new cars was enormous; more than half the 26 million cars in the United States were more than ten years old and well overdue for replacement. While it would be unjust to say that *any* car sold, whatever its quality, the early postwar years were a sellers' market par excellence, and all car and truck makers flourished.

With the scramble to get back into production, it is hardly surprising that there were few novelties among the 1946 models. Without exception they were warmed-over 1942 designs with modified grilles and bits of extra chromework here and there. Plymouth boasted 50 new features and improvements over its 1942 models, but these were mostly limited to new interior trims, front bumpers that wrapped around the fenders to the wheel arches, and improved synchromesh gears. Under the hoods there were improvements, thanks to wartime experience: Ford and Mercury V8 engines had new aluminum pistons, larger and higher capacity oil pumps, nickel-chrome alloy valves, and other developments that had been tried on wartime truck engines, while GM's HydraMatic drive was improved thanks to experience with tanks.

Ford and Mercury had new body styles in the form of a wood-paneled two-door convertible called the Sportsman. Made at Ford's Iron Mountain plant, the body consisted of mahogany panels attached to a steel inner frame. Otherwise the Sportsman was the same as the regular convertibles, although the rear fenders came from the 1941 sedan delivery, as the postwar fenders wrapped around too much and would have cut into the wooden trunk lid. The Sportsman convertibles were the most expensive of both the Ford and Mercury ranges, costing $1,982 with Ford badging and $2,263 as Mercurys. The latter were very rare, only 205 being made in 1946, but the Ford Sportsman sold 3,487 in three seasons, 1946–48.

The Sportsman was the idea of Henry Ford II (1917–1987), who took over as president of the Ford Motor Company from his grandfather in September 1945 (his father Edsel had died in 1943). The 28-year-old ex-naval ensign had a formidable task on his hands, for the company was heavily in debt — accounting procedures were so haphazard and primitive that in one department costs were estimated by weighing a pile of invoices on a scale. He also faced the hostility of his grandfather's henchman Harry Bennett. Within a few days he fired Bennett, who responded with the ungracious but undeniable comment: "You're taking over a billion-dollar organization here that you haven't contributed a damned thing to."

In February 1946 Henry II brought in a group of talented young men who had decided to hire themselves out as a ready-made management team. They included Charles (Tex) Thornton, at 32 one of the youngest colonels in the U.S. Army Air Force, and two academics, Ed Lundy from Princeton and Robert McNamara from the Harvard Business School, later to become U.S. Defense Secretary. Ten in all, they were nicknamed

STUDEBAKER BROUGHT OUT RADICALLY RESTYLED
CARS IN 1946, FEATURING WRAPAROUND REAR
WINDOWS ON SOME MODELS, SHORT HOODS, AND
LONG TRUNKS. IN FACT ON THE ORIGINAL CHAMPION
COUPE, HOOD AND TRUNK WERE OF ABOUT EQUAL
LENGTH, GIVING RISE TO THE NICKNAME "COMING OR
GOING STUDEBAKERS." THE BULLET-NOSE FRONT END
CAME WITH THE 1950 MODELS, WHICH ALSO HAD
COIL-AND-A-ARM INDEPENDENT FRONT SUSPENSION.

OWNER: JIM BABB   (PHOTO NICKY WRIGHT)

"the Whiz Kids." Together with accountant Ernest Breech, they set about turning Ford's fortunes around. This they did to a considerable extent, selling more than 1 million cars (including Lincoln and Mercury) in 1949, the first time the million mark had been passed since 1930. However, they never achieved their aim, which was to beat their great rival, General Motors.

Chrysler's equivalent to the Sportsman was the Town & Country, which was built in several models, closed and open. The 1946 catalog shows five styles, a roadster, a brougham, a two-door club coupe, a four-door sedan, and a convertible. The roadster was never built and only one brougham and seven club coupes saw the light of day, but the sedan and convertible went into production, the former mostly on the six-cylinder Windsor chassis, and the latter on the eight-cylinder New Yorker. In 1946 exactly 100 eight-cylinder sedans were made. Unlike the Ford Sportsman, which used wood strips on metal panels, the Town & Country had structured wood framing of white ash, with shaped plywood panels, and plenty of leather and Hylander wool graced the interior. This handwork was reflected in the price, $2,366 for the sedan, compared with $1,561 for a regular steel-bodied sedan, and $2,743 for the convertible, $550 more than was asked for the regular convertible.

There was little change in the years 1946 to 1948, except for price increases for 1948. The Town & Country models attracted a great deal of attention, and even if Chrysler made little profit on them their publicity value was excellent. Chryslers were restyled for 1949, and only the convertible was made in the Town & Country style, replaced by a hardtop for 1950. This had less wood in its construction, with ash framing on an all-steel body. Only 993 '49s and 698 '50s were made, and from 1951 onward the Town & Country name was used on station wagons.

1947 KAISER K-100 PINCONNING SPECIAL TWO-DOOR SEDAN ▼ ▶

THE LOWER-PRICED CAR IN THE KAISER-FRAZER LINE-UP, THE KAISER WAS PLANNED TO HAVE FRONT DRIVE, BUT THIS WAS NEVER IMPLEMENTED. ONLY FOUR-DOOR MODELS WERE OFFERED TO THE PUBLIC, BUT THIS ONE-OFF TWO-DOOR SEDAN WAS SPECIALLY BUILT FOR THE HANDICAPPED WIFE OF ED HUNT, HEAD OF PRODUCTION AT KAISER-FRAZER, AND NAMED FOR HUNT'S BIRTHPLACE, PINCONNING, MICHIGAN. IT HAS A SWIVELING FRONT PASSENGER SEAT TO ENABLE THE OCCUPANT TO CONVERSE WITH REAR PASSENGERS FACE-TO-FACE.

OWNER: NATIONAL AUTOMOBILE MUSEUM, RENO, NEVADA

(PHOTO NICKY WRIGHT)

GENUINE POSTWAR CARS

Although most auto manufacturers delayed their postwar designs until 1948 or later, there were two new shapes to be seen on the streets by the end of 1946. These came from Studebaker and from the new Kaiser-Frazer organization.

When Studebaker revived the prewar Champion, it was very much a stopgap model, and only 19,275 were made between December 1945 and March 1946 when it gave way to the radical-looking "coming or going" models styled by Raymond Loewy and Virgil Exner. Loewy ran an independent design studio that had been retained by Studebaker since the 1930s. As well as the short hoods and long trunks that gave the cars their nicknames, they had wraparound rear windows and the straight-through lines from front to rear fenders that would soon become universal, although at the time these were only seen on Kaiser-Frazer cars.

The box-section Studebaker frame was designed for front or rear location of the engine but, so far as is known, no rear-engined model ever reached the prototype stage. However, air- and water-cooled flat-6s were tried before opting for the familiar 80bhp 169.6-cubic-inch Champion engine, joined by the 94bhp 226.2-cubic-inch unit from the prewar Commander. The same names were used, and both models came in four-door sedan, two-door coupe, and convertible forms. Although the Champion was compact in size, at 193 inches in length and weighing 2,600–2,875 pounds, it seated three passengers on front and rear seats thanks to the full-width styling.

The new Studebakers were launched in May 1946 as 1947 models; 1946 calendar year production was 77,567 and by 1949 this had risen to 228,402, putting Studebaker in eighth place and in the lead over other independent manufacturers. Assembly took place in eleven overseas plants, and a full manufacturing plant was opened at Hamilton,

Ontario, in 1948. Sixteen years later this would keep Studebaker production going when it had ceased in the United States. The peak year for output and workforce was 1950, when more than 23,000 workers at South Bend turned out 268,229 cars and more than 50,000 trucks. Up to 1952 the styling was little changed, apart from a pointed, missile-inspired grille in 1949. The Commander engine went up to 245.6 cubic inches and 100bhp for 1949, and independent front suspension by coils replaced the transverse leaves for 1950.

The other new cars of 1946 came from a new company, the Kaiser-Frazer Corporation, which was formed on July 23, 1945, only eight days after the two founders met for the first time. Henry J. Kaiser

(1882–1967) was a millionaire sand and gravel entrepreneur who had been chairman of the Hoover Dam project in the 1930s and whose seven shipyards had built 1,490 Liberty, Victory, and other ships during World War II. He was also a car buff who had an experimental lab at Emeryville, California. Joseph W. Frazer (1892–1971) had direct auto industry experience, having been with the Chrysler Corporation from 1924 to 1939, then served as president of Willys-Overland to 1943, after which he bought into the Graham-Paige Corporation, which had ceased car making in 1941 but still had an active plant. Their joint project would be the last attempt by an independent to challenge Detroit for a significant slice of the popular car market.

The design of the car came from Frazer, or rather from Howard Darrin and Bill Stout who worked for him, and the basic lines were established before he teamed up with Kaiser. From the Emeryville studio came two ideas that were soon abandoned, front-wheel drive and a fiberglass body. The initial idea was that an inexpensive front-drive car would be made in California under the Kaiser name, and a more expensive and conventional Frazer would be made in the Graham-Paige plant in Detroit. However, Joe Frazer decided that he needed bigger facilities than Graham-Paige could provide, so he leased the enormous 1-million-square-foot Willow Run plant where Ford had built Liberator bombers.

The front-drive Kaiser and rear-drive Frazer were shown to the public at New York's Waldorf-Astoria Hotel in January 1946, although both had to be sent there by train as neither was in a state to run. It is doubtful if the front-drive Kaiser ever ran, and it was soon dropped. When deliveries to dealers began in June, the cars were basically the same, the Frazer having more luxurious trim, a dual-choke carburetor, and overdrive; it cost $185 more than the $1,868 Kaiser Special. Both cars used a Continental flathead-6 of 226-cubic-inch displacement, which gave 100bhp and a top speed of 84mph. At first the engines were bought from Continental, but later Kaiser-Frazer made them themselves, in a former Hudson plant.

With the postwar car shortage, the slab-sided and modern-looking Kaisers and Frazers sold well to start with, 144,490 in 1947 and 181,316 in 1948. More expensive models were added in the Frazer Manhattan and Kaiser Custom, whose prices were in the $2,300–$2,746 range. The lowest-priced 1948 Kaiser cost $2,244, which put it in competition with

1950 FORD CUSTOM CONVERTIBLE ▼ ▶

FORD'S FIRST POSTWAR CARS, WHICH DEBUTED IN JUNE 1948 AS 1949 MODELS, WERE RADICALLY RESTYLED BY AN OUTSIDE TEAM HEADED BY GEORGE WALKER. FORD WAS SO PLEASED WITH THE RESULTS THAT IN 1955 WALKER BECAME CHIEF DESIGNER FOR ALL FORD COMPANIES. THE 1950 MODELS WERE WIDELY FACE-LIFTED AND QUALITY WAS IMPROVED. SIXES AND EIGHTS WERE OFFERED, BOTH IN DE LUXE AND CUSTOM SERIES. THIS V8 COUPE CONVERTIBLE COST $1,948.

OWNER: ARLEN MADLAND (PHOTO NICKY WRIGHT)

1950 CHEVROLET STYLELINE COUPE ▲
LIKE MOST AMERICAN AUTO MAKERS, CHEVROLET INTRODUCED ITS NEW POSTWAR MODELS FOR THE 1949 SEASON, SO 1950 MODELS WERE LITTLE CHANGED. THERE WERE TWO LINES, THE STYLELINE, WITH PROJECTING TRUNK, AND THE FASTBACK FLEETLINE, MADE ONLY IN TWO- OR FOUR-DOOR SEDAN FORMS. PRICES WERE THE SAME AS FOR THE STYLELINE, $1,482 FOR A TWO-DOOR AND $1,529 FOR A FOUR-DOOR. THIS STYLELINE COUPE COST $1,498.
OWNER: BARNEY SMITH (PHOTO NICKY WRIGHT)

Hudson, Mercury, and the more expensive Buicks rather than with the low-priced Ford or Chevrolet. (During the war Henry Kaiser had envisaged a sort of latter-day Model T to sell at no more than $365.) Up to 1949 only four-door sedans were offered, but then new models appeared in the form of the Frazer Manhattan four-door convertible, Kaiser Virginian hardtop, and the Kaiser Traveler utility sedan. This had a hatchback at the rear, although unlike modern one-piece hatchbacks it opened in two parts, being hinged at top and bottom. The rear seat back could be folded down to give maximum carrying space and the left rear door was welded shut. Kaiser never made a station wagon, but the Traveler offered many of its advantages, while still looking like a sedan.

Kaiser-Frazer never did as well again as in 1947, when a profit of $20 million was recorded, although output for 1948 was higher. The problem was that Detroit's big guns all had new models for 1949 and suddenly the cars from Willow Run seemed old-fashioned. Always undercapitalized, Kaiser-Frazer did not have the funds to come up with a new body style until 1951, by which time sales had dropped to 99,343. Rivals like Oldsmobile and Chrysler had new, powerful V8 engines, while K-F could never afford to replace the old Continental-designed flathead-6, which was really a prewar design. The only other company using it in 1950 was taxicab maker Checker Motors.

The 1949 model year saw genuine postwar designs from all of America's auto makers. The high, prewar style bodies gave way to lower, wider styles with fenders faired into the doors, while suspensions went independent even on Fords. Few cars were completely new, though, and engines remained generally unchanged, with the notable exceptions of Cadillac and Oldsmobile, who offered their valve-in-head V8s in 1949.

The 1949 Fords, announced in June 1948, were more innovative than any since the Model A replaced the T. Engineered by Harold Youngren and styled by Richard Caleal working for consultant George Walker, they had low, wide-looking bodies with straight-through lines from front to rear fenders. Although they seemed larger all round, they were fractionally shorter and narrower than the '48s, and the roof line was 3 inches lower. They were also lighter than their predecessors by up to 500 pounds. The old beam front axle with transverse leaf suspension gave way to an independent system by coil springs and wishbones; at the rear, suspension was by longitudinal leaf springs as in most other contemporary cars. The cruciform frame was replaced by a ladder type, except on the

▼ IN 1950 THE WHITE HOUSE RENEWED ITS VEHICLE FLEET, TAKING DELIVERY OF TEN LINCOLNS, ALL ON THE 145-INCH WHEELBASE. NINE WERE LIMOUSINES WITH BODIES BY HENNEY, AND THE TENTH WAS THIS SEVEN-PASSENGER CONVERTIBLE BODIED BY DIETRICH CREATIVE INDUSTRIES OF GRAND RAPIDS, MICHIGAN. IT WAS PART OF THE WHITE HOUSE FLEET FOR 18 YEARS, SERVING PRESIDENTS TRUMAN (SEEN HERE), EISENHOWER, KENNEDY, AND JOHNSON.
FORD MOTOR COMPANY, MIRCO DE CET COLLECTION

TWO GENERATIONS OF BUICK
STATION WAGON ▲▼

THE 1952 ROADMASTER (BELOW) STILL HARKS BACK
TO THE WOODY ERA, MAKING USE OF MAHOGANY,
ASH, AND BIRCH IN ITS CONSTRUCTION. THE 1964
SKYLARK SPORTWAGON (ABOVE) WAS OF ALL-METAL
CONSTRUCTION, AND WAS A DISTINCTIVE DESIGN WITH
ITS VISTA-DOME ROOF. IT USED A WHEELBASE 5 INCHES
LONGER THAN OTHER SKYLARKS, AND CAME WITH THE
OPTION OF A 155bhp 225-CUBIC-INCH V6 OR A 210bhp
300-CUBIC-INCH V8. THE ROADMASTER USED A 320-
CUBIC-INCH STRAIGHT-8 ENGINE GIVING 170bhp.

ABOVE: GENERAL MOTORS BELOW: MIRCO DE CET COLLECTION

1950 MERCURY COUPE ▲▼

MERCURY HAD A COMPLETELY NEW BODY AND CHASSIS IN 1949, WITH X-BRACED
FRAME, INDEPENDENT FRONT SUSPENSION, AND LOWER LINES. CONSEQUENTLY, FEW
CHANGES WERE MADE FOR 1950, APART FROM A NEW INSTRUMENT PANEL AND MINOR
MODIFICATIONS TO THE GRILLE. A NEW MODEL IN MID-SEASON WAS THE MONTEREY
COUPE WITH PADDED CANVAS OR VINYL TOP AND CUSTOM LEATHER INTERIOR. THIS IS
THE STANDARD COUPE, WHICH SOLD FOR $1,980.

OWNER: ARLEN MADLAND (PHOTO NICKY WRIGHT)

convertible, and the engine was moved 5 inches forward in the frame, which enabled the rear seats to be positioned well forward of the axle, giving a much better ride. Just about the only major components unchanged were the engines, which remained the familiar 95bhp six and 100bhp flathead V8. Ford did not adopt a valve-in-head V8 until 1954. A planned compact Ford with a small V8 engine was never made in the United States, but became the French-built Ford Vedette.

Mercury and Lincoln accompanied their sister marque with new models for 1949, using the same suspension and new bodies based on wartime-styled models by Gregorie. Mercury had a larger V8 engine of 255.4 cubic inches and 110bhp, while Lincoln abandoned its V12 in favor of a new 336.7-cubic-inch 152bhp V8. Mercurys became heavier and more expensive, taking on the role of junior Lincolns rather than senior Fords; this reinforced the decision taken by Henry Ford II in 1945 to create a Lincoln-Mercury Division.

General Motors' cars were less radically styled than Ford's, but were substantially changed in appearance. All had the wider, lower look, with straight-through lines from front to rear fenders, and low, horizontal grilles. Among the styling highlights was Buick's Riviera coupe, a hardtop styled to look like a convertible. The idea is said to have originated with Sarah Ragsdale, wife of assistant body engineer Ed Ragsdale, who drove a convertible because she liked its sporty lines but never had the top down as she said it spoiled her hairdo. Another Buick stylist, Ned Nickles, might have disputed that, as he had been working on the idea since 1945 and it was a feature of the seven Chrysler Town & Country coupe prototypes built in 1946. Nevertheless Buick was the first to put the

idea into large-scale production. There were also Cadillac and Oldsmobile hardtops, known respectively as the Coupe de Ville and Holiday.

Another characteristic of 1949 Buicks was the row of portholes just ahead of the front doors. These were Nickles' idea. He had cut them in his own 1947 Buick convertible, rigging up lights in them which flashed at increasing speed as the engine revved up. On being told that Nickles had ruined his car with these portholes, Buick's general manager Harlow Curtice asked to see them and was so impressed that he ordered them to be part of the 1949 models, three on Supers and four on Roadmasters. This became the quickest way of identifying the top model and doubtless encouraged the sales of Roadmasters. With some changes in shape, portholes were Buick features until 1958, and again on some models from 1960 into the early 1970s.

The first of the new GM bodies came from Cadillac and Oldsmobile, introduced on their 1948 ranges. Together with the 1949 Chevrolet, Buick, and Pontiac, they looked remarkably alike in

1951 OLDSMOBILE 88 SEDAN ▲▼
A NEW MODEL FOR 1949, THE OLDS 88 COMBINED THE NEW ROCKET V8 ENGINE WITH THE LIGHTWEIGHT FUTURAMIC 76 BODIES, SO WAS QUITE A PERFORMER. SIX BODIES WERE OFFERED ORIGINALLY, BUT BY 1951 THE REGULAR 88 WAS DOWN TO TWO, A TWO-DOOR AND A FOUR-DOOR SEDAN. THE SUPER 88, OF WHICH THIS IS AN EXAMPLE, WAS MADE IN FIVE STYLES, INCLUDING A HARDTOP COUPE AND A CONVERTIBLE.

OWNER: BILL GOODSENE (PHOTO NICKY WRIGHT)

1949 CADILLAC COUPE DE VILLE ▲▶

CADILLACS WERE UPDATED IN TWO STAGES BETWEEN 1947 AND 1949. NEW BODIES APPEARED FOR 1948, AND THE 1949 SEASON SAW THE TREND-SETTING OVERHEAD VALVE V8 ENGINE, WHICH GAVE 160bhp FROM A SMALLER DISPLACEMENT THAN ITS 140bhp PREDECESSOR. LARGELY ON THE STRENGTH OF THE ENGINE, THE 1949 CADILLACS WERE CHOSEN AS *MOTOR TREND* MAGAZINE'S FIRST CAR OF THE YEAR. THE SERIES 62 COUPE DE VILLE WAS A NEW STYLE FOR 1949, AND COST $3,496. ONLY 2,150 WERE BUILT, MAKING IT THE RAREST STYLE IN THE 1949 RANGE.

OWNER: LES STERLING (PHOTO NICKY WRIGHT)

1954 CHRYSLER NEW YORKER DE LUXE SEDAN ▼

IN 1954 CHRYSLER STYLING WAS STILL INFLUENCED BY KAUFMAN T. KELLER'S DEMAND FOR PLENTY OF HEADROOM. "MANY OF YOU CALIFORNIANS MAY HAVE OUTGROWN THE HABIT," HE TOLD A STANFORD UNIVERSITY AUDIENCE IN 1948, "BUT THERE ARE PARTS OF THIS COUNTRY, CONTAINING MILLIONS OF PEOPLE, WHERE BOTH THE MEN AND THE LADIES ARE IN THE HABIT OF GETTING BEHIND THE WHEEL, OR ON THE BACK SEAT, WEARING HATS." THIS 1954 NEW YORKER WAS ONE OF THE LAST "HIGH-HAT" CARS, FOR THE NEXT YEAR'S MODELS WERE STYLED BY VIRGIL EXNER, WHO GAVE CHRYSLER A LOWER APPEARANCE CALLED "THE 100 MILLION DOLLAR LOOK."

OWNER: VIRGIL MYERS (PHOTO NICKY WRIGHT)

profile, and in fact the same doors were shared by Buick, Cadillac, and Oldsmobile. The 1948 Cadillacs were the first to sport fins at the back of the rear fenders, although these were quite modest compared with later appendages. Fins became as much a Cadillac trademark as portholes were for Buick. Although Cadillac's bodies were new for 1948, their engines remained the familiar 346-cubic-inch flathead V8s that had been around since 1936.

In 1949 both Cadillac and Oldsmobile Divisions introduced their all-new valve-in-head high-compression V8 engines. Cadillac's displaced 331 cubic inches and developed 160bhp, while the Oldsmobile Rocket was slightly smaller at 303 cubic inches and 135bhp. With a compression ratio

of 7.25:1, these engines marked the beginning of the horsepower race that pushed outputs to more than 300bhp in less than ten years. Buick received its new V8 in 1953, Chevrolet and Pontiac in 1955. Pontiac replaced its venerable straight-8, which was the last engine of this layout to be made in the United States.

Chrysler Division cars were less radically restyled than their rivals, as Chrysler boss Kaufman T. Keller favored a fairly high roof line. An inveterate hat wearer, he stuck to the principle that the roof should be high enough to accommodate a man wearing a hat. "We build cars to sit in," he said, "not to piss over." The result was generally uninspired styling for the 1949 Chrysler, De Soto, Dodge, and Plymouth; the six-window sedans were

▲ WHETHER THE "STEP DOWN" HUDSON WAS AMERICA'S MOST BEAUTIFUL CAR IS DEBATABLE, BUT IT WAS CERTAINLY ONE OF THE MOST INNOVATIVE DESIGNS OF THE POSTWAR ERA.

MIRCO DE CET COLLECTION

replaced by four-window models with larger trunks in all four lines, although six-window eight-passenger sedans and limousines were continued in the bigger Chrysler ranges, Windsor and Crown Imperial. Dodge advertised its new models as "higher inside, lower outside, shorter outside, longer inside." The regular models were shorter by only 1.6 inches, but there was a new Wayfarer series, which was 8.2 inches shorter. A new model in the Wayfarer range was a two/three-passenger roadster in the 1930s idiom, even down to its detachable windows, although these were soon discontinued. Roadster production in 1949 was 5,420 out of a total of 298,399 Dodges made that year. Another new style was Plymouth's De Luxe Suburban, a two-door station wagon with no wood trim.

Among the independents, Hudson and Nash both had dramatically styled new models. Hudson's, announced in October 1947 as a 1948 model, featured semi-unit construction and a very low line, which gave it the nickname the "step down" Hudson. It had been planned before the war and in 1941 chief stylist Frank Spring had shown a prototype to Hudson president A. E. Barit. The conservative Barit had growled "too low," and the prototype was consigned to the roof of the Hudson plant where it rusted away for the duration of the war. In about 1946 Spring retrieved his car, smartened it up, and re-presented it to Barit, who drove it home one evening and was so delighted that he ordered it into production.

The new Hudsons were only 60 inches high, 7 inches lower than a Buick and 6 inches lower than a Chrysler, and had the lowest center of gravity of any American car. The floor dropped below the frame sides, being the lowest part of the structure. There was still a frame, although it was welded to the body, giving semi-unit construction rather than a full monocoque. The rear wheels were actually mounted inside the side members of the frame. They were big cars, 207 inches long and 77 inches wide, but had excellent roadability. The latter was praised by the British magazine, *The Motor*, which often criticized American cars for

1952 HUDSON COMMODORE EIGHT SEDAN ◄
HUDSON OFFERED FOUR LINES FOR THE 1952 SEASON: PACEMAKER, WASP AND COMMODORES SIXES, AND COMMODORE EIGHT. ALL HAD THE SAME GENERAL APPEARANCE AS THE FIRST "STEP DOWNS" OF 1948, WHICH LASTED UNTIL AFTER THE 1954 MERGER WITH NASH. AS WELL AS FOUR-DOOR SEDANS, THERE WERE COUPES AND CONVERTIBLES. COMMODORE SIXES AND EIGHTS SHARED A 124-INCH WHEELBASE AND WERE ALMOST IDENTICAL IN APPEARANCE APART FROM UPHOLSTERY, CARPETS, AND "6" OR "8" ABOVE THE FRONT WHEELS. THIS EIGHT COST $2,769. THE YEARS 1951–53 SAW HUDSON DOMINANT IN STOCK CAR RACING, WITH 105 WINS IN MAJOR NASCAR EVENTS.

OWNER: DICK GINTHER (PHOTO NICKY WRIGHT)

their soft suspension and habit of rolling on corners. Unchanged was the familiar 128bhp flathead straight-8 engine, although this was supplemented by a new 123bhp six, also a flathead. At 262 cubic inches, this had a larger displacement than the eight. Four-door sedans, two-door coupes, and convertibles were offered in both series.

Although "step down" prices were well up on those of the 1947 Hudsons, sales were up too, from just over 100,000 to 143,697 for the calendar year 1948. They dipped slightly in 1949, when Hudson was hit by several strikes, including one in August occasioned by a heatwave. The basic design of the "step down" was not changed until 1955, when the 1954 merger with Nash led to Hudsons being made at the Nash Kenosha plant. A larger engine was introduced in 1951, a 308-cubic-inch flathead-6 giving 145bhp, which enabled Hudson to dominate stock car racing for three years.

Nash's postwar car was just as striking as Hudson's, but with less satisfactory handling. Its official name was Airflyte, but it soon acquired the nickname "bathtub," due to its all-enveloping fastback styling with partial fairings over front and rear wheels. It featured full-unit construction, a curved, one-piece windshield, and a pod above the steering column that contained all the instruments, known as the Uniscope. Front seats folded back to make a double bed, as in previous Nashes. The Airflyte was available in two series, with names carried over from earlier models, the 600 and the Ambassador. The 600 rode on a 112-inch wheelbase with a small six engine of only 172.6 cubic inches, while the Ambassador had a 121-inch wheelbase and was powered by a 234.8-cubic-inch six with overhead valves. Both these engines were carried over from the 1946–48 Nashes, and were continued until 1955 when the Ambassador was given a Packard V8 engine. Because of the unit construction, there were not many body variations in the Airflyte range, only two- and four-door sedans and a two-door brougham, with no convertibles. In 1950 Nash brought out a compact car, the Rambler, to be described later in this chapter.

The only other independent, eventually to become Studebaker's partner, was Packard. The venerable Detroit company abandoned the luxury field when it sold the dies for the big 180 series to the Soviet Union, so it entered the postwar market

1947 PACKARD CLIPPER CUSTOM SUPER 8 SEDAN ▼

THE CLIPPER LINE WAS INTRODUCED IN MID-1941 AND WAS A RADICAL DEPARTURE FROM PREVIOUS PACKARD STYLING, WHICH HAD BEEN MORE CONSERVATIVE THAN OTHER DETROIT MAKES. POSTWAR PACKARDS WERE ALL CLIPPERS, AND WERE MADE IN FOUR SERIES, A SIX AND THREE EIGHTS. THE CUSTOM SUPER 8 WAS THE TOP OF THE RANGE, AND UNLIKE OTHER CLIPPERS CARRIED NO IDENTIFYING FRONT DOOR SCRIPTS; IT HAD LUXURIOUS INTERIOR TRIM, WITH SPECIAL CARPETING, RICH BROADCLOTH AND LEATHER UPHOLSTERY, AND IMITATION WOOD PANELING. THIS SEDAN COST $3,274. A BASIC CLIPPER SIX COULD BE HAD FOR $1,745.

OWNER: JOHN J. POVINELLI (PHOTO NICKY WRIGHT)

1948 CHEVROLET STATION WAGON ▲
THE TRADITIONAL "WOODY" STATION WAGON
WAS STILL PART OF THE CHEVROLET RANGE IN 1948.
THIS EIGHT-PASSENGER MODEL IN THE FLEETMASTER
SERIES WAS THE MOST EXPENSIVE CHEVROLET
THAT YEAR, AT $2,013.

(PHOTO NICKY WRIGHT)

1947 CHRYSLER TOWN & COUNTRY SEDAN ▶
THE TOWN & COUNTRY WAS MORE OF A GENUINE WOODY THAN THE FORD SPORTSMAN,
FOR THE FRAME WAS OF WHITE ASH, WITH PLYWOOD PANELS. ALTHOUGH FIVE BODY
STYLES WERE PLANNED, ONLY THE CONVERTIBLE AND THE FOUR-DOOR SEDAN WERE
PRODUCED IN ANY NUMBERS. THIS SIX-CYLINDER SEDAN WAS MADE FOR THE THREE YEARS
OF THE TOWN & COUNTRY'S LIFETIME, 1946—1948, WITH 3,994 DELIVERED. ONLY 100 EIGHT-
CYLINDER SEDANS WERE MADE, ALL OF THEM IN 1946. THIS 1947 SEDAN COST $2,713.

OWNER: BLAINE JENKINS (PHOTO NICKY WRIGHT)

1947 FORD SPORTSMAN CONVERTIBLE ◄
THE SPORTSMAN WAS HENRY FORD II's IDEA OF
ADDING SOME SPICE TO THE IMMEDIATE POST-WORLD
WAR II CARS, BEFORE ALL-NEW MODELS COULD APPEAR.
DEVELOPED FROM BOB GREGORIE'S WARTIME
SKETCHES, THE SPORTSMAN HAD WHITE ASH AN
MAHOGANY PANELS OVER A STEEL FRAME. THEY
ATTRACTED PLENTY OF ATTENTION AT FORD
DEALERSHIPS, BUT A PRICE THAT WAS $500 MORE
THAN THAT OF THE REGULAR CONVERTIBLE WAS A
DETERRENT TO SALES. ONLY 1,209 SPORTSMEN
WERE MADE IN 1946, 2,250 IN 1947, AND 28 IN 1948.
THE COMPANION MERCURY MODEL WAS EVEN
RARER, FOR ONLY 205 WERE MADE.

OWNER: BLAINE JENKINS (PHOTO NICKY WRIGHT)

1949 CROSLEY CD WAGON ▲

CROSLEY WAS THE ONLY SUCCESSFUL MAKER OF SMALL CARS IN THE POSTWAR ERA AND EVEN IT
EXPERIENCED A BAD SLUMP IN SALES IN 1949, TO ONLY 7,431 FROM 29,184 THE PREVIOUS YEAR.
THIS STATION WAGON WAS THE MOST POPULAR OF FOUR STYLES, WITH 3,803 DELIVERED.

OWNER: AUBURN-CORD-DUESENBERG MUSEUM (PHOTO NICKY WRIGHT)

with the middle-class Clipper, priced from $1,680 for the cheapest six to $3,047 for a Custom Super Eight sedan. Wheelbases were 120 or 127 inches, although there was an extended wheelbase model in the Super Eight series that ran to 148 inches and was available as a limousine at $4,496. For 1948 the Clippers were restyled, with longer hoods, bolder grilles, and rounded styling; like Nash's Airflyte, they earned the epithet of "bathtub" or "pregnant elephant." There were three series, Standard Eight, Super Eight, and Custom Eight, with engines of 288, 327, and 356 cubic inches respectively. With a 165bhp output, the latter was America's most powerful engine until the arrival of the 180bhp Chrysler hemi-head V8 for 1951.

Convertibles were back for the first time since 1942, and a new style in the Standard Eight range was the Station Sedan, a woody-styled car which nevertheless used mostly sedan body stampings. The only items of wood about the exterior were the bolted-on ribs over simulated woodgrain panels on the doors. These required fungus-killing treatment and regular varnishing, as did the wooden cargo deck inside, so the Station Sedan needed as much upkeep as a real woody. At $3,350 it was the most expensive Standard Eight by a wide margin, costing more than many Super Eights. It was listed through the 1950 season, after which totally new Packard bodies were introduced.

A MINOR LEAGUE REVOLT AGAINST DETROIT

In 1949 the Big Three and the major independents accounted for 19 marques, but there were, in theory, at least 40 for American car buyers to choose from. All over the country postwar euphoria saw a host of mainly small concerns making small cars. Together they made up what *Popular Mechanics* magazine called "a minor league revolt against Detroit." Not that they caused many headaches in the Motor City; with few exceptions, the newcomers were not competing in the mass-produced family car market, but catered to what turned out to be a non-existent demand for small shopping cars, or what would be called 30 years later the sub-compact class.

Typical of the smallest class was the San Diego-built Towne Shopper, a doorless open two-

passenger runabout with a horizontally-opposed twin Onan engine selling at just under a dollar a pound ($595 for a 600-pound car). Others included the Airway, also from San Diego, a three-passenger sedan or two passenger coupe with aluminum and plastic body and two-cylinder engine, and the Brogan three wheeler from Rossmoyne, Ohio. Slightly larger were the Del Mar, a five-passenger convertible powered by a 162-cubic-inch Continental engine, and the Gregory, a real weirdo with a rear-mounted Continental engine driving by shaft to the front wheels.

More serious ventures which ultimately came to nothing were the Keller and Playboy. The Keller originated in San Diego in 1945 as the Bobbi-Kar, a rear-engined runabout in the Towne Shopper class, powered by a 16hp Briggs & Stratton engine. This was soon replaced by a 25hp Hercules four, and in this form it attracted the attention of ex-Studebaker sales vice-president George Keller. He convinced a group of Alabama investors that the car would be better produced in their state, where there was a lot of unemployment due to closure of wartime aircraft factories. The cars to be produced at Huntsville under the Keller name were a rear-engined convertible, essentially the four-cylinder Bobbi-Kar renamed, and a front-engined station wagon with a 49hp 162-cubic-inch Continental engine. The Huntsville plant was an assembly operation, for practically all components of the Keller were bought out; it had Ross steering, Wagner brakes, and a Carter carburetor, the transmission was the same as that in a 1941 Studebaker, the wheels were shared with the Crosley, and so on. The only parts made by Keller were the seats and the wooden station wagon body.

By September 1949 Keller Motors Corporation had signed up 1,523 dealerships, but only 18 prototypes had been made. The heart attack that killed George Keller on October 4 proved a fatal blow for the company, which had been promoted on the man rather than the car. No more Kellers were made, and finances were so tight that the Hotel Buckingham in New York was forced to sell the Keller on display in the lobby to cover outstanding bills. The design had a short further life in Belgium, where George Keller had acquired a dealership, Poelmans and Merksen of Antwerp. A few station wagons, sold under the name Pullman,

were assembled at this European location.

The Playboy also started as a rear-engined convertible, with all-independent suspension as well. One prototype was built in this form, by designer Charles Thomas, but by the time he had obtained financial backing for its manufacture, the engine had moved to the front and suspension was by conventional semi-elliptic springs at the rear, although at the front it was still independent by horizontal coil springs. Backing came from Buffalo Packard dealer Louis Horwitz and service station owner Norman Richardson. They started Playboy production in the old Brunn coachbuilding plant in Buffalo, with 125 workers assembling the cars by hand. In 1948 Playboy Motor Car Corporation leased a huge former aero-engine plant at Tonawanda, New York, which was too large, just as the Brunn premises had been too small. The administration building alone offered double the space the Playboy needed.

The Playboy price was set at $985, which seemed good value compared with the Ford Super De Luxe convertible at $1,740, but this was only when comparing one convertible with another. Playboy was aiming at the bottom end of the market, regardless of body style. Here a basic Ford De Luxe six two-door sedan cost $1,212 and a similar Chevrolet $1,313. It is doubtful if Playboy could have held the price at $985, and if the $1,000 or $1,100 mark had been broached, the Playboy's price tag would have been perilously close to the Big Three, which produced much more substantial cars. However, the sale of Playboy stock was hit by the Tucker scandal, and despite plans to merge sales operations with Kaiser-Frazer, Horwitz filed for bankruptcy in July 1948. Playboy production was just 97 cars.

Crosley's postwar history was much more of a success story. Among its many wartime contracts was one to make a copper-brazed six-cylinder engine for powering generators, and Powel Crosley built a four-cylinder adaptation of this for his postwar car. It displaced only 44 cubic inches, developed 26.5bhp, and weighed only 59 pounds. Unusual was the single overhead camshaft, the first use of this on an American car since the demise of Stutz in 1935. The car had an all-new body style, with a slab-sided two-door sedan and rolltop sedan. Despite the absence of synchromesh in the three-speed transmission, the little Crosleys sold well, 4,999 in 1946 and 19,344 in 1947 when a station wagon was added. Crosley's best year was 1948, with 29,184 passenger cars sold, as well as 2,411 vans and pick-ups. Of the cars, the great majority, 23,489, were station wagons, indicating where Crosley's best market lay.

The only dark cloud on the horizon was the copper-brazed (COBRA) engine, where electrolysis was causing small holes to appear in the block, letting the cooling water escape. There was no way in which the process could be stopped, nor could the holes be repaired, so after a number of engines had been rebuilt at the factory, a switch was made to a cast-iron block (CIBA).

As the postwar sellers' market evaporated, so Crosley's sales dived to 7,431 in 1949 and 6,792 in 1950. The range was enlivened by the Hotshot, a low-built doorless two-passenger roadster on an 85-inch wheelbase, 5 inches longer than other Crosleys. Top speed was 77mph, although tuned competition versions could exceed 90mph. Special versions of the Hotshot competed at Le Mans and at Sebring, winning the Index of Performance there in 1951. In 1951 the Hotshot was joined by the Super Sport, the same car with doors and a 10:1 compression ratio. Only 2,498 sports cars were made in four seasons, 1949–52. Another new model was a small, Jeep-like vehicle with six forward and two reverse speeds, and optional dual rear wheels. Named the FarmOroad, it could be fitted with a plow or disk harrow or tow a mower. Crosley sales dwindled through 1951 and 1952, with Powel Crosley putting in $3 million of his own money, but labor costs rose more than the price he could charge for the car. This had risen from $888 in 1947 to $1,033 five years later. On July 3, 1952, Crosley closed his plant and America's most successful small car was no more. The FarmOroad design was revised by Crofton Marine Engineering of San Diego in 1959, and about 250 were sold under the name Crofton Bug.

Among all the small manufacturers who sought a place in the sun of the immediate postwar years, only one proposed a full-sized six-passenger sedan which could have mounted a serious challenge to Detroit. His name was Preston Thomas Tucker (1903–56). Having started his working life as an office boy for Cadillac engineer D. McCall White,

he went on to become a policeman, a salesman for Dodge and Studebaker, and a brewery official. During World War II he made a lot of money from a gun turret he designed, and this was the basis of the finance for his postwar car.

He had many discussions about the car with the famous race car designer Harry Miller, and when Miller died in 1943 the basic layout of the Tucker car had been decided, or so said Ben Parsons who joined Tucker in 1945 to, as he put it, "just clean up" the design. This was over-modest, for Parsons was responsible for the radical flat-6 engine and all the chassis engineering. The body was designed by former Auburn-Cord-Duesenberg stylist Alex Tremulis. Miller had suggested the rear engine location, and that it should be a flat-6; its enormous displacement (589 cubic inches) was Parsons' idea,

the theory being that it would be a really low-stressed unit turning at no more than 1,800rpm even when the car was at its maximum of 110mph. At 60mph the engine would be turning at 1,000rpm. The design was full of advanced features, including fuel injection, hemispherical combustion chambers, and hydraulic valve actuation which used columns of oil in place of cams and pushrods. The idea was that the absence of mechanical valve train would enable Parsons to design an ideal cylinder head. Unfortunately the valves wouldn't open until sufficient oil pressure had been pumped up by the engine, which clearly wouldn't start unless the valves could open. This was overcome by using the massive 24-volt battery for several seconds, but it was never satisfactory. Drive to the rear wheels was by two torque converters.

1948 TUCKER SEDAN ▼▶
ALTHOUGH PLENTY OF COMPACTS, SUB-COMPACTS, AND SHOPPING CARS CHALLENGED DETROIT
IN THE EARLY POSTWAR YEARS, THE ONLY FULL-SIZED SIX-PASSENGER SEDAN TO DO SO CAME FROM PRESTON
TUCKER. THE ORIGINAL DESIGN CALLED FOR A 589-CUBIC-INCH FLAT-6 ENGINE, BUT THE POWER UNIT ACTUALLY
USED WAS MUCH SMALLER, AT 334 CUBIC INCHES, ABOUT THE SAME AS A CONTEMPORARY V8 CADILLAC.
ITS 166bhp GAVE A TOP SPEED OF 120mph, BUT THE CONCENTRATION OF WEIGHT AT THE REAR OF THE CAR
MADE FOR TRICKY HANDLING. ONLY 51 TUCKERS WERE MADE, OF WHICH THIS IS #47.
OWNER: GILMORE CAR MUSEUM, KALAMAZOO, MICHIGAN (PHOTO NICKY WRIGHT)

Away from the engine, the Tucker Torpedo was no less radical, with all-independent suspension by rubber, disk brakes, seat belts, a popout windshield, and a third headlight that turned into corners. Only one chassis and one full-bodied car were made in original form, and subsequent Tuckers were more conventional, although the low (49-inch) body and cyclops headlight remained. Parsons' engine was replaced by a much smaller flat-6 made by Air Cooled Motors (formerly Franklin) of Syracuse, N.Y. Converted to water cooling, it displaced 334.1 cubic inches, about the same as a V8 Cadillac, and gave 166bhp at 3,200rpm. The torque converters gave way to a preselective transmission as used in the Cord 810; Tucker scoured junkyards to locate these for the first production cars, although later he made his own, based on the Cord design, and called them the Y-1. The seat belts went too; Tucker was strongly in favor of them but his vice-president of sales, Fred Rockelman, said that putting belts in a car implied that it was unsafe to begin with. However, the value of belts was shown when a test driver at Indianapolis rolled a Tucker several times and stepped out completely unscathed. Top speed was around 120mph, and in 1954 a Tucker out-accelerated an Oldsmobile 88, the hottest mass-produced car of the late 1940s, at the Pomona Strip, California.

For making his new car Tucker leased the world's biggest building under one roof, running to 93 acres, with two foundries and 30 to 40 separate cafeterias. Located in Chicago and even bigger than Kaiser-Frazer's Willow Run plant, this was the building that had been used by Dodge to build B-29 aircraft engines, and came with more machine tools than the whole of Switzerland. Before he could use even a fraction of this space for car production, Tucker ran into problems with the Securities Exchange Commission, the government agency that regulates the stock market. Unhappy about many of Tucker's promises, the SEC OK'd the offer of $20 million stock, but warned the public to be cautious. Tucker was also required to pay $500,000 as his first year's rent on the factory to its owners, the War Assets Administration. This wasn't too onerous as stock sold well at first, but Tucker made a great mistake in promising in September 1947 that by March 1948 he would be making 1,000 cars a day, a clear impossibility.

To obtain desperately needed cash Tucker applied for a loan to the Reconstruction Finance Corporation, a government body that helped companies to re-establish themselves after war work. The RFC asked the SEC for advice; don't do it, said the SEC, so the RFC didn't. From early 1948 things went from bad to worse for Preston Tucker; he was investigated by Michigan Senator Homer Ferguson, and suspected that Ferguson was motivated by Detroit to sabotage his efforts to establish a rival marque. The influential radio commentator Drew Pearson said that the car was a hoax, that only one had been built, out of Oldsmobile parts, and that it couldn't back up (this last accusation was true of the original prototype because fluid couplings had been used instead of the planned torque converters with reverse stators). At the time of the broadcast, Tucker had built at least eight cars, and he rushed three to Washington where he parked them outside Pearson's office. With his attorney he asked Pearson to look out of his window and retract the statement, but Pearson refused to move from his desk.

Confidence in Tucker stock, and in his car, fell, and dealers began suing him for not providing cars for them to sell. Only 51 Tuckers were ever built, and everything in the enormous factory was auctioned off in 1950, bringing in only 18 cents on the dollar. Tucker later tried to make a popular-priced car in Brazil. He died of lung cancer on December 26, 1956.

Two frequently made charges about Tucker deserve attention: that he was a fraud more interested in making money than cars, and that his woes were the result of Detroit's big guns being out to get him. In 1972 *Special-Interest Autos* magazine put the question of fraud or hoax to seven men qualified to speak on the subject, from former associates Ben Parsons and Alex Tremulis to General Motors president Ed Cole and experienced journalists John R. Bond, Maurice Hendry, and Karl Ludvigsen. No one upheld the suggestion of fraud, which had been started by Drew Pearson and others, but there was a general feeling that Tucker was sadly short of auto industry experience and that he was too enthusiastic about untried designs. Too much of his limited capital was wasted on gimmicks such as the torque converter. Also he misread the market; his car was undoubtedly way ahead of the competition, but the American public did not want what he had to offer. If the engineering and marketing might of General Motors could not make a success of the rear-engine flat-6 Corvair, what hope was there for Preston Tucker?

The suggestion that Tucker scared the daylights out of Detroit and that they resorted to underhanded methods to suppress him is equally improbable. For one thing, the late 1940s were a sellers' market and Detroit was too busy obtaining steel to meet the enormous pent-up demand for new cars to worry about a way-out design from an unknown. The Tucker was projected to sell at $2,450, so it would have been up against the Buick Roadmaster and Chrysler New Yorker, both of which appealed to traditional buyers. Kaiser-Frazer might have worried Detroit, although not for long; Tucker could hardly have cost all the Big Three executives five minutes' sleep between them.

Special-Interest Autos editor Mike Lamm summed it up as well as anyone: "Preston Tucker," he said, "was essentially a small-time promotor who'd gone big-time. He was out of his pond."

COMPACTS AND THE CONTINUING DECLINE OF THE INDEPENDENTS

In recent years the American motorist has become accustomed to a variety of sizes and ranges within each make—sub-compacts, compacts, pony cars, intermediates, and so on. Up to 1950 such variety was practically unknown; a typical make like Oldsmobile had three series, 76, 88, and 98, with two different engines, a six for the 76 and a V8 for the others, but they looked almost alike, and differences in size were very small, an extra 2.5 inches on the wheelbase and 2 inches on the front tread between the bottom and top of the range. Among the popular makes in 1950, Ford had two engines and a single wheelbase, while Chevrolet and Plymouth made do with a single engine and wheelbase.

In the 1930s several companies had tried making smaller cars, often under different names, such as Studebaker's Rockne, Buick's Marquette, and Marmon's Roosevelt, but the only one that had any lasting success was the Studebaker Champion, made from 1939, which differed in styling as well as size from the big Studebakers. Studebaker was, of course, an independent company (not part of the Big Three and not even Detroit-based), and the three small cars which emerged in the early 1950s, and of the size which would later be called "compacts," also came from independents.

Nash's Rambler was firmly supported by the company president George Mason, who reasoned

1952 ALLSTATE MODEL A-2304 SEDAN ▲▶
THE ALLSTATE WAS THE SECOND ATTEMPT BY SEARS ROEBUCK TO MARKET ITS OWN BRAND OF AUTOMOBILE (THE FIRST WAS THE SEARS MOTOR BUGGY OF 1908-1912). BUILT BY KAISER-FRAZER FOR SEARS, THE ALLSTATE WAS A HENRY J WITH A MODIFIED GRILLE AND BETTER QUALITY UPHOLSTERY, USING SEARS' OWN BRAND OF SPARK PLUGS, BATTERIES, AND TIRES. THE CHEAPEST ALLSTATE UNDERCUT THE HENRY J BY JUST $12, BUT ON THE WHOLE SEARS CUSTOMERS PAID SLIGHTLY MORE THAN THOSE WHO BOUGHT FROM K-F DEALERS. THIS SEDAN HAS THE FOUR-CYLINDER 68bhp WILLYS ENGINE, BUT THE 80bhp SIX WAS ALSO AVAILABLE.
OWNER: NATIONAL AUTOMOBILE MUSEUM, RENO, NEVADA (PHOTO NICKY WRIGHT)

that an independent car maker had to be different, to offer something not available from the Big Three. He also thought that the reason small cars had generally failed in America in the past was that they sold on price, and therefore marked down the owners as people of limited means. If you could get people to buy small cars because they wanted them, not because they could afford nothing else, you could capture a useful slice of the market.

This philosophy gave rise to the Rambler, regarded as a separate marque within the Nash Corporation and for which the name of a Nash predecessor made from 1902 to 1913 was revived. Launched in April 1950, it had a 100-inch wheelbase unitary construction body which bore a family resemblance to the bigger "bathtub" Nashes, with partially covered front as well as rear wheels, and was powered by the 172.6-cubic-inch 600 engine. Initially, the only model was a convertible with a price tag of $1,808; this was America's second lowest-priced convertible, after the Crosley, and cheaper than Ford or Chevrolet convertibles. It was, however, several hundred dollars above the lowest-priced Chevrolet or Ford sedan, so it escaped the label of being a cheap car. Its image was that of a chic second car for well-off suburbanites, and first year sales were an encouraging, although not spectacular, 9,330 convertibles and 1,712 station wagons (introduced in June 1950).

A "Country Club" hardtop was added to the 1951 Rambler range, and sales went up to 70,002, more than 36 percent of total Nash sales. The original Rambler never did as well again, being hit by rival compacts from Kaiser, Hudson, and Willys, and after 1955 it was dropped. However, three years later the new president George Romney relaunched the car under the name Rambler American, and this time it really was a basic automobile, offered only as a sedan and business coupe. By then George Mason was dead, and so was Nash, which had merged with Hudson in 1954 to form American Motors. All cars were called Ramblers, but the American remained the compact version and sold very well in the years 1959–61, helping Rambler into third place, behind Chevrolet and Ford, in 1960 and 1961. Its success undoubtedly influenced the Big Three into speeding up the launch of their own compact

designs in time for the 1960 auto season.

The Rambler's rivals from Kaiser, Hudson, and Willys were less stylish and aimed more at the economy market than the chic suburbanite. Henry Kaiser had dreamed of a really low-priced car, a latter-day Model T, before he launched his full-sized cars in 1946. He spoke of a target price of $385, which was quite unrealistic by any standards, but it showed that he thought a car could be sold on price alone. This was the thinking behind the Henry J, launched for 1951 as a two-door sedan on a 100-inch wheelbase (the same as the Rambler), with a choice of engines, 68bhp 134.2-cubic-inch four-cylinder or 80bhp 161-cubic-inch six. Both engines were bought from Willys, the four being that which powered the Jeep, although Kaiser did not disclose this in its publicity. The target price was $1,195 and the Henry J was not much above this when it went on sale at $1,363 for the four and $1,499 for the six.

Unfortunately a basic Ford six two-door coupe cost less than a Henry J four ($1,324) and was also a full-sized car from an established maker. Many Henry J owners complained of poor body

1950 NASH RAMBLER ▲
BORN OF PRESIDENT GEORGE ROMNEY'S BELIEF THAT INDEPENDENT AUTO MAKERS NEEDED TO OFFER SOMETHING DIFFERENT FROM THE BIG THREE IF THEY WERE TO GAIN A NICHE IN THE MARKET, THE NASH RAMBLER SHARED THE "BATHTUB" STYLING OF THE LARGER NASHES, BUT HAD A 100-INCH WHEELBASE. AT $1,808 IT WAS AMERICA'S SECOND LOWEST-PRICED CONVERTIBLE AFTER THE CROSLEY, WHICH WAS HARDLY IN THE SAME LEAGUE.

MOTOR VEHICLE MANUFACTURERS' ASSOCIATION

1953 WILLYS AERO SEDAN ▲
STYLED BY PHIL WRIGHT AND ENGINEERED BY CLYDE PATON, THE AERO WAS THE FIRST WILLYS SEDAN MADE SINCE 1942. A COMPACT IN THE RAMBLER/HENRY J MARKET, IT HAD GOOD PERFORMANCE AND FUEL ECONOMY, BUT WAS EXPENSIVE, COSTING MORE THAN A FULL-SIZE FORD OR CHEVROLET; 1953 PRICES RAN FROM $1,646 FOR A LARK TWO-DOOR SEDAN WITH 72bhp FOUR-CYLINDER L-HEAD ENGINE TO $2,157 FOR THE EAGLE HARDTOP WITH 90bhp SIX-CYLINDER F-HEAD ENGINE. THIS WAS $106 MORE THAN A CHEVROLET BEL AIR HARDTOP.

NICK GEORGANO COLLECTION

workmanship, and even of windows breaking if the doors were closed too hard. Kaiser managed to sell just over 124,000 Henry Js over a four-year period, but many people thought that his money would have been better spent on a V8 engine for the regular-sized Kaiser.

A curious venture was the Allstate, a Henry J with different grille supplied to the Sears Roebuck store chain for sale through its outlets, using Sears' own brands of tires, batteries, and spark plugs. Prices were slightly higher than for virtually the same car bought from a Kaiser-Frazer dealer, and despite the name Allstates were sold in only ten states, all in the South and Southwest. Only 2,363 were sold.

The other compacts represented two different lines of thinking: Hudson's Jet was a smaller, low-priced version of the regular Hudsons, while

Willys' Aero was a return to the passenger car field after more than a decade spent making the Jeep and its derivatives. Hudson was no stranger to smaller cars, having had a lot of success with the Essex in the 1920s and the 112 in the late 1930s. The company hoped to recreate these successes with the Jet, but was too late with its introduction, which did not happen until November 1952, with no cars reaching customers until March 1953.

By then the market was dropping, as Nash and Kaiser were discovering. The Jet was rather a dumpy-looking car, with a family resemblance to the larger "step down" Hudsons, although unfortunately the Hudson board, notably Ed Barit, wanted to step into rather than down, and the Jet had a standard height floor. Wheelbase was 105 inches and power was provided by a 202-cubic-inch L-head six which gave 104–114bhp according to carburetion and compression ratio. Although in the compact class, the Jet was wide enough to accommodate six passengers, although the rear seat legroom was strictly limited. In height it was 1 inch taller than the full-sized Hornet and Wasp. The Jet was originally offered as a four-door sedan or two-door club coupe. It was not particularly cheap, at $1,858–$1,933, but the 1954 season saw a new budget-priced Jet two-door "Family Club Sedan" at $1,621. However, the Nash-Hudson merger on May 1, 1954 put an end to the Jet, its place being taken by the Rambler which had previously been a competitor. Jet production was 21,143 in the 1953 model year, and 14,224 for 1954. As with the Henry J, the Jet was not a success for its makers. Indeed some say it killed the Hudson company. Certainly a shortage of finance prevented the development of the regular Hudson, leading to falling sales, but whether a resoundingly successful Jet would have forestalled the merger with Nash is less certain.

Production of regular passenger cars had ceased at Willys at the outbreak of World War II, during which the company became world famous for the Jeep, of which 361,000 were made between 1941 and 1945. After the war Willys continued the Jeep in modified form as the Universal, and supplemented it by a station wagon on a longer wheelbase (1946) and a sports roadster called the Jeepster (1948). Several proposals for small sedans came and went, but it was not until 1950 that

1956 PACKARD EXECUTIVE SEDAN ▲

A NEW LINE IN MID-SEASON OF 1956, THE EXECUTIVE WAS INTENDED TO FILL THE $1,000 GAP BETWEEN THE CLIPPER CUSTOM AND THE SENIOR PACKARD LINE. MADE ONLY AS A FOUR-DOOR SEDAN OR TWO-DOOR HARDTOP, IT HAD A PACKARD GRILLE AND SIDE BODY TRIM, BUT USED CLIPPER BODY PRESSINGS AND A 352-CUBIC-INCH V8 ENGINE. THIS SEDAN COST $3,465, WHICH PLACED IT CONVENIENTLY BETWEEN THE $3,069 CLIPPER AND $4,160 PACKARD.

OWNER: ROY D. CROWE (PHOTO NICKY WRIGHT)

president Ward Canaday ordered work to start. The design he approved was by Clyde Paton, who had worked on Ford's small car that became the French Ford Vedette and who by then had his own consulting firm. The unitary body was styled by Paton's partner Phil Wright, and was made as a two-door sedan or hardtop coupe. Power came from the 161-cubic-inch six-cylinder engine which had been used in the Jeep station wagon since 1948. The car was available in two forms, an L-head giving 75bhp and an F-head giving 90bhp. Wheelbase was 108 inches and overall length 181 inches, making the Willys slightly larger than the Rambler or the Henry J.

Introduced in March 1952, the new Willys line was called the Aero, the Aero Lark having the L-head engine and the more up-market Aero Wing, Aero Ace, and Aero Eagle the F-head. The Eagle hardtop was the most expensive, at $1,979, while a Lark could be had for $1,588. The press loved the cars, and Griff Borgeson was so delighted with the one he tested for *Motor Trend* that he bought one for his own use. He later wrote that he covered 25,000 miles without spending a cent on maintenance, averaging 20.5mpg on a 1,600-mile trip that included some flat-out runs on the Bonneville salt flats in Utah.

The only trouble with the Willys Aero was its price. Even the basic Lark was undercut by the Ford six at $1,525 and Chevrolet at $1,533. For 1953, when a four-door sedan joined the range, Willys prices went up to $1,732–$2,157. Sales were good to start with, 31,362 in 1952 and 41,814 in 1953, but the public taste was for powerful V8s rather than economy cars, and 1954 sales dived to 8,240. By this time Willys had been taken over by Kaiser-Frazer, although Willys was the more prosperous of the two firms and tried to underpin ailing Kaiser, with all car production transferred to Toledo. The only effect on the Willys Aero was availability of the 226.2-

cubic-inch Kaiser engine, but this made for less improvement in performance than one might have imagined—better acceleration but only 1.5mph on the top speed, heavier steering, and worse handling. Sales plummeted further to 5,897 in the 1955 model year, which Kaiser-Willys halted in April. The Aero later surfaced in Brazil, where it was made from 1957 to 1964, and was then restyled by Brooks Stevens for a further lease of life as the Aero 2600. This lasted until 1972, latterly as a Ford after Ford's take-over of Willys-Overland do Brasil.

INDEPENDENTS MERGE FOR SURVIVAL

In 1929 the independents enjoyed 20 percent of the U.S. car market. In 1952 their market share had dropped to 13 percent. In 1954 it was barely over 4 percent. The output of the Big Three received a tremendous boost with the end of government controls after the Korean War, and to the beleaguered boards of America's remaining six independent auto companies, mergers seemed the only answer.

Nash Kelvinator's George Mason had approached A. E. Barit of Hudson and Alvan Macaulay of Packard as early as 1946 about a merger. Rebuffed, he tried again in 1948 and in 1951, when he outlined two mergers that eventually took place, Nash with Hudson and Studebaker with Packard. His plan was that the two groupings would then merge, giving a four-make line-up from a compact to a high-priced luxury car. Secret plans were made in 1954 for three basic bodies and major sheet metal parts, with the make and series characterized by trim. They were envisaged as 1957 models, with the Nash Rambler representing the compact, various Studebakers, Hudsons, Nashes, and the Packard Clipper in the middle, and the Packard Patrician at the top of the line. But this never happened, because Studebaker-Packard never merged with American Motors.

The birth of American Motors took place between January and March 1954. The essential aspects of the merger were worked out by Mason and Barit over a two-hour lunch in June 1953. The Hudson and Nash boards of directors agreed to a merger on January 14, 1954, and the shareholders on March 24, with American Motors officially coming into being on May 1. Packard might have been included in the group, but its president, James Nance, wanted the presidency of American Motors, which Mason would not give up. Barit, wanting to phase into retirement, was content to be a director with a four-year consulting contract. This seems to have been a wise step, for he lived another 20 years, whereas George Mason died the following October.

With debts of $30 million, Hudson had to take second position in the new corporation, and shareholders were invited to trade three Hudson shares for two in AMC. One of the largest single blocks of Hudson stock (11 percent) was held by the Netherlands Royal Family. It is likely that they sold rather than accept the swap. Although Mason stressed that Hudson had equal status with Nash, Hudson employee Don Butler said that there was a definite feeling in the styling and engineering departments that they had to adapt to Nash ways. This became evident with the 1955 models, which were basically Nashes with different grilles made alongside their former rivals in Nash plants at Kenosha and Milwaukee. Six-cylinder engines were still Hudson's, and there was a new V8 supplied by Packard. The "Hashes," as they were called, survived until the end of the 1957 season, when they and Nashes were dropped in favor of the Rambler lines.

A curiosity from American Motors was the Metropolitan, a sub-compact car on an 85-inch wheelbase which used Nash styling and a 42bhp 73-cubic-inch four-cylinder engine made by the British Austin Motor Company. Although they looked like baby Nashes, the Metropolitans were made by Austin in England, with unitary bodies by Fisher & Ludlow Ltd. They carried both Hudson and Nash badges, and cost $1,455 for a two-passenger convertible with limited rear accommodation for children or parcels. Metropolitans sold surprisingly well, 97,000 of them up to 1961, when they were discontinued. Advertised as "milady's perfect companion for shopping trips," they were also popular with American servicemen; the British historian Michael Sedgwick observed that the sight of Metropolitans in Britain tended to indicate the nearby presence of an American air base. From 1957, Metropolitans

1959 RAMBLER AMBASSADOR SEDAN ▲▼
HUDSON AND NASH DISCONTINUED THEIR FULL-SIZE CARS AFTER THEIR MERGER INTO AMERICAN MOTORS, AND FOR 1958 LAUNCHED A SINGLE CAR, THE RAMBLER AMBASSADOR. THIS HAD A 9-INCH FRONTAL EXTENSION TO THE COMPACT RAMBLER CHASSIS, AND A NEW 327-CUBIC-INCH V8 GIVING 270bhp. IT WAS MADE AS A SEDAN, STATION WAGON, AND AN UNUSUAL HARDTOP STATION WAGON, OF WHICH ONLY 294 WERE MADE IN 1958 AND 4,341 IN 1959. AMBASSADOR SALES WERE LOWER THAN THOSE OF THE SMALLER RAMBLERS.

OWNER: C. J. OWENS (PHOTO NICKY WRIGHT)

$5,932). The top model was the limited-production Caribbean convertible, with a 352-cubic-inch V8 engine, with two four-barrel Rochester carburetors giving 275bhp, and an overall length of 220 inches and a wheelbase of 122 inches. It was said that the Caribbean's rear deck was large enough to land a helicopter on! Similar models were made in 1956, although the Clipper was marketed as a separate line in order to reassert Packard as a luxury make. The Caribbean came as a hardtop in addition to the convertible, and refinements included twin electric radio aerials and reversible seat cushions, fabric on one side, leather on the other. For 1956, displacement and power were raised to 374 cubic inches and 310bhp.

Fine cars though the 1956 Packards were, and better made than the '55s, they were too late. The company suffered a severe blow when its body supplier, Briggs, sold out to Chrysler who, not unnaturally, vetoed the supply of bodies to a rival. Packard had to settle for a cramped body plant on Detroit's Conner Avenue, which led to supply and quality problems. In addition, Packard had lost valuable defense contracts, as had Studebaker, when the demand for military trucks dried up, and there was no money to finance new Packards. Studebaker-Packard was bought up by Curtiss-Wright in August 1956, primarily as a tax loss operation; the 1957 Packards were badge-engineered Studebakers, with this make's 289-cubic-inch V8 engine. A McCulloch supercharger, available only on the Studebaker Golden Hawk coupe, was used on all Packards, boosting power from 225 to 275bhp. Only two bodies were offered, a Town Sedan and a Country Sedan, the latter being a station wagon. Although prices were around $800 higher than those of the equivalent Studebakers, no one was fooled that they were buying a proper Packard, and only 4,809 were made. The same models were offered in 1958, plus a Packardized Studebaker Hawk coupe which cost $3,995 compared with $3,182 for the Studebaker

1961 STUDEBAKER LARK VIII REGAL CONVERTIBLE ▲

THE LARK WAS STUDEBAKER'S ENTRY IN THE COMPACT FIELD, AND ANTICIPATED THOSE OF THE BIG THREE BY A YEAR. THIS GAVE THE SOUTH BEND COMPANY A WELCOME BOOST IN SALES, WITH A TOTAL OF 153,823 DELIVERIES IN 1959, OF WHICH 129,950 WERE LARKS. SIX- AND EIGHT-CYLINDER ENGINES WERE OFFERED IN LARKS, CALLED RESPECTIVELY THE LARK VI AND VIII. THIS IS A LARK VIII CONVERTIBLE, THE MOST EXPENSIVE 1961 STUDEBAKER AT $2,689.

OWNER: STEVE PIPER (PHOTO NICKY WRIGHT)

were sold on the British market as well.

The Studebaker-Packard merger followed close on the formation of American Motors. It was the idea of Packard's James Nance, who saw the need for diversification from his company's largely expensive cars. Studebaker seemed an attractive partner, for it not only made cars in the medium-price range, but also trucks, and had valuable defense contracts. For Studebaker the merger offered fresh capital to modernize their aging and underused plant at South Bend. The merger agreement was signed on June 22, 1954, by Nance for Packard and Paul Hoffman for Studebaker, and on October 1 the Studebaker-Packard Corporation came into existence.

The merger produced a less immediate effect on the cars than at American Motors; 1955 Packards and Studebakers continued to be distinct designs, Packard making its upper medium price Clippers ($2,586–$3,076) and luxury Senior models ($3,390–

variety. Apart from a bolt-on fiberglass grille, special features included a tire impression stamped on the rear deck, leather interior and sports car type instrumentation, and Packard emblems on the hub caps. Only 588 Hawk coupes were made, together with 2,038 other 1958 Packards, and that was the end. James Nance had already left, shortly before the Curtiss-Wright take-over.

Studebaker was working well below its plant capacity of 250,000 vehicles per year when Curtiss-Wright bought the company. Its sedans had no particular distinction, but the Hawk coupes, derived from Raymond Loewy's 1953 Starliner, had a niche market among enthusiasts, and in recent years have become significant collector cars. They were not enough to keep Studebaker afloat, however, and for 1959 the company turned to the low-priced compact idea with its Lark.

The brainchild of new president Harold E. Churchill, the Lark looked like an all-new car, which is what the stylists hoped for, although it was based on the Champion's center section, with a wraparound windshield from the 1955 Studebakers, a steering wheel from the '57s, and hardtop doors from the '58s. At 108.5 inches, the wheelbase was quite large for a compact, but very limited overhang gave a handy overall length of 175 inches. Interior space was very good, with seating for six passengers.

Two engines gave the Lark a dual character; the Lark VI was an economical budget car with a 90bhp 169-cubic-inch six-cylinder engine, while the Lark VIII had a sparkling performance with 106mph top speed, thanks to its 180bhp 259-cubic-inch V8. Two- and four-door sedans and a station wagon were offered in 1959, prices ranging from $1,925 for a VI two-door sedan to $2,590 for a VIII wagon. A convertible was added for 1960.

Thanks to the Lark, Studebaker production increased by 381 percent between 1958 and 1959, and 70 percent of the cars traded in on new Larks came from rival makes. Overall sales in 1959 totaled 153,823 units, but Studebaker could not hold this, or its tenth position, in the years that followed. The problem was twofold: imports on the one hand, and on the other new compacts from the Big Three, Corvair, Falcon, and Valiant, all of which debuted for the 1960 season. For 1961, Detroit brought out four more compacts, in a higher price range than the original cars. The Dodge Lancer, Olds F-85, Pontiac Tempest, and Buick Special competed on performance and price with the Lark VIII. Studebaker had a lot of shared dealerships with Chrysler, Ford, and GM, and when the Big Three launched their compacts dual dealers were forced to give up Studebaker. Thus Lark sales declined during the 1960s, to only 44,232 in 1964. By then the South Bend plant had closed and Studebakers were made only at the Canadian plant at Hamilton, Ontario. Production continued for a further three years, although the Lark name was dropped after 1964. Total Lark production (including the

1963 STUDEBAKER GT HAWK COUPE ▶

THE HAWK LINE DATED FROM 1956,
ALTHOUGH THE CONCEPT REALLY ORIGINATED
IN THE STARLINER COUPE OF 1953,
DESIGNED BY ROBERT G. BOURKE OF
THE LOEWY STUDIOS. THE CAR WAS
RESTYLED BY BROOKS STEVENS FOR 1962
AS THE GT HAWK, AND 1963 MODELS
CAME WITH 210bhp 289-CUBIC-INCH ENGINES
AS STANDARD. OPTIONAL WERE
THE 240bhp R1 AND 290bhp R2 ENGINES.
WITH THE LATTER, A GT HAWK
COULD EXCEED 140MPH.

OWNERS: CHUCK AND CHRIS COLLINS   (PHOTO NICKY WRIGHT)

1963 STUDEBAKER AVANTI COUPE ▼

ANOTHER DESIGN FROM THE LOEWY STUDIOS, THE AVANTI WAS QUITE UNLIKE ANY OTHER STUDEBAKER.
THE INTERIOR FEATURED FOUR SEPARATE BUCKET SEATS, AN AIRCRAFT-TYPE CONTROL PANEL, AND AMPLE CRASH
PADDING. THE BENDIX CALLIPER DISK BRAKES WERE THE FIRST OF THEIR KIND ON AN AMERICAN-BUILT CAR.

OWNER: CHRIS COLLINS (PHOTO NICKY WRIGHT)

Canadian cars, which were lineal descendants although called Cruiser and Daytona) was 563,960, and in addition Kaiser-Illin assembled about 3,500 in Israel between 1959 and 1965. One of these was a convertible lengthened by 25 inches to make a parade phaeton for Israel's President Zalman Shazar.

Hawk coupes continued in production until the end of 1963, and there was also the strikingly different Avanti coupe. This was dreamed up by Studebaker's new president Sherwood Egbert, who replaced Churchill in February 1961, with body styling by Raymond Loewy. It had razor-edged front fenders, a jacked-up rear end, and no radiator grille, the air intakes being concealed under the front bumper. The Avanti's chassis was taken from the shorter chassis (109-inch) of the Larks and the engine was the 240bhp 289-cubic-inch V8 from the Golden Hawk. With a Paxton supercharger, power went up to 290bhp, giving a top speed of 124mph.

In order to publicize the Avanti's performance, Egbert had a special car prepared with which Andy Granatelli broke 29 stock car records at Bonneville in October 1962. The following year Granatelli returned to Bonneville with an even more powerful Avanti, whose twin-supercharged engine developed an almost unbelievable 575bhp. Little streamlining was needed since the Avanti body was so slippery,

1965 CHECKER MARATHON SEDAN ▲

AN INDEPENDENT WITH A DIFFERENCE WAS THE KALAMAZOO-BASED CHECKER MOTORS CORPORATION, FAMOUS
FOR ITS TAXICABS SINCE 1923. IN 1959 THE COMPANY LAUNCHED A VERSION OF ITS CAB FOR THE PRIVATE BUYER.
THE SAME BODY SHELL AND SIX-CYLINDER CONTINENTAL ENGINE WERE USED, AND THE INTERIOR HAD TAXI-LIKE JUMP
SEATS GIVING ACCOMMODATION TO EIGHT PASSENGERS. AN OVERHEAD VALVE VERSION OF THE ENGINE WAS OFFERED
AT NO EXTRA COST, WHICH RAISED POWER FROM 80 TO 122BHP, AND IN 1961 THIS ENGINE BECAME STANDARD
ON THE STATION WAGONS. THE TOP MODEL SUPERBA SPECIAL WAS RENAMED MARATHON IN 1961, AND FROM 1965
V8 CHEVROLET ENGINES WERE OFFERED AS ALTERNATIVES TO THE CONTINENTAL. CHECKER PASSENGER CAR
PRODUCTION WAS ALWAYS LOW, GENERALLY NOT MORE THAN 20 PERCENT OF TOTAL OUTPUT, WHICH SELDOM
EXCEEDED 6,000 UNITS PER YEAR. CHECKER BOWED OUT OF THE CAR AND TAXI FIELD IN 1982.

OWNER: JOHN R. OWEN (PHOTO NICKY WRIGHT)

but the rear wheels were enclosed. The car was christened the Due Cento (Italian for 200) as 200mph was the top speed hoped for, but Granatelli's best figure was 196.62mph.

Unfortunately the Avanti did not move so quickly in the showrooms, largely because production problems with the fiberglass body delayed its appearance, and many who ordered an Avanti in late 1962 or early 1963 canceled and bought a Corvette instead. A total of 3,834 Avantis were built in the 1963 model year, and 809 '64s, all of which were delivered before the move to Canada. However, the Avanti didn't die, for two Studebaker-Packard dealers, Nate Altman and Leo Newman, purchased the dies, parts, and rights to the Avanti, bought a small part of the Studebaker factory, and restarted production in 1965, using 327-cubic-inch Chevrolet Corvette engines. With several changes of ownership, the Avanti is still being made at the time of writing; the original shape is little changed, although there are two styles never made by Studebaker, a convertible and a four-door sedan.

The third merger of the independents took place in April 1953, when Kaiser Industries bought Willys-Overland to form the Kaiser-Willys Sales Corporation. Kaiser sales had been falling since their peak in 1948, and the Frazer name had been dropped after the 1951 season. The Henry J and restyled 1951 Special and De Luxe kept the firm going in the early 1950s, but the lack of a V8 engine was a growing drawback for a medium-priced car competing against such performers as the Oldsmobile 88 with 145–160bhp. The old Continental six gave only 115bhp, and there was not much Kaiser could do with it until 1954 when a McCulloch supercharger was added, boosting power to 140bhp. This was only available on the top Manhattan model, which cost nearly $300 more than the other Kaisers.

The engineering department experimented with V8 engines bought in from Oldsmobile and Cadillac, but there was no way that GM would sell such engines for production, although the corporation did let Kaiser use its HydraMatic transmission. Henry Kaiser drove a Manhattan with a Cadillac engine, although this fact was not publicized at the time.

The Willys purchase gave Kaiser a better small car than its own Henry J and also the profitable Jeep operation. (The Jeep has been an attraction for successive corporate take-overs; American Motors in 1970, Renault in 1978, Chrysler in 1987, all were lured to acquisition by the chance of getting their hands on the successful Jeep business.) The enormous Kaiser factory at Willow Run was sold to General Motors, and all car production relocated to Willys' headquarters in Toledo. Then in 1955, after only 1,000 cars had been made, Kaiser announced that it was pulling out of the passenger car business in the United States. The majority of the 1955 models were sold to Argentina, and later in the year body dies and manufacturing equipment also went to Argentina, where the design was made for a further seven years. Latin America also received the Willys Aero, which went to Brazil and had an even longer career. Only the Jeeps in their various forms continued to issue from Toledo. Officially they were Willys Jeeps until 1963, when the maker's name became Kaiser-Jeep Corporation and Jeep became a marque in its own right. The Kaiser-Frazer Corporation was changed to Kaiser Industries Corporation and continued to be active in cement, steel, engineering, and sand and gravel, which Henry Kaiser had dealt in long before he got mixed up with automobiles.

Thus in the long run, with the exception of American Motors, mergers failed to save the independent car makers. Even AMC eventually succumbed to take-over by Chrysler, while at the time of writing even Chrysler seems none too healthy.

1956 IMPERIAL SEDAN ▲▶

ALTHOUGH THE NAME IMPERIAL HAD BEEN USED BY CHRYSLER SINCE 1924, IT DID NOT BECOME A RECOGNIZED
SEPARATE MARQUE UNTIL 1955. ENGINES AND BODIES WERE SHARED WITH LESSER CHRYSLER MODELS, BUT THE
IMPERIALS WERE DISTINGUISHED BY THEIR OWN TWO-PIECE SPLIT GRILLES AND FREE-STANDING TAILLIGHTS ABOVE THE
REAR FENDERS. THREE MODELS MADE UP THE 1956 IMPERIAL RANGE, THE FOUR-DOOR SEDAN ILLUSTRATED HERE, AND
TWO HARDTOPS, TWO- AND FOUR-DOOR VERSIONS. THERE WERE ALSO THE ENORMOUS CROWN IMPERIALS, EIGHT-
PASSENGER SEDAN AND LIMOUSINE, ON A 149.5-INCH WHEELBASE.

OWNER: CARL W. REID (PHOTO NICKY WRIGHT)

1968 CROWN IMPERIAL SEDAN ▶

IMPERIAL WAS THE TOP LINE OF CHRYSLER, AND WAS
PROMOTED TO THE STATUS OF AN INDIVIDUAL MARQUE
FROM 1955 THROUGH 1975. THE 1968 CROWN AND
LEBARON MODELS USED THE SAME 440-CUBIC-INCH V8
AS THE CHRYSLER 300 AND NEW YORKER. THIS CROWN
FOUR-DOOR HARDTOP SEDAN WAS THE MOST POPULAR,
WITH 8,492 DELIVERED; BY CONTRAST, THE TWO-DOOR
CONVERTIBLE ACCOUNTED FOR ONLY 474 DELIVERIES.
THE RAREST MODEL OF ALL WAS THE IMPERIAL
LEBARON LIMOUSINE WITH WHEELBASE STRETCHED
BY STAGEWAY OF FORT SMITH, ARKANSAS, TO 163
INCHES. FEWER THAN 12 OF THESE WERE MADE, AT
A PRICE IN EXCESS OF $12,000.

OWNER: ALLAN S. MURRAY (PHOTO NICKY WRIGHT)

V8 ENGINES AND THE HORSEPOWER RACE

The V8 engine had been around for a long time,
but in 1946 it featured in only three makes of
American car, Cadillac, Ford, and Mercury.
Fourteen years later it was offered by every
manufacturer and was standard for larger cars. Its
rise to popularity also saw a remarkable growth in
output, popularly known as "the horsepower race."

The first of the new generation of V8s came
from Cadillac in 1949. Under development for
more than ten years, its chief novelties were
overhead valves, slightly oversquare dimensions
(3.81 x 3.63 inches), and slipper pistons, in which
the lower sides of the pistons were cut away so the
piston nested between the crankshaft
counterweights at the bottom of the stroke. This
allowed shorter connecting rods and a consequent
reduction in size and weight. The new V8 weighed
220 pounds less than its flathead predecessor, and
displaced 331 cubic inches compared with 345, yet
it gave 10bhp more, at 160. Its compression ratio
was higher, at 7.5:1, and had risen to 10.5:1 by 1959.
The engine was developed through the 1967
season, by which time it had been bored out to 429
cubic inches and gave 340bhp. Not many people
realized at the time what an important engine this
was; one who did was *Motor Trend* editor John
Bond, who chose the 1949 Cadillac as the first Car
of the Year selected by his magazine. Cadillac's
bodies had been completely restyled for 1948, with

the first of the famous fins, so the '49 Cadillac really was an all-new car compared with its predecessor of two years earlier.

Oldsmobile also came out with an overhead valve oversquare V8 for 1949, but it was smaller at 303 cubic inches and 135bhp. It was strongly influenced by the Cadillac design, and a heavier F-head V8 that Olds engineers had been working on was abandoned when they had a good look at what Cadillac was doing. The Olds was called the Rocket V8 and gave the Lansing make a change of image, with 100mph obtainable from the 98 convertible. By 1954, displacement was up to 324 cubic inches and power to 185bhp, raised to 202 for 1955.

The next important V8 engine came from Chrysler for 1951. Also an oversquare unit with the same dimensions as the Cadillac, it had hemispherical combustion chambers which gave more efficient breathing, and accounted for the extra 20bhp it yielded. The valves were inclined on either side of the combustion chamber, which necessitated four rocker shafts in place of two, and eight intake pushrods, eight exhaust pushrods, and eight intake and eight exhaust rocker arms. A conventional V8 such as Cadillac's needed 16 identical pushrods and rocker arms. The cost of making two sets of everything pushed up the price of the hemi engine to unacceptable levels, and it was eventually dropped, in 1959, but not before it had provided America with some of the most powerful and dramatic automobiles ever seen.

During the 1950s the V8 became established as the logical power unit for American cars. The straight-6 was relegated to the lowest-priced lines and the straight-8 was consigned to oblivion. Studebaker brought out a V8 in 1951, Buick, De Soto, and Dodge in 1953, Chevrolet, Hudson, Nash, Packard, Plymouth, and Pontiac in 1955. The last straight-8s were made by Packard and Pontiac in their 1954 models. Lincoln went to overhead valves in 1952, Ford and Mercury in 1954, and all the other new units also had ohv.

The adoption of V8s by Chevrolet and Plymouth sealed the success of the layout. Chevrolet's was a 265-cubic-inch unit which owed much to the '49 Cadillac, and was designed by Ed Cole and Harry Barr who had worked on the Caddy. Like its more costly sister, it had slipper pistons, but advances in manufacturing techniques made it cheaper to build. Lighter than the old six, which gave 125bhp at best, it was considerably more powerful, with 170–180bhp in 1955 and 225 in 1956. A larger 283-cubic-inch V8 was an additional option for 1957, and this gave up to 280bhp. The power race was on, even for the low-priced makes, with Ford offering a 312-cubic-inch 254bhp engine for 1957, going up to 352 cubic inches and 300bhp for 1958, while Plymouth started with a modest 177bhp from 260 cubic inches in 1955, going up to 315bhp from 350 cubic inches for 1958.

Among the larger cars, the race was between

Cadillac and Chrysler, with the latter making the more exciting cars from 1955 onward. In that year they brought out the 300, a lowered New Yorker hardtop with grille from the top line Imperial, powered by a modified 331-cubic-inch hemi engine, with twin quadrajet carburetors, a racing type camshaft, and twin exhausts. This gave 300bhp and propelled the 4,000-pound car at 130mph. The colorful auto writer Tom McCahill pronounced it "as solid as Grant's tomb, and 130 times as fast."

The 1956 300 was the 300B, the first of the family that became known as the "letter cars," the

1957 CHEVROLET BEL AIR HARDTOP ▼

THE 1955/57 CHEVROLETS ARE AMONG THE MOST POPULAR OF ALL CHEVYS WITH TODAY'S COLLECTORS, AND OF THESE THE '57s PROBABLY COMMAND THE GREATEST ENTHUSIASM. COMPLETELY RESTYLED AND GIVEN A NEW V8 ENGINE FOR 1955, THE '57s WERE MORE POWERFUL, WITH OPTIONAL FUEL INJECTION AND INCREASED DISPLACEMENT GIVING 283bhp, OR 1 HORSEPOWER PER CUBIC INCH. THE BEL AIR LINE WAS THE TOP OF THE RANGE AND WAS MADE IN SEVEN BODY STYLES, SEDANS, HARDTOPS, CONVERTIBLE, AND STATION WAGON. THIS TWO-DOOR HARDTOP SPORTS COUPE WAS THE SECOND MOST POPULAR BEL AIR, WITH 166,426 UNITS DELIVERED IN THE 1957 MODEL YEAR.

OWNER: BILL GOODSENE (PHOTO NICKY WRIGHT)

1957 PLYMOUTH FURY HARDTOP ▲

"SUDDENLY IT'S 1960," CLAIMED PLYMOUTH ADVERTISING IN 1957. FOR THAT YEAR PLYMOUTHS WERE COMPLETELY RESTYLED, WITH A WIDER GRILLE, QUAD HEADLIGHTS (ONE PAIR OF WHICH WERE PARKING LIGHTS), AND FINS WHICH GAVE A LOWER LOOK. MECHANICALLY, THEY WERE DISTINGUISHED BY TORSION BAR FRONT SUSPENSION. THE FURY WAS A HIGH-PERFORMANCE MODEL WITHIN THE BELVEDERE RANGE AND WAS MADE ONLY AS A TWO-DOOR HARDTOP. IT USED A 235bhp V8 ENGINE, WITH A 290bhp OPTION, AND WAS THE MOST COSTLY '57 PLYMOUTH AT $2,935. IT WAS ALSO THE LOWEST IN HEIGHT (53.4 INCHES) AND IN PRODUCTION, WITH JUST 7,438 MADE.

OWNER: BOB SCHMIDT (PHOTO NICKY WRIGHT)

series going up to the 300L of 1965. The V8 was bored out to give 354 cubic inches and 340bhp, but the appearance of the 300B was similar to that of the 300 apart from slightly upswept fins. Cadillac was now up to 365 cubic inches and 305bhp, but never went in for stock car racing, as Chrysler did. In 1955 a team of 300s led by Karl Kiekhafer won 32 out of 52 NASCAR (National Association for Stock Car Auto Racing) races, taking the trophy, while in 1956 Kiekhafer's drivers took all three stock car championships. A Detroit housewife, Vicky Wood, took the Women's Speed Trial Championship in her 300B with a one-way run of 143.827mph. The 1957 300C was, like other Chryslers that year, completely restyled by Virgil Exner, and had a 392-cubic-inch engine giving 390bhp. For the first time, a convertible was made in the 300 series.

The peak of power was reached in 1962 with the 405bhp 300H, but by this time the hemi engine had been replaced by a more conventional and cheaper-to-build wedge-shaped combustion chamber. In the mid-1960s Chrysler revived the hemi design for stock car racing, and a very limited number of Plymouth and Dodge street cars were equipped with hemi engines. The 300s were never big-selling cars; total production over 11 years was only 17,007, the best single year being 1964 when 3,647 300Ks were built. Convertibles were scarcer than coupes.

Cadillac dropped out of the horsepower race

1968 CHRYSLER NEW YORKER HARDTOP ▶

AS IN PREVIOUS YEARS, THE NEW YORKER FOR 1968 WAS THE TOP MODEL IN THE CHRYSLER RANGE, ALTHOUGH EXCEEDED IN PRICE AND LUXURY BY THE SEPARATE IMPERIAL LINE. THE 440-CUBIC-INCH V8 WAS THE LARGEST ENGINE CHRYSLER EVER BUILT AND GAVE 350 OR 375bhp. THERE WERE THREE MODELS IN THE NEW YORKER RANGE, OF WHICH THIS HARDTOP SEDAN WAS THE MOST EXPENSIVE, AT $4,500, AND ALSO THE MOST POPULAR, WITH 26,091 DELIVERED.

OWNER: CARL W. REID (PHOTO NICKY WRIGHT)

after 1958, when the more powerful version of its 365-cubic-inch engine gave a matching 365bhp. After that, although displacement went up to 390 cubic inches in 1959 and to 429 in 1964, power stayed around the 325–340bhp level. 1968 saw a new Cadillac V8 of 472 cubic inches, and the 1970 derivative of this, standard in the front-drive Eldorado, displaced 500 cubic inches, a record for a postwar American car. By then, however, the horsepower race was being contested by a very different kind of automobile, the Muscle Car, to be described later.

1958 PONTIAC BONNEVILLE HARDTOP ▲

PONTIAC FIRST USED THE NAME BONNEVILLE IN 1957 FOR A LIMITED-EDITION FUEL-INJECTED CONVERTIBLE, AND IN 1958 IT BECAME A LINE NAME INSTEAD OF A SINGLE MODEL DESIGNATION. TWO STYLES WERE OFFERED IN THE BONNEVILLE LINE, A HARDTOP KNOWN AS THE CUSTOM SPORT COUPE AND A CUSTOM CONVERTIBLE. BOTH WERE AT THE TOP OF THE PONTIAC RANGE, WITH 255 OR 285bhp STAR CHIEF V8 ENGINES AND DE LUXE STEERING WHEEL, CHROME WHEEL DISKS, AND SPECIAL UPHOLSTERY.

OWNER: JIM diGREGORIO (PHOTO NICKY WRIGHT)

1955 CHRYSLER C300 HARDTOP ▲

"AS SOLID AS GRANT'S TOMB AND 130 TIMES AS FAST," SAID TOM McCAHILL OF THE CHRYSLER 300, ALLUDING TO ITS 130mph TOP SPEED. IT WAS THE SENSATION OF 1955, WITH ITS 300bhp HEMI V8 ENGINE WITH TWIN QUADRAJET CARBURETORS, NEW YORKER NEWPORT BODY, AND IMPERIAL GRILLE. THE 300 WAS STYLED BY VIRGIL EXNER, WITH ENGINEERING BY CHRYSLER'S CHIEF ENGINEER, BOB ROGER. ONLY 1,725 WERE MADE OF THE 1955 MODEL. KNOWN AS THE C300, IT WAS FOLLOWED BY THE 300B FOR 1956 AND THE 300C FOR 1957, THE LATTER WITH NEW STYLING ALSO BY EXNER.

OWNER: OTTO ROSENBUSCH (PHOTO NICKY WRIGHT)

1958 CADILLAC ELDORADO BROUGHAM ◄

LAUNCHED IN 1957, THE ELDORADO BROUGHAM WAS A HAND-BUILT, LIMITED-EDITION VERSION OF THE SERIES 62, AND AMERICA'S FIRST COMPLETELY PILLARLESS FOUR-DOOR SEDAN. THE PRICE WAS A WHOPPING $13,074 (AN ORDINARY 1958 SERIES 62 FOUR-DOOR SEDAN COST $4,891), BUT BUYERS GOT ALL THE OPTIONS, INCLUDING DUAL FOUR-BARREL CARBURETORS AND AIR SUSPENSION. INTERIOR FITTINGS INCLUDED A DUAL HEATING SYSTEM, AIR CONDITIONING, CIGARETTE AND TISSUE DISPENSERS, AND AN ATOMIZER WITH LANVIN PERFUME. ONLY 400 BROUGHAMS WERE MADE IN 1957 AND 304 IN 1958; ALTHOUGH THE NAME SURVIVED TO 1960, LATER ELDO BROUGHAMS WERE MUCH LESS DISTINCTIVE.

OWNER: ED OBERHAUS (PHOTO NICKY WRIGHT)

THE NEW GENERATION AMERICAN SPORTS CAR

The sports car, roadster, speedster — call it what you will — flourished in the second and third decades of the century, and struggled into the 1930s, but after the death of the Auburn 851 in 1936, the breed went into limbo. Not for long, though, for in 1949 Californian Frank Kurtis, who had built a number of successful Indianapolis racing cars, brought out a two-passenger sports car with a fiberglass body. Engines were the customer's choice, although Ford V8s were the normal, with Cadillacs or Chryslers for richer speed freaks. Even with a Ford engine, a Kurtis cost $4,700, more than most Cadillacs and all Chryslers or Lincolns.

After building 36 cars, Kurtis sold the design to television maker Earl Muntz, who lengthened the frame so as to accommodate four passengers, standardized on a Cadillac engine, and sold his Muntz Jet for $4,450. Most Muntz Jets, of which 394 were made, had Lincoln V8 engines. Like Preston Tucker, Earl Muntz was keen on safety, and his cars featured padded dashboards, padded tops on the hardtop, and seat belts.

With its four seats the Muntz was more of a sporty convertible (or hardtop) than a sports car, but other makers soon began to cater to a growing demand. Frank Kurtis returned to the fray in 1954 with a very hot sports car with a tubular frame patterned after the Indy car that Bill Vukovitch drove to victory in 1953. It had a simple fiberglass body with a wrap-around windshield, and was sold as the 500KK in kit form, or the 500M fully built-up. With a 250bhp Cadillac V8, it was capable of 135mph, justifying Kurtis' claim that it was "guaranteed to outperform any other sports car on the road." Kurtis' manufacturing facilities were limited, and he was busy building Indy and midget race cars, so only 30 500KKs and 20 500Ms were made.

On the other side of the continent, at West Palm Beach, Florida, millionaire sportsman Briggs Swift Cunningham began

to build Chrysler-powered sports cars with the intention of winning an American victory at the Le Mans 24-Hour Race, at that time the world's premier sports car event. He had entered two Cadillacs at Le Mans in 1950, a stock Series 62 coupe and a custom two-seater which the French called "Le Monstre," and 1951 saw his Chrysler-powered C-2R open sports car with De Dion rear axle. It finished eighteenth at Le Mans, but several replicas were sold to racing enthusiasts.

Cunningham entered cars at Le Mans each year to 1955, his best place being third in 1953, but the only production cars sold for road use were the Chrysler-powered C-3s with aluminum coupe bodies by Vignale of Italy; 26 were built in 1953 and 1954, selling for the very high price of $9,000.

Numerous other sports cars appeared in the early 1950s, their makers encouraged by the successes of imports such as the MG Midget, Jaguar XK120, and Allard J2, the latter fitted with Cadillac, Mercury, or Chrysler engines when it was sold in the United States. Kaiser-Frazer built the Kaiser-Darrin 161, which had a pretty fiberglass

body styled by Howard Darrin and sliding doors. However, it was under-powered with a 90bhp Willys Six engine, and at $3,668 (more than a Corvette) was no bargain. Kaiser built only 435 in 1953-54, but then Howard Darrin bought the remaining 50 bodyshells, fitted them with Cadillac engines at his Hollywood plant, and sold them as Darrins over the next four years.

Another user of the Willys engine was Woody Woodill of Downey, California, who made about 315 Woodill Wildfire sports cars, later ones being offered in kit form, to take Ford engines and transverse spring front suspension. To demonstrate that assembly need take no more than 14 hours, Woodill once built a car in front of a TV audience. He also offered a child's version on a 63-inch wheelbase, called the Brushfire. Other entrants in the field included Brooks Stevens' Excalibur-J (1952) with a Henry J chassis and Willys engine, the Edwards America (1954–5) with a Mercury chassis and with Lincoln or Oldsmobile engines, the Multiplex (1952–4) with its Willys four or six engines, and the Ford-powered Rockefeller

1958 OLDSMOBILE SUPER 88 TWO-DOOR HARDTOP ◄
OLDSMOBILES WERE REDESIGNED FOR THE SECOND YEAR RUNNING FOR 1958, AND WERE LONGER AND MORE CHROME-LADEN THAN EVER. INNOVATIONS INCLUDED QUAD HEADLIGHTS, FEATURED BY ALL OTHER GM DIVISIONS THAT YEAR. THE SUPER 88 WAS THE MIDDLE SERIES, SHARING ITS 125.5-INCH WHEELBASE WITH THE DYNAMIC 88, AND ITS 305bhp V8 ENGINE WITH THE 98. FIVE BODY STYLES WERE OFFERED, TWO SEDANS, A HARDTOP, CONVERTIBLE, AND STATION WAGON. THIS HARDTOP HOLIDAY COUPE COST $3,262.
OWNER: DEAN ULLMAN
(PHOTO NICKY WRIGHT)

Yankee (1949–54) and Story (1950) models.

Although none of these sports cars sold in any numbers, they and, more importantly, sports car imports made the major auto firms think that maybe there was something in this hitherto ignored field. The first was Nash, whose Nash-Healey came about as a result of a shipboard meeting in 1949 between George Mason and the British sports car maker Donald Healey. Healey was on his way to Detroit to try to buy Cadillac engines in order to give his Silverstone sports car more power, and as a result of this casual meeting on board the Queen Elizabeth, he stayed with the Masons in Detroit. George Mason told him that if he failed to get Cadillac engines, he should come to him. As it happened, Cadillac was having difficulty making engines for its own use, so Healey took up Mason's offer. The stark-looking Silverstone was redesigned with an all-enveloping body and a Nash grille, and went into production at Healey's Warwick factory in 1951. Bodies were made by Panelcraft of Birmingham, so although American in design and

styling, the car was fully assembled in England.

The Anglo-American Nash-Healey was soon to acquire three nationalities, for in 1952 the rather uninspired Panelcraft body was replaced by one styled and built by Pininfarina in Italy. The complicated manufacturing process went like this: engines, transmissions, and other components were shipped from the Nash plant at Kenosha to the Healey plant at Warwick, where they were mated to the Healey chassis and shipped on to the Pininfarina coachworks in Turin, Italy; from there the completed cars went direct to the United States, for Nash-Healeys were not sold in Europe. The price was a hefty $5,128 at the port of entry, although this represented no profit to Nash. What with all the shipping costs, it has been estimated that Nash lost around $9,000 on each Nash-Healey sold! No wonder production was kept low, only 506 being made between early 1951 and August 1954. However, the Nash-Healey acted as excellent bait to draw customers into showrooms to buy production Nash cars, and in this they fulfilled George Mason's original plans. They also rescued Donald Healey from possible bankruptcy, enabling him to design the Healey Hundred, which became the Austin-Healey, a much more successful and famous sports car than the Nash-Healey ever was.

▲ THE FIRST HAND-MADE PRODUCTION MODEL OF THE CORVETTE ABOUT TO LEAVE THE LINE AT FLINT ON JUNE 10, 1953. THE FIRST 300 CARS WERE ALL IN WHITE, WHICH GAVE SOME PEOPLE THE IDEA THAT YOU COULD NOT HAVE FIBERGLASS IN ANY OTHER COLOR.
MIRCO DE CET COLLECTION

CORVETTE AND THUNDERBIRD

By the time the Nash-Healey had been laid to rest, General Motors already had a sports car in production and Ford was about to launch another. Chevrolet's Corvette was the idea of GM's styling chief Harley Earl, who envisaged a low-priced sports car for his college-age son and his friends. He began to make sketches in 1951 and, aided by a young sports car enthusiast, Bob McLean, full-size drawings were followed by a plaster mock-up. Earl originally planned a V8 engine, but owing to the popularity of the Jaguar XK120, he and McLean changed their ideas to a six.

Since 1951 General Motors had been launching its new models at an extravagant display called Motorama which toured major cities. Alongside production cars were dream cars to test out new ideas on the public. Buick, Cadillac, Oldsmobile, and Pontiac all had their dream machines, but humble Chevrolet did not, until 1953. Then it was decided to exhibit Earl's sports car as Chevy's contribution and, what is more, it was given running gear by GM's chief of engineering, Ed Cole. It was more of a functioning automobile than many other dream cars.

Cole and his team shortened the stock Chevrolet frame by 13 inches to 102 inches, and moved the engine back in the frame by 7 inches.

▲ ▶ GENERAL MOTORS STYLIST HARLEY J. EARL, WHO BEGAN HIS CAREER WITH THE DON LEE STUDIOS IN THE 1920S, IS PICTURED HERE WITH TWO DREAM CARS, THE BUICK LE SABRE OF 1951 (ABOVE) AND THE PONTIAC FIREBIRD III GAS TURBINE CAR OF 1959 (RIGHT). FEW OF LE SABRE'S STYLING INNOVATIONS EVER APPEARED ON PRODUCTION BUICKS, ALTHOUGH FINS BECAME FAMILIAR ON CADILLACS, AND THE CENTRAL AIR INTAKE WAS COPIED BY SEVERAL EUROPEAN CUSTOM BODY STYLISTS AND APPEARED ON AT LEAST ONE BUS. THE BIRD DESIGN ON THE PONTIAC'S HOOD WAS USED ON PRODUCTION FIREBIRDS FROM 1973 ONWARD.
GENERAL MOTORS ARCHIVES, MIRCO DE CET COLLECTION

This meant that the driver could touch the rear wheels from his seat. The engine was a stock 235-cubic-inch Chevy six with power boosted from 115 to 150bhp thanks to triple Carter carburetors, high-lift cams, twin exhausts, and other modifications. Transmission was a two-speed Powerglide automatic, far from ideal for a sports car but the only one available that could cope with the power.

Three show cars were built, a roadster called Corvette, a fastback coupe called Corvair, and a station wagon called Nomad. The last two remained prototypes, but the Corvette was so enthusiastically received by the public that Chevrolet decided to go into limited production. The first cars came off the line at Flint in June 1953, and by the year's end 315 had been made. They had fiberglass bodies in white, which led people to think that this was the only color you could have fiberglass in. Most of these early 'Vettes were given to VIPs or used for publicity, although a price of $3,440 was fixed. This was much more than the $1,000 college kids' car Earl had dreamed of, and made the Corvette a specialty car, nearly double the price of any other Chevrolet. One of the first private buyers was Briggs Cunningham, who gave the car to his wife.

In 1954 production was transferred to St. Louis, where it has remained ever since. Only minor improvements were made, but additional colors were introduced, Pennant Blue and Sportsman Red, although 80 percent of buyers opted for white, with red and white interiors. Of the 3,640 built in 1954, not much above 2,000 found buyers, which was disappointing after the car's rapturous reception the year before. At the end of the season, dealers had around 1,500 Corvettes in stock. Because of this, only 674 '55 models were sold. The Corvette had fallen between two stools; the enthusiasts rejected it because of the automatic transmission and simulated knock-off wheels, while those who were used to convertibles disliked the side curtains which had to be pushed aside to gain access to the interior door handles, as there were none on the outside. Also the cars leaked water and dust. A senior, though unnamed, Chevrolet source said in the 1980s: "Quite frankly, those early 'Vettes weren't very good cars. I know they're highly praised now by collectors, but we had nothing but headaches from them, and in 1954 and 1955 it really looked like there wouldn't be any '56s."

However, Ed Cole had an ace up his sleeve, the

1967 CHEVROLET CORVETTE STING RAY COUPE ▶

THE DISTINCTIVE FASTBACK STING RAY COUPE, INTRODUCED IN 1963, IS A VERY POPULAR MODEL WITH COLLECTORS, ALTHOUGH IT WAS OUTSOLD BY THE CONVERTIBLE WHEN NEW. THE STANDARD ENGINE WAS A 300BHP V8, BUT SEVERAL MORE POWERFUL OPTIONS WERE AVAILABLE, UP TO THE L-71 TRI-CARB WHICH GAVE 435bhp FROM 427 CUBIC INCHES. A THREE-SPEED MANUAL TRANSMISSION WAS STANDARD, BUT ONLY 1.9 PERCENT OF BUYERS CHOSE IT; 83 PERCENT WENT FOR THE FOUR-SPEED MANUAL, AND 10.1 PERCENT FOR THE POWERGLIDE AUTOMATIC TRANSMISSION.

OWNERS: SKIP AND KATHY MARKETTI (PHOTO NICKY WRIGHT)

1969 CHEVROLET CORVETTE STINGRAY CONVERTIBLE ▲

CORVETTES WERE RESTYLED FOR 1968 WITH A MORE AERODYNAMIC FRONT END AND A NEW TUNNELBACK COUPE REPLACING THE SPLIT-WINDOW FASTBACK. ALTHOUGH THE WHEELBASE WAS THE SAME, 98 INCHES, OVERHANG MADE THE NEW CORVETTE 7 INCHES LONGER. THE STING RAY NAME WAS DROPPED, BUT REAPPEARED FOR 1969 AS ONE WORD, STINGRAY. POWER STEERING WAS AN INCREASINGY POPULAR OPTION, UP FROM 13.7 PERCENT IN 1965 TO 59.2 PERCENT IN 1969.

(PHOTO NICKY WRIGHT)

V8 engine which powered all Corvettes from 1956 onwards. This 265-cubic-inch overhead valve unit gave 195bhp in its mildest 1955 form, and up to 225bhp in 1956. Combined with a three-speed manual transmission, this made the Corvette into a more serious sports car, reinforced in 1957 when the V8, enlarged to 283 cubic inches, gave 220–283bhp, the latter the psychologically and promotionally valuable figure of 1 horsepower per cubic inch. Corvette sales increased to 3,467 in the 1956 season, 6,339 in 1957, and 9,168 in 1958. By 1960, sales were well into five figures, where they have remained ever since.

Belgian-born and Russian-educated Zora Arkus-Duntov was the man really responsible for the Corvette's success, working on the improved suspension of the '56 model, and introducing fuel injection and four-speed transmission options on the '57. Whereas the original Corvette had taken 11 seconds to reach 60mph, the '57 fuelie did it in 5.7 seconds, a respectable figure for a sports car even today; 240 fuel-injected 1957 Corvettes were made, as many buyers just did not want that amount of performance, or to pay the additional $675.

By 1962 the Corvette engine was up to 327 cubic inches and a maximum of 360bhp. Then, in the following year came the Sting Ray, which, apart from its engine, was an all-new car. The body was completely restyled, and in addition to the roadster there was a striking split-window fastback coupe. Suspension was all-independent, by coil springs at the front (from the stock passenger cars) and by transverse leaf springs and lower wishbones at the rear. The wheelbase was 4 inches shorter, rear tread 2 inches narrower, and frontal area reduced by 1 square foot. Front/rear weight distribution was 48/52 compared with 53/47 for previous Corvettes. Ride and handling were significantly improved, with the most powerful engine option giving 360bhp and a top speed of 147mph.

Chevrolet now had a sports car which could compare well with European competition, at the quite reasonable price of $4,037 for the roadster and $4,252 for the coupe. Sting Ray sales were well up on previous Corvettes, at 21,513, divided equally between the open and closed models. The Sting Ray was steadily developed during its five-year lifespan, notably in 1965 when disk brakes were fitted and a 396-cubic-inch engine was the largest option. This grew again to 427 cubic inches in 1966, when maximum output was 425bhp. This gave 0–60mph in around 5 seconds and a theoretical top speed with the 3.08:1 rear axle of 170mph. Most powerful of all was the L88 competition coupe with aluminum cylinder head, four-barrel carburetor, and a compression ratio of 12.5:1. This developed 560bhp. Only 20 Corvettes used this engine. No price was quoted, but the 435bhp tri-carb engine cost $947 above the standard coupe price of $4,663.

The Sting Ray name was discontinued for the 1968 Corvettes, to be revived by the single word, Stingray, for 1969. Stingrays were roomier, longer, and heavier than their predecessors, and their styling lasted up to 1983. Engine size and power were drastically reduced, though, the 1982 models having just one 350-cubic-inch unit giving 200bhp.

Ford's Thunderbird was made in larger numbers than the Corvette, but only for the first three years of its life could it really be considered a sports car. Thereafter it grew into a four-passenger personal convertible. The idea of a two-passenger sports car had been around at Ford for some time, but only crystallized when Chevrolet showed the Corvette at the GM Motorama in February 1953. It was the work of a team acting under Ford design director, Franklin Q. Hershey, and encouraged by general manager Lewis D. Crusoe. A mock-up remarkably similar to the production Thunderbird was shown at the January 1954 Detroit Auto Show, and the cars began to come off the assembly lines on September 9, 1954.

Although it was compared to the Corvette in having two seats, the Thunderbird was a very different car in other ways. Hershey shunned the Corvette's crude side curtains for proper roll-up windows, used conventional steel instead of fiberglass for the body, and installed a larger and more powerful V8 engine. This gave it a better performance than the Corvette, 112 as against 107mph top speed, and 0–60 in 9.3 seconds as against the 11 seconds needed by the Corvette. No wonder it sold well, for it performed better without the sports car crudities of the Corvette. At $2,944, it was $496 less than its GM rival. More of a conventional American car than a European imitation, it shared the Corvette's 102-inch wheelbase, yet its substantial rear overhang gave it 18 inches more length. At 3,850 pounds curb weight, it was 730 pounds heavier. Sales of the first model year were 16,155, nearly four and a half times the Corvette's figures.

Impressive though they were for the first year of a new model, Thunderbird's sales figures were not good enough for divisional general manager Robert McNamara, who thought that a popular car

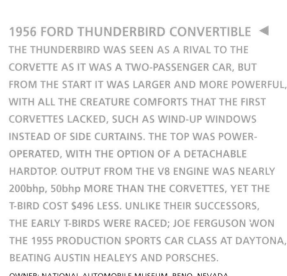

1956 FORD THUNDERBIRD CONVERTIBLE ◄
THE THUNDERBIRD WAS SEEN AS A RIVAL TO THE CORVETTE AS IT WAS A TWO-PASSENGER CAR, BUT FROM THE START IT WAS LARGER AND MORE POWERFUL, WITH ALL THE CREATURE COMFORTS THAT THE FIRST CORVETTES LACKED, SUCH AS WIND-UP WINDOWS INSTEAD OF SIDE CURTAINS. THE TOP WAS POWER-OPERATED, WITH THE OPTION OF A DETACHABLE HARDTOP. OUTPUT FROM THE V8 ENGINE WAS NEARLY 200bhp, 50bhp MORE THAN THE CORVETTES, YET THE T-BIRD COST $496 LESS. UNLIKE THEIR SUCCESSORS, THE EARLY T-BIRDS WERE RACED; JOE FERGUSON WON THE 1955 PRODUCTION SPORTS CAR CLASS AT DAYTONA, BEATING AUSTIN HEALEYS AND PORSCHES.
OWNER: NATIONAL AUTOMOBILE MUSEUM, RENO, NEVADA
(PHOTO NICKY WRIGHT)

1959 FORD THUNDERBIRD CONVERTIBLE ◄
FOR 1958 THE THUNDERBIRD WAS REDESIGNED AS A
FOUR-PASSENGER CONVERTIBLE, LOSING WHATEVER
CLAIMS IT MIGHT HAVE HAD TO BE A SPORTS CAR. THE
WHEELBASE WAS LENGTHENED FROM 102 TO 113 INCHES
AND THE ENGINE WAS A NEW 352-CUBIC-INCH V8 GIVING
300bhp. THIS CONVERTIBLE SOLD FOR $3,979. THERE
WAS ALSO A HARDTOP AT $3,696 WHICH PIONEERED
THE SQUARE-CUT FORMAL-LOOK BODY LATER USED
ON OTHER FORD MODELS.
OWNER: DR. ROSS BEWLEY (PHOTO NICKY WRIGHT)

TWO CURIOSITIES FROM FORD—
EDSEL AND CONTINENTAL MARK II
By the mid-1950s Ford had come a long way from
their parlous postwar state, thanks to Ernest
Breech, the "Whiz Kids," and, not least, Henry
Ford II. However, the company still lagged behind
General Motors, by 1,187,033 cars in 1954, and
Breech felt Ford needed more marques to match
the five offered by GM. The middle price class was
catered to by three GM marques, Pontiac,
Oldsmobile, and Buick; Ford had only Mercury, so
a new marque was planned that would bracket
Mercury at either end, giving a wide spread of
models and engines.

The new project was christened the E-car (for
Experimental) and was to be all new, with its own
engines and body shells. Ford engineers soon
realized that this would be too expensive, so
existing Ford and Mercury bodies were used, Ford
in the lower-priced Ranger and Pacer models,
Mercury for the more expensive Corsair and
Citation. Two engines were offered, both from the
new family of overhead valve V8s, a 361-cubic-inch
which was not used by either Ford or Mercury, and
a 410-cubic-inch from the middle of the Mercury
range. If the bodies and engines were familiar, a
note of distinction had to be sounded somewhere,
and this was in the grille, a vertical shape when all
contemporaries were horizontal, and generally
likened to a horse collar. It was certainly unusual,
but whether it conveyed the right messages is
another matter.

The naming of the new car caused more

---

should seat at least four passengers. His attitude
highlighted a fundamental difference between the
thinking behind Corvette and Thunderbird. The
Corvette was intended to earn publicity for GM
through a performance image, not to make money.
For McNamara, every automobile carrying the
Ford name was expected to make money.

Work on a four-passenger Thunderbird went
ahead in 1955, and for the 1958 season the two-
passenger car was dropped. It had not been greatly
changed, although a 312-cubic-inch engine was an
option for 1956, and for 1957 this came in three
versions, 245, 270, or 285bhp. These were
introduced to counter the greatly improved and
more powerful Corvettes that were coming on the
market. There were also the McCulloch
supercharged versions giving 300–340bhp, of which
only 208 were made; 300bhp was probably the
maximum output from a customer car, with 340
being reserved for the T-birds that Ford entered in

NASCAR racing during the 1950s.

The four-passenger Thunderbird which
debuted for 1958 was a different car, 11 inches
longer in wheelbase and 20 inches longer overall.
Styling was closer to that of other Fords, although
no T-bird was as distinctive as the Corvette was
from regular Chevrolets. The four-passenger
convertible or hard-top, known as the Square Bird
or Big Bird, was a great success, selling nearly
38,000 in its first year, nearly double the Little
Bird's best figure, and going on to 90,843 in 1960. It
lost whatever sporting image it had in the mid-
1960s, when a four-door sedan was made, but by
the late 1980s the T-bird was again a performance
car, with a turbocharger from 1984 to 1988, and then
a supercharger.

1958 EDSEL CITATION HARDTOP ▲

THE CITATION WAS THE TOP MODEL OF EDSEL, SHARING THE BODY OF THE CORSAIR BUT WITH MORE DELUXE TRIM AND
INTERIORS. BOTH THE CITATION AND THE CORSAIR HAD MERCURY-BASED BODIES ON A 124-INCH WHEELBASE EXCLUSIVE
TO EDSEL. ASSEMBLED IN THE MERCURY FACTORY AT WAYNE, MICHIGAN, THEY WERE KNOWN INTERNALLY AS EMs
(EDSEL MERCURY) TO DISTINGUISH THEM FROM THE LOWER-PRICED FORD-DERIVED EFs. THIS CITATION TWO-DOOR
HARDTOP COUPE SOLD 2,535 UNITS IN THE 1958 MODEL YEAR, AT A PRICE OF $3,535.

OWNER: MIKE SAYER (PHOTO NICKY WRIGHT)

1961 LINCOLN CONTINENTAL FOUR-DOOR CONVERTIBLE ▲

THIS STRIKING CAR MARKED A RETURN TO THE FOUR-DOOR CONVERTIBLE STYLE LAST SEEN IN THE 1930s. IT WAS A BIG CAR, 212.4 INCHES LONG AND WEIGHING 5,215 POUNDS, BUT SHORTER THAN THE MASSIVE 1960 PREMIERE AND CONTINENTAL MARK V. THERE WERE ONLY TWO STYLES IN THE 1961 LINCOLN RANGE, THE CONVERTIBLE AND A SEDAN WITH SIMILAR LINES. THE CONVERTIBLE COST $6,713, MAKING IT AMERICA'S MOST EXPENSIVE CAR IN 1961, APART FROM THE LIMITED-PRODUCTION CADILLAC 75 LIMOUSINE. IT WAS IN AN EXTENDED VERSION OF THE 1961 CONTINENTAL THAT PRESIDENT KENNEDY WAS RIDING WHEN HE WAS ASSASSINATED IN NOVEMBER 1963.

OWNER: BLAINE JENKINS (PHOTO NICKY WRIGHT)

1957 FORD RETRACTABLE SKYLINER ▲

OTHER COMPANIES BUILT SO-CALLED HARDTOP CONVERTIBLES, BUT FORD'S SKYLINER REALLY WAS THAT: THE HARD METAL TOP COULD BE FULLY RETRACTED IN JUST OVER 1 MINUTE. THE SYSTEM INVOLVED THREE DRIVE MOTORS AND FOUR LOCK MOTORS, TEN POWER RELAYS, TEN LIMIT SWITCHES, EIGHT CIRCUIT BREAKERS, AND 610 FEET OF WIRING. IN ORDER TO FIT THE MECHANISM, THE FUEL TANK HAD TO BE RELOCATED BEHIND THE REAR SEAT, AND THE SPARE TIRE WAS RECESSED IN THE TRUNK FLOOR. THE REAR FENDERS WERE 3 INCHES LONGER THAN ON THE STANDARD CONVERTIBLE. WITH ALL THIS COMPLEXITY, THE SKYLINER WAS ONLY $337 MORE THAN THE $2,605 REGULAR CONVERTIBLE. ALL SKYLINERS HAD V8 ENGINES AND WERE MADE FOR THREE SEASONS ONLY, 1957 THROUGH 1959.

OWNERS: RANDY AND CINDY ANKLE (PHOTO NICKY WRIGHT)

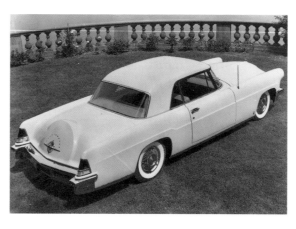

1957 CONTINENTAL MARK II COUPE ▲

MARKETED AS A SEPARATE MARQUE FROM LINCOLN, WHICH THE FIRST CONTINENTAL HAD NEVER BEEN, THE MARK II HAD TOTALLY FRESH STYLING AND A NEW CHASSIS DIPPED BETWEEN FRONT AND REAR AXLES TO GIVE PLENTY OF HEADROOM WITHOUT A HIGH ROOF LINE. THE ENGINE WAS THE STANDARD LINCOLN V8, ALTHOUGH EACH UNIT WAS SELECTED FROM THE ASSEMBLY LINE AND INDIVIDUALLY BALANCED. ALL 2,989 PRODUCTION MARK IIs WERE COUPES, ALTHOUGH A SOLITARY CONVERTIBLE WAS MADE FOR MRS. WILLIAM CLAY FORD, WHOSE HUSBAND HEADED THE CONTINENTAL DIVISION.

LEFT, OWNER: PETE GARBE (PHOTO NICKY WRIGHT); RIGHT, FORD ARCHIVES, MIRCO DE CET COLLECTION

headaches, dissension, and working hours than any other car in history. Guidelines were laid down by merchandising and public relations that it should have two or three syllables, be clear and distinct, and not be prone to obscene double-entendres or translate into anything objectionable. Some of the suggestions made were later adopted as model names, including Citation, Pacer, and Ranger, but the marque name was still unchosen. Advertising agents Foote, Cone & Belding came up with a list of 6,000 names; project chief Dick Krafve exclaimed, "My God, we don't want six thousand names, we only want one," which left FC & B distinctly crestfallen, although presumably they collected their fee just the same.

One who would not accept a fee ("My fancy would be inhibited by acknowledgment in advance of performance") was Brooklyn poet Marianne Moore, whom market research manager David Wallace contacted with a request for suitable names. He recalled that an entertaining

1970 LINCOLN CONTINENTAL MARK III COUPE ◀

LINCOLN REVIVED THE CONTINENTAL MARK SERIES IN 1968, BUT THE MARK III WAS LESS DISTINCTIVE THAN ITS PREDECESSOR, SHARING A CHASSIS AND BODYSHELL WITH THE FORD THUNDERBIRD. IN STYLING IT WAS DISTINGUISHED FROM OTHER LINCOLNS BY ITS RECTANGULAR GRILLE AND SPARE TIRE MOTIF ON THE REAR DECKLID. MORE MODESTLY PRICED THAN THE MARK II AT $6,585, IT SOLD MUCH BETTER; THE FIRST HALF-SEASON FIGURE (IT WAS NOT INTRODUCED UNTIL APRIL 1968) OF 7,710 EASILY EXCEEDED OUTPUT OF THE FIRST CONTINENTAL AND MARK II ADDED TOGETHER.

OWNER: PETE GARBE
(PHOTO NICKY WRIGHT)

correspondence ensued, but none of Miss Moore's suggestions was remotely suitable. They included "The Intelligent Whale" (after a pioneer submarine shaped like a sweet potato), "Resilient Bullet," "Mongoose Civique," "Taper Racer," "Taper Acer," and as a final fling "Utopian Turtletop." Miss Moore never received a fee, but eventually $25 worth of red roses were dispatched to her, with the message "Merry Christmas to our favorite Turtletopper."

As David Wallace recalled, the final choice of name went to the man with the most power, Ernest Breech, who was deputizing for Henry Ford, vacationing in the Bahamas. "Why don't we call it Edsel?" he asked, and when told that Ford family members had expressed their distaste for their father's name to be spinning on countless hubcaps across the nation, he replied "Don't worry about that; I'll take care of Henry."

And so the new car was launched as the Edsel on September 4, 1957, with a TV spectacular starring Bing Crosby with Frank Sinatra as principal guest. This was a significant event in itself, as it marked Crosby's rather belated transition from radio to TV. The trouble was that, after all the hype swallowed and propagated by such wide-selling magazines as *Time* and *Life*, it was not a new car in the sense that the Corvette or Thunderbird were. Apart from its curious grille, its

chief innovation was push-button gear selection in the center of the steering wheel. There were 13 models in four series on three wheelbases, 116 (station wagons), 118, and 124 inches. In addition to the wagons there were two- and four-door sedans, hardtops, and convertibles. Prices ran from $2,519 for a two-door Ranger sedan, a little above the Ford Fairlane 500 on the same wheelbase but with a smaller engine, to $3,801 for a Citation convertible, $317 less than a Mercury Park Lane convertible. Compared with rivals from other groups, these prices were lower than De Soto or Oldsmobile, about on a par with Pontiac, and slightly higher than Dodge.

Although Krafve was given a small assembly plant devoted exclusively to Edsels, most of them rolled off the same lines as Fords and Mercurys, which was logical as they used basically the same bodies and chassis. The trouble was that Edsel was a separate division at first, so Krafve had to pay the Ford or Mercury divisions for every Edsel they

made. If they had been genuine outside suppliers he could have refused to accept a defective car, but as it was he could only complain. There was plenty to complain about. Edsel production was squeezed in at the end of each hour of Ford work, with the inevitable lowering of quality associated with rushed work. Despite McNamara's efforts to rectify matters, dealers and buyers began to see Edsels as being of inferior quality to Fords or Mercurys.

Worse than quality control, which was rectified as time went on, was the shift in American car-buying patterns. During the years when the Edsel was being developed, medium-sized cars accounted for about 40 percent of the market, but by the end of 1957 this had dropped to 25 percent, the balance being taken up by economy cars such as the Rambler American and by imports, which quadrupled between 1956 and 1958. It is debatable whether the Edsel was the right car for any time; certainly the late 1950s were the wrong time. Another factor was the dealer network. Of 2,400 dealers selling Edsels, only 118 had exclusive franchises; the rest were shared with Mercury, or even De Soto, which was not a Ford product at all. With cars in that price range becoming harder to sell, it is not surprising that dealers pushed the well-known makes rather than the newcomer.

Even before the end of 1957 it was evident that the Edsel was not selling well enough to sustain a separate division, so in January 1958 it was merged with Lincoln-Mercury to form the M-E-L Division, which also had responsibility for selling small imports from British and German Ford factories. Edsel production for the 1958 model year was 63,110, putting it in twelfth place. Mercury, in contrast, made 133,271 cars. To break even, Ford needed to sell 650 Edsels a day; for the first ten days the daily average was 409, but then it dropped to around 300.

The Edsel range was cut for the 1959 season to three lines, Ranger, Corsair, and station wagons; only one 120-inch wheelbase was offered, and a 145bhp six joined the V8s as a sop to the economy market. Production slipped to 44,891, and for 1960 the horse collar grille was dropped. This may have deprived comedians of jokes, although most of them had found other sources of humor after the first few months anyway, but it robbed the Edsel of any individuality. The new horizontal grille looked rather like last year's Pontiac, while the bodies were mildly restyled Fords. Only 2,846 '60 Edsels were made, and production ended on November 19, 1959. Customers who had already placed their orders for Edsels were given a $300 voucher toward the purchase of any other Ford product. The Edsel venture is said to have lost Ford more than $250 million, and gave the language a new word for failure.

Ford's other new marque of the 1950s was the Continental Mark II, a response to Lincoln dealers who were asking for a new Continental to replace the much-loved V12 coupes and convertibles that had gone out of production in 1948. Market research indicated that there were some 250,000 to 300,000 families in the United States whose disposable incomes would justify spending $10,000 on a car. At the time of the survey, the most expensive domestic product was the Cadillac Series 75 imperial sedan at $5,643. Some imports such as Rolls-Royce and Ferrari cost over $10,000, but their sales amounted to no more than 200 units a year. The Continental was going to be a gamble, but Ford was willing to take it, and set up a separate division under Henry's younger brother, 26-year old William Clay Ford.

Several body designs were put forward, and the chosen one was by John Reinhart. It was a low, wide four-passenger coupe with no family resemblance to the contemporary Lincoln, which made it a more distinctive design than the former Continentals. A spare wheel motif was molded into the rear deck and actually held the spare wheel. Bodies were not made by Ford's usual supplier, Briggs, but by Mitchell-Bentley of Ionia, Michigan. The Continental Mark II was a big car, 218.5 inches long and weighing 4,825 pounds. The engine was Lincoln's new 368-cubic-inch V8 which developed 285bhp. Experiments had been made with fuel injection, which would have given increased power, but the budget would not allow it.

The Continental Mark II was launched in June 1955 as a 1956 model, the model year running for fifteen months. The price was just under the envisaged $10,000, at $9,695, but customers did not flock to the showrooms. Of the estimated 250,000 families who could have afforded one, only 1,325 actually paid up. The Mark II cost more than twice as much as a Lincoln Premiere ($4,601), but it was clearly not twice the car. Few changes were made for 1957, although power went up to 300bhp, and

1964 FORD FALCON SPRINT HARDTOP ▼

UNDER THE GUIDANCE OF LEE IACOCCA THE FALCON BEGAN TO CHANGE FROM PLAIN-JANE COMPACT TO MUSCLE CAR IN 1963, WHEN V8 POWER WAS AVAILABLE FOR THE FIRST TIME. THE SPRINT WAS THE HIGH-PERFORMANCE VERSION OF THE FALCON FUTURA, AND CAME IN TWO-DOOR HARDTOP AND CONVERTIBLE FORMS, ALL WITH 260-CUBIC-INCH V8 ENGINES. MOST SPRINTS HAD BUCKET SEATS, ALTHOUGH 626 CONVERTIBLES WERE DELIVERED WITH BENCH SEATS.

OWNER: MIKE MYERS (PHOTO NICKY WRIGHT)

production was discontinued on May 13 that year. The total number made was 2,989, plus 23 prototypes, for an overall figure of 3,012. Among the prototypes was a solitary convertible by Derham. Made in 1956 and updated to 1957 specifications, it became the property of Mrs. William Clay Ford. It is estimated that Ford lost $1,000 on each Mark II sold, but at least this was better than Cadillac's estimated loss of $10,000 on each of its Eldorado Brougham rivals to the Continental.

Continental was retained as a separate marque for 1958, but the car was really a de luxe Lincoln with similar styling to other Lincolns, and sold for a more modest $5,800–$6,200. For 1959 it was absorbed into the Lincoln range. A separate Continental series was revived in 1968 with the Mark III, but it was not so distinctive as the Mark II and is generally regarded as a model of Lincoln.

THE SIXTIES: COMPACTS, PONY CARS AND MUSCLE CARS

While independents such as Kaiser, Studebaker, and American Motors built smaller cars in the 1950s, the Big Three left well enough alone until the very end of the decade. The subject was being thought about, though, and two compact designs rejected by Detroit went on to successful careers abroad. These were a Chevrolet tested in four- and six-cylinder form, which inspired the Australian Holden of 1948, and the 1945 compact Ford, which became the French Ford Vedette, also in 1948. Chevrolet began tooling in 1946 for a compact car to be called the Cadet and built in Cleveland, only to drop it because regular-sized Chevies were selling so well.

It was not until October 1959 that the Big Three launched their compacts, and a very diverse trio they turned out to be. Ford's Falcon was the most conventional, using regular Ford engineering with simple, unadorned styling, Chevrolet's Corvair was the most unorthodox with its rear-mounted flat-6 air-cooled engine, while Chrysler's Valiant was front-engined but had completely fresh styling, a tilted engine, and unitary construction. The impetus to bring them out came from the 1958 season, which had been poor for large cars but very successful for the compact Rambler American. The standard size American car had been growing over the previous

few years, so that the 1960 Ford Fairlane stretched 214 inches from bumper to bumper, 16 inches longer than its counterpart of 1954. The Falcon was only 181 inches long, yet offered as much interior space as the regular '54 Fords.

In 1957/58 Fords had been offered in two wheelbases, 116 inches for the Custom line and 118 inches for the Fairlanes. The larger cars had sold better, and 1959, when all Fords rode on a 118-inch wheelbase, was one of the very rare years when Ford outsold Chevrolet. This led the company to favor a two-pronged attack, with its large Fairlane and a considerably smaller car, the Falcon. This used a new 144-cubic-inch 90bhp six-cylinder engine which contained 120 fewer parts than its predecessor. Transmission was three-speed manual, with two-speed Fordomatic optional for an extra $180. Four bodies were offered, two- and four-door sedans, and equivalent station wagons, at prices from $1,912 to $2,287. These were about $300 lower than a six-cylinder Fairlane and more than $700 below the top line V8 Galaxie.

The Falcon may have looked dull in its specification and appearance, but it sold better than the other two compacts, with 435,676 units in its first year. This represented nearly 50 percent of all Ford sales. Within the next few years the Falcon became more exciting, with convertibles and V8

engines from 1963. This was largely the idea of Lee Iacocca, who took over the presidency of Ford in 1960 from the more conservative Robert McNamara. The Falcon was dropped after 1970, but it sired numerous famous Fords, including the Mustang, Comet, and Maverick. At the time of writing it is still being made in Argentina, complete with 1962 styling.

The Corvair had a longer gestation than the Falcon, and it needed it, considering its radical design. Robert Benzinger, who was in charge of engine design, said: "We started with probably about the blankest piece of paper we'd had in a long time." The flat-6 engine was the basis of the design, around which the rest of the car grew. Its layout was possibly inspired by the similarly designed Continental engine that powered the

M42 tank, for Chevrolet's general manager Ed Cole had supervised tank production at Cadillac during the Korean War. Also Cole's private Beechcraft Bonanza used a flat-6. Another factor was the growing success on the U.S. market of Volkswagen, which also featured a rear-mounted air-cooled horizontal engine.

Cole was never a man to shy away from innovation, and the Corvair certainly had the kind of innovations never seen before on a mass-production American car. Up to then no one had seriously questioned the dogma that an automobile must have its engine up front, vertically mounted and water-cooled, driving the rear wheels. The Corvair upset all that, and threw in all-round independent suspension by coil springs as well. The Tucker had several of the Corvair's features, but was hardly an example to follow. Ed Cole wanted the Corvair to be as different as possible from regular Chevrolets, so as not to steal sales from them. He saw it competing against the Rambler and Studebaker Lark, and against the VW and other imports. In fact, because the Corvair appealed to enthusiasts who liked a car that was sporty and fun to drive, it became something of a niche car before the end of its run, but that was not how its creator saw it at the start.

The 140-cubic-inch flat-6 had an aluminum block and separate cylinder barrels. A four-cylinder engine was considered briefly, and would have been much simpler to make, but a 140-cubic-inch four would have been unacceptably rough; apart from Jeep, which was not a regular passenger car, no other American auto maker was offering a four in 1959. In its original form, the Corvair engine gave 80 or 95bhp according to the number of carburetors. Transmission was three-speed manual with floor shift (very unusual at that time), or a two-speed Powerglide. A four-speed manual was optional on the Monza coupe, which came onto the market in May 1960. Initial Corvair bodies were a four-door sedan and two-door coupe. With no tunnel for the drive shaft, they could be full six-passenger automobiles and unusually low as well. Height was 51.5 inches, 3 inches lower than a Falcon. Prices were $1,984–$2,049 for the coupe and $2,038–$2,103 for the sedan, the higher prices being for the De Luxe 700 Series, which accounted for many more sales than the basic 500 Series. The

1961 CHEVROLET CORVAIR MONZA SEDAN ▲
THE MONZA NAME WAS FIRST USED FOR A SPORT COUPE VERSION OF THE CORVAIR, BUT FOR 1961 THERE WAS A MONZA SEDAN WITH BUCKET SEATS, FRONT ARM RESTS, CARPETING, BACK-UP LIGHTS, AND MANY OTHER FEATURES EITHER NOT AVAILABLE ON THE LESSER CORVAIRS OR ONLY AT EXTRA COST. THREE-SPEED MANUAL TRANSMISSION WAS STANDARD, BUT A FOUR-SPEED FLOOR TRANSMISSION WAS A $65 OPTION, WHILE A THREE-SPEED AUTOMATIC COST $157 EXTRA. IN THE BACKGROUND IS A MONZA CONVERTIBLE.
OWNER: LEE ROWE (PHOTO NICKY WRIGHT)

more powerful Monza coupe was priced at $2,265.

First year sales of the Corvair were 250,007, not much over half the Falcon's figure, but well ahead of the Valiant's 182,274. The Corvair received the best press reports, and the editors of *Motor Trend* named it their Car of the Year in April 1960. For 1961 a station wagon was added, and in addition there was the Greenbriar, a forward-cab six-door sports wagon also made in half-ton panel delivery and pick-up form.

April 1962 saw important changes in the Corvair range. The Lakewood station wagon was dropped because it was facing heavy competition from the conventional Falcon-like Chevy II which had arrived the previous fall. This simple car, which used Chevrolet's first four-cylinder engine since

1928, was an acknowledgment that GM could not rely on the unorthodox Corvair to challenge the Falcon and Valiant as basic transportation. With the Chevy II taking that role, at prices slightly below those of the Corvair, the latter was pushed into the role of a sporty car for the enthusiast. The station wagon was withdrawn, but in its place came the first Corvair convertible, the Monza, offered with a turbocharger which raised power from 90 to 150bhp. This was the world's first use of a turbocharger in a production car, although it differed from most later designs in that the turbo was mounted between the carburetor and intake manifold, drawing air through the carb, whereas modern turbos blow air into the carb or fuel injection system. The turbo version was called the Monza Spyder, and cost an extra $317.45, this being part of a package that included a heavy-duty clutch, four-speed transmission, and strengthened suspension.

The Monza Spyder soon attracted a cult following, but it had two serious drawbacks. Like all early turbos, there was a lag of up to 2 seconds between flooring the accelerator and any reaction from the engine, which took some getting used to. Once going, though, the Spyder was brisk, with 0–60mph taking 9.7 seconds compared with a snail-like 23.2 seconds for the original 80bhp Corvair. The other problem was handling with a high proportion of weight in the rear. Original weight distribution was to be 40/60 front/rear, but when the spare tire was moved from under the hood this went up to 37/63. Tire pressures were critical; the makers recommended 15psi at the front and 26psi at the rear, and these inflations, combined with the heavy-duty suspension, made for pretty good handling. Not every driver bothered too much about tire pressures, though.

For 1964 the Spyder became a standard model instead of an option package, and displacement went up to 164 cubic inches. With the turbo, power was now 180bhp and top speed 114mph. The convertible price was $2,811 — expensive for a Corvair, but more than $1,200 below a Corvette. The Monza was considered the poor man's equivalent to the Corvette. Indeed, for nimbleness and sense of driver control, it was more enjoyable than the more powerful front-engined car. All Corvairs were restyled for 1965, but by then sales were dropping. From a peak of 329,632 in 1961 they fell to 207,114, in 1964, and the restyling only lifted them slightly to 237,056 for 1965. Thereafter they dropped rapidly, to 103,745 in 1966, 27,253 in 1967, and only 6,000 in 1969, the last Corvair leaving the line on May 14 that year.

Much has been written about the death of the Corvair, the blame being laid on Ralph Nader. A crusading young lawyer (who didn't hold a driver's license), Nader published an article in *The Nation* magazine in November 1965 entitled "The Corvair Story." This formed the first chapter of his book *Unsafe at any Speed*, which came out the same month. His charges were that the swing axle, under the severe lateral forces produced by cornering, tended to lift the rear wheels of the car so that both wheels leaned outward, the angle increasing from

an acceptable 4° to a dangerous10° or 11°. The wheels tucked under in an instant causing rollover. Maurice Olley, an ex-Rolls-Royce GM engineer, had warned of this when he saw the swing axle designs before the Corvair project was launched, but his warnings were ignored. He had studied European cars with rear engines and swing axles, such as the Volkswagen Beetle and Renault Dauphine, and pronounced them "a poor bargain." The Corvair was heavier than either of these, with a higher proportion of weight at the rear. There were certainly a number of one-car accidents involving Corvairs, including the one which cost comedian Ernie Kovacs his life. Nader pointed out that GM could easily have afforded safety research, as their net income as a percentage of sales was 10.2 percent (Ford, 5.6 percent) and their return on invested capital was 20.4 percent (Ford 11.3 percent).

Nader certainly influenced some Corvair owners to shop elsewhere for their next car, but his book was not crucial. The problem was that the complex Corvair was not as profitable as more conventional Chevrolets. As early as May 1965, when Nader was still at his typewriter, word went down the line to stop further development on the Corvair, just to do enough to satisfy Federal smog and safety requirements. The Mustang, which debuted in April 1964, was the biggest threat to the Corvair, for its wide hood could accommodate any size of V8 engine. The Corvair flat-6 could not be enlarged much without a complete redesign, and when a 283-cubic-inch V8 was tried the handling was so terrible that the idea was quickly forgotten.

1972 PLYMOUTH DUSTER ◀
THE DUSTER WAS A NEW PLYMOUTH FOR 1970, AIMED AT THE FORD MAVERICK MARKET. IN BASIC FORM, IT WAS AN ECONOMY COMPACT, ALTHOUGH THERE WAS A PERFORMANCE VERSION, THE 340, WITH 275bhp V8 ENGINE. WONDER HOW MANY CARS THIS CUTESY AD SOLD?
CHRYSLER CORPORATION

Many special versions of the Corvair were made, including three which were regarded as separate makes. John Fitch's Phoenix of 1966 was a two-passenger convertible with a body built in Italy by Intermeccanica. It had an electrically operated rear window and a removable metal roof panel that could be stowed in the trunk. A tuned engine gave 170bhp without the need for a turbocharger. The really high-performance Corvairs were called Yenko Stingers. Built by Don Yenko of Canonsburg, Pennsylvania, they came in several degrees of performance, the hottest having an engine bored out to 176 cubic inches and giving 240bhp. About 130 Stingers were made between 1965 and 1969, and they won many races, the last in 1973, four years after Corvair production ended.

The most bizarre of all Corvair conversions was the Lost Cause, offered by former mayor of Louisville, Kentucky, Charles Peaslee Farnsley. Using a 1963 four-door sedan, he had Derham do some customizing of the bodywork and equipped the interior with such delights as altimeter, compass, picnic hamper, lap robes, matching luggage, and vermeil mint julep cups. If you dared sip your mint julep at 115mph, a John Fitch

conversion was available to provide this speed. Even without the Fitch conversion, the cost was $19,600, more than eight times that of a regular Corvair sedan.

The third competitor for the compact market was Chrysler's Valiant, which appeared on October 29, 1959 — 27 days after the Corvair. Built by Dodge and sold mainly by Plymouth dealers, it was considered a separate brand for the 1960 season only, after which it became a Plymouth. A new Plymouth-DeSoto-Valiant Division was created, and the Valiant was promoted as "Nobody's kid brother — this one stands on its own four tires." It was certainly different, with totally fresh styling dominated by a rectangular grille and sculptured rear end with simulated spare wheel cover molded into the trunk lid. The spare wheel actually lived under the trunk floor, but the effect was stylish, recalling the Continental Mark II.

The Valiant's engine was a 170-cubic-inch over-head valve six tilted at 30° to allow a lower hood. It gave 110bhp, or 148bhp with a four-barrel carburetor, and featured alternator ignition, not used by Plymouth. Two bodies were offered initially, a four-door sedan and a station wagon

called the Suburban. The latter was made in two versions, with two or three rows of seats; the third row, for two passengers, was rear-facing. Like the other compacts, the Valiants came with a three-speed manual transmission as standard, with a two-speed automatic as a $172 option. Prices were $2,033 for a basic sedan and $2,546 for a de luxe nine-passenger Suburban; although listed as a nine-passenger, the rear seat of the de luxe Suburban would not comfortably accommodate more than two adults, whereas the larger Plymouth Suburban was a genuine nine-passenger car.

The Valiant changed little until 1963, when it lost its distinctive styling in favor of a blander look somewhat reminiscent of a Rambler. A convertible was offered and a 225-cubic-inch six was an alternative engine. The 1964 Valiant-based Barracuda coupe was hastily developed to meet the Mustang challenge. Upon learning that Ford was working on a sporty car based on the Falcon, Chrysler set to work on a rival. Having less money and time, for the Mustang project was well advanced before the rumors started, Chrysler could not afford an all-new body, so used the regular Valiant shell back to the windshield, and grafted onto it a two-door coupe with an enormous wraparound rear window; this was the Barracuda's most distinctive feature — with an area of 2,070 square inches, it was the largest piece of glass ever used in an automobile. A choice of three engines was offered, the 170 or 225-cubic-inch sixes, and a new 180bhp 273-cubic-inch V8.

As a Mustang rival, the Barracuda was a pony car, while installation of the larger V8s put it in the muscle car category, to be considered later. Meanwhile the Valiant sedans, convertibles, and Suburbans were continued as the lowest-priced Plymouth line up to 1976. Some were very plain-Jane cars in styling and performance, but in 1971 you could have a 275bhp 340-cubic-inch V8 in your Valiant Duster coupe.

The 1960 compacts catered well for the low-priced market, but the buyer who wanted a little more style and performance in a small package got nothing from the Big Three. He did not have long to wait, however, for the 1961 season saw three new cars from Buick, Oldsmobile, and Pontiac, as well as the Valiant-related Dodge Lancer. The GM cars were very interesting, for while they shared the same basic bodies, they incorporated plenty of technical innovation in engines and transmissions. Somewhat larger than the Big Three compacts, they rode on 112-inch wheelbases.

The Buick Special and Oldsmobile F-85 appeared in the first week of October 1960, with the Pontiac Tempest following on November 3. Buick and Oldsmobile shared a 215-cubic-inch V8 with aluminum blocks and cylinder heads, but the engines were not identical. Output was the same, at 155bhp, but combustion chamber differences gave the Buick slightly better torque. Pontiac, on the other hand, used a 194.5-cubic-inch four which was essentially half of the big 389 V8. More than 120 parts were common to both engines, with only 16 non-common parts, including the fuel pump. Standard output was 110bhp, but higher compression ratios and four-barrel carbs gave 120, 130, 140, or 155bhp, and the Buick V8 was also available in the Tempest, though only 2 percent of buyers chose it in the first season. The Tempest's transmission was unconventional, with a curved driveshaft driving to a rear axle mounted three-speed manual transmission. The shaft was arched just under 3 inches at its center (if the arch were a

1961 PONTIAC TEMPEST SEDAN ▲▼
THE TEMPEST WAS THE LEAST CONVENTIONAL OF GM'S SECOND GENERATION OF COMPACTS, WHICH INCLUDED THE BUICK SPECIAL AND OLDSMOBILE F-85. THE ENGINE WAS A 194.5-CUBIC-INCH FOUR, EFFECTIVELY HALF OF PONTIAC'S 389 V8, AND THE TRANSMISSION WAS VIA A CURVED DRIVESHAFT TO A THREE-SPEED MANUAL GEARBOX LOCATED ON THE REAR AXLE. WITH FIRST SEASON SALES OF OVER 100,000, THE TEMPEST BEAT ITS RIVALS FROM BUICK AND OLDSMOBILE.
PONTIAC MOTOR DIVISION, GENERAL MOTORS (PHOTO NICKY WRIGHT)

segment of a complete circle, it would have had a diameter of 73 feet) and absorbed much of the torsional vibration associated with a four-cylinder engine.

Although it had the same body as Olds and Buick, the Tempest had a strong Pontiac appearance thanks to its divided grille. Sedans, coupes, and station wagons were available, and Tempest sales were the best of the three makes, at 100,783. For comparison, the Buick Special sold 86,868 and the Olds F-85 59,674.

For 1962, a 198-cubic-inch cast-iron V6 joined the V8 in the Buick, and convertibles were added to all three ranges. From Spring 1962 to summer 1963, the Olds F-85 was offered with a turbocharger similar to that of the Corvair; 215bhp from 215 cubic inches allowed Olds to boast of

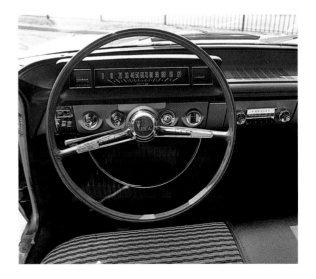

being the first U.S. manufacturer to offer 1 horsepower per cubic inch. However, Chevrolet had achieved this with the 1957 Corvette, and the turbo Corvair gave a better ratio, 150bhp from 145 cubic inches. An advantage of the Olds turbo was that it incorporated a wastegate, in effect a safety valve which "blew off" when pressure threatened to damage the engine. To combat build-up of carbon deposits in the cylinders, Olds injected a 50-50 mixture of methyl alcohol and water between the carburetor and turbocharger, calling the mixture "turbo rocket fluid." However, it was found that at the top end of the speed range, acceleration faded away, so that a Jetfire was slower than a four-barrel carb non-turbo car. The Jetfire, made as a two-door coupe only, was dropped after 9,607 had been made.

Fine engine though it was, the aluminum V8 proved uneconomical to make, so it was dropped after the 1963 season. It was subsequently sold to Rover in England, where it featured in Rover cars, Range Rovers, Morgan, and TVR sports cars. In its place came the cast-iron V6 in both Buicks and Oldsmobiles, although larger V8s were also available, 300 cubic inches in the Buick and 330 in the Olds F-85 Cutlass. The Pontiac Tempest lost its four in favor of a 215-cubic-inch six, and there were also V8 options. The cars were growing in size, and were called intermediates rather than compacts. The year 1964 was the first in which Pontiac used the magic letters GTO (Gran Turismo Omologato, or homologated Grand Touring), which were to appear on the company's powerful muscle cars.

1964½ FORD MUSTANGS ▲ ▶

THE FIRST SERIES MUSTANGS ARE CALLED 1964½ MODELS, AS THEY WERE INTRODUCED IN MID-SEASON, APRIL 17, 1964, SEVEN MONTHS LATER THAN OTHER 1964 FORDS. A COMPACT CAR WITH A VARIETY OF CHARACTERS FROM TAME TO FIERCE ACCORDING TO THE ENGINE FITTED, THE MUSTANG WAS DETROIT'S GREATEST SUCCESS OF THE 1960s. AT ONE TIME THERE WERE 15 ORDERS FOR EVERY AVAILABLE MUSTANG AND DEALERS TOOK TO AUCTIONING OFF THE CARS THEY HAD. THE FIRST MUSTANG WAS GIVEN THE TIFFANY AWARD FOR EXCELLENCE IN AMERICAN DESIGN, THE ONLY TIME AN AUTOMOBILE HAS BEEN SO HONORED. SEEN HERE ARE THE FIRST SEASON CONVERTIBLE AND COUPE.

CONVERTIBLE OWNER: BILL GOOSENE (PHOTO NICKY WRIGHT)

COUPE: FORD ARCHIVES, MIRCO DE CET COLLECTION

PONY CARS AND MUSCLE CARS

The 1960s saw a widening of American car ranges that has continued up to the present day. In the early 1950s there was generally one body shell made in traditional models such as sedan, coupe, convertible, and station wagon, and more often than not, only one engine. By the end of the decade there were usually several engine options from a humble six to a powerful V8, but only one size of car on a single wheelbase. Then came the compacts which grew into intermediates, and two new types emerged, the personal two-door four-passenger coupe and the high-performance machine which resulted from installing the most powerful V8 from the full size range in an intermediate body shell. The former were nicknamed "pony cars," while a powerful engine in an intermediate sedan body shell was called a "muscle car."

The first of the pony cars was the Ford Mustang; doubtless the name was derived from that of the Mustang, although the word pony was appropriate to their size and nimbleness. Interestingly, the term "pony car," used to designate a comparatively small sporty car, was current in the United States back in the 1920s. Some historians have called the Mustang the most significant American car of the 1960s; certainly it captured the trends of the decade, a brilliant piece of market identification as successful as the Edsel was disastrous.

Although many people were responsible for its design, the Mustang owed its existence to one man, Lee Iacocca. The Pennsylvania-born son of an Italian immigrant, Iacocca became a Ford salesman in Allentown, and vowed that he would be a Ford vice-president by his 35th birthday. He didn't quite make it, although 18 days after the birthday Henry Ford II invited him to become Vice-President of Cars and Trucks, with overall responsibility for Lincoln-Mercury as well as Ford. This was in January 1965, by which time the Mustang had been on the market for nearly a year.

If the Mustang idea had any ancestors, the two-passenger Thunderbird and the Corvair Monza were among them. Ever since the "baby 'bird" had been dropped, Ford customers and dealers had been calling for a replacement, while the bucket-seated Monza accounted for 76 percent of all Corvair sales. Iacocca was devoted to the philosophy of Thinking Young and had been responsible for Ford's re-entry into NASCAR events as well as dropping a V8 engine into the Falcon. He saw the growing purchasing power of the young and of women. The postwar baby boomers were coming up to driving age by the mid-1960s and were increasingly likely to want a car different from that of their parents. Women had traditionally influenced their menfolk in the choice of a car, but were now actually buying cars for themselves, particularly young, professional women such as teachers, accountants, and doctors. In Iacocca's mind it all added up to the need for an individually styled car, smaller than the regular models but without the family sedan image of the existing compacts.

A lot of market research figures have been published concerning the expected growth of the 15–29 year old sector of the market, its preference for sporty cars, floor shifts, and so on, and these have been given as the impetus for the Mustang project. However, according to Donald Frey, Iacocca's manager of product planning, most of the encouraging market research figures came after the project was under way. "They made it all up afterward — somebody did — in order to sanctify the whole thing. The market research that you read of is a bunch of bull."

The original Mustang prototype had a German-built Ford V4 engine mounted transversely behind the driver and passenger. It was tested at Watkins Glen by racing driver Dan Gurney, who loved it, as did the rest of the racing fraternity. However, Iacocca knew that a car that pleased the racing buffs would never sell in the volume he wanted, so it was abandoned. The car that came to the market in April 1964 was a front-engined coupe or convertible

with a long hood and a relatively short passenger compartment that seated four. Iacocca saw to it that it covered as wide a market as possible, with five engines, six transmissions, three suspension packages, three brake systems, three wheel sizes, and many other options in the comfort and performance fields. This blanket market coverage was later used in the Anglo-German Ford Capri, although not with such a wide range of options.

Mustang engines in the first year were a 101bhp 171-cubic-inch six, a 260-cubic-inch V8 (164bhp), and three variations of the 289 V8, giving 210, 220, and 271bhp. Only 26.9 percent of customers chose the six, but this rose to 41.7 percent the following

year. In view of the supposed preference of the young for floor-shift manual transmissions, it is surprising to find that in the first year 49.2 percent of Mustangs were sold with automatic transmission, rising to 62.6 percent on the 1965 models, and to 90.4 percent by 1973.

The Mustang's target price was $2,500, but Ford managed to start at $2,368 for the base six-cylinder coupe. The V8 options added between $75 and $442.60, while four-speed manual transmission was an extra $75.80. Thus a Mustang with the most powerful V8 engine and all the handling and performance options could cost over $3,850, but this fitted perfectly with Iacocca's aim. The young, economy-minded schoolteacher could buy a Mustang for $2,368, while the speed enthusiast could also be a Mustang customer. This reasoning certainly worked, for more than 100,000 Mustangs were sold in the first four months of production, while the first 24 months accounted for over 1 million. For 1965, the six went up to 200 cubic inches, front disk brakes were available (at $58), and a fastback coupe joined the hardtop and convertible. Power options went up over the next few years to keep pace with competition from Plymouth's

Barracuda and Chevrolet's Camaro. For 1968 there were seven engine choices, from a 115bhp six to a 390bhp 427-cubic-inch V8. The most powerful Mustangs were the Boss 429s of 1969, which developed 375bhp in standard form, and up to 515bhp when tuned for Trans Am racing.

Distinctive Mustangs, although not the most powerful, were those assembled by Carroll Shelby and marketed as a separate make from 1965 through 1970. The first 100 were built in Ford's San Jose, California, plant and had a number of Shelby-requested modifications. These included the hi po (high power) 289 engine with stronger con rods and crankshaft, and a Shelby-designed camshaft. The engines were delivered to Shelby's plant near Los Angeles airport, where they were further developed, with four-barrel Holley carburetor and improved exhaust manifolding. Handling was improved by stiffer anti-roll bars, new steering arms, and modified suspension. The

1970 FORD MUSTANG BOSS 302 COUPE ▲▶

NAMED FOR ITS ENGINE DISPLACEMENT, THE BOSS 302 WAS A HIGH-PERFORMANCE MUSTANG LAUNCHED IN MID-1969 AS A ROAD-GOING VERSION OF THE TRANS AM RACING MUSTANGS. OUTPUT WAS RATED AT 290bhp, BUT 350bhp WAS A MORE REALISTIC FIGURE. MADE ONLY IN COUPE FORM, THE 302s HAD SPECIAL STRIPING, A FRONT "CHIN" SPOILER, AND DISTINCTIVE REAR WINDOW LOUVERS. STANDARD EQUIPMENT INCLUDED HEAVY-DUTY SPRINGS, FOUR-SPEED MANUAL TRANSMISSION, AND POWER-ASSISTED FRONT DISK BRAKES; 1,934 BOSS 302s WERE MADE IN 1969 AND 6,318 IN 1970.

OWNERS: TOM AND CAROL PODEMSKI (PHOTO NICKY WRIGHT)

rear seat was replaced by a shelf, and a fiberglass hood took the place of the metal one. Externally the Shelby Mustangs were distinguished by a thin blue stripe running between front and rear wheel arches, incorporating the letters GTO 350, and two wide blue stripes running from the front of the hood over the top and down the rear deck. In standard form a GT 350 gave 306bhp, but Carroll Shelby soon brought out the Competition version with 350bhp. About 25 of these were sold, and they became SCCA (Sports Car Club of America) "B" Production Class champions in 1966 and 1967.

GT 350 production was only 562 in 1965, but the next year 2,378 were made, including 936 bought by Hertz Rent-A-Car. Hirers had to be aged over 25 with a clean license; rates were $17 a day and 17 cents a mile. Most of the Hertz cars except the very earliest had automatic transmissions, whereas the regular GT 350 came with a four-speed manual.

In 1967 the GT 350 was joined by the GT 500, which offered such refinements as a rear seat, air conditioning, and power steering and brakes. To cope with the additional weight the 429-cubic-inch engine was used, and performance was similar to that of the smaller cars. The luxury/GT package with seating for four seemed to appeal more than the stark 350, and 1967 sales of the GT 500 were 2,950, nearly double the 1,175 350s sold. Late that year Shelby lost the lease on the Los Angeles airport site, and later Shelby Mustangs were built in the Ford plant. Problems with insurance, emission, and safety regulations, common to all high-performance cars, brought Shelby production to an end in 1970.

We have seen that Plymouth's Barracuda began as a hastily produced rival to the Mustang, but in its early days it was not offered with such a wide variety of options. Stirred into action by the challenge of the Mustang, Pontiac GTO, and Oldsmobile 4-4-2, Plymouth offered a 235bhp V8 for $146 extra in the 1965 Barracuda and enhanced its sporting character by an all-synchro four-speed transmission with Hurst floor gearshift. For 1967 the Barracuda was restyled to distance it from the prosaic Valiant, and three bodies were offered, fastback and notchback coupes, and a convertible. The body was 11/2 inches wider, which meant that the hood could accommodate the 383-cubic-inch V8 giving 280 or 325bhp. A year later the fabulous 425bhp 426 hemi engine could be had in the Barracuda, although very few were so equipped and those mostly for drag racing.

The years 1970 and 1971 were the last for the big-engined Barracudas, when a wide range was offered. The car had been nicknamed the 'Cuda, and for 1970 this became the official name for the high-performance versions, carried in script on the rear end. Models included the AAR 'Cuda, named for the All-American Racers developed for Dan Gurney and the Plymouth Trans Am team. This used the 290bhp 340-cubic-inch V8, but 'Cudas could be had with a 383, 440, or 426 hemi engine. The 440 was less powerful than the 426, as it did not have the hemi head, but still delivered 390bhp. It was known as the six-pack, from its three two-barrel carburetors; 0–60mph took 5.9 seconds, pretty impressive for a 3,720-pound car. Nor was it very expensive. Base price for a 440 six-pack was $3,414, but this could be inflated by options such as power steering and brakes. Singer Richard Carpenter bought a 440 six-pack with every possible option except air conditioning, not available on the 440 as there was no space under the hood for the compressor, and paid $4,400.

With Ford and Chrysler offering increasingly powerful pony cars, GM had to get in on the act too, which it did in 1967 with the Chevrolet Camaro and Pontiac Firebird. When the Mustang first appeared, GM management was not very

1968 CHEVROLET CAMARO SS CONVERTIBLE ◀▲
THE CAMARO WAS GM'S ANSWER TO FORD'S PHENOMENALLY SUCCESSFUL MUSTANG, AND FOLLOWED THE SAME PHILOSOPHY OF A SPORTY FOUR-PASSENGER CAR WITH A WIDE RANGE OF ENGINES, IN THIS CASE FROM A 140bhp SIX TO A 350bhp V8. THE LETTERS SS INDICATE A SPORT PACKAGE; THIS INCLUDED STIFFER SPRINGS AND SHOCK ABSORBERS, WIDER TIRES, DISK BRAKES, AND A MODIFIED HOOD WITH EXTRA SOUND INSULATION.
(PHOTO NICKY WRIGHT)

1969 PONTIAC FIREBIRD TRANS AM COUPE ▲▶

THE FIREBIRD WAS PONTIAC DIVISION'S VERSION OF THE CAMARO, AND USED THE SAME SHEET METAL, WITH ITS OWN DISTINCTIVE FRONT END. ENGINES WERE NOT SHARED WITH THE CAMARO, BEING PONTIAC UNITS FROM A 165bhp SIX TO A 325bhp V8. THE TRANS AM VERSION WAS INTRODUCED IN MARCH 1969 AND FEATURED A 345bhp ENGINE, HEAVY-DUTY THREE-SPEED MANUAL GEARBOX, AEROFOIL ON THE REAR DECK, AND FULL-LENGTH BODY STRIPES ON HOOD, TOP, AND REAR DECK. THIS IS A RARE CAR, AS ONLY 607 TRANS AMS WERE MADE IN 1969. IT WAS PRICED AT $3,556, WHILE A REGULAR FIREBIRD COUPE COST $2,831.

OWNER: KEITH WILSON (PHOTO NICKY WRIGHT)

interested, thinking that it had a good competitor in the Corvair Monza. However, by the time the Mustang had sold 100,000 cars in four months, rethinking was suggested, and a program was hurriedly set in motion which resulted in the Camaro for the 1967 season. It was in many ways a similar concept to the Mustang, being a hardtop coupe or convertible with two standard engines, a 230-cubic-inch six and a 327-cubic-inch V8. The latter could be had in various models from 210 to 325bhp, and another option was the 350bhp 396-cubic-inch V8. The six-cylinder coupe was priced just $5 above the Mustang at $2,466, while the V8s were up to $70 more.

While the F-car, as it was called before being named Camaro, was being developed by Chevrolet, GM reasoned that it could sell more pony cars through two divisions than one (Ford was already doing the same with the Mustang-based Mercury Cougar) and that the second model should come from Pontiac. This was a logical choice, for

Pontiac already had a sporty image with the GTO, and its General Manager John Z. DeLorean was performance-minded and had recently submitted proposals for a two-passenger sports car. This was killed off by the Pontiac F-car, on which work started only six months before the Camaro's debut in September 1966. It was to have been called the Banshee, a name Pontiac had used for some of its show cars, but when an ad agency did a dictionary check and found that a banshee (a spirit in Irish folklore) foretold a death in the family, a hasty search for other names began. Firebird, which had also been used for General Motors prototypes, was ultimately chosen.

The Firebird used the same sheet metal as the Camaro for all major body panels, but managed a distinctive front end appearance by adding a large grille/bumper ahead of the fender, common to both models. Engines were Pontiac's own, a 165bhp 230-cubic-inch six and V8s of 326 and 400 cubic inches, giving 250–285 and 350bhp. The latter

breached GM's internal rule that power should not exceed a ratio of 10 pounds/horsepower, so the 350 was reduced to 325bhp by a small metal tab in the throttle linkage. Once the car had been sold with a limit of 325bhp, there was nothing GM or anyone else could do to prevent those tabs being removed. Ride characteristics were better on the Firebird, which had different spring rates and two adjustable traction bars connecting the rear axle to the floorpans rather than the Camaro's one.

The Firebird was launched in mid-season on February 23, 1967. Prices were about $200 higher than the Camaro right through the range. Both cars were soon given high-performance models, the Camaro Z/28 appearing in December 1966 and the Firebird Trans Am in March 1969. Both were suitable for street or track, and won many races in the Trans Am series. These were started in 1966 by the Sports Car Club of America for sedans in two classes, up to 2.5 liters (152.5 cubic inches) and up to 5 liters (305 cubic inches). The small class was dominated by foreign cars such as Alfa Romeo, but the larger was just right for the pony cars, and promoted much rivalry between Mustangs, Camaros, Firebirds, Barracudas, Challengers, and AMC Javelins. Z/28s took 18 out of the 25 races in 1967, and won the class championships in 1968 and 1969, while the Trans Am was third in the 1969 series. Both cars had 302-cubic-inch engines, the largest permitted under SCCA rules.

Street Z/28s and Trans Ams could be had with larger engines, up to 400 cubic inches. Only 697 Trans Ams were built in 1969, and of these precisely eight were convertibles. These were the only convertible Trans Ams ever built. The next Firebirds were not introduced until February 1970, which led to them being called 1970½ models. They had restyled bodies with lower, meaner lines, and six engines from a 155bhp six to a 345bhp V8. With the latter, 0-60mph took only 5.4 seconds.

1967 AMERICAN MOTORS MARLIN COUPE ▶

THE MARLIN WAS AMC'S ENTRY INTO THE MUSTANG/CAMARO PERSONAL CAR MARKET, BUT IT MET WITH MUCH LESS SUCCESS THAN THESE. ORIGINALLY STYLED THE RAMBLER MARLIN IN 1965, IT WAS A FASTBACK COUPE DERIVED FROM THE RAMBLER CLASSIC SEDAN ON A 112-INCH WHEELBASE. THE 1967 MARLIN WAS LONGER AND BETTER LOOKING, BEING BASED ON THE 118-INCH AMBASSADOR, BUT SALES WERE SLUGGISH: ONLY 4,547 IN 1966 AND 2,545 IN 1967. ENGINE OPTIONS WERE A 145bhp SIX AND V8s OF 235 OR 280bhp, AND SPORTY ITEMS SUCH AS FOUR-SPEED MANUAL TRANSMISSION, BUCKET SEATS, AND TACHOMETER WERE ALSO AVAILABLE.

(PHOTO NICKY WRIGHT)

1964 FORD GALAXIE 500 SEDAN ▲

THE FULL-SIZE FORDS WERE COMPLETELY RESTYLED FOR 1964 WITH A MORE COMPLEX GRILLE AND SCULPTURED LOWER BODY PANELS. THE BASE MODEL WAS THE CUSTOM, FOLLOWED BY THE GALAXIE AND GALAXIE XL, THE LATTER WITH FLOOR TRANSMISSION, BUCKET SEATS, AND OTHER SPORTY APPURTENANCES. AVAILABLE ENGINES COULD BE ANYTHING FROM A 138bhp SIX THROUGH FIVE V8s, TOPPED BY THE 425bhp 427-CUBIC-INCH UNIT THAT POWERED THE SUCCESSFUL NASCAR RACERS.

OWNER: JEFFREY HODDER (PHOTO NICKY WRIGHT)

1961 PONTIAC BONNEVILLE CONVERTIBLE ▲

PONTIAC'S TRANSFORMATION FROM A STAID "AUNTIE" CAR TO AN AUTO HIGH IN PERFORMANCE AND STYLE WAS ALMOST COMPLETE BY 1961. A LARGE CAR ON A 123-INCH WHEELBASE WITH AN OVERALL LENGTH OF 217 INCHES, THE BONNEVILLE WAS PONTIAC'S TOP LINE. THREE BODIES WERE OFFERED, SEDAN, HARDTOP, AND CONVERTIBLE, OF WHICH THE CONVERTIBLE WAS THE MOST COSTLY AT $3,905. THE CUSTOM SAFARI STATION WAGON WAS A SEPARATE SERIES. THE BASE ENGINE WAS A 303bhp 389-CUBIC-INCH V8, WITH THE 348bhp TRI-POWER V8 AS AN OPTION.

OWNER: BARRY BALES (PHOTO NICKY WRIGHT)

1954 LINCOLN CAPRI CUSTOM COUPE ◄

LINCOLN'S RACING PROGRAM PRECEDED THAT OF FORD BY THREE YEARS, AND WAS CONCENTRATED ON THE CARRERA PANAMERICANA, A 1,938-MILE RACE ACROSS THE OFTEN UNMADE ROADS OF MEXICO. LINCOLNS TOOK THE FIRST FOUR PLACES IN THE PRODUCTION CAR CLASS IN NOVEMBER 1952 AND 1953, AND THE FRIST TWO PLACES IN 1954. THIS CAPRI COUPE, DRIVEN BY RAY CRAWFORD, WAS THE WINNER, FOLLOWED BY WALT FAULKNER. CADILLACS TOOK THE NEXT TWO PLACES.

OWNER: NATIONAL AUTOMOBILE MUSEUM, RENO, NEVADA

(PHOTO NICKY WRIGHT)

1964 DODGE POLARA 500 HARDTOP ▲

INTRODUCED IN 1960, THE POLARA WAS THE TOP MODEL OF DODGE, AND IN 1964 WAS AVAILABLE IN FOUR BODY STYLES, SEDAN, HARDTOP SEDAN, HARDTOP COUPE, AND CONVERTIBLE. THE POLARA 500 WAS A SPECIAL TRIM OPTION WITH BUCKET SEATS, "SPORTS INTERIOR TRIM," AND EXTERIOR IDENTIFICATION NAMEPLATES. A VERY SMALL NUMBER OF POLARA 500s, OF WHICH THIS IS ONE, WERE FITTED WITH THE 426 HEMI ENGINE, GIVING 415 OR 425bhp ACCORDING TO COMPRESSION RATIO.

OWNER: JIM DONALDSON (PHOTO NICKY WRIGHT)

The front air dam and rear spoilers on the Trans Am were made of fiberglass, and were developed not in a wind tunnel but by running on a dry lake. The Trans Am name has been retained for the top model of Firebird up to the present day.

American Motors was not going to be left out of the pony car field, and in 1966 sorely needed a change from its "sound and sensible" image. The answer was the Javelin, launched in September 1967. It had a new four-passenger coupe body with a choice of three existing AMC engines, a 232-cubic-inch six, and 290 or 343 V8s, the latter with four-barrel carburetor and dual exhausts. Heavy-duty suspension, front disk brakes, and wide tires made it a good performer, with a top speed approaching 120mph. At $2,482 for the six and $2,588 for the smaller V8, the Javelin was lower in price than the Mustang, Camaro, or Barracuda. Unlike its rivals, it was never offered in convertible form.

First year sales for the Javelin were 55,124, quite encouraging for an independent car maker, but after that they dropped instead of climbing. By 1972 sales were down to 26,184, and although they recovered to over 27,000 in the next two years, AMC dropped the Javelin at the end of 1974 because it could not meet Federal bumper standards without a drastic redesign.

From mid-1968 to the end of the 1970 season, there was a shorter companion to the Javelin called the AMX. Unique among pony cars in that it seated only two passengers, it was 12 inches shorter in wheelbase. To reinforce its sporty image the AMX was not available with the six-cylinder engine; the 225bhp 343 V8 was standard, with optional 280bhp 343 and 315bhp 390 V8s. Richard

Teague, vice-president of styling at AMC, recalled that the AMX gave the Corvettes a really hard time in local races, and feels that with a little more time for development and styling improvements, it could have been a great car; not a big seller, but a useful addition to AMC's prestige. Unfortunately sales were very modest, only 6,725 in 1968 and 8,293 in 1969. AMC president William Luneburg

complained that it was cluttering up the line, and killed it at the end of 1970. Total production of AMXs was 19,134, and of Javelins 236,379.

1968 PONTIAC GTO COUPE ▲▼
OFTEN CITED AS THE FIRST OF THE MUSCLE CARS,
THE GTO WAS A GOOD EXAMPLE OF THE OLD FORMULA
OF LARGE ENGINE IN MID-SIZED BODYSHELL. THE GTO
BEGAN LIFE IN 1964 AS A SUB-MODEL OF THE TEMPEST,
BUT BY THE TIME THIS 1968 COUPE WAS BUILT IT
WAS A LINE OF ITS OWN, AND ONE OF THE MOST
EXCITING OF ALL PONTIACS. FOUR ENGINE OPTIONS
WERE OFFERED, FROM 265 TO 366bhp, THE MORE
POWERFUL HAVING FOUR-JET CARBURETION AND
10.75:1 COMPRESSION RATIOS. COUPES WERE BY FAR
THE MOST POPULAR, WITH 77,704 DELIVERED,
COMPARED WITH 9,980 CONVERTIBLES.
OWNER: BARRY BALES (PHOTO NICKY WRIGHT)

MUSCLE CARS

Precise definitions are seldom accurate, but it is generally considered that two-door purpose-built coupes like the Mustang and Camaro are "pony cars," no matter how powerful their engines, while intermediates or full-size cars with the same engines under the hood are "muscle cars." Competition has reinforced the distinction, for pony cars competed in SCCA Trans Am races, while muscle cars ran in the NASCAR events. These dated back to 1947 when dirt track races were held for stock production sedans and coupes. Purpose-built tracks which became banked oval superspeedways followed, mostly in the Southeastern states which were the birthplace and spiritual home of stock car racing.

During the 1950s auto makers began to develop cars for NASCAR events, encouraged by the slogan "The sedan that wins on Sunday sells on Monday." Plymouth began supporting NASCAR in 1949, Dodge in 1953, Ford in 1955, and Pontiac in 1957. Their regular sedans became increasingly powerful, so it is not easy to say where or when the

AMERICA'S FIRST PRODUCTION FRONT-DRIVE CAR SINCE THE 1937 CORD, THE TORONADO WAS A PERSONAL FOUR-PASSENGER COUPE POWERED BY A 425-CUBIC-INCH V8 ENGINE, OLDSMOBILE'S LARGEST THAT YEAR. WITH 385bhp, IT WAS THE MOST POWERFUL VERSION OF THIS ENGINE. LOCATED SLIGHTLY TO THE RIGHT OF CENTER, IT HAD A TORQUE CONVERTER TO THE REAR, CONNECTED VIA CHAIN DRIVE TO THE AUTOMATIC TRANSMISSION. EARLY TORONADOS (1966) GOT THROUGH FRONT TIRES AT AN ALARMING RATE, BUT IMPROVED SUSPENSION ON THE '67s RESULTED IN A HIGHER TIRE MILEAGE. THIS 1967 TORO SOLD FOR $4,945.

(PHOTO NICK GEORGANO)

muscle car breed began. The Pontiac Tempest GTO of 1964 is often cited as the first, but what about the Chevrolet Impala SS 409, the Pontiac Grand Prix 421, the Ford Galaxie 500 XL, all cars of 1962 or 1963, and all delivering more than 400bhp? They were production cars, but their ancestors were the tuned and lowered custom cars of the 1950s, the first fruits of the marriage between youth culture and the automobile.

Some of the customs were purely performance cars, hot rods designed for straight-line acceleration, while others were styling exercises of which the peak was represented by the creations of George Barris. Most were something of both, for to gain the admiration of the pack, you needed Go as well as Show. A new car culture emerged in the late 1950s, riding on the back of growing national prosperity and youth independence. The car had always been an important status symbol for the family, but now the young wanted something quite different from their parents. Some went for foreign sports cars, but these were always expensive, and too small. Youth culture flourished in groups rather than exclusive couples; if your friends were temporarily carless you could take six of them around in your Galaxie, which you certainly couldn't do in an MG or Jaguar XK120. And if you wanted privacy with your girlfriend, the Galaxie was also fine, and a lot warmer and more comfortable than the MG.

The hot rod and custom car movement began, like so many trends, in California, but by 1960 had spread to virtually every town across the nation.

The growing suburbs, with miles rather than blocks between home and school, shops, restaurants, and drive-in movie houses, made the need for personal transportation ever more important. The car and its nurture soon became a way of life for millions of Americans between the ages of 15 and 25. As Dave Emanuel said: "The entire legacy of human interaction could be experienced from the front seat of a one-and-a-half ton three hundred horsepower womb. Heroes and villains, damsels in distress and gallant knights, courtesans, jesters, and pretenders could all play out their roles as the wombs rolled from stoplight to drive-in to parking lot."

Music, too, took up the theme. Groups such as the Beach Boys and Jan and Dean came up with "Little Deuce Coupe," "Shutdown," "409," "Dead-man's Curve," and "Little GTO," a best seller from the never-heard-from-again group Ronnie and the Daytonas. Dave Emanuel again: "The religion of the automotive sub-culture was now complete. It had its own icons, high priests, rubric, argot, and finally, its very own hymns."

Despite the popularity of hopped-up full-size sedans and coupes, the market welcomed the Pontiac GTO with wild enthusiasm. It was the idea of John DeLorean and his team and followed the age-old theme of a big engine in a small body. The engine was the 389-cubic-inch V8 from the Pontiac's Catalina/Bonneville line in 325 or 348bhp versions, and the body was the Tempest coupe. This had grown somewhat from its launch as a compact for 1961, but was still 17 inches shorter than the full-size Pontiacs. To round out the sporting specification,

THE 4-4-2 ORIGINATED IN 1964 AS A PERFORMANCE PACKAGE ON OLDS' F-85 COMPACT CAR. THE NUMBERS INDICATE FOUR-ON-THE-FLOOR TRANSMISSION, FOUR-BARREL CARB, AND TWIN EXHAUSTS. ALSO INCLUDED IN THE PACKAGE, EARLIER OFFERED ON POLICE CARS, WERE HEAVY-DUTY SPRINGS AND SHOCK ABSORBERS, A SPECIAL AIR CLEANER, AND SPECIAL FENDER EMBLEMS. BY 1970, THE YEAR OF THIS 4-4-2 COUPE, A 455-CUBIC-INCH 365bhp ENGINE WAS USED, BUT FROM 1971 ONWARD EMISSION CONTROL LAWS ENFORCED A DECLINE IN POWER.

(PHOTO NICKY WRIGHT)

1970 DODGE CHALLENGER R/T COUPE ▲

THE CHALLENGER WAS DODGE'S ANSWER TO THE MUSTANG AND THE CAMARO, AND WAS A SMALLER COMPANION TO THE CHARGER MUSCLE CAR. A NEW MODEL FOR 1970, IT WAS OFFERED AS A HARDTOP OR CONVERTIBLE, WITH TWO REGULAR ENGINE OPTIONS, A 145BHP SLANT-6 AND A 230BHP V8. THERE WERE SIX OTHER OPTIONS UP TO THE FORMIDABLE 425BHP 426 HEMI. R/T REPRESENTS ROAD/TRACK, AND WAS APPLIED TO THE HIGHER-PERFORMANCE CHALLENGERS WITH 383 OR LARGER V8 ENGINES. 1970 CHALLENGER OUTPUT WAS 83,032 CARS, OF WHICH 60 PERCENT HAD THE STANDARD V8 AND 26 PERCENT OPTIONAL V8s; 14.4 PERCENT WERE SIXES.

OWNER: LARRY BELL (PHOTO NICKY WRIGHT)

were 32,450 the first year, 75,352 the second, and 96,946 the third. Research revealed that the average age of a GTO buyer was 25.7 years, compared with 43.3 years for all other new car buyers; that 30 percent were living with their parents (6 percent of all new car buyers); that 60 percent had attended college (46 percent of all new car buyers); and that 43 percent were unmarried. Roughly the same figures probably applied to purchasers of the GTO's rivals, which sprang up between 1965 and 1970.

Chevrolet and Oldsmobile responded to the GTO with the Chevelle SS-396 and the Cutlass 4-4-2, both of which had intermediate body shells with powerful V8 engines. Output started at 375bhp in the Chevrolet and 290 in the Olds, but quickly went up to 425bhp in the 1966 SS-396 and 390bhp in the 1968 4-4-2. This designation signified four-on-the-floor transmission, four-barrel carb, and dual exhausts. The ultimate 4-4-2 was the Hurst/Olds of 1968; this began as a special for gearbox manufacturer George Hurst, but was offered as a limited production model prepared by Lansing industrialist John Demmer. He received the 4-4-2s from the Olds assembly line, and in his own workshops fitted the Hurst four-speed transmission or HydraMatic with Hurst floor shifter, and high-performance cylinder heads which gave 390bhp from the 455-cubic-inch engine. Only 515 Hurst/Olds were made in 1968, all coupes, and 906 in 1969. No convertibles received the Hurst treatment, and indeed convertible muscle cars were generally few and far between. The GTO was made in a special version called The Judge in 1969; of 6,833 made, only 108 were convertibles.

Convertibles were never offered on the Chrysler Corporation's muscle cars, which were some of the most dramatic of all. Dodge's Charger began in 1965 as a fastback coupe derived from the mid-sized Coronet, and was available with the usual choice of engines from a relatively mild 230bhp 318-cubic-inch V8 to a blistering 425bhp from the 426 hemi V8. This remarkable engine was developed for NASCAR events in 1964 and was so successful that NASCAR stipulated that all engines should be available in production cars. Because of this, Dodge and Plymouth took a year out from NASCAR racing in 1965 and came up with the "street hemi" for 1966, used in the Charger,

the GTO had a four-speed floorshift transmission and beefed-up suspension and brakes. It nearly didn't happen at all, for DeLorean knew that the GM hierarchy would not approve the idea, so he went ahead quietly. "When the corporation management got wind of the car shortly before it was introduced, it was mad. But the GTO was too late in its development to be stopped."

As we have seen, the letters GTO stood for Gran Turismo Omologato, the designation used by Ferrari for the cars it had manufactured in sufficient numbers to be homologated for production car racing. As might have been expected, sports cars enthusiasts objected to the use of the hallowed letters on a mass-produced American car, but as *Car & Driver* pointed out, the Pontiac could beat the Ferrari in a straight line, and with NASCAR suspension, even on corners. "The Ferrari costs at least $20,000; with every conceivable option on a GTO it would be difficult to spend more than $3,800. That's a bargain."

Strictly speaking, the GTO was an option package on the Tempest Le Mans for 1964 and 1965, becoming a line in its own right in 1966. Sales

1970 DODGE CHARGER RT/SE HEMI COUPE ◄

CHRYSLER CORPORATION'S HEMI ENGINES OF
THE 1960s WERE THE SECOND GENERATION OF THIS
DESIGN, AND WERE ALWAYS LIMITED EDITIONS.
THIS RT/SE (*ROAD & TRACK*, SPECIAL EDITION)
COUPE IS VERY RARE, ONLY FOUR HAVING BEEN MADE
IN 1970. THE 426 STREET HEMI POWER UNIT COST
AN ADDITIONAL $618 OVER THE $3,711 PRICE
OF THE CHARGER WITH 400 ENGINE. THE SE PACKAGE
INCLUDED SPECIAL EXTERIOR AND INTERIOR TRIM,
AND WAS NOT CONCERNED WITH PERFORMANCE.
PROBABLY THE MOST FAMOUS CHARGER R/T WAS
"THE GENERAL LEE," THE FOUR-WHEELED STAR
OF THE "DUKES OF HAZZARD" TV SERIES.
THE WHOLE STOCK CAR RACING SCENE GREW UP
IN THE COUNTRY DISTRICTS OF THE SOUTHEASTERN
UNITED STATES, TYPIFIED BY HAZZARD COUNTY.

OWNER: STEVE WITMER (PHOTO NICKY WRIGHT)

1974 PLYMOUTH ROAD RUNNER 440 COUPE ►

1974 SAW THE END OF BOTH THE HIGH-PERFORMANCE
PLYMOUTH LINES, BARRACUDA AND SATELLITE,
THE ROAD RUNNER BEING A MEMBER OF THE
SATELLITE FAMILY. THE STANDARD ENGINE
IN THE ROAD RUNNER WAS A 318-CUBIC-INCH V8
GIVING ONLY 170bhp, ALTHOUGH THE 440 WAS
AN OPTION. EVEN THIS DEVELOPED ONLY 275bhp,
COMPARED WITH 390bhp FOUR YEARS EARLIER.
THE ROAD RUNNER WAS IDENTIFIED BY THE STRIPES,
POWER BULGE ON THE HOOD, AND CARTOON BIRD
EMBLEM ON THE VERTICAL PART OF THE STRIPE,
JUST BEHIND THE WINDOWS. IT WAS PRICED AT $3,545,
AND 11,555 WERE MADE IN THE 1974 SEASON.

OWNER: GILMORE CAR MUSEUM, KALAMAZOO, MICHIGAN

(PHOTO NICKY WRIGHT)

Plymouth Belvedere, and Satellite, and later in the Barracuda, Road Runner, and GTX. The fastback Charger gave way to a notchback design for 1968, of which the muscle version was the Charger R/T (Road/Track), available with the 426 hemi or the larger but less powerful (375bhp) 440-cubic-inch V8. Along with other sporting Dodges such as the Super Bee, Dart GTS, and Coronet R/T, it came with bumble bee stripes running round the rear deck and on the quarter panels. These cars were collectively known as Dodge's Scat Pack. The Charger was the most performance-oriented, with stiffer springs and shock absorbers, and larger front disk brakes than its stablemates. When *Road & Track* editors tested an automatic version they

1964 AND 1971 BUICK RIVIERA COUPES ◀▼▲▶

ONE OF THE MOST IMPORTANT POSTWAR BUICKS, THE RIVIERA ORIGINATED IN A BILL MITCHELL PROJECT TO REVIVE THE LASALLE. MITCHELL TOOK OVER FROM HARLEY EARL AS GM's STYLING CHIEF IN 1958, AND PENNED A FRESHLY STYLED PERSONAL SPORT COUPE WHICH WENT INTO PRODUCTION AS A SEPARATE BUICK LINE FOR 1963. IT REMAINED A SEPARATE LINE, MADE ONLY AS A HARDTOP COUPE, THROUGH THE 70s. BY 1971 THE WHEELBASE HAD INCREASED FROM 117 TO 122 INCHES, AND MITCHELL HAD GIVEN IT A VERY DRAMATIC BOATTAIL REAR DECK; SOME THOUGHT IT THE MOST BEAUTIFUL CAR TO APPEAR IN YEARS, WHILE OTHERS HATED IT. THE 455-CUBIC-INCH V8 ENGINE GAVE 315 OR 345bhp.

OWNER: ED BEHLE (PHOTO NICKY WRIGHT)

recorded a top speed of 156mph and 0–60mph in 4.8 seconds, a figure hardly equaled by any of today's supercars from Lamborghini or Ferrari. However, Chrysler had reservations about the hemi's longevity; the normal five-year or 50,000-mile warranty was reduced to 12 months or 12,000 miles for any car equipped with the hemi engine, and even then only if the engine had not been modified in any way.

Plymouth's hemi-powered cars were the Road Runner and GTX coupes. The former was named after the cartoon bird, whose "beep-beep" call was imitated by the car's horn. The GTX was similar in appearance, but more luxuriously equipped, hence the $3,355 price, $459 above the Road Runner. The 426 hemi was an option in both cars, but few were fitted compared with the 383 or 440 engines. The most dramatic-looking Road Runners were the

Superbirds of 1970. These were replicas of the NASCAR racers, with extended streamlined noses and large rear stabilizers. Regulations dictated that Plymouth build half as many of these cars as the total number of dealers, so 1,920 were made. The hand-built Superbird was priced at $4,298, while a regular Road Runner coupe cost $3,204. There was a very similar-looking Dodge, the Charger Daytona, of which 505 were made in the 1969/70 season.

For the muscle car, 1970 was the high point. After that the pony cars took over briefly as the favorite choice of performance-minded youngsters. Then the whole scene changed. Environmental pressures forced power-reducing controls on engine design and the oil crisis intervened. In some cases the names lingered on lesser cars, such as the Barracuda (to 1974), BD Charger (to 1978), and the 4-4-2 to the present day. Only the Firebird, Camaro, and Corvette survived the 1970s, to receive a new lease of life and power in the next decade.

1991 CHEVROLET CAPRICE SEDAN ▼

CHEVROLET DIVISION, GENERAL MOTORS (PHOTO NICKY WRIGHT)

CHAPTER SEVEN

THE AMERICAN AUTOMOBILE AT BAY

1970 – 1992

"Americans are fat and happy, but that doesn't mean America is finished. When it gets tough they will straighten out."

Lee Iacocca, chairman of Chrysler, 1988

1979 AMC PACER LIMITED STATION WAGON ▲

THE PACER WAS LAUNCHED IN 1975 AS A COMPETITOR FOR FORD'S PINTO AND CHEVROLET'S VEGA, ALTHOUGH AT $3,299 IT WAS MORE EXPENSIVE THAN EITHER. THE PLANNED POWER UNIT WAS A GM-BUILT WANKEL ROTARY ENGINE, BUT WHEN THIS WAS DROPPED THE PACER HAD TO USE A RELATIVELY HEAVY AMC-BUILT SIX, WHICH DAMAGED PERFORMANCE AND ECONOMY. BY 1979, WHEN THIS STATION WAGON WAS MADE, A 304-CUBIC-INCH V8 WAS AN ALTERNATIVE TO THE SIX. THIS LIMITED WAGON COST A HEFTY $6,189 WITH THE SIX-CYLINDER ENGINE, AND $6,589 WITH THE V8. THE PACER WAS DROPPED AFTER THE 1980 SEASON.

OWNER: EBER SCHMUCKER (PHOTO NICKY WRIGHT)

THE PAST TWO DECADES have been more traumatic for the American auto industry than anything that went before. The Depression of the 1930s saw a more drastic drop in production, but it was a worldwide phenomenon. America still turned out more than twice as many cars as its nearest rival (Britain), and the Depression bottomed out within three years, after which there was a cautious climb to renewed prosperity. There are few signs of such a climb back today. American complacency, Arab self-assertiveness, and Japanese drive and ingenuity have wrought mighty and irreversible changes in the American auto scene.

In 1970 the industry was riding high, with production of more than 6.5 million passenger cars, more than double that of its nearest rival, Japan. Luxury cars such as the Cadillac Eldorado had the world's largest engine at 500 cubic inches and Chrysler's Hemi 426 was the world's most powerful at 425bhp. When John Q. Public bought a Ford, Chevrolet, or Pontiac (or almost any other make), he knew he was buying an American-designed and American-built car and giving employment to American workers. Twenty years later a Ford Festiva was a Korean-built Japanese Mazda design, a Chevrolet Turbo Sprint was a Japanese-built Suzuki, and a Pontiac Le Mans was a German-designed Opel Kadett built in Korea. The best-selling American-built model in 1989 and 1990 was a Honda Accord.

Ever since 1906, when France fell from its commanding position, America had built more cars than any other nation, and even in 1970 there was no reason to suppose that this position would change. America was the natural leader, and although exports were not as large as they had been in the 1920s and 1930s, U.S. companies made cars throughout Europe, Latin America, and Australia. No foreign companies were building cars on American soil.

IMPORTS AND THE AMERICAN RESPONSE

Until well into the 1950s the imported car was a grace note on the American scene, not an important economic factor. Before World War II imports were largely confined to luxury cars such as Mercedes, Minerva, Renault, and Rolls-Royce, although there were some improbable imports such as Fiat's tiny 500 Topolino (Mickey Mouse); 434 were sold in 1938/39, making it the best-selling imported car. Almost every corner of the world wanted American cars, but America had no need of the products of the rest of the world.

In the early postwar years imports meant sports cars, first MG Midgets, then Allard J2s, which were fitted with American engines, and Jaguar XK120s. The first family car to make any impact on the U.S. market was the Volkswagen Beetle, early examples

of which reached these shores in 1949. Sales were negligible the first year, but in 1950 New York dealer Max Hoffmann managed to move 157 of the funny little foreign cars. In 1954 the figure had jumped to 6,343, and VW chief Heinz Nordhoff was able to describe the Beetle as the symbol of German recovery. In 1955, 35,581 Volkswagens found buyers in the United States; the 500,000th was sold in June 1960 and the 5 millionth in September 1971. In 1962 there were 687 VW dealers across the nation.

Although the most successful of the foreign imports, the Volkswagen was not the only small foreign car to change the ingrained habits of American drivers. Renault, Simca, and Fiat all sold in reasonable numbers in the late 1950s, leading to total imports of 100,000 in 1956, which doubled in 1957 and again in 1958. Buick dealers started selling Opel Olympias from GM's German factory in 1957, and Pontiac did the same with British-built Vauxhalls from 1958. These sold well for a while,

but were badly hit by the compact cars from 1960 onward. Who wanted a 55bhp four-cylinder Vauxhall station wagon for $2,367 when he could get an 85bhp six-cylinder Ford Falcon station wagon for $2,287? From 1961 Vauxhalls were available on a special order basis only, and not many orders materialized.

The Japanese made a very hesitant start. The first Toyotas reached the West Coast in 1957, against the wishes of designer Kenya Yakamura, who felt that Toyota was not ready to challenge the U.S. market. Ford's Donald Frey tried a Toyota and pronounced it to be "a piece of junk." By U.S. standards, Toyotas were poorly made and so underpowered that they could not accelerate safely when joining freeways. You had to be pretty desperate to take on a Toyota dealership.

Robert Krause of Schnecksville, Pennsylvania, lost his Dodge and Plymouth agency when the main distributor switched to Ford in 1959. Needing something to sell, he took on a franchise for the Toyopet Crown Custom, purchasing six of the 65bhp 88-cubic-inch four-door sedans, plus $800 worth of parts, special tools, and a small sign. Selling Toyopets was no bed of roses; people asked if they were made of beer cans, and once on the

1975 CHEVROLET COSWORTH VEGA SPORT COUPE ▲

THE VEGA WAS CHEVROLET'S CANDIDATE IN THE SUBCOMPACT FIELD, AND WAS MADE FROM 1970 THROUGH 1977. OF THE 1,988,933 BUILT, 3,508 HAD A TWIN-CAM 16-VALVE ALUMINUM CYLINDER HEAD DESIGNED BY COSWORTH ENGINEERING, THE BRITISH COMPANY FAMED FOR ITS 3-LITRE DFV V8, WHICH POWERED MANY FORMULA 1 RACE CARS. FUEL SUPPLY WAS BY BENDIX ELECTRONIC FUEL INJECTION CONTROLLED BY A COMPUTER LOCATED IN THE GLOVEBOX. UNFORTUNATELY THE "COSVEG" NEVER DEVELOPED ENOUGH POWER TO MATCH THE EXPECTATIONS RAISED BY ITS "GO FASTER" STRIPES, WIDE RADIAL TIRES, ANTIROLL BARS FRONT AND REAR, AND CAST ALUMINUM WHEELS. PERFORMANCE WAS LITTLE BETTER THAN A VOLKSWAGEN RABBIT. THE "COSVEG" WAS PRODUCED FOR THE 1975 AND 1976 SEASONS ONLY.

OWNER: NATIONAL AUTOMOBILE MUSEUM, RENO, NEVADA (PHOTO NICKY WRIGHT)

road they suffered broken valves at 55–60mph and seized overdrives after 300 miles. Krause sold 12 cars his first year, but stayed with Toyota. He was still with them in 1990, having one of the oldest Toyota franchises in the country. He describes it as "the next best thing to owning a McDonalds."

The Japanese studied the U.S. industry very carefully. In the early 1950s Eiji Toyoda of Toyota spent three months at Ford, remarking when he left: "I realize this is the way to produce perfect cars. Toyota has much to learn here. . . Because we are such a little company, we managers have to be involved in all the manufacturing areas."

Before long Japanese engineers began to see ways in which they could improve on American techniques. Take, for example, the design of stamping machines. In America machines tended to make the same parts for weeks at a time, which led to stockpiling. This meant that capital was tied up for a long time. The Japanese were determined to turn materials into money as soon as possible, so Toyota's production manager Taiichi Ohno developed machines that could be changed easily, making 100 units of one shape, then turning to another. Such changes took up to three hours in Detroit, hence the reluctance to make frequent

changes, but Ohno got them down to a few minutes. The enormous capital investment for such machinery was met by low-cost loans from the Japan Development Bank and the World Bank.

Other Japanese firms moved into the U.S. market, Datsun with its Bluebird in 1960, Mitsubishi with the Colt, sold by Dodge from 1971, and Honda with the Civic from 1973. These and, more important, Volkswagen prompted Detroit to move into a still smaller market than had been attempted hitherto, the "sub-compact" sector. True to its custom of innovation, American Motors was first in this field with the Gremlin, announced as a mid-season model on April 1, 1970. It rode on a 96-

inch wheelbase and from the doors forward was similar to the compact-sized Hornet. The rear end was very short, with a sharply sloping fastback and very little overhang. Two- and four-passenger models were available, the latter with a fold-down rear seat. The standard engine was a 323-cubic-inch six, also used in the Hornet, Javelin, and Matador, but a larger six of 258 cubic inches was an option.

Despite controversial styling, which meant that a sizable minority of potential buyers couldn't stand it, the Gremlin sold well enough, 26,000 in the half season to September. Stylist Richard A. Teague maintained that it needed to look different. "Nobody would have paid it any attention if it had looked like one of the Big Three."

In September 1970 the Big Two had answers to the Gremlin. Chevrolet's Vega debuted on September 10 and Ford's Pinto eight days later. Chrysler's planned sub-compact never appeared, but instead the British Hillman Avenger was imported and sold under the name Plymouth Cricket. The Pinto and the Vega were generally similar, with two-door sedan bodies on wheelbases of 94.2 and 97 inches respectively. Both ranges included a station wagon, the Pinto's not until 1972. The Pinto was another of Lee Iacocca's babies and took less than three years from original conception to showroom. Both engines were European-built fours, a British 75bhp 98.6-cubic-inch unit with pushrod overhead valves, or a German 100bhp 122-cubic-inch with single overhead camshaft. The Vega was more American in content, with a specially designed 140-cubic-inch four with cogged belt drive to the single overhead camshaft, made in 90 or 110bhp forms. The Pinto cost $1,919–$2,062 compared with the Vega's $2,090–$2,328.

In its first season the Pinto outsold the Vega by 352,402 to 269,905, and continued to do so until the Vega was dropped after 1977. Neither model was free from problems, the Pinto suffering severe criticism with regard to safety, and the Vega dogged by body rust, rough engines, oil leaks, and cylinder head warping. The Vega also suffered from something of an identity crisis, as the Corvair had done. Intended as a mass-market low-price sedan, it acquired the image of a sporty small car for a specialty market, an image reinforced by its hatchback coupe. In 1975 there was an overtly sporting model, the Cosworth-Vega, which used a 16-valve twin-overhead cam engine developed by the British firm Cosworth Engineering Ltd. Ironically, Cosworth was famed mainly for its work with Ford in the 3-liter engine used in countless Formula One racing cars, and in the 16-valve four of today's Cosworth Sierra Sapphire 144mph sedans.

Cosworth's involvement with GM was not a happy one. The development time was very long, for John DeLorean had planned a Cosworth engine

for the Vega in 1969, more than twelve months before the car was launched, yet the Cosworth-Vega did not come onto the market until May 1975. By then emission controls had seriously eroded the engine's power. The first development engines of 1971 gave 180bhp, which augured really dramatic performance, but the production engine of 1975 gave no more than 110bhp and 0–60mph in 12.3 seconds was on a par with the Volkswagen Rabbit, hardly the BMW rival that Chevrolet anticipated. The Cosworth's price was much higher than the Rabbit, though, at $5,916, and nearly double that of the regular Vega hatchback. The youth market at which the car was aimed either couldn't afford the price or preferred to pay another $900 and buy a Corvette. GM planned to sell 5,000 Cosworth-Vegas per year, but only managed 3,508 in two seasons; 1,500 unused engines were scrapped.

The Vega stayed in the Chevrolet range until 1977, but in 1976 it was supplanted at the lower-priced end by the Chevette. This was GM's first world car, and was soon made in five different countries, Brazil, the United States, Britain, Germany, and Japan. Called a Chevette in the first three countries, in Germany it was the Opel Kadett and in Japan the Isuzu Gemini. It was a

▼ BUILDING, REPAIRING, AND IMPROVING ROADS WENT ON ALL THROUGH THE 1970s, AS IN PREVIOUS DECADES. THESE PHOTOS SHOW M-84 AT SAGINAW, MICHIGAN, BEFORE AND AFTER REPAIRS THAT TOOK PLACE IN THE FALL OF 1975.
MICHIGAN DEPARTMENT OF HIGHWAYS

1990 CADILLAC FLEETWOOD SEDAN ▲▶
FLEETWOOD HAD BEEN CADILLAC'S "CAPTIVE" COACHBUILDERS SINCE THE LATE 1920s AND THE NAME WAS USED FOR MANY POSTWAR CLOSED MODELS, ESPECIALLY THE LONG-WHEELBASE LIMOUSINES. THE 1990 FLEETWOOD SEDAN WAS A FRONT-DRIVE C-BODY CAR WITH A 272.5-CUBIC-INCH FUEL-INJECTED V8 ENGINE GIVING 185bhp. IN THE BACKGROUND ARE EARLIER CADILLACS OF (LEFT TO RIGHT) 1939, 1946, 1954, 1967, AND 1976.

CADILLAC DIVISION, GENERAL MOTORS

conventional small car (94.3-inch wheelbase) in the European mold, with a front engine, rear drive, and unit body construction, and was originally made in three-door hatchback form only. A five-door on a 97.3-inch wheelbase arrived for 1978. Two four-cylinder engines were offered, an 85-cubic-inch 52bhp and a 98-cubic-inch 60bhp. These were more conventional than the Vega's, with iron cylinder blocks in place of aluminum, although they used the cogged rubber belt for driving the overhead camshaft.

The Chevette sold for a modest $2,899 in its stripped Scooter form, although most customers preferred to pay an extra $199 for the more fully equipped version. Chevrolet geared up for 275,000 Chevettes in 1976, but actually sold only 187,817. The first impact of the oil shortage was receding and Americans were turning to larger cars again. In the long term, though, the Chevette was a success, selling 451,161 units in 1980 and 433,600 in 1981, when a diesel option was added. But it never reached these figures in later years, when it was overtaken by more advanced front-drive small cars such as Ford's Escort and various imports. The

1990 CHEVROLET BLAZER 4 X 4 STATION WAGON ▲▼

THE RUGGED 4 X 4 WITH GOOD CROSS-COUNTRY ABILITY WAS A POPULAR MODEL WITH ALL AMERICAN
MANUFACTURERS FROM THE 1960s. THEY FOLLOWED THEIR REGULAR COUSINS IN REDUCTION IN SIZE IN THE EARLY
1980s, AND CHEVROLET'S SMALLER BLAZER S JOINED THE BIGGER BLAZER IN SEPTEMBER 1982. IT WAS MADE THROUGH
1990 WITH A 262-CUBIC-INCH V6 ENGINE IN TWO- AND FOUR-DOOR MODELS.

CHEVROLET DIVISION, GENERAL MOTORS

Chevette soldiered on into 1987, when only 46,208 were made, but by then the sub-compact end of the Chevrolet range had been taken over by the three-cylinder Sprint, actually a Japanese-built Suzuki Swift. For 1989 the Sprint was rebadged as a Geo Metro, part of the Geo range which was a subdivision of Chevrolet. Other Geos were the imported Spectrum (Isuzu) and Tracker (Suzuki 4x4), and the California-built Toyota-designed Nova.

Ford continued the Pinto through the 1980 season, by which time 3,150,313 had been made. A 170-cubic-inch V6 engine originating from Ford's German division was an optional alternative to the four from 1975 through 1979. Styling evolved gradually, but the round-backed body of 1980 was clearly recognizable as the same design that had appeared in the fall of 1970. A Mercury version called the Bobcat appeared in 1975. Costing around $400 more than the equivalent Pintos, Bobcats were better trimmed and were distinguished by what the auto editors of *Consumer Guide* called "a pretentious little stand-up grille." Like the Pinto, the Bobcat survived to the end of the 1980 season.

For 1981 Ford replaced the Pinto with its own world car, the Escort. This was a new design with transverse-mounted engine driving the front wheels, although the Escort name had been carried on rear-drive British and German Fords since 1968. Code-named Erika, the new small Ford was conceived by Ford's powertrain research group in Dearborn, but was engineered for production in Europe, where there was more experience in small displacement four-cylinder engines. Like the Chevette, the Escort engine had a cast-iron block with aluminum intake manifolds and crossflow heads. Combustion chambers were hemispherical, as in the Chrysler muscle cars of the 1960s although nobody made much fuss about it. The engine had a 97.6-cubic-inch displacement, giving 65bhp, and this was upped to 72 or 88bhp for 1983, and to 120bhp on the turbo version of 1984.

Transmission was four-speed automatic, with a five-speed manual arriving for 1983. Escort bodies were similar in appearance to the European varieties, three-door hatchbacks or four-door station wagons, with a five-door hatchback coming in 1982. Mercury equivalents at slightly higher prices were called Lynx. The Escort convertible and high-performance XR3, both popular models in Europe, were never made in the United States.

For 1982 a new coupe derived from the Escort appeared, under the name EXP. Ford's first two-seater since the original Thunderbird, it used the same wheelbase and engines as the Escort, but new body panels disguised the hatchback's appearance completely. However, it did not sell too well. Everyone realized that it was just a re-skinned Escort costing around $1,000 more. The EXP lasted until 1988, but a companion Mercury, the LN7, did not survive beyond 1983.

The Escort was Ford's best-selling model in the United States for several years, but profit margins on each car were very low and for a while it was a net drain on company resources. For 1990 Ford decided to shop abroad for the Escort's replacement. Still called an Escort, the new model launched in mid-season was a rebodied Mazda 323

with a 116-cubic-inch Ford four in the base model, and a 110-cubic-inch twin cam Mazda four in the GT. The latter gave 127bhp. Despite the fact that the engineering work was done in Japan, the new Escort program still cost Ford $2 billion. No wonder more and more American auto makers are sharing their new models with foreign firms.

Chrysler's sub-compacts were all foreign-based from 1970 onward. From 1971 through 1977 they relied on imports, the Hillman Avenger-based Plymouth Cricket from 1971 through 1973, and various Mitsubishi designs sold as Plymouth Arrow or Dodge Colt from 1971 through 1977. For 1978 Chrysler launched the Dodge Omni and Plymouth Horizon, very similar front-drive five-door hatchbacks with styling based on that of the European Chrysler Horizon. Unlike the Cricket and Colt, the Horizon and Omni were made in the United States and had U.S.-designed four-cylinder 104.7-cubic-inch engines based on a Volkswagen unit. For 1979 Chrysler followed Ford in offering a sporty-looking coupe derived from its sub-compact. Known as the Dodge 024 or Plymouth TC3, it was 2½ inches shorter in wheelbase and offered 2+2 seating at an extra cost of up to $400 above the hatchback. In 1982, however, Plymouth offered Miser models of both designs at an identical $5,299. In 1983 the 024 and TC3 became the Charger and Turismo, and were continued until 1989. The Omni/Horizon hatchbacks lasted until December 1989, after which they were replaced by Chrysler-distributed Mitsubishis and the Dodge Shadow/Plymouth Sundance sedans. These, introduced in 1986, were 2 inches shorter in wheelbase, but increased overhang gave them greater overall length than the Horizon.

DESIGNED IN WASHINGTON?

Until the late 1960s car design was largely dictated by two interests, consumers on the one hand and manufacturers' accountants on the other. Engineers and stylists juggled with what they perceived to be consumer tastes and the limitations imposed by accounts and general management. Sometimes they got public taste wrong, as with the Chrysler Airflow. Often they had to bow to financial necessity and abandon cherished technical advances. Then, suddenly, a third factor loomed: the bureaucrats in Washington, whose dictates alarmed engineers and accountants alike.

It is hardly an exaggeration to say that in the 1960s much of the decision-making power passed from Detroit to Washington. By setting standards for fuel consumption, exhaust emissions, and safety the legislators mandated whole new fields of

1980 CADILLAC SEVILLE SEDAN ▲

ONE OF THE CARS OFFERED WITH A DIESEL ENGINE FROM 1978 TO 1985 WAS THE SEVILLE. IT WAS THE FIRST CADILLAC TO BE BUILT TO COMPETE WITH AN IMPORTED CAR IN THE INTERMEDIATE SIZE, THE MERCEDES-BENZ 450. ALTHOUGH CONSIDERABLY SMALLER THAN ANY OTHER CADILLAC, WITH A WHEELBASE OF 114.3 INCHES (THE DE VILLE AND CALAIS WERE 130 INCHES), IT WAS MORE EXPENSIVE THAN ANY BUT THE ENORMOUS 75 SEDAN AND LIMOUSINE. THE 1975 PRICE OF A SEVILLE WAS $12,479, AND THIS CONSIDERABLY RESTYLED 1980 MODEL SOLD FOR $20,477. THE RAZOR-EDGE STYLING OF THE REAR BODYWORK WAS REMINISCENT OF SOME CUSTOM BODIES ON PRE-WORLD WAR II ROLLS-ROYCES, AND GAVE THE SECOND GENERATION SEVILLES MORE DISTINCTION THAN THE ORIGINAL SEDANS. THE STYLE LASTED THROUGH 1985; AFTER THIS THE SEVILLE NAME WAS CARRIED BY A NEW FRONT-DRIVE SEDAN, WHICH SHARED A 108-INCH WHEELBASE WITH THE ELDORADO.

OWNERS: BRENT AND NANCY STEWART (PHOTO NICKY WRIGHT)

research into engine design, bumpers, seat belts, air bags, and so on.

Concern about exhaust emissions first surfaced in California, specifically in Los Angeles where the combination of sunshine and exhausts produced notorious smogs, so endangering the health of young children and susceptible elderly people that they were advised not to go out of doors on some days. In 1988, even after two decades of anti-pollution regulation, there were 75 such days, leading to more drastic decisions such as banning gasoline-burning vehicles from the city by 2007. Martin Wachs, professor of urban planning at UCLA, doubted whether this was possible, but said that at least by setting such a goal, people's minds would be concentrated on the problem.

The main preoccupation of the legislators was to reduce the amount of hydrocarbons, carbon monoxide and oxides of nitrogen being emitted in exhausts. The most effective way of doing this was by catalytic converter, familiarly known as a cat. An uncontrolled engine produces 84 grams per milliliter of carbon monoxide; this has been reduced to 3.4gm/ml under current federal regulations, with a target figure of 1.7gm/ml for the year 2000. The equivalent figures for hydrocarbon emissions are 10.6gm/ml unrestricted, 0.41gm/ml current, and 0.125gm/ml for 2000, showing how effective a cat can be. Two drawbacks exist, however: the cat converts unwelcome emissions into water, carbon dioxide, and nitrogen, and carbon dioxide is considered to be the main element in the greenhouse effect leading to global heating. Also the effectiveness of a cat decreases with use; according to the Environmental Protection Agency (EPA), after 50,000 miles a cat might be letting virtually untreated gases through. To control this would require regular compulsory exhaust check-ups; these are already available on a voluntary basis, and are especially popular in Los Angeles.

Emission control began in California in the mid-1960s with the PCV (positive crankcase ventilation) valve. In 1973 came mandatory exhaust gas recirculation to control nitrogen oxide emissions. Coupled with lower compression ratios, this led to drastic reductions in power output, especially from large engines. A 460-cubic-inch Lincoln engine gave 365bhp in 1971, but only 224bhp a year later, and 202bhp in 1976. Dramatic engines like the 426 Hemi were dropped altogether after 1971, and Chrysler's 440 fell from 385bhp in 1971 to a miserable 195 in 1977, after which it ceased to be made.

Up to the 1950s America had produced all the oil she needed, but a massive increase in consumption in the next decade was not accompanied by increased output, so the country became more dependent on imported oil, most of which came from the Arab countries. The Arab-Israeli war of 1973 led to an enormous price increase and a reduction in supplies to countries thought to be favorable to Israel. When the oil companies offered a 15 percent increase in price the producers demanded 70 percent and got it, together with a 5 percent reduction in output.

The immediate effect of the gas shortage was a downturn in sales of large cars. Worst hit were large-sized, medium-priced cars such as Mercury, whose model year production of Monterey/Marquis models fell from 184,346 to 88,593 between 1973 and 1974. At one point the St. Louis plant was shut down completely, since the daily supply of cars far exceeded requirements for the rest of the model year. Although nothing could be done immediately, there was a noticeable downsizing of large cars during the late 1970s, both in engine displacement and overall length. The 1977 Cadillac De Ville sedan was 8.5 inches shorter in wheelbase than the previous year's, and 900 pounds lighter. By 1981 it had lost a further 200 pounds, and the 1985 models were shorter by another 10.7 inches.

This was the era when fuel consumption, never a great concern to makers of larger cars, began to interest the U.S. government. In 1976 the Energy Conservation and Oil Policy Act was passed, mandating Corporate Average Fuel Economy (CAFE) for all manufacturers. The initial level for 1978 was 18 miles per gallon, and by 1992 it had risen to 27.5mpg. This is an average figure for all models, and auto makers can apply credits from the three previous years or the next projected three. However, there are strict penalties, $5 per 0.1mpg

diesel fuel had been used in European trucks since the early 1930s, and were offered in a Mercedes-Benz passenger car in 1936. America was slow to take to the diesel engine, even in heavy trucks, and there were no diesel passenger cars until 1978 when Oldsmobile offered a 350-cubic-inch diesel which shared dimensions with the equivalent gas engine, although block, heads, crankshaft, and pistons were all modified. Fuel economy was 25 percent better than with the gasoline engine, but there was a penalty in price ($735–$895) and power was 50bhp down at 120bhp.

For 1979 Olds offered a 260-cubic-inch V8 diesel as well as the 350, and from 1982 a 262-cubic-inch V6. Olds made all the diesels for GM, and the same units were offered by Buick, Cadillac, Chevrolet, and Pontiac. However, the drawbacks of low specific output, noisy running, and slow cold-weather starting damped down the diesel engine's popularity, and after the fuel crisis passed sales

shortfall, multiplied by the number of cars produced. Imports are calculated separately in CAFE figures; any car with less than 75 percent local content is considered foreign-made. This has led to the ridiculous situation of Ford loading its standard-size Crown Victoria and Mercury Marquis with non-U.S. content components so that the high consumption of these cars can be factored out of

the domestic CAFE. Today there is also a Gas Guzzler Tax on the car's list price, triggered at anything below 22.5mpg. In 1986 the revenue from this tax was $116.8 million.

Another approach to fuel economy and pollution was the use of alternative fuels, particularly diesel for the former, unleaded gasoline and methanol for the latter. Compression ignition engines burning

dropped. GM offered its last diesels in 1985, although Ford listed a small four-cylinder unit in the Escort, Tempo, and Mercury Lynx from 1984 through 1987, and a turbocharged diesel in the 1984/85 Lincolns. In 1991 the only diesels on the U.S. market were in imports, the Volkswagen Jetta and Mercedes-Benz 190. The attraction of diesel in cutting carbon dioxide emissions has not yet made an impact in the United States, although diesel cars are being built in growing numbers in Europe.

Tetraethyl lead (TEL) was added to gasoline in the 1920s as a remedy for knocking and pinking in the long and shallow combustion chambers of side-valve engines. It was added without arousing much comment until the 1960s, when the growing use of cats made it essential to remove it, because it rapidly destroys the elements of a cat. Even so-called unleaded gasoline contains a very small amount of TEL, but the proportion was limited by the EPA to 0.4 grams per gallon, reduced to 0.2gm/g in December 1986 and to 0.1gm/g in September 1988. Leaded fuel was still available, but in decreasing amounts, and by 1989 some larger urban areas were completely without it.

Methanol is a high octane fuel produced from coal or natural gas which produces little in the way of hydrocarbons, so it is not a smog creator, although it is high in carbon dioxide output. At the end of the 1980s Ford and GM both offered engines adapted to run on methanol as well as gasoline, or a mixture of the two. Expectations are that by 1993 at least 100,000 variable fuel cars, light trucks, and buses will be made per year. Two gas companies, Arco and Chevron, plan to offer methanol from many of their outlets.

The other area in which Washington played an increasing part in auto design was safety. For years it had been an accepted axiom in the auto industry that safety doesn't sell cars. Some manufacturers had made half-hearted gestures in the safety direction — Chrysler rolled Airflows in public to demonstrate the rigidity of their unitary bodies and Muntz installed seat belts in its 1952 convertibles. The main theme of Ralph Nader's *Unsafe at any Speed*, published in 1965, was that the industry did not make use of available technology in the service of safety. He complained that Buick was indifferent to failures of its power brake system, and that Cadillac did nothing to modify its fins until several pedestrians and cyclists had been impaled on them. There may have been some truth in his accusations against the Corvair, but the Pinto almost certainly involved more painful deaths and payouts by its makers than the Corvair ever did.

In May 1972 California housewife Lily Gray pulled out onto a freeway in her new Pinto, the engine died, and before she could restart, another car rear-ended her. The fuel tank, crushed between the rear bumper and axle, burst, filling the car with gasoline vapor which exploded. Lily died soon afterward and her passenger, 13-year-old Richard Grimshaw, was so badly burned that he spent the rest of his teenage years in operating theaters where surgeons made heroic attempts to rebuild his face.

Over the next few years, at a conservative estimate, 59 Pinto drivers and passengers died in the same way as Lily Gray. The problem was that, in order to keep the weight below 2,000 pounds, Ford engineers had eliminated rear subframe members on the car, leaving the gas tank more vulnerable than on heavier cars. Also the Pinto had a filler neck that was very likely to be ripped out in a collision, pouring fuel into the passenger compartment.

The cost of economizing on safety was high. In the case of Richard Grimshaw vs. the Ford Motor Company the judge awarded Grimshaw $3.5

1988 CHEVROLET CAVALIER RS COUPE ▶

THE CHEVROLET CAVALIER, ONE OF GM's J-CAR FAMILY,
WAS LAUNCHED FOR 1982 AS A MONZA REPLACEMENT.
LIKE ITS SISTERS IT HAD A TRANSVERSELY MOUNTED
FOUR-CYLINDER ENGINE DRIVING THE FRONT WHEELS,
AND IN ITS CHEVROLET GUISE A CHOICE OF FOUR
BODIES: TWO- AND FOUR-DOOR SEDANS, THREE-DOOR
HATCHBACK COUPE, AND FIVE-DOOR STATION WAGON.
A FIVE-SPEED MANUAL TRANSMISSION AND FUEL
INJECTION CAME WITH THE 1983 MODELS, AND THE V6-
POWERED Z24 CONVERTIBLE AND HATCHBACK FOR 1985.
THIS 1988 RS COUPE COST $9,175.

CHEVROLET DIVISION, GENERAL MOTORS

million in compensation and $125 million in punitive damages. On appeal the latter were reduced to $3 million, but the case still cost Ford $6.5 million, plus interest. This was substantial, as the case was not finally settled until March 1986, when Grimshaw was 27 years old. Numerous other cases followed, including one in which Ford was charged with reckless homicide, the first time any auto maker had been accused of a criminal offense. The company was finally cleared, but the affair did not make pretty headlines, particularly when Henry Ford II's contemptuous views about safety became known.

The Pinto's frame was duly strengthened, at a cost of an extra 600 pounds weight. The Pinto saga concentrated the minds of auto makers on the safety question, and by the mid-1970s federal legislation dictated bumper height and front/rear end deformation after 30mph collisions. A decade later, side impact standards were also set, for a vehicle traveling at 15mph being struck by one traveling at 30mph. There was a brief fashion for safety features to be combined in special cars called Experimental Safety Vehicles (ESV). In June 1970 Secretary of Transportation John Volpe offered multi-million dollar incentives to build such cars, which had to be capable of withstanding 10mph front and rear impacts with no damage to the bumpers, and 50mph impacts without injury to passengers. Some of the results were quite grotesque, for example a front bumper which extended automatically by 12 inches when the car's speed exceeded 25mph. GM's contribution had interior padding to give protection at impact speeds

**1991 CHEVROLET CAVALIER Z24
TWO-DOOR SEDAN ◀ ▶**

THE CAVALIER FIRST APPEARED IN CHEVY'S 1982 RANGE,
AS ONE OF THE INTERNATIONAL J-CARS OFFERED (FOR
THE FIRST TIME FOR ANY MODEL) BY ALL FIVE GM
DIVISIONS, AS WELL AS IN BRITAIN, GERMANY, AND
AUSTRALIA. IMPROVEMENTS DURING THE DECADE
INCLUDED A FIVE-SPEED MANUAL TRANSMISSION FOR
1983, A CONVERTIBLE AND NEW FRONTAL STYLING FOR
1984, AND THE Z24 "MINI-MUSCLE CAR" FOR 1985. THIS
HAD A 173-CUBIC-INCH V6 ENGINE GIVING 125bhp. THE
1991 Z24 SEEN HERE HAD A LARGER V6 OF 189 CUBIC
INCHES, SPORT SUSPENSION, AND FIVE-SPEED
TRANSMISSION AS STANDARD.

CHEVROLET DIVISION, GENERAL MOTORS

1990 PONTIAC SUNBIRD LE CONVERTIBLE ▼▶
SUNBIRD WAS PONTIAC'S VERSION OF THE J-CAR,
ALTHOUGH IT WAS CALLED THE J-2000 UNTIL 1984 WHEN
IT BECAME THE 2000 SUNBIRD, AND THEN PLAIN
SUNBIRD. THE CONVERTIBLE RETURNED TO THE RANGE IN
1984 AND WAS STILL MADE IN 1990, ALONG WITH A
FOUR-DOOR SEDAN AND TWO-DOOR COUPE. THE
ENGINE WAS A 121-CUBIC-INCH FOUR THAT GAVE 95bhp,
OR 165bhp IN TURBO FORM.

PONTIAC DIVISION, GENERAL MOTORS (PHOTO NICKY WRIGHT)

up to 30mph, after which airbags took over. The downside of all these ESVs was their greatly increased weight. In the wake of the fuel crisis they were all quietly forgotten.

Two safety devices that did make it into production were seat belts and airbags. The former were first seen on Nash and Muntz cars in 1952, and by 1970 active belts (which the wearer had to put on) were standard equipment in all new cars, as they were virtually everywhere else in the world. Compulsory belt-wearing took longer to be applied, dating from 1971 in the Australian state of Victoria, and spreading throughout Europe, West and East, during the 1980s. In America a good many states mandated the wearing of belts, and manufacturers were required to install passive belts, which fitted automatically. This regulation was to have been mandatory by 1990, but the

deadline has been extended to 1994.

The airbag was a supplementary device which inflated within about 40 milliseconds of a collision, and protected the driver from impact on the steering column and windshield. Ideal in a head-on collision, an airbag is only helpful within a range of 30° on either side, and of no use at all in a side-impact collision. There were fears that the great increase in pressure might blow out windows or rupture passengers' eardrums, although neither of these eventualities has actually happened. A number of Mercurys were fitted with airbags for the Allstate Insurance Company as early as 1974, and airbags were offered by Oldsmobile for several years from 1974, proving to be one of the least popular options in the accessory book. By the late 1980s they were seen on a number of models by the Big Three. Usually for the driver only, bags have been offered for the front passenger on a few cars, but not yet for passengers in the back.

One of the casualties of the growing safety movement, and also of a preference for air conditioning and stereo systems, was that

quintessential American dream car, the convertible. Chrysler made its last ragtop in 1970, and associates Dodge and Plymouth in 1971. The last convertible from the Ford Motor Company was a Mercury Cougar XR-7, which left the line on July 7, 1973. GM carried on somewhat longer, Buick, Chevrolet, Oldsmobile to the end of the 1975 season, and Cadillac to 1976. The day the last Cadillac convertible came down the line — Wednesday, April 21, 1976 — was a sad one, marking not only the end of the famous Eldorado convertible, but of all U.S. convertible production.

The factory was besieged with orders for the last convertible, and produced 200 identical "last" cars, painted white with white tops, leather upholstery, and wheel covers. Prices quickly shot up (and as quickly came down later), and many were the Eldorado coupes that lost their tops to earn their owners a few more bucks. The actual last car was retained by Cadillac for its historical collection.

Although there did not seem to be sufficient demand for the big manufacturers to continue making convertibles, clearly some people still wanted them, and within a year custom firms began to fill the gap. Convertibles Inc. of Lima, Ohio, offered an Eldorado convertible for $6,500 above the list price of a coupe, and American Custom Coachworks of Beverly Hills, California, made an open-top version of the new downsized Coupe de Ville. This retailed for $37,000, while a coupe cost only $9,810. The following year American Custom Coachworks offered a wider range of convertible Cadillacs, on two- and four-door models, while another firm made an open-top Seville. One of the best-known of the conversion firms, Hess & Eisenhardt, famed for ambulances and funeral cars, made more than 300 converted Coupe de Villes in 1978 and 1979. They sold for $29,000 and were marketed through 60 Cadillac dealers.

By the early 1980s the customizers were working not only on Cadillacs but on Lincolns, Pontiacs, Buicks, and other makes. Even the compact Pontiac Phoenix was offered in convertible form by American Custom Coachworks from 1980. This tempted Detroit back into the market, and Chrysler, the first corporation to abandon the ragtop, was the first to return, offering two convertibles in the compact LeBaron line for 1982. This was the decision of Lee Iacocca, who moved from Ford to Chrysler in 1978. Convertibles were also offered on the companion Dodge 400.

Once Chrysler had given the lead, others followed. Cadillac brought back the Eldorado convertible for 1984, while two of GM's J-cars, the Chevrolet Cavalier and Pontiac Sunbird, were made in convertible form from 1984. The Chevrolet Corvette had a convertible in 1986 and the Camaro in 1987. Lowest-priced of all the new generation convertibles, at $10,295, was American Motors' Alliance of 1985. This was actually a French-designed Renault, made in closed form as the Alliance sedan and Encore hatchback, but the French never got a convertible.

1985 BUICK REGAL GRAND NATIONAL COUPE ▲

THE REGAL WAS A REAR-DRIVE COUPE MADE FROM 1978 TO 1987, AND ITS T-TYPE WAS ONE OF THE SPORTIER BUICKS WITH STRONGER CHASSIS AND SUSPENSION, AND FAT TIRES. THE GRAND NATIONAL WAS A LOW-PRODUCTION COMMEMORATIVE MODEL NAMED FOR THE NASCAR GRAND NATIONAL RACES, AND WAS MADE FROM MID-1982 THROUGH 1987. T-TYPE AND GRAND NATIONALS HAD A TURBOCHARGED 321-CUBIC-INCH V6 ENGINE GIVING 200bhp. ONLY 2,102 GRAND NATIONALS WERE MADE IN 1985, OUT OF TOTAL REGAL PRODUCTION OF 124,546.

OWNER: PAT JANISCH (PHOTO NICKY WRIGHT)

STANDARDIZATION: LATTER-DAY LETTER CARS

Bodies began to be standardized before World War II, but in the past 20 years standardization has extended to engines and transmissions as well. In the 1980s there was much less difference between a Buick, Pontiac, or Oldsmobile J-car than between a Buick J and a Buick H. Toward the end of the decade models more individual to a particular marque began to appear, Buick's Reatta for example, and Chevrolet's Beretta and Corsica.

In the early 1970s GM's production was already highly standardized. All bodies were produced by Fisher Body Division; Chevrolet shared the A-body (Chevelle) and B-body (Impala) with all but Cadillac, the X-body (Nova) with Oldsmobile and Pontiac, the F-body (Camaro) with the Pontiac

Firebird, and so on. Other components were also shared as it was uneconomical for each division to make its own. Thus Oldsmobile was responsible for steering design (the actual gears and linkages were made by Saginaw), Buick for brakes (made by Delco-Moraine), Chevrolet for front suspension, and Pontiac for rear suspension. A similar situation obtained at Chrysler, where four bodies and seven engines were combined to make up 35 models of Chrysler, Dodge and Plymouth.

As the cost of new models escalated, it became necessary to share designs more thoroughly, and this was typified by GM's J-cars introduced for 1982. In the United States the J-cars were aimed at the quality small imports, particularly the Honda Accord, but the design was international, also made in Britain as the Vauxhall Cavalier, in Germany as

1988 CHEVROLET CORSICA SEDAN AND BERETTA COUPE ◀▼

ANNOUNCED IN MARCH 1987 AS 1988 MODELS, THE CORSICA AND BERETTA BROKE WITH RECENT GENERAL MOTORS CUSTOM IN HAVING NO EQUIVALENTS IN OTHER GM DIVISIONS. THEY HAD A NEW PLATFORM ON A 103.4-INCH WHEELBASE, AND USED COMPONENTS FROM J- AND N-CARS, INCLUDING INDEPENDENT COIL FRONT SUSPENSION WITH McPHERSON STRUTS, AND FRONT DISK/REAR DRUM BRAKES. ENGINES ALSO CAME FROM THE J-CAR RANGE, A 90bhp 121-CUBIC-INCH FOUR OR A 120/135bhp 173-CUBIC-INCH V6. THEY WERE PRICED AT AROUND $1,500–$2,000 ABOVE EQUIVALENT CAVALIERS, BUT SOLD VERY WELL. IN 1991 THEY WERE STILL AMONG THE MOST SUCCESSFUL CHEVROLETS.

CHEVROLET DIVISION, GENERAL MOTORS

the Opel Ascona, and in Australia as the Holden Camira. For the first time all five GM divisions used a single design, known as the Buick Skyhawk, Chevrolet Cavalier, Oldsmobile Firenza, and Pontiac J-2000. Cadillac was rather cagey about its J-car, calling it Cimarron by Cadillac rather than a Cadillac Cimarron. No Cadillac badge featured on the car.

All J-cars rode on a common wheelbase of 101.2 inches, but body variations allowed for slight differences in overall length, from 169.4 inches for the Pontiac and Chevrolet hatchback copies to 175.3 inches for the station wagons offered by all but Cadillac. Engines were 112- or 121-cubic-inch fours giving 84 or 98bhp. The smaller was an overhead cam unit built by GM in Brazil, while the larger had pushrod overhead valves and was made by Chevrolet. The overhead cam engine was turbocharged from 1984, and enlarged to 121 cubic inches in 1987, when the 150bhp turbo engine was dropped. All engines were transversely mounted and drove the front wheels.

J-car prices ran from $6,966 for the base Cavalier coupe to $12,131 for the Cimarron. As one would expect, the Chevrolet sold the best, more than 270,000 in the 1982 model year, rising to more than 462,000 for 1984. It was followed by Pontiac, Buick, Oldsmobile, and Cadillac, whose Cimarron managed only 25,968 for 1982, and fell thereafter, whereas other J-cars improved their sales. The

1991 CHEVROLET BERETTA COUPE ▶ ▼

THE BERETTA COUPE, LAUNCHED IN MARCH 1987, CONTINUED TO BE INDIVIDUAL TO CHEVROLET, REVERSING THE EARLIER GM TREND TOWARD SHARING MODELS BETWEEN ALL THE DIVISIONS. ALTHOUGH 8½ INCHES LONGER THAN THE CAVALIER, THE BERETTA WAS NEVERTHELESS CLASSED AS A COMPACT. ENGINES WERE A 140bhp V6 OR A MORE POWERFUL, ALTHOUGH SMALLER, 180bhp TWIN-CAM FOUR. BERETTAS WERE MADE AT THEIR OWN PLANT AT WILMINGTON, DELAWARE.

CHEVROLET DIVISION, GENERAL MOTORS

Cimarron was aimed at younger, affluent buyers who had never entered a Cadillac showroom before, but such buyers were not taken in by a car which wasn't all that different from a Buick Skyhawk, yet sold for $4,200 more than a Skyhawk with all options. The Cimarron had a few exclusive features such as the leather upholstery and, from 1983, a sliding glass "Astroroof," but these were clearly not enough, and Cimarron sales skidded down to 6,454 in 1988, its last year. One advantage for Cadillac was that the modest fuel consumption of the Cimarron helped its CAFE figures until new downsized models could be made.

The J-cars were gradually improved over the years, with a convertible coming to the Cavalier and J-2000 Sunbird in 1984, and V6 engines in some models from 1986. Cavalier and Sunbird were still being made in 1992. There were numerous other "letter cars" in the 1980s. GM's first front-drive designs were the X-cars launched in mid-1979 as the Buick Skylark, Chevrolet Citation, Oldsmobile Omega, and Pontiac Phoenix. They featured transverse 151-cubic-inch 90bhp four-cylinder engines built by Pontiac, with a 173-cubic-inch 115bhp V6 optional on most models. Bodies included three- and five-door hatchbacks, and two-door coupes. In August 1985 the X-cars gave way to the N-cars — Buick Skylark, Oldsmobile Cutlass, and Pontiac Grand Am — with slightly more powerful four- and six-cylinder engines.

Chevrolet's individual cars, not shared with any other division, were the Beretta coupe and Corsica sedan which debuted in March 1987. Although they employed a new body platform of 103.4-inch wheelbase, their engineering owed much to the J- and N-cars, notably the suspension. The standard engine was the Cavalier's 90bhp four, but the 120/135bhp V6 was an option. Corsica and Beretta found a useful niche in the import-dominated market for more individual smaller cars; in 1988 they were the second and third best-selling Chevrolets after the Cavalier, with 291,163 Corsicas and 275,098 Berettas finding buyers.

Chrysler had been famous for its "letter cars" in the 300 series of the 1950s, but its offerings 30 years later were less interesting. Smallest was the L-car, the European-designed Dodge Omni/Plymouth Horizon sub-compact hatchback, then came the K-car, badged as a Chrysler LeBaron, Dodge Aries, and Plymouth Reliant. Made as a sedan, coupe, and station wagon, with a convertible in the LeBaron range, it was a compact car on a 100.1-inch wheelbase, with a choice of Chrysler-built 135-cubic-inch or Mitsubishi-built 156-cubic-inch fours under the hood. The K-platform was used for a

wide variety of cars, from the sporty coupes badged as Chrysler Lasers or Dodge Daytonas, through the Chrysler GTS/Dodge Lancer five-door hatchback, which had an H-body on a K-platform, to the Executive sedan and limousine with wheelbase stretched to 124.3 or 131.3 inches. The latter cost $26,318 in 1985, when you could get a LeBaron sedan for $9,309.

Even more expensive was the Chrysler TC by Maserati, a two-passenger convertible on a shortened version of the K-platform, using the 135-cubic-inch four with a 16-valve twin cam head designed and made by the famous Italian firm in which Chrysler acquired a minority interest in 1984. The turbocharged engine gave 200bhp, but despite disk brakes all round it did not handle as well as a $30,000 car should, and sales were slow. Later models had a 183-cubic-inch V6 engine and automatic transmission in place of the five-speed manual of the first. Production was phased out early in 1991.

Other Chryslers of the 1980s were the P-body replacements for the Omni/Horizon, which debuted in 1987 and ran alongside the older designs for a while. They were badged as Dodge Shadow and Plymouth Sundance. There was also the K-car replacement, the A-body Chrysler Saratoga/Dodge Spirit/Plymouth Acclaim. The big rear-drive Fifth Avenue, the last of what had been the standard models, was dropped for 1990, making Chrysler the only one of the Big Three to offer an all-front-drive range.

Over at Ford the most important model of the 1980s was the mid-sized Taurus, also badged as a Mercury Sable, originally known as the DN5 project (D for the class of car, N for North America). Launched for 1986, its development dated back to 1979 and involved study of all domestic, European, and Japanese cars in the same class. The result was

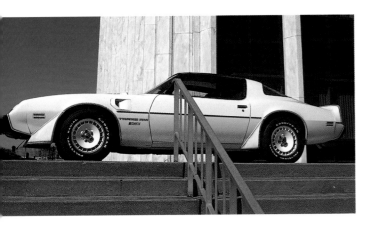

1980 PONTIAC FIREBIRD TRANS-AM COUPE ▲▶

PONTIAC BROUGHT OUT A TENTH ANNIVERSARY FIREBIRD FOR 1979, AND THE 1980 MODELS WERE LITTLE CHANGED. THE 1979/80 CARS WERE CHARACTERIZED BY THE BOLDER FRONTAL AIR DAM, WITH SEPARATE COMPARTMENTS FOR THE FOUR HEADLIGHTS, BUT THE BODY WAS CARRIED OVER FROM THE 1976 MODELS. THE FIREBIRD MOTIF ("THE CHICKEN") HAD CHANGED CONSIDERABLY SINCE ITS INTRODUCTION IN 1973, GETTING LARGER WINGS AND BREATHING FIRE FROM ITS MOUTH. ALTHOUGH IT WAS THE MOST EXPENSIVE, THE TRANS-AM WAS THE MOST POPULAR FIREBIRD IN 1980. THE 301-CUBIC-INCH V8 COULD BE HAD WITH TURBOCHARGER, WHICH RAISED POWER FROM 140 TO 210BHP.

PONTIAC MOTOR DIVISION, GENERAL MOTORS

(PHOTO NICKY WRIGHT)

the most aerodynamic American sedan ever made, with a drag coefficient of 0.33 for the Taurus and 0.32 for the slightly longer and sleeker Sable. Even the station wagon achieved 0.35. Engine options were a 88bhp 153-cubic-inch four or a 140bhp 182-cubic-inch V6, both new engines specially developed for the new cars.

With an investment of more than $3 billion, the DN5 project was crucial for Ford, which had lost $1 billion a year for two years in a row. Fortunately the new cars were a runaway success; in spite of a shortened season (they were launched on December 26, 1985), sales of the 1986 Taurus reached 236,362 and the Sable 95,638. The 1987 Taurus was the best-selling Ford (beating the Escort by just seven cars to reach 374,772), while Sable sales totaled 121,313. In 1989 the Taurus was the best-selling American-designed car, though just beaten to first place by the Honda Accord. The 1989 season included a high-performance Taurus called the SHO (Super High Output), with a Yamaha-engineered 24-valve V6 engine with single camshaft to each bank of cylinders. This developed 220bhp and propelled the six-passenger sedan to 60mph in 7 seconds. Features included disk brakes all round and larger antiroll bars. The SHO sold for $19,739, more than $4,000 above the price of a Taurus LX sedan.

INDIVIDUALITY FIGHTS BACK

But the auto scene wasn't all standardization in the 1980s. There were several models individual to particular makes, such as the Pontiac Fiero, Cadillac Allante, and Buick Reatta, while evergreens like the Corvette, Camaro, Firebird, and Mustang carried on, gaining fresh performance and power by the end of the decade. There was also a growing fashion for 1930s-styled neo-classics and replica cars.

Once a staid "schoolteacher's car," Pontiac had a performance image from the mid-1960s, and the

Firebird was a hot performer 20 years later. In 1973 the first of the firebird motifs, familiarly known as "the chicken," was seen on the hood. At first opposed by GM's Bill Mitchell, the motif soon became inseparably associated with the Firebird Trans Am. In 1989 the most powerful engine option in the Firebird was a 225bhp V8. However, the lower-priced two-passenger sports car was an attraction which would not go away, and a mid-engined Firebird concept car was built as early as 1971. Locating the engine behind the driver gave the best handling characteristics for a sports car, but

1987 FORD TAURUS SEDAN ▲

FORD'S MOST IMPORTANT CAR OF THE 1980s, THE TAURUS WAS LAUNCHED FOR 1986 AND INCORPORATED A COMPLETELY FRESH AERODYNAMIC BODY, AND NEW FOUR-CYLINDER AND V6 ENGINES. BODIES WERE LIMITED TO TWO, A FOUR-DOOR SEDAN AND A FIVE-DOOR STATION WAGON. THEY SHARED McPHERSON STRUT AND COIL FRONT AND REAR SUSPENSION; BUT WHEREAS THE SEDAN HAD PARALLEL CONTROL ARMS AT THE REAR THE WAGON USED TWIN ARMS, WHICH WERE MORE SUITABLE FOR THE WIDE VARIATION OF LOAD WEIGHT CARRIED BY THIS CATEGORY OF CAR. THE HIGH-PERFORMANCE SHO TAURUS CAME IN 1989, AND IMPROVEMENTS FOR 1991 INCLUDED SEQUENTIAL FUEL INJECTION AND AN ELECTRONICALLY CONTROLLED FOUR-SPEED AUTOMATIC TRANSMISSION ON ALL MODELS BUT THE SHO.

FORD MOTOR COMPANY

EXTERNALLY THE MID-ENGINED FIERO WAS A COMPLETELY NEW CAR, ALTHOUGH IT USED THE TRANSVERSE ENGINE AND TRANSMISSION FROM GM's X-CARS, SUCH AS THE PONTIAC PHOENIX. FRONT SUSPENSION CAME FROM THE CHEVETTE. THE FIRST NEW VOLUME PRODUCTION TWO-PASSENGER CAR FROM DETROIT SINCE THE ORIGINAL FORD THUNDERBIRD, THE FIERO USED THE SAME BASIC LAYOUT AS THE FIAT X1/9 AND THE TOYOTA MR2. IT WAS NOT SO LONG LIVED AS THESE IMPORTED CARS, HOWEVER, FOR IT WAS DROPPED AFTER FIVE SEASONS. GOVERNMENT-MANDATED RECALLS AND A GREAT INCREASE IN INSURANCE PREMIUMS FOR SPORTS CARS HASTENED ITS DEMISE. THE FIERO WAS ANNOUNCED AS A 1984 MODEL; THIS IS A 1983 PROTOTYPE.

PONTIAC MOTOR DIVISION, GENERAL MOTORS

(PHOTO NICKY WRIGHT)

finding a suitable drive train was a problem, and Pontiac could not afford to engineer one from scratch. Then, in 1980, came the X-car, with transverse engine and front drive, which could be adapted to a mid-engined rear-drive sports car. This was the essence of the Fiero, largely developed for Pontiac by Turkish-born Hilki Aldikacti, head of Pontiac's Advanced Engineering.

The Fiero had a spaceframe chassis to which plastic body panels were attached, and rode on a short wheelbase of 93.4 inches. The engine was the 151-cubic-inch cast-iron block four known as the "Iron Duke," and transmission also came from the X-cars. The Chevette's front suspension was used. Although the Fiero looked a sporty little thing, the public realized that it used many components from standard sedans, and this, coupled with a none-too-inspiring top speed of 97mph, prevented it from being the sales success that Pontiac hoped for.

Even at the modest base price of $7,999, Fiero sales disappointed, although the first year (1984) was quite promising at 136,840. They dropped to 76,371 in 1985 and to 46,581 in 1987, despite the option of the 173-cubic-inch V6 engine which pushed top speed up to 112mph. A series of engine fires in 1984 models prompted a government-ordered recall of 20 percent of that year's production, and this was followed by a sudden increase in insurance rates for two-passenger sports

cars. It was all too much for the Fiero, which registered only 26,402 sales in 1988, and GM announced that there would be no 1989 Fieros.

A measure of the imported car threat was that a number of new American models were aimed directly at competing with imports rather than domestic cars. One such was Cadillac's Allante two-passenger convertible with which the makers hoped to dent sales of Mercedes-Benz's 560SL convertible. The car had an Eldorado frame shortened from 108 to 99.4 inches and a 249-cubic-inch V8 engine tuned to give 170bhp. The frames were flown out to Pininfarina in Turin, Italy, where the convertible bodies were built in a separate plant from Pininfarina's other activities. The complete cars were then flown back to Detroit for drive train installation and final finishing. Specially equipped Boeing 747s were used for this operation, dubbed "the longest production line in the world."

The Allante's exotic origins were reflected in its price, $54,000, well over double that of an Eldorado convertible. It was difficult to justify such a price differential except in terms of exclusiveness. In 1973 the staff of *Automobile Quarterly* commented: "We know the real reason why people buy Eldorados, and logic has nothing to do with it. This is status, conspicuous consumption, a highly visible declaration of what its owner thinks of himself, and what he would like other people to think about him. But it's a free country, and everybody has the right to make a fool of himself." No doubt they would have said the same about the Allante.

Cadillac hoped to sell 4,000 Allantes in 1987, but managed only 1,651, and 2,569 of the 1988 models. The large stock of unsold cars meant that, unlike the Mercedes, the Allante depreciated as soon as it left the showroom. Also there were criticisms of water leaks, squeaks and rattles, horns that didn't work, and heaters that worked too well — a sorry catalog of woe for America's most expensive domestic car. For 1989 engine displacement went up to 273 cubic inches, giving 200bhp, and so did the price, to $57,183. The 1993 Allante promised to be a much improved car, with the new 32-valve Northstar V8 engine giving 290bhp, and with four-speed automatic transmission and improved brakes, steering and suspension. The price was now $65,000, but this was still $30,000 below the rival Mercedes-Benz.

Another two-passenger car, this time exclusive to Buick, was the Reatta, introduced for the 1988 season. It was based on a shortened Riviera platform with a 98.5-inch wheelbase. Also from the Riviera came the 231-cubic-inch V6 engine, transmission, suspension, brakes, steering, and instrument panel. The Reatta's novelty lay in its

body, which gave it the character of a mature sporty car likely to appeal to America's aging baby boom generation now around 40 years old. By no means cheap at $25,000, it was conceived by Buick as a "halo car," enhancing the corporate image and luring into showrooms buyers who might place an order for a more prosaic sedan or station wagon. The cars were hand-assembled at the Reatta Craft Center in Lansing, Michigan. Sales never reached the Center's capacity of 25,000 a year, and little more than 20,500 were made between October 1987 and May 1991, when the Reatta was discontinued. The plant was to be used for the manufacture of GM's Impact electric car.

Chevrolet's Corvette was little changed in the 1970s, apart from inevitable reductions in engine size and power. These reached a low point in 1975 when the only engine was a 350-cubic-inch V8 giving 190 or 210bhp. Five years earlier there had been a 454-cubic-inch giving 465bhp. The last convertible Corvette for 11 years came in 1975. Yet despite its aging body and emasculated engine it became more popular than ever in the late 1970s, with a record 53,807 sales in 1979.

Officially there was no 1983 Corvette, for the completely revised car that appeared in March was classed as a 1984 model. The body was restyled with much smoother lines; there was a forward-opening alligator hood and a hatchback rear window; the frame was a Lotus-like backbone chassis welded to an upper birdcage for added strength; and the body was of fiberglass, like all previous Corvettes. A convertible returned to the range in 1986, engineered by the American Sunroof Corporation of Bowling Green, Ohio, which also aided GM with the J-car convertibles and American

Motors with the Alliance.

The next big step in Corvette development came for 1989 with the LT5 engine. This had the same displacement, 350 cubic inches, as existing engines, but was a completely new design with shorter bore and longer stroke, twin camshafts for each bank of cylinders, and four valves per cylinder. Developed by GM's recent acquisition, Lotus of Norfolk, England, the LT5 developed 385bhp yet delivered up to 22.5mpg and complied with all current emission regulations. An unusual feature was the "granny switch" by which the secondary ports could be deactivated so that only three valves were working in each cylinder. The second intake valve moved but did not admit any mixture to the combustion chamber. The switch was operated by a key.

The ZR1 also featured Selective Ride Control (optional on lesser Corvettes) and a six-speed manual transmission which shifted automatically at light throttle openings (below 35 percent) and low speed (12–19mph). This gave better fuel consumption, which helped Chevrolet with their CAFE figures, but most Corvette owners were likely to floor the throttle, in which case the automatic shift did not come into effect. The ZR1 was a limited edition Corvette, and the first season's production was not expected to exceed 1,500, out of a total Corvette output of about 27,000. Its price was around $60,000, as against $31,545 for a regular coupe. The sticker price for a ZR-1 in 1991 was $64,138, but recession-hit dealers were offering it for around $13,000 below this figure. The 1992 sales are likely to be hit further by the greatly improved regular Corvette, the LT1. Although still with only two valves per cylinder, the engines had greatly improved breathing, giving 300bhp. Prices started at only $33,635.

NEO-CLASSICS AND REPLICAS

In 1964 stylist Brooks Stevens was working as a consultant for Studebaker. In order to liven up its image he built a two-passenger roadster styled after the 1930 Mercedes-Benz SSK, using a Lark Daytona chassis and an Avanti V8 engine. The car was scheduled to debut on the Studebaker stand at the New York Show in April 1964, but before it reached the show Studebaker vetoed it on the grounds that a replica classic did not fit the common sense image that it was trying to project. Stevens and his sons found themselves with a car and nowhere to show it, so they hired a small stand of their own.

Christened Excalibur after a sports car Stevens had built in the early 1950s, the car was a hit, and in August 1964 the Stevens formed SS Automobiles in Milwaukee to build it commercially. One of the first orders came from Chevrolet dealer Jerry Allen, the show organizer who had found Stevens his last-minute stand. He wanted 12 cars, but as a Chevy dealer with showrooms on the ground floor of New York's General Motors building he could hardly sell a car with a Studebaker engine. "One day the

directors are going to stop off at my showroom out of curiosity on their way to lunch, and I'm going to have my ass kicked. Couldn't you put a Chevrolet engine in it?"

This wasn't too difficult as Stevens was friendly with GM's Ed Cole, and all production Excaliburs were Chevrolet-powered. The Studebaker chassis, however, was used up to 1969. Bodies were originally of hammered aluminum, later of fiberglass. Stevens could not obtain the burnished outside exhaust pipes in the United States, but managed to track down the German firm that had made them for the original Mercedes, and placed an order.

As production did not begin until August 1964, the first Excaliburs were 1965 models; 56 cars were

sold at a price of $7,250, followed by 90 in 1966, when a four-passenger phaeton with full fenders and running boards was added. A new 111-inch chassis came in 1970, and the standard engine went up from 327 to 350 cubic inches. By then competitors had appeared. Oklahoma schoolteacher Glenn Pray began building replicas of the Cord 810 in ⅞th size of the original, powered by a Corvair engine. The necessary restyling was done by the car's original designer, Gordon Buehrig. After he had sold 91 Cords, Pray decided that the Auburn 851 speedster would be a better-selling replica, so he sold the Cord project to another Oklahoma company, which made a few more Cord 810s powered with Ford or Chrysler V8 engines.

The Auburn proved to be a better proposition,

not only for Pray but for numerous other companies who jumped on the bandwagon. Pray's Auburn-Cord-Duesenberg Company stayed in business into the 1980s, by which time at least four other companies had offered Auburn speedsters, one making a four-passenger dual-cowl model which Auburn itself never built. Most used Ford V8 running gear, though one was based on a VW Beetle frame!

The Auburns were full-size replicas, quite difficult to distinguish from the originals. Soon numerous other companies began to offer similar replicas of classics such as the Duesenberg Model J and SSJ, the 1934 Ford V8 roadster (the Canadian-built Timmis), and the 1932 Packard (Second Chance). Postwar sports cars also came in for the replica treatment, notably the Cobra (by far the most popular, with around 20 companies worldwide

making replicas), Mercedes-Benz 300SL gull-wing, and original Corvette and Thunderbird. These are intentional replicas, whereas the Excalibur was never such a close copy of the Mercedes, and became less so as the years passed.

The Excalibur was really the first of the neo-classics, a breed that proliferated from the late 1970s onward. Most were not based on any real classic but aimed to recapture the style of the 1930s continental luxury coupe — long, long hood, sweeping fenders, shallow windshield, relatively small two-passenger coupe body. Some had side-mounted spare wheel covers and/or outside exhausts, although these were strictly ornamental, with a conventional exhaust system under the floor and a spare wheel at the rear.

One of the first neo-classics, after Excalibur, was the Clenet built in Goleta, California, by

French-born Alain Clenet. This used a center section from an MG Midget, with a very long hood and exhaust pipes emerging under the fenders. The hood seemed long enough to house a straight-12 or at least a straight-8, but in fact there was just a compact Lincoln V8. Behind the tiny two-passenger convertible body was a small trunk and a separate spare wheel cover. The price when the Clenet was introduced in 1976 was $83,000, high enough, but not a top price for a neo-classic, which could go as high as $130,000.

Most neo-classics seemed to emanate from either California or Florida, where most of their customers were to be found. One cannot imagine many canny Vermonters investing in Clenets or Zimmer Golden Spirits! The Golden Spirit, made by a mobile home manufacturer from Pompano Beach, was the best-known Florida neo-classic. The recipe was to take a Mustang coupe, chainsaw the monocoque in half, and add in an extension to give an extra 3 feet at the front. The floor, doors, window glass, and roof of the center section were retained, and a period body in fiberglass was built around them. Looking at the long, low coupe, one would never guess its Mustang origins, but it was clearly less of an original car than the Excalibur, which had its own ladder chassis.

For $90,000 the Golden Spirit owner got a luxurious interior, with walnut fascia, Italian leather upholstery, and Bohemian crystal vases in the rear compartment. For such a high-priced car, the Golden Spirit sold quite well, about 1,400 between 1980 and 1988, but then the firm got into difficulties, turned to making an expensive customized Pontiac Fiero called the Quicksilver, and nearly went out of business, although the Golden Spirit was revived in 1990.

Bankruptcies and changes of name and ownership were frequent in the neo-classic world. The Clenet disappeared in 1982, reappearing a few years later as the Roaring Twenties. The Scepter sports car was made at Goleta by the Scepter Motor Car Company, then went out of production, only to reappear as the Gatsby Griffin from San Jose, one of a range of neo-classics offered by Gatsby Coachworks. Most neo-classics were two-door coupes or convertibles, but four-door sedans were made by Excalibur (from 1988) and Zimmer, among others, and there were a few stretched

1991 CHEVROLET CAMARO Z-28 COUPE ◄▼
THE Z-28 DESIGNATION WAS FIRST USED FOR THE TOP
MODEL OF CAMARO IN 1983, DROPPED FOR 1988, AND
REVIVED FOR 1991. HOT CAMAROS IN THE LATE 1980s
WERE DESIGNATED Z-IROC, FOR THE INTERNATIONAL
RACE OF CHAMPIONS IN WHICH THEY COMPETED. THE
1991 CARS SPORTED A TALLER REAR WING, BOLDER-
LOOKING ALLOY WHEELS, AND A CHOICE OF 230 OR
245bhp V8s. THE LATTER WAS ONLY AVAILABLE
WITH AUTOMATIC TRANSMISSION.

CHEVROLET DIVISION, GENERAL MOTORS (PHOTO NICKY WRIGHT)

limousines in neo-classic style, by Baroque from
Omaha, Nebraska, and Excalibur. Most of the
breed used the largest available V8 engine,
although power was inevitably down compared
with 1976. However, the Knudsen Baroque used a
turbocharged Buick V6 and the Spartan from San
Marcos, California, took its engine and central body
section from the Nissan 300X.

There was inevitably a heavy mortality among
neo-classic manufacturers; of the 40 or so models
announced between 1976 and 1990, only 5 were
listed for 1992. Excalibur went bankrupt in 1986,
but the company was taken over by the Acquisition
Company of Illinois, which continued the range
and later added the sedan and limousine.

A specialty car which falls neither into the
replica or neo-classic category is the Avanti,
continued after the demise of Studebaker by two
former dealers, Leo Newman and Nathan Altman.
Like Excalibur, they turned to Chevrolet power,
using the 327-cubic-inch V8 until 1969, when it was
enlarged to 350 cubic inches. They gradually
upgraded the Avanti's equipment, with electric

1990 CHEVROLET CORVETTE ZR-1 ▲▼▶
POWER AND PERFORMANCE RETURNED TO THE
CORVETTE WITH THE ZR-1, A LIMITED PRODUCTION CAR
THAT HAD A COMPLETELY NEW LOTUS-DESIGNED 32-
VALVE FOUR-CAM V8 ENGINE. KNOWN AS THE LT-5, THIS
ENGINE GAVE 385bhp FROM 350 CUBIC INCHES,
COMPARED WITH 240–245bhp FROM THE REGULAR L69
ENGINE. THE LT5 POWER UNIT WAS ENGINEERED TO FIT
THE EXISTING CORVETTE CHASSIS WITHOUT ALTERATION,
BUT THE ZR-1 COULD BE RECOGNIZED BY SQUARED-UP
TAILLIGHTS AND A WIDER BODY BEHIND THE DOORS TO
ACCOMMODATE THE FATTER TIRES.
CHEVROLET DIVISION, GENERAL MOTORS (PHOTO NICKY WRIGHT)

window lifts, optional leather trim, and tinted windshield, while colors could be anything the customer wanted. This lifted prices from the original $6,550 ($1,100 more than the Studebaker-built Avanti) to $18,995 by 1980. Inflation contributed to this increase, of course, but the Avanti's makers deliberately pushed it into a higher class to compete with the Cadillac Eldorado.

The 1980s saw two changes of ownership, in 1982 and 1985, and a move to Youngstown, Ohio, which marked the end of car making in South Bend. The original Avanti shape was continued with hardly any change, and was still made in 1991, but two new models were introduced, a convertible in 1985 and a four-door sedan in 1989. At the end of 1990 Avanti was in deep trouble, with complaints over unpaid bills from dealers, suppliers and its advertising agency, and 80 percent of its workforce laid off.

1977 AVANTI II COUPE ▲

AFTER STUDEBAKER MOVED PRODUCTION TO CANADA IN 1963, THE AVANTI DESIGN WAS CONTINUED BY LEADING STUDEBAKER DEALERS LEO NEWMAN AND NATHAN ALTMAN. THE STUDE ENGINE WAS REPLACED BY A CHEVROLET V8. THE BASE PRICE IN 1977 WAS $13,195, BUT THIS WAS FREQUENTLY INCREASED BY OPTIONS SUCH AS HURST FOUR-SPEED FLOOR TRANSMISSION, AIR CONDITIONING, POWER STEERING, LEATHER TRIM, AND MANY OTHER FEATURES. KNOWN AS THE AVANTI II UNTIL 1981, IT BECAME PLAIN AVANTI AFTER A CHANGE OF OWNERSHIP. CONVERTIBLE AND FOUR-DOOR SEDAN VERSIONS WERE ADDED IN 1985 AND 1989.

OWNER: DAN KUHL (PHOTO NICKY WRIGHT)

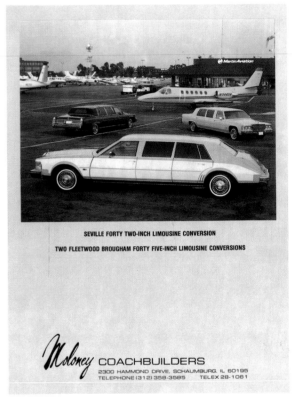

▼ IN 1980 MOLONEY COACHBUILDERS OFFERED A LIMOUSINE DERIVED FROM THE CADILLAC SEVILLE, WITH A 42-INCH EXTENSION. IN THE BACKGROUND ARE TWO OTHER MOLONEY OFFERINGS, FLEETWOOD BROUGHAMS EXTENDED BY 45 INCHES.

MOLONEY COACHBUILDERS, (PHOTO WALTER McCALL)

THE STRETCHED LIMOUSINE

The 1980s saw a boom in both the quantity and size of limousines built on lengthened standard chassis. The basic idea had been around since the early 1920s, when stretched Cadillacs and Pierce-Arrows were often used on bus routes that did not warrant full-size buses. Later, six- and even eight-door limousines were built for airport and hotel work, but they were relatively utilitarian vehicles, with no luxuries. The typical stretched limo that began to appear at the end of the 1970s had only four doors, with a fixed panel between front and rear doors behind which were located the bar, tape and compact disk player, cellular telephone, radio, and TV, all essential amenities in such cars. Instead of the forward-facing jump seats of the old style limousine, there were now rear-facing seats that were just as luxurious as those opposite.

The usual base for limo conversions has been the Cadillac Fleetwood Brougham and the Lincoln Town Car, although some smaller front-drive models have been given similar treatment, their advantage being that there is no need to extend the drive shaft. However, they lack the dignity of the traditional rear-drive Cadillacs and Lincolns which are the favorite for hire work. It is the growth of private hire that has given such a boost to the stretched limo trade, for many hire companies offer such cars, giving Hollywood-style luxury for little more than double the price of a regular cab. Production doubled to 5,000 between 1983 and 1984, and has run at around 6,000 a year since then.

One of the first companies to offer luxury limousine conversions was A.H.A. (Andrew Hotten Associates) of Brampton, Ontario, which began stretching Lincolns in 1977, later working on Buick Electra, Cadillac, Chrysler, and Mercedes-Benz chassis platforms. For those who wanted a compact limousine, a Honda Accord or Volvo 264 would be stretched. A.H.A.'s boss Andrew Hotten has the world's largest collection of classic Lincolns. Other specialists in this field were American Custom Coach of Beverly Hills, Armbruster of Fort Smith, Arkansas, Bradford Coach Works of Boca Raton, Florida, Hess & Eisenhardt of Cincinnati, Ohio, Moloney of Schaumberg, Illinois, National Coach of Port Sanilar, Michigan, and O'Gara of Simi Valley, California. The latter builds presidential Lincolns and specializes in armored bodywork.

A typical stretch involved adding a center section of 36 or 42 inches, extending a Lincoln

1987 LINCOLN TOWN CAR LIMOUSINE ▲

THE LINCOLN TOWN CAR HAS BEEN THE MOST POPULAR BASE FOR STRETCH LIMOUSINES. THEY WERE SUPPLIED IN
ORDINARY FORM TO THE COACHBUILDER BUT WITH A DELETE TRIM OPTION. THIS WAS DONE SO THAT, IN ADDITION TO
STRETCHING THE FRAME, THE COACHBUILDER COULD ADD HIS OWN INTERIOR TRIM. THE COMPANY RESPONSIBLE FOR
THIS LIMOUSINE WAS NOT IDENTIFIED IN THE LINCOLN CATALOG, BUT IT COULD WELL BE A.H.A. OR BRADFORD.

LINCOLN-MERCURY DIVISION, FORD MOTOR COMPANY

Town Car wheelbase from 117.3 to 153.3 or 159.3 inches, giving an overall length of up to 261 inches. For those who wanted such things, more extensive stretching could be done. When the length became too great to be reasonably supported on four wheels, the makers added an extra axle at the rear. Several New York hire companies offered six wheelers by the end of the 1980s, overall length running to more than 300 inches. In Los Angeles (where else?) Ed Tillman had an eight-wheeled Lincoln with a floorplan stretched by 83 inches and a swimming pool (actually no bigger than a large bath) where the trunk would normally be. The ultimate in long cars is probably a 26-wheeled 100-foot creation by Jay Ohrburg of Burbank, California, containing not only a swimming pool with a diving board, but also a king-size water bed. It is powered by two Cadillac engines.

HOW AMERICAN IS AN AMERICAN CAR?

Up to the 1970s it was taken for granted that a car bearing any of the well-known names would be an American design built in America. However, the situation has changed greatly in the past decade, largely because the enormous cost of retooling for a new model can be bypassed if an already-developed foreign design is used instead. The first American Ford Escort was an international car engineered in Europe as well as the United States, while the second, introduced in 1990, was engineered in Japan by Mazda. In 1988 cars badged as Fords, Lincolns, and Mercurys came from five different countries: Korea (Ford Festiva), Mexico (Mercury Tracer), Canada (Mercury Topaz and Grand Marquis, Ford Tempo and Crown Victoria), Germany (Merkur), and the United States (Ford Escort, Tempo, Taurus, Mustang, Thunderbird, Mercury Topaz, Sable and Cougar, all Lincolns). A sixth country was added in 1990, when Mercury started selling the Australian-built Capri sports car, although the poor-selling German-made Merkur was dropped.

Mercury had a tradition of selling imported cars, beginning in 1970 with the European Ford Capri

coupe. This was a junior Mustang in conception, with a variety of engines from tame to hot, but the one Mercury sold started with a British-sourced 97.6-cubic-inch four-cylinder engine. Although introduced in mid-1970 as a 1971 model, sales during the calendar year 1970 were 17,300, a record for an import in its first year. For 1972 the engine range was extended to include a 122-cubic-inch four and a 158.6-cubic-inch V6 billed as "the sexy European in a more passionate version." In 1971 Mercury dealers began selling an even more passionate European, the Italian-built mid-engined De Tomaso Pantera, offered with a choice of three Ford V8s up to 330bhp. U.S. sales were discontinued after 1974, although the same design was still being built in Italy in 1992.

The Capri, on the other hand, continued to sell well, its V6 engine being shared with the Mustang from 1974. Another example of international cooperation was that while the American-built Mercury Bobcat used engines from Lima, Ohio, those in the Canadian Bobcat were sourced to a Ford plant in Brazil. Capri imports ended in 1977 when the name went on a hatchback coupe that shared a body with the Ford Mustang. However, Lincoln-Mercury dealers had another import to sell in 1985, the German-built Merkur, the "hot" model of the European Ford Sierra range. A slippery three-door hatchback coupe with grille-less front end and biplane spoiler at the rear, the Merkur XR4Ti was powered by a 140-cubic-inch turbocharged four similar to that used in the Thunderbird and Cougar. Selling for $16,361, the Merkur (German for Mercury) was predicted to be a great success. "I've never seen a vehicle attract as

1988 CHEVROLET NOVA, TURBO SPECTRUM, AND TURBO SPRINT ▲

CHEVROLET'S THREE SMALL CARS FOR 1988: THE TWIN-CAM NOVA SEDAN (FOREGROUND) WAS A TOYOTA DESIGN BUILT IN CALIFORNIA BY NUMMI; THE SPECTRUM (CENTER) AND SPRINT (BACKGROUND) WERE BUILT IN JAPAN, THE SPECTRUM BY ISUZU AND THE SPRINT BY SUZUKI. THE LATTER HAD A FOUR-CYLINDER TURBOCHARGED ENGINE GIVING 101bhp AND A TOP SPEED OF 105mph. FOR 1989 THESE CARS WERE RENAMED GEO PRIZM, GEO SPECTRUM, AND GEO METRO.

CHEVROLET DIVISION, GENERAL MOTORS

much attention as the XR4Ti in America," enthused Egon Goegel, Ford's European chief engineer for vehicle development in Europe.

In May 1987 the three-door hatchback was joined by a five-door model called the Merkur Scorpio powered by a 177-cubic-inch V6. Riding on a 108.7-inch wheelbase, this was classed as a mid-sized car, whereas the XR4Ti was a compact. Neither sold as well as was hoped, probably because they were high-priced, and the Scorpio in particular had little to offer that could not be found on the roomier Taurus and Sable for less money.

GM's foreign involvement, after the importation of Vauxhalls and Opels in the 1960s and 1970s, has centered on Japan. (The Chevette, although a foreign design, was built in the United States.) In 1971 GM acquired a 34.2 percent stake in Isuzu, which resulted in the Japanese company's light pickup being sold in the United States as the Chevrolet LUV (Light Utility Vehicle) from March 1972 through the 1982 season. By the mid-1980s it was evident that the rear-drive Chevette was coming to the end of its career; for its replacement, the three- or five-door front-drive hatchback called the Swift, Chevrolet went to Suzuki. In its 61-cubic-inch three-cylinder form, the Swift was sold

THE AMERICAN AUTOMOBILE: A CENTENARY 1893 – 1993

1990 GEO STORM COUPE ◄

GEO WAS A NEW BRAND NAME FOR 1989, A
SUBDIVISION OF CHEVROLET THAT COVERED THE
CALIFORNIA-BUILT NOVA (GEO PRIZM), AND THE
IMPORTED SUZUKI SPRINT (GEO METRO) AND SAMURAI
(GEO TRACKER). THE STORM WAS A 1990 ADDITION TO
THE GEO RANGE, BEING A REBADGED ISUZU IMPULSE
2 + 2 COUPE WITH 125bhp 16-VALVE TWIN-CAM FOUR
ENGINE. A COMPETITOR FOR THE HONDA CRX, THE
STORM WAS 18 INCHES LONGER THAN ITS RIVAL, ABOUT
EQUAL IN PRICE ($11,650), AND SOMEWHAT INFERIOR IN
PERFORMANCE. STYLING WAS CONTROVERSIAL AND
COMMENTS VARIED FROM "...REALLY TURNS HEADS" TO
"AT BEST, UNUSUAL LOOKING, AT WORST, ODD."

GEO DIVISION, CHEVROLET

on the U.S. market as the Chevrolet Sprint. In 1986 the twin cam 16-valve turbocharged Turbo Sprint appeared. It was joined by the Isuzu-built Chevrolet Spectrum and the Nova, a rebadged Toyota Corolla built by a joint GM-Toyota operation called NUMMI (New United Motor Manufacturing Company Inc.) at Fremont, California.

Although all three were good cars, sales were slower than anticipated. One reason was that buyers of Hondas, Nissans, and the like were used to purchasing fully equipped cars, whereas the traditional Chevy dealer offered a base model with a long list of options. Chevrolet General Manager Jim Perkins observed: "Generally speaking, the people who look at and buy these cars are a little different from those we would see in a Chevrolet dealership."

To set up a new dealer network in competition with Chevrolet's nearly 5,000 locations was clearly out of the question, so GM compromised with a new brand name which they called Geo. This was a sub-division of Chevrolet, and all Chevy dealers had the opportunity to add Geo cars to their line. Two of the three Chevrolets were renamed, the Sprint becoming the Geo Metro and the Nova the Prizm. Another model was added, the Suzuki Samurai 4x4 light cross-country vehicle, which became the Geo Tracker. Geo models debuted in 1989. Later additions to the range included a Metro convertible and the Storm, a GT coupe derived from the Isuzu Impulse. The Metro is the most frugal car on the U.S. market and the lowest-priced, at $5,995 undercutting the Ford Festiva by $500. At around $10,000, the Metro convertible is the lowest-priced open-top car currently on the U.S. market.

Chrysler took a 15 percent stake in Mitsubishi in 1970, which led to the latter's Colt small cars being sold under the Dodge Colt name from 1971.

In 1978 Chrysler sold 25 percent of all Mitsubishi's passenger car output. Starting in 1982, Mitsubishi engines were alternatives in the K-cars, Chrysler LeBaron, Dodge Aries, and Plymouth Reliant, and have been continued in subsequent models up to the present.

In 1988 Chrysler and Mitsubishi set up a joint factory at Normal, Illinois, under the name Diamond Star. The product was a very sleek sports coupe with a choice of four-cylinder engines from a 110bhp 109.7-cubic-inch single cam to a 195bhp 122-cubic-inch twin cam turbocharged engine, five-speed manual transmission, and full-time four-wheel drive on the top GSX models. Mechanical elements were designed and built by Mitsubishi and the body by Chrysler, and the cars were marketed under three names with only minor differences, Mitsubishi Eclipse, Eagle Talon, and Plymouth Laser. The Mitsubishi models sold the best, according to Lee Iacocca, because Americans have an inferiority complex about American-brand cars in the sporty field. Prices were very close, from around $10,800 for the base model two-wheel drive to $13,400 for a turbo model, with an extra $3,600 for four-wheel drive.

For 1990 the Mitsubishi models were joined by the V6-powered Dodge Stealth, a close cousin of the Mitsubishi 3000GT/HSX. This was a more

1978 DODGE ASPEN COUPE ◄

INTRODUCED FOR 1976, THE ASPEN WAS A COMPACT: A
SLIGHTLY LARGER, ROOMIER, AND HEAVIER VERSION OF
THE DART, MUCH AS FORD'S GRANADA WAS OF THE
MAVERICK. ORIGINALLY MADE AS A SEDAN, COUPE OR
WAGON IN SEVERAL SERIES, THE ASPEN WAS DOWN TO
THREE MODELS BY 1978. THIS COUPE CAME ON A 108.7-
INCH WHEELBASE; THE FOUR-DOOR SEDAN AND WAGON
WERE 4 INCHES LONGER. THE ASPEN'S TWIN IN THE
PLYMOUTH RANGE WAS THE VOLARE, AND BOTH CARS
WERE SUBJECT TO MASSIVE RECALLS TO THE FACTORIES
BECAUSE OF POOR QUALITY CONTROL AND RUSTING.
THEY WERE MADE THROUGH THE 1980 SEASON, AFTER
WHICH THEY WERE REPLACED BY THE DODGE
ARIES/PLYMOUTH RELIANT.

(PHOTO NICKY WRIGHT)

sophisticated and expensive car, with steering as well as drive to all four wheels, and a twin-turbocharged engine giving 280bhp. Much of the mechanical content came from the Mitsubishi Galant sedan, which is not made in the United States. A Stealth was selected as the 1991 Indianapolis Pace Car, a choice seen by some as a symbol of America's automotive decline. Bill Osos, director of the United Auto Workers' Union Region 3, said: "I think it's morally wrong to use a 100 percent Japanese-built car right here in the heart of Indiana. It's a slap in the face of the American auto worker." As a result of this and other protests, the Stealth was replaced by a Dodge V10 Viper driven by Carroll Shelby.

Other American-badged Mitsubishis were the Dodge and Plymouth Colts, both small hatchbacks with four-wheel drive at the top of the range, selling from $6,995 to $14,700.

The only other major American car maker, American Motors, also came under foreign influence when the French Renault company began to buy into AMC in 1978. Renault eventually acquired 46.9 percent of the stock, and in 1982 gave AMC an entry in the sub-compact market with its four-cylinder sedans and hatchbacks, badged as Alliance and Encore. AMC's president in 1983 was a Renault man, Jose Dedeurwaerder, and the Renault-based cars were soon outselling the American-designed four-wheel drive Eagles by ten to one. Jeeps still remained the most profitable part of AMC's business, and it was interest in Jeep

which led Chrysler to acquire AMC for $600 million in 1987. Chrysler discontinued the old Eagle designs but set up a new Jeep-Eagle Division which made the Renault 21-based Eagle Premier and Eagle Talon coupe as part of the Diamond Star program.

Foreign penetration into U.S. car manufacturing has been very deep. In fact it is almost impossible to quantify the exact American content of models such as those described here. Foreign auto companies are also manufacturing under their own name in the United States. This trend began with Volkswagen setting up a plant in New Scranton, Pennsylvania, in 1978 to make Rabbits, the American name for the Golf. The first to start, VW was also the first, and so far the only, company to abandon U.S. manufacture, giving up in 1988 after serious problems with quality control. Honda opened its plant at Marysville, Ohio, in 1983, the same year that Nissan started production at

1991 OLDSMOBILE 98 TOURING SEDAN ◄▲►
THE NUMBER 98 HAS LONG INDICATED THE TOP MODEL OF OLDSMOBILE, SINCE 1941 IN FACT, AND THE 50TH ANNIVERSARY OF THE NAME BROUGHT A LARGE FRONT DEIVE SEDAN WITH GENERAL MOTORS' C-BODY AND A 231-CUBIC-INCH 170bhp V6 ENGINE. ALTHOUGH IN THE SAME SIZE CATEGORY AS BUICK'S PARK AVENUE, THE 98 DID NOT SHARE A SINGLE BODY PANEL WITH ITS COUSIN FROM FLINT. THE OLDSMOBILE'S SUSPENSION IS FIRMER THAN THE BUICK'S. THE BASE PRICE FOR THE TOURING SEDAN WAS $28,595.

OLDSMOBILE DIVISION, GENERAL MOTORS (PHOTO NICKY WRIGHT)

Smyrna, Tennessee. Mazda began its operations at Flat Rock, Michigan, in 1985, and Toyota at Georgetown, Kentucky, in 1988. Not only did these factories build cars for the U.S. market, they also started exporting U.S.-built Japanese cars to Japan. Diamond Star shipped its first 3,000 Eclipse coupes in November 1989, and in 1990 Toyota began building right-hand-drive Camry sedans for export. These operations reduced to some extent the trade imbalance between the United States and Japan, brought about by the enormous volume of imports from Japan, not only of cars but of electrical goods, televisions, videos, and cameras.

In 1990 Honda took an important step toward becoming a fully-fledged domestic manufacturer, with the introduction of its Accord station wagon. This was styled by Honda's research and development facility at Torrance, California, and engineered at Marysville. Engines were built at Honda's other Ohio plant, at Anna. The 134-cubic-inch all-aluminum 16-valve unit was also used in Accord sedans and coupes. Production for 1991 was set at 30,000–35,000 cars: 10,000 earmarked for export, 5,000 to Japan and 5,000 to Europe — the first time a U.S.-made Japanese car has been exported other than to Japan. Honda's marketing in the United States has been double-pronged, the Ohio-built Civic and Accord being sold under the Honda name, and the higher-priced Legend sedan and coupe and NSX sports car carrying the Acura name and being sold by a different dealer network. The same strategy is employed by Nissan and Toyota, whose Infiniti and Lexus luxury sedans are marketed quite separately from their lower-priced cars. The Lexus even uses a different advertising agency from Toyota.

Korea is also making inroads into the North American market, with Hyundai having a Canadian plant at Bromont, Quebec, whose cars are sold in the United States through Chrysler/Eagle dealers. GM's Korean arm, Daewoo, builds the Opel Kadett-based Pontiac LeMans compact sedan and coupe, and has considered marketing its cars in the United States under its own name.

A TROUBLED DECADE, AND THE WAY AHEAD

The American auto industry took a real battering at the beginning of the 1980s. In the wake of the fuel consumption regulations that reduced the appeal of the traditional big American car, imports surged ahead, particularly those from Japan. Domestic production, which had been 9.7 million in 1973, dropped to little over 6 million in 1980, the year in which America took second place to Japan in overall production. And between 1978 and 1982 32 manufacturing and assembly plants across the nation closed. In 1987 imports accounted for 3,197,000 cars, 31.1 percent of the total sold in the United States.

The relative decline of American car makers vis-à-vis the Japanese began in the 1960s, when American confidence slipped into complacency, and the Japanese were exerting themselves to build up an industry from nothing. The cost-accounting dominance of men like Ford's Whiz Kids led to a short-sighted policy where year-end profits were the sacred cow and capital investment which would lower those profits was severely discouraged. Thus both new machine tools and research and development were starved of funds. By the early 1980s Japan's level of automation was double that of America. Of course high profits and low investment suited the American work force. Executives' annual profits-linked bonuses

sometimes exceeded their salaries, and blue collar workers, in the late 1970s, took home 60 percent more than the average industrial wage. Each year would bring a substantial rise in their standard of living, wouldn't it?

Ford entered the 1980s in bad shape; between June 1979 and the end of 1981 its white-collar workforce was cut by a quarter, and the blue-collar payroll was reduced from 190,000 to 115,000. Personal differences between Henry Ford II and Lee Iacocca led to the latter's departure in August 1978, and Henry himself stepped down from the three-man "office of chief executives" on October 1, 1980. His brother, William Clay Ford, and

Donald Petersen stepped up to take the vacant places, and Philip Caldwell, who was already there, made up the third. Caldwell had made a great success with Ford trucks and, although unkindly described as "uncharismatic" and "a gray, cold-blooded bean counter," he did the same with the whole company, achieving profits of $187 million in 1984 after three years of serious losses.

Iacocca moved to Chrysler and had much the same success there. When he took over, U.S. passenger car sales were only 1.25 million, and the 1978 loss was $208 million. The introduction of the K-cars achieved a turnaround, putting Chrysler in profit again in 1983. Since then the corporation has had several milestones — the reintroduction of the convertible, the purchase of American Motors and Lamborghini in 1987, and the Diamond Star joint venture with Mitsubishi from 1988.

By the end of the decade Chrysler was in a healthier position than it had been at the beginning, but as the smallest of the Big Three it was still vulnerable in a world difficult for all Detroit car makers. In 1989 the corporation was forced to sell $300 million worth of Mitsubishi

shares to cover losses, and a year later was trying to divest itself of the Technologies Group and other non-automotive businesses. There were rumors, strongly denied by vice-president Bob Lutz, that Lamborghini would have to be sold, and a merger with Fiat was discussed. One growth field for Chrysler was exports, particularly to Europe, where American cars have been little represented in recent years. The medium-sized Chrysler Saratoga and LeBaron went to France, Switzerland, Germany, and other markets at prices somewhat below the similar-sized BMW 5 Series. The 1990 export sales, including Jeep products, were 41,000, with an anticipated 55,000 for 1991. In December 1990 California billionaire Kirk Kerkorian bought nearly 10 percent of Chrysler stock, which led to rumors of a takeover. However, it seems more likely that he was simply investing in stock that was very low ($12.25 compared with $48 in 1987) and could only move upward.

General Motors also had a roller coaster ride in the 1980s, rising from a poor start to record sales in 1984/85, when it had three makes in the top five best sellers, Chevrolet in first place, Oldsmobile in third, and Pontiac in fifth. GM also made its mistakes, particularly in the Cadillac Division, where the V-8-6-4 engine, which could be run with a varying number of cylinders according to driving conditions, flopped after one season. A good idea, it was too complex to be reliable and brought many customer complaints. The automated Hamtramck body plant, where Cadillac Sevilles, Olds Toronados, and Buick Rivieras were made, gave a lot of trouble to start with (robots painted each other instead of the cars). Cadillac suffered from a severe loss of image, having too little to distinguish it from other GM products. The Allante was an attempt to rectify this but has not been a marked success so far. However, GM increased its market share in 1990 to 35.7 percent, 0.5 per cent up on 1989.

Although GM's small car imports in the Geo range sold quite well, they made very little profit. In order to meet the imports head on, a new division making an all-new car was announced in 1983, with production slated to start in the summer of 1990. Named Saturn in tribute to the rocket that carried America to the moon, it was located in a new 2,450-acre complex at Spring Hill, Tennessee. Unlike GM plants which work in collaboration with

1988 CHEVROLET ASTRO CL ◀

VARIOUSLY CALLED THE PEOPLE CARRIER OR MPV (MULTIPURPOSE VEHICLE) THE HIGH-ROOF, SHORT-HOOD DESIGN COMBINED THE VIRTUES OF A STATION WAGON AND A VAN. MPVs WERE BUILT IN EUROPE AND JAPAN FROM THE EARLY 1980s, AND THE LAYOUT APPEARED IN THE UNITED STATES IN 1984 WITH THE DODGE CARAVAN. THIS WAS FOLLOWED BY THE CHEVROLET ASTRO FOR 1985 AND THE FORD AEROSTAR FOR 1986. THE ASTRO USED A STANDARD V6 ENGINE AND REAR DRIVE, AND CAME IN PANEL VAN OR STATION WAGON FORM. THE CL PACKAGE INCLUDED CUSTOM STEERING WHEEL, WHEEL TRIM RINGS, AUXILIARY LIGHTING, CIGAR LIGHTER, AND CARPETS. IN FIVE-PASSENGER FORM IT COST $9,359.

CHEVROLET DIVISION, GENERAL MOTORS

others, using engines from one source, transmissions from another, and steering gears from a third, Spring Hill is a complete producer, with its own foundry, body-stamping shop, and paint, interior and general assembly shops. No components are shared with other GM cars, although, surprisingly, 65 percent of the Saturn's content comes from outside suppliers. Bought-in items include spark plugs, seats, and tires, which the auto industry traditionally buys from specialists.

Working conditions at Saturn are above average for the industry, including complete air conditioning throughout the complex, electrically powered tools rather than air-driven ones, and less demarcation between management and workforce. Taking a lead from the NUMMI plant at Fremont, California, which is said to have the best quality control of any GM installation, there is less dependence on robots than in some Detroit plants.

The Saturn is a generally conventional car made

in sedan and coupe forms, with two 116-cubic-inch four-cylinder engines, a single cam developing 85bhp and a twin cam giving 123bhp. The sedan's wheelbase is 104.2 inches, identical to the Honda Accord and Toyota Camry. Construction is a pressed steel spaceframe and steel top and hood, with doors and side panels of molded plastic screwed to the frame.

Saturn marketing is new, too, with one dealer for each of 250 geographical areas, who sells only Saturns. He may handle other cars, but only from a different location. Saturn stresses a high degree of customer friendliness, with as much prominence being given to service as to sales. Market research has shown that many customers feel intimidated in car showrooms and have a low level of trust in salespeople. Initial sales were to be confined to

1990 PONTIAC TRANS SPORT MPV ◀

ONE OF A GENERAL MOTORS FAMILY OF MPVs THAT INCLUDED THE CHEVROLET LUMINA AND OLDSMOBILE SILHOUETTE, THE TRANS SPORT HAD A 191-CUBIC-INCH FUEL-INJECTED V6 MOUNTED TRANSVERSELY UNDER THE SHORT HOOD AND DRIVING THE FRONT WHEELS. DESPITE ITS NAME IT WAS NOT PARTICULARLY SPORTING: "MORE TRANS THAN SPORT" AS *AUTOWEEK* MAGAZINE REPORTED. THERE WAS A SINGLE DOOR ON THE DRIVER'S SIDE, TWO ON THE PASSENGER SIDE, WITH SEATING FOR FIVE OR SEVEN.

PONTIAC DIVISION, GENERAL MOTORS

1991 SATURN SEDAN AND COUPE ▲ ▶

PRODUCTS OF AN ALL-NEW GM DIVISION LOCATED IN TENNESSEE, THE SATURN MODELS WERE DESIGNED TO MEET
IMPORTS SUCH AS THE HONDA ACCORD AND TOYOTA CAMRY HEAD-ON. IT WAS OFFERED IN FOUR MODELS:
THE BASE SL AND BETTER-TRIMMED SL1 SEDANS (BACKGROUND) WITH SINGLE-CAM FOUR-CYLINDER ENGINES; THE
SL2 SEDAN (RIGHT FOREGROUND) WITH TWIN-CAM ENGINE; AND THE SC COUPE (LEFT FOREGROUND), ONLY
AVAILABLE IN TWIN-CAM FORM. ALL HAD TRANSVERSE ENGINES DRIVING THE FRONT WHEELS. IN THE EXPLODED
DRAWING, THE DETACHABLE HOOD AND TOP PANELS ARE OF STEEL, THE BODY SIDE, FRONT AND REAR PANELS
OF MOLDED DENT-RESISTANT POLYMER PLASTIC.

SATURN CORPORATION

California, the prime market for imported cars, and to the home state of Tennessee. Production started up on July 31, 1990, and dealers received their first sedans in December. In February 1991, 50 percent of the 3,000 Saturns made up to that date were subject to recall because of possibly faulty seat recliners. However, overall 1991 sales were encouraging, at nearly 75,000. Saturn was ranked first among 24 small cars in a J. D. Power customer satisfaction survey. A station wagon was added to the range in 1992. Exports to Canada began in 1991, and entry into the Japanese market is planned for the mid-1990s.

An interesting recent development has been the revival of the traditional large rear-drive V8 sedan, which even as recently as 1988 seemed doomed to extinction. The genre was gradually marginalized in the ranges of all Big Three manufacturers. GM offered only station wagons in the Buick, Oldsmobile, and Pontiac lines, and production was among the lowest of any of its models. Chrysler kept alive the Fifth Avenue and its sisters the Dodge Diplomat and Plymouth Grand Fury because their development costs had long since been amortized, and big cars generally make more profit than small ones. They, and equivalents from Ford and Chevrolet, were popular with taxi operators and police forces.

However, a wider market for a large six-passenger car clearly still existed, and so, despite concern over CAFE figures, Chevrolet brought out a completely restyled Caprice for 1990. Launched in January as a 1991 model, it preserved the 305-cubic-inch V8 engine and rear drive via automatic transmission that dated back to 1976, but it was clothed in a new aerodynamic body. A large car at 214 inches overall length and weighing 3,935 pounds, it gave neither sparkling performance nor a taut ride, yet it clearly struck a chord with the American public. To the amazement of European commentators, who referred to its "Moby Dick school of styling," the Caprice was named Car of the Year by *Motor Trend* magazine.

At the end of 1990 other GM divisions followed Chevrolet; Oldsmobile announced the Custom Cruiser eight-passenger station wagon, and Buick revived the Roadmaster name, unused since 1958, for a similar wagon. A Roadmaster sedan joined it in spring 1991, powered by a larger engine of 348 cubic inches. The wagons were really big, with 87 cubic feet of cargo space, yet prices were quite reasonable, around $18,000 for a fully equipped Caprice to $25,000 for a Buick Roadmaster. Cadillac continued its old-style Brougham, which used the same platform as the Roadmaster/Caprice, but a restyle was announced for 1993.

Over at Ford there was a similar revival of the large car, with the Crown Victoria and Mercury Grand Marquis completely restyled to look like grown-up versions of the Taurus/Sable. Unlike the GM cars, the Fords had new engines as well, 281-cubic-inch overhead cam V8s giving 190 or 210bhp with dual exhausts. These were 40 and 50bhp better than the larger pushrod V8s in the previous big Fords. Prices started at $19,200 for the Crown Victoria. Careful choice of components enabled these Fords to be classed as imports, having just over 25 percent imported parts. Thus their fuel consumption could be averaged with more economical Ford imports such as the Festiva and Mercury Capri.

Despite all these new models, the outlook for the American auto industry at the beginning of 1992 is not encouraging. The recession began to hit in the second half of 1990, and overall U.S. production of cars and light trucks was down on 1989. Yet the Japanese, both with imports and transplants, mostly registered an increase on 1989. Mitsubishi's sales jumped by 29.6 percent, Toyota's by 15.1 percent, and Honda's by 9.2 percent. For the second year running, the Honda Accord was the best-selling model, beating the Taurus by more than 100,000 units, while Chrysler only just held onto third place, selling only 6,000 more cars than Honda. The Accord again registered first place in 1991. In 1990 the domestic car makers had 60 percent of the market, with the Japanese taking 27.5 percent and European imports 12.5 percent. In January 1991 the Big Three temporarily closed 24 of 62 main plants, laying off 62,000 workers. A year later GM announced closure of 21 U.S. plants over the next four years.

In order to boost sales in a market where cars are a fairly expensive item, more expensive relative to family income than at any time in the last two decades, almost all dealers offered discounts on the list price. This applied not only to domestic models

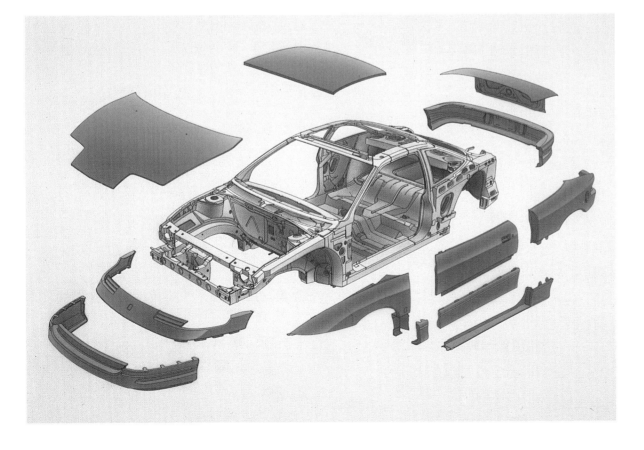

1991 CHEVROLET CAPRICE SEDAN ▲ ▶
ONE OF GENERAL MOTORS' NEW GENERATION OF FULL-SIZE, REAR-DRIVE CARS, THE 1991 CAPRICE WAS BASED ON A WIDENED VERSION OF THE 1990 CHASSIS, WITH AN ALL-NEW BODY WHOSE DRAG COEFFICIENT WAS ONLY 0.33, COMPARED WITH 0.41 FOR THE 1990 SEDAN. OVERALL LENGTH WAS NEARLY 18 FEET AND TRUNK VOLUME 20.4 CUBIC FEET. OTHER CARS IN THE SAME FAMILY WERE THE BUICK ROADMASTER SEDAN AND OLDSMOBILE CUSTOM CRUISER STATION WAGON.

CHEVROLET DIVISION, GENERAL MOTORS

(PHOTO NICKY WRIGHT)

but to supposed popular imports such as the Lexus luxury sedan, officially priced at $38,000 but available for $30,400 to a determined bargainer. Discounting may help to move cars, but it is no way to make profits. Even the sticker price, which hardly anybody pays, represents a loss to manufacturers. In 1989 it was estimated that GM lost around $1,200 per car on average, Chrysler $1,000, and Ford $800. In 1990 GM lost $1.6 billion and Ford $519 million, although Chrysler recorded a $31 million profit. Even more depressing was 1991. July–September losses were $1.1 billion for GM, $574.4 million for Ford, and around $82 million for Chrysler. Analysts predicted that overall 1991 losses might be the worst in the history of the industry. One of the victims was Roger Penske's

1991 CHEVROLET CAPRICE SEDAN ▲◄

THE CAPRICE AND ITS SISTER, THE BUICK ROADMASTER, MARKED A RETURN TO THE TRADITIONAL FULL-SIZE, REAR-DRIVE AMERICAN AUTOMOBILE, AND GM'S COMMITMENT TO SUCH CARS WAS UNDERLINED BY BRAND-NEW BODIES THAT WERE CLEARLY PLANNED TO HAVE SEVERAL YEARS OF LIFE. PRICES BEGAN AT JUST UNDER $16,000, AND BUYERS GOT A LOT OF CAR FOR THEIR MONEY. AN UPGRADED F41 SUSPENSION PACKAGE WENT SOME WAY TO ELIMINATING THE WALLOW ASSOCIATED WITH THESE CARS. CHEVROLET OFFERED POLICE AND TAXI PACKAGE VERSIONS OF THE CAPRICE, THE LATTER PRICED AT $19,283.

CHEVROLET DIVISION, GENERAL MOTORS (PHOTO NICKY WRIGHT)

1992 FORD CROWN VICTORIA AND MERCURY MARQUIS SEDANS ◄▼

FORD AND MERCURY COMPLETELY MODERNIZED THEIR LARGE REAR-DRIVE CARS FOR 1992, THE NEW MODELS BEING ANNOUNCED IN DECEMBER 1990. STYLING BORE A CLOSE FAMILY RESEMBLANCE TO THE FORD TAURUS AND MERCURY SABLE, AND THERE WAS A NEW ENGINE IN THE MODULAR OVERHEAD-CAM V8. THIS WAS 37 POUNDS LIGHTER THAN ITS PREDECESSOR, YET GAVE 40bhp MORE IN SINGLE EXHAUST FORM AND 50bhp WITH TWIN EXHAUSTS. THE ALL-NEW ALUMINUM CYLINDER HEAD ACCOUNTED FOR PART OF THE WEIGHT REDUCTION, AIDED BY ALUMINUM PISTONS AND INTAKE MANIFOLD. NOT SO MUCH "CARS FOR THE SHUFFLEBOARD SET" AS THEIR PREDECESSORS HAD BEEN, THE NEW BIG FORDS HAD GREATLY IMPROVED RIDE AND HANDLING.

FORD MOTOR COMPANY

huge Cadillac-Buick-Chevrolet dealership in Manhattan, which closed in the spring of 1991.

Recession apart, much of the malaise in the American auto industry stems from a massive loss of confidence on the part of the American car-buying public. At one time, enthusiasm and snobbery were the main motives for buying imported cars, but over the past decade or so, budget-minded drivers worried about every cent of repair and running costs, and trade-in values, have been the main customers for foreign cars. A 1988 survey of customer satisfaction put the top U.S. car (Cadillac) in fifteenth place, beaten by Acura, Range Rover, and Mercedes-Benz (first, second, and third respectively), and also by such minor imports as Daihatsu and Hyundai. However, at least Cadillac beat Volkswagen! The Acura has been so reliable that a dealer complained that he could make no money in his service department. "These cars just do not break. You know, we said that in the beginning, too, and everyone thought it was because the cars were brand new. Well, they can't say that any more, and we still don't have any service business." In 1991 Japan again topped the list, the Lexus gaining 146 points, but U.S. makes were much higher. Cadillac was second with 140 points and Lincoln fourth with 136.

Yet industry leaders see several gleams of hope. Lee Iacocca thinks that hard times will concentrate the American mind on efficiency and quality:

1992 BUICK ROADMASTER STATION WAGON ▲

BUICK REVIVED THE ROADMASTER NAME, DORMANT SINCE 1958, FOR THE NEW FULL-SIZE SEDAN AND STATION
WAGON. THE BUICK WAGON SHARED PLATFORM AND 305-CUBIC-INCH V8 ENGINE WITH CHEVROLET'S CAPRICE
AND OLDS' CUSTOM CRUISER, WHILE THE SEDAN HAD A LARGER ENGINE. THE WAGON WAS DESCRIBED BY
ROAD & TRACK AS "DECIDEDLY UNTRENDY, WITH ITS FLOATING RIDE AND VINYL WOODGRAIN APPLIQUÉ," BUT
ITS ACCOMMODATION FOR EIGHT PASSENGERS AND 87 CUBIC FEET OF CARGO SPACE CLEARLY APPEALED
TO MANY AMERICANS TIRED OF SHOEBOX-SIZED COMPACTS.

BUICK DIVISION, GENERAL MOTORS (PHOTO NICKY WRIGHT)

◀▼ TWO OF THE MOST INTERESTING CONCEPT CARS OF RECENT YEARS WERE THE ZIG (LEFT) AND ZAG (BELOW) FROM FORD WITH STYLING BY GHIA. BASED ON A FIESTA FLOORPAN SHORTENED BY 6 INCHES, THEY WERE RESPECTIVELY A TWO-PASSENGER ROADSTER AND A MINIVAN. GHIA STRESSED THAT OTHER STYLES COULD BE HAD ON THE SAME FLOORPAN: THREE- OR FIVE-DOOR SEDANS OR A STATION WAGON. A SARICH-DESIGNED TWO-CYCLE ENGINE WAS A PLANNED POWER UNIT, AS WERE ELECTRIC MOTORS.

MIRCO DE CET COLLECTION

"When it gets tough they will straighten out." This applies just as much to the parts industry, which has to compete with imported parts when supplying to transplants like U.S.-built Hondas and Toyotas. Iacocca sees hope here, too. The annual Detroit Auto Shows have become increasingly important for new "concept cars," which reach the marketplace within a few years, just as Japanese concept cars have been doing. Pontiac's Trans Sport multipurpose vehicle was a concept in 1986 and in the showrooms four years later. Buick's Essence concept of 1989 became a reality with the 1991 Park Avenue Ultra, described by international journalist Peter Robinson as "one of the most promising of American cars." With radical ideas like two-stroke engines and electric motors now actually powering running cars, Detroit seems more in the engineering vanguard that it has been for many years. Let us hope that Henry Ford, Alfred Sloan, and Walter Chrysler can rest in peace, in the knowledge that their legacies will continue to flourish.

1992 FORD TAURUS ▲◄

ALTHOUGH THE 1992 TAURUS AND SABLE REPRESENT THE BIGGEST SINGLE MODEL YEAR CHANGE SINCE THEIR INTRODUCTION, PROGRESS HAS BEEN EVOLUTIONARY RATHER THAN DRAMATIC. BODY PANELS ARE ALL NEW APART FROM THE DOORS, YET APPEARANCE IS NOT RADICALLY CHANGED. SUSPENSION AND TIRES ARE SOFTER, GIVING A SMOOTHER RIDE. ON THE ENGINE SIDE, THE FOUR HAS BEEN DROPPED, LEAVING TWO PUSHROD V6 AND THE TWIN-CAM 24-VALVE V6 USED IN THE HIGH-PERFORMANCE SHOW MODEL.

FORD MOTOR COMPANY

1930 RUXTON ROADSTER ▼

(PHOTO NICKY WRIGHT)

CHAPTER EIGHT

OLD BANGERS TO BLUE CHIP INVESTMENTS

"I warn you that in ten years most of you guys will be standing
outside the hobby, looking in."

Parke-Bernet spokesman, 1962

save cars from the scrappers, and some newspapers demanded that the cars be barred from the streets as dangerous old wrecks. Sometimes there was justification for this, for the meticulous care for authenticity and safety that characterizes nearly all old car lovers today was not so evident 50 years ago. Old tire sizes were unobtainable until the Firestone Company stepped in to make replicas after World War II, so bald tires were frequently seen at early meets.

The AACA formed its first regional chapter in 1945, in northern Illinois, followed by Cleveland. By 1960 more than 80 chapters spanned the United States and Canada, with more than 9,000 members. Two big meets were held each year, Spring and Fall, and the latter seemed to attract the most entrants. Held at the Devon (Pennsylvania) Horse Show Grounds from 1946 through 1953, meets grew too large when more than 200 cars were entered, so a move was made to the stadium at Hershey, home town of the famous chocolate bars. The first Hershey Meet took place in October 1954, and the Fall Meet has been held there annually ever since and now occupies a vast area outside the stadium. The swap meet, in which parts, literature, photographs, and phonograph records as well as cars change hands, occupies far more space than the car show.

Meanwhile other clubs had been formed. The second was the Horseless Carriage Club of America headquartered in Downey, California, which began in November 1937. Formed by automotive engineer and designer of a teardrop three-wheeled car, W. Everett Miller, it had a number of active women members from the start, including Miller's

IN JANUARY 1931 THE Philadelphia Automobile Trade Association, which organized the annual auto show in the city, was looking for inexpensive publicity to spice up the unveiling of new models in Convention Hall. Someone suggested inviting owners of early cars to come along, the definition of "early" being 25 or more years old. The number of owners who turned up has not been traced, but the occasion was considered enough of a success to be repeated annually.

The Antique Automobile Derby, as it was called, attracted more entries each year, and by 1936 at least 40 cars rallied to Philadelphia from points which had to be 25 or more miles away. The contestants were not too happy, though, as they received little prize money and were regarded as

comic relief by the public and the show organizers. In 1935 two of the participants, Ted Fiala and Frank Abramson, suggested the formation of a club for old car enthusiasts, and in November 1935 this became a reality as the Antique Automobile Club of America, with 14 paid-up members (annual dues $1). This was the second such organization in the world, the first being Britain's Veteran Car Club formed in November 1930.

Membership grew only slowly in the pre-war years, but among the club's supporters was pioneer automobilist Charles Duryea, who donated a mimeograph machine to the club in 1938. By 1944, there were 400 paid-up members. The war saw many antique cars melted down in the scrap drive, but this also gave an impetus to enthusiasts to save what they could. Although they had a lot of fun at meets, they were labeled unpatriotic for trying to

wife Katherine, who suggested the club name, Margaret Lewerenz, and Doris Twohy. They encouraged the wearing of period costume at meets, although this has always been a controversial subject. Some enthusiasts feel it introduces a carnival atmosphere unsuited to the serious use of old cars. The HCCA flourished after the war, and has 27 regions across the United States and one in New Zealand.

The third national club was formed in the Boston area in December 1938, under the name Veteran Motor Car Club of America. This had 107 members by 1940, and in 1949 acquired the cars

belonging to the Larz Anderson estate at Brookline, Massachusetts. They also had the use of the Coach House on the estate, whose mansion is modeled after the Château de Chaumont in France, as club headquarters.

▲ A 1935 AUBURN 851 CONVERTIBLE AMONG OTHER PRODUCTS OF THE AUBURN-CORD-DUESENBERG GROUP AT MEADOWBROOK IN 1991.

(PHOTO NICKY WRIGHT)

CLUBS FOR LATER CARS

Prior to World War II, collector interest was confined to cars made before 1920. Model Ts were just acceptable if they had brass radiators (pre-1917), but later ones were of no interest. The loss to the scrapman of so many expensive cars of the 1920s alerted enthusiasts to the idea that collectible cars did not have to be Brass-Age antiques. Immediately after World War II a number of big old Lincolns, Cadillac V16s, Pierce-Arrows, and Rolls-Royces came out of hibernation. Many of them were quickly sold by their well-heeled owners as soon as new cars became available, and they were snapped up by young enthusiasts for a few hundred dollars. Keith Marvin, later a founder member of the Automobilists of the Upper Hudson Valley, bought his first Rolls-Royce, a 1930 Phantom I, for $500 in 1946. Giants of the 1920s could be had for less than this. In 1953 autobook publisher George Dammann was able to buy a 1936 Lincoln V12 Brunn Brougham in reasonable shape for $10.

The Classic Car Club of America (CCCA) was founded late in 1951. At the 1952 International Motor Sport Show in New York City, a 1931 Cadillac V16 displayed by a CCCA member attracted so much attention that club membership

rose from around 20 to almost 90 before the show closed. The club's definition of a classic was a car of recognized quality made between 1925 and 1942. Definitions of "recognized quality" were not always easy to establish, but certain makes were accepted unconditionally for all models. These included Cord, Duesenberg, duPont, Mercer, Pierce-Arrow, and Stutz, as well as foreign makes such as Alfa-Romeo, Bugatti, Isotta-Fraschini, Rolls-Royce, and others. For some other makes, the club was more selective. Most Packards were allowed, but not the

120s or 110s. The big Lincolns and Continentals were accepted, but not the Zephyr. The acceptance of the Continental necessitated a date extension to 1948, as the postwar cars were essentially the same as the prewar ones. No Chevrolets, Fords, Oldsmobiles, or Pontiacs were admitted — unless with custom coachwork and a special application had been made — and among Buicks, only the 90 or Limited series from 1931 to 1942. Classics are ideal tour cars. The CCCA, with its 27 regions, organizes regular long-distance journeys, with some

▲ POST-WORLD WAR II CARS AT A MEET AT THE SLOANE MUSEUM, FLINT, MICHIGAN, IN 1991. IN THE FOREGROUND ARE A 1953 STUDEBAKER AND A 1951 CHEVROLET.
(PHOTO MIRCO DE CET)

◄ ANOTHER CORNER OF THE SLOANE MUSEUM MEET; IN THE FOREGROUND, A CORVETTE, BEHIND IT A CUSTOMIZED 1939 CHEVROLET AND BEYOND THAT A DE TOMASO PANTERA.
(PHOTO MIRCO DE CET)

▶ A PRISTINE EXAMPLE OF A 1956 MERCURY CONVERTIBLE AT MEADOWBROOK.
(PHOTO NICKY WRIGHT)

or one-model clubs. In fact there are clubs for almost every make one can think of, from the prestigious Auburn-Cord-Duesenberg Club to the King Midget and Eshelman Registry. There are at least 23 Ford clubs as well as separate ones for Mustangs and Thunderbirds. At first only the two-passenger T-Birds were thought worth collecting, but soon a club for the four-passenger "Square

◄ RICHARD KUGHN IS A LEADING CAR COLLECTOR WHO ALSO HAS A MAGNIFICENT COLLECTION OF LIONEL MODEL TRAINS. HERE HE IS DRIVING HIS 1935 AUBURN PHAETON.

(PHOTO NICKY WRIGHT)

▼ A 1937 CORD 812 SEDAN.

(PHOTO NICKY WRIGHT)

members driving hundreds of miles to the start of the event. Like the other clubs mentioned, the CCCA publishes a fine magazine, *The Classic Car*.

By the late 1960s it was felt that humbler cars of the classic period should be recognized. By then there were many one-make clubs which catered to Ford V8s, Chevys, and Plymouths, but an umbrella organization for all cars made between 1928 and 1948, the Contemporary Historical Vehicle Association, was formed in 1967. Then, in 1971, came the Indianapolis-based Milestone Car Society "For the Great Post-war Cars." Founded by historian Richard M. Langworth, it covered a later period still, 1945 through 1967 (recently extended to 1972). American and foreign cars are eligible, and are selected by a committee, of which the author has the honor to be a member. Names are put forward by club members, who are usually owners of the cars they propose; if they achieve sufficient votes in five areas, Styling, Engineering, Performance, Innovation, and Craftsmanship, they are admitted. Among more than 170 Certified Milestones in 1992 were early postwar cars such as Chrysler Town & Country, Frazer Manhattan, and Tucker, and recent ones have included Ford Mustang Boss 302, Plymouth Roadrunner, and Pontiac GTO.

Nearly all the domestic makes in the Classic and Milestone clubs also have their own one-make

THE AMERICAN AUTOMOBILE: A CENTENARY 1893–1993

Birds" appeared as well. There are also clubs for trucks, motorcycles, and foreign cars, so that the total currently listed — and it is changing all the time — is around 550.

▲ THIS GATHERING OF WOODIES AT MEADOWBROOK SHOWS SOME UNUSUAL CARS. ON THE LEFT IS A 1941 CADILLAC WITH A CUSTOM BODY, POSSIBLY BY BOHMAN & SCHWARTZ (CADILLAC NEVER CATALOGED A STATION WAGON). ON THE RIGHT IS A 1941 PACKARD WHICH WAS CATALOGED, THOUGH FEW WERE MADE. VISIBLE IN THE BACKGROUND BETWEEN THEM IS A 1941 OR '42 CHRYSLER.

(PHOTO NICKY WRIGHT)

THE COLLECTORS

The backbone of the old vehicle movement is the individual enthusiast who owns one or two cherished cars, but some enthusiasts have a great many more and a few are collectors on a grand scale. The first big collector was probably Henry Ford, who began amassing cars in the early 1920s, along with a great many other pieces of American rural life, particularly plows and other items of farm equipment, which went to make up the Henry Ford Museum and Greenfield Village. The historical complex opened on October 21, 1929, with Thomas Alva Edison, Orville Wright, and President Hoover on hand for the celebrations. Among highlights of the car collection were

Sylvester Roper's pioneer steamer of 1863, Ford's first quadricycle of 1896 and his massive 999 racer of 1903, and cars associated with personalities, such as Charles Lindbergh's Franklin and President Taft's 1912 Baker Electric.

Another pioneer collector, in a very different mold from Henry Ford, was Detroit entrepreneur (coal and coke, asphalt paving, excavating) Barney Pollard, whose collection eventually totaled over 1,000 cars. He acquired the first, a 1910 Cadillac, in 1938, but the real volume came during World War II, when two or three car carriers would come in daily. This continued after the war, when old cars would be brought in on back hauls from delivering new cars all over the country. The cars were

stacked vertically in sheds and remained thus until Pollard began to sell them off, starting in 1976. About 40 remain to this day in the Pollard family. They are now well housed in purpose-built accommodation.

Henry Austin Clark Jr., one of the great figures of the old car world, bought his first antique, a 1915 Ford Model T, in 1937 when he was a freshman at Harvard. By the outbreak of World War II, when he went into the Navy, he had acquired five more antiques, and has subsequently owned more than 400 vehicles. He was one of the first to appreciate the interest and fun in collecting old trucks, buses, and fire engines. In 1948 he opened the Long Island Automotive Museum at Southampton.

Another collector who eventually opened a museum was Briggs Cunningham, whose assembly of mostly sporting machines opened at Costa Mesa, California, in the 1960s. Early collectors who saved countless cars from the crusher included D. Cameron Peck of Chicago and opera singer James Melton, who had more than 100 cars by 1946, which he displayed in a museum.

The best known collector of them all, and founder of the world's largest auto museum, was Reno casino owner William Fisk Harrah. Beginning in 1948 with a Model T Ford and a two-cylinder Maxwell, Harrah amassed an enormous collection before he opened to the public. Within a few years he had around 1,400 cars, trucks, and fire engines, of which 1,100 were on display. Countless makes, both domestic and foreign, were represented. Among the highlights were more than 100 Fords (at least one for every year from 1903 to 1951) and more than 50 each of Franklin and Packard, two of Bill Harrah's favorite makes. He personally tested every car before it went on display, and his restoration workshops and library were world famous. Unfortunately he left no instructions about the fate of his collection after his death, which occurred in June 1978. There were plans to disperse the collection completely, and objectors to this took their appeals as far as President Reagan.

Eventually a series of sales was arranged to bring the collection down to more manageable proportions. These took place in 1984 and 1985, and a nucleus of about 225 cars was rehoused in downtown Reno. The collection is now known as the National Automobile Museum, which has made available for photography many of the cars illustrated in this book.

As well as broad spectrum collectors there are many who specialize in one make or model. Their dedication is amazing. Everitt White of Middletown, Wisconsin, had 150 Corvairs in the late 1970s, although about 50 were parts cars and others were bought and sold as part of his used car business. Don Schneider of Mansfield, Ohio, had 60 Corvairs, mostly 1964–66 models, which were part of a permanent collection. Pennsylvania farmer Hugh Lesley must have the world's largest collection of Edsels, with about 150 at the last count. One way to economize on space is to collect small cars. Paul Gorrell of Burlington, Iowa, restricts himself to Crosleys, of which he has 41, as well as a few King Midgets. He can haul four of these small cars on a trailer behind a van, with a fifth on the van roof, and even squeeze a sixth inside. He has nearly every body style and color Crosley built, and at least three of each year.

Some one-make names may have physical origins. Milwaukee Buick dealer Wally Rank was knocked out cold at the age of three by a Pierce-Arrow. Although he made a full recovery, he says he cannot see a Pierce-Arrow today without wanting to buy it. His last total was 18. One of the most specialized collections is that of Dick de Vecchi of San Lorenzo, California. He has concentrated on 1941 Chevrolets and now has seven, one of every style Chevy offered for that year, including a sedan delivery. Is he content? Not quite. He would like the one-and-only 1941 convertible sedan, a car built up by another enthusiast from two sedans and two convertibles.

A one-year collection which earned its keep was that of the Santa Ynez, California, airport rental fleet, all of which were 1958 Chevrolets. Most were sedans, with a few wagons and a Bel Air hardtop. They were active in 1978, but it is not known if you can still rent a 1958 Chevy at Santa Ynez today.

THE PROFESSIONALS

For many years the old car hobby was just that, a pastime that provided hundreds of happy hours of tinkering and driving for enthusiasts. Nobody made any money out of it, the reverse in fact, although when prices were low, it was more costly in time than in dollars and cents. However in

▼ 1957 PONTIAC BONNEVILLE CONVERTIBLE WITH FUEL INJECTION ENGINE —
A PRIZE WINNING CAR.
(PHOTO NICKY WRIGHT)

famous international auction houses such as Sotheby's and Christies from London. Sotheby's worked in conjunction with the New York house of Parke-Bernet, but the best known purely American company is the Indiana-based Kruse Classic Auction Company. Well known for real estate and farm equipment auctions, Kruse made headlines in January 1973 when it sold an armor-plated Mercedes-Benz limousine from the Adolf Hitler stables for $153,000. The following year a Duesenberg Model J broke the $200,000 barrier, and in 1979 Christie's sold the Hitler Mercedes-Benz for $400,000. Throughout the 1980s Kruse held around 40 auctions annually across the United

the past 30 years or so a growing number of people have made satisfactory livings out of restoring, dealing in, and auctioning collector cars of all ages.

The first important American auction took place in May 1962, when the Wallace C. Bird collection of classic cars was sold by O'Reilly Brothers on Long Island. Nine cars realized $37,850, and the prices of $5,300 for a Duesenberg, $3,700 for a Hispano-Suiza, and $1,850 for a Bugatti Type 43 were regarded as very high at the time. An observer from Parke-Bernet predicted that this was only the beginning; "Friend, I would advise you to buy your heart's desire now. I warn you that in ten years most of you guys will be standing outside the hobby looking in."

He was right. Prices soon escalated. But even modest hobbyists were not excluded, for rising prices meant that the capital value of even a small collection appreciated accordingly. By the late 1960s a Mercer 35 Raceabout was fetching $45,000, and during the next decade the importance of old cars was validated by the entry into the field of

States. Kruse auctions more than 13,000 cars annually, representing more than 75 percent of all collector cars offered for sale in the United States. Including property auctions, their annual volume of sales approaches $1 billion. The current U.S. auction record is the $6.5 million paid by Jerry Moore for a Bugatti Royale in 1986. This car later changed hands privately for $8.1 million, the new owner being pizza king Tom Monaghan. The Bugatti joined his collection of 20 Ferraris, 20 Rolls-Royces, and 28 Duesenbergs.

If one adds to the auctioneers the dealers and professional restorers of old cars, the cars of yesteryear are certainly a multi-million dollar industry, yet for all those who earn a living from it, there are far more who put money into one of the fastest growing hobbies of the late twentieth century.

BIBLIOGRAPHY

Among my reference books, some have been constant and indispensible companions, in particular:

The Standard Catalog of American Cars 1805–1942 by Beverly Rae Kimes and Henry Austin Clark Jr.; Krause Publications, 1989

The Standard Catalog of American Cars 1946–1975 by The Editors of Old Cars publications; Krause Publications, 1982

Fifty Years of American Automobiles from 1939 by The Auto Editors of *Consumer Guide*, 1989

Also the magnificent series of one-make books published by Crestline Publishing, Sarasota, Florida

Seventy Years of Buick by George Dammann, 1973

Cadillac and La Salle by Walter McCall, 1982

Seventy Years of Chrysler by George Dammann, 1974

The Dodge Story by Thomas A. McPherson, 1976

The History of Hudson by Don Butler, 1982

The Cars of Lincoln and Mercury by George Dammann and James K. Wagner, 1987

Seventy Five Years of Oakland and Pontiac by John Gunnell, 1982

The Cars of Oldsmobile by Dennis Casteele, 1981

The Plymouth and De Soto Story by Don Butler, 1979

Many other books consulted include:

American Automobile Manufacturers by John B. Rae, Chilton, Philadelphia, 1959

American Cars, 1930–1942 by James H. Moloney, Crestline, Sarasota, Florida 1977

The American Car Since 1775 by the Editors of *Automobile Quarterly*, New York, 1971

The American Rolls-Royce by Arthur W. Soutter, Mowbray, Providence, Rhode Island, 1976

Automania — Man and the Motorcar by Julian Pettifer and Nigel Turner, Collins, London, 1984

The Automobile and American Culture edited by David L. Lewis and Laurence Goldstein, University of Michigan Press, 1983

Automobiles of America Wayne State University Press, Detroit, 1962

Beetle — the Chronicles of a People's Car by Hans-Rudiger Etzold, Haynes, England, 1988

Cars of Canada by Hugh Durnford and Glenn Baechler, McClelland & Stewart, Toronto, 1973

Cars of 1923 by Keith Marvin and Arthur Lee Homan, Automobilists of the Upper Hudson Valley, Troy, N.Y., 1957

Cars of the 1930s by Michael Sedgwick, B.T. Batsford Ltd, London, 1970

Chevrolet, 1911–1985 by the Auto Editors of *Consumer Guide*, 1984

The Classic Cord by Dan R. Post, Dan Post Publications, Arcadia, California, 1952

The Complete Handbook of Automobile Hobbies edited by Beverly Rae Kimes, Princeton Publishing Inc, Princeton, N.J., 1981

Duesenberg — the Pursuit of Perfection by Fred Roe, Dalton Watson, London, 1982

Encyclopedia of American Cars, 1945–1970 by Richard M. Langworth, Beekman House, New York, 1980

The Fabulous Firebird by Michael Lamm, Lamm-Morada Press, Stockton, California 1979

Fit for the Chase — Cars and the Movies by Raymond Lee, A.S. Barnes & Co, New York, 1969

Ford, 1903–1984 by the Auto Editors of *Consumer Guide*, 1984

Ford, the Dust and the Glory by Leo Levine, Collier-Macmillan, Toronto, 1968

Ford, the Men and the Machine by Robert Lacey, Heinemann, London, 1986

The Great Old Cars, Where Are They Now? by Stanley K. Yost, The Wayside Press, Mendota, Illinois, 1960

Last Onslaught on Detroit by Richard M. Langworth, Automobile Quarterly Publications, New York, 1975

The Motor Car, 1945–1956 by Michael Sedgwick, B.T. Batsford Ltd, London, 1979

Pierce-Arrow by Marc Ralston, A.S. Barnes & Co, New York, 1980

A Record of Motor Racing, 1984–1908 by Gerald Rose, Motor Racing Publications, Abingdon, England, 1949

Rolls-Royce in America by John Webb de Campi, Dalton Watson, London, 1975

The Shell Book of Firsts by Patrick Robertson, Ebury Press, London, 1974

Standard Catalog of Light Duty Trucks edited by John Gunnell, Krause Publications, Iola, Wisconsin, 1987

The Studebaker Century by Asa E. Hall and Richard M. Langworth, Dragonwyck Publishing, Contoocook, New Hampshire, 1983

They Don't Build Cars Like They Used To by Stanley K. Yost, The Wayside Press, Mendota, Illinois, 1963

Turbo — an A to Z of turbocharged cars by Graham Robson, Apple Press, London, 1988

Unsafe at any Speed by Ralph Nader, Grossman Publishers, New York, 1965

US Military Wheeled Vehicles by Fred Crismon, Crestline, Sarasota, Florida, 1983

The VW Beetle by Jonathan Wood, Motor Racing Publications, London, 1983

What was the McFarlan? by Keith Marvin and Alvin J. Arnheim, published privately, 1967

World Guide to Automobiles by Nick Baldwin, Nick Georgano, Brian Laban and Michael Sedgwick, Orbis, London, 1987

Magazines consulted include:

Antique Automobile, Autocar & Motor, Automobile Quarterly, The Upper Hudson Valley Automobilist, Autoweek, Bulb Horn, Car, Car & Driver, Motor Trend, Road & Track, the Society of Automotive Historians Journal and Automotive History Review, Special Interest Autos, Top Wheels

Figures in *italics* refer to captions to illustrations.

ACKNOWLEDGMENTS

Nick Georgano would like to thank the numerous people who helped in the research for this book, especially Keith Marvin and Beverly Rae Kimes, who answered a barrage of queries with kindness and good humour. Also Lynda Springate and her staff at the Library of the National Motor Museum, Beaulieu, Hampshire, England.

Others who helped include Charles L. Betts Jr., James T. Billings Public Relations Director of Kruse International, Homer D. Brown, Christopher Foster, Jack Heald, Wade Hoyt, editor of *MoTor* magazine, Linda Huntsman, Research Librarian at the National Automobile Museum, Reno, Nevada, Richard Langworth, Professor David Lewis of the University of Michigan, Walter McCall, G. Marshall Naul, and Barney C. Pollard.

Nicky Wright would like to thank the following museums and people for the special help they gave:
Auburn-Cord-Duesenberg Museum, Auburn, Indiana
Gilmore Car Museum, Kalamazoo, Michigan
Jim Ransom
National Automobile Museum, (William F. Harrah Foundation), Reno, Nevada
Western Reserve Historical Society, Cleveland, Ohio

He would also like to thank: Chris Anderson, Harvey Anderson, Tom & Karen Barnes, Patricia Beck, Jim Bell, Larry Bell, Russ Bell, Steve & Evelyn Benn, Mr. & Mrs. James Beversdorf, Dan Blakely, Rod Butler, Dell Casters, Dick Choler, Randy Daniels, Jonathan Day, Fuji Film, Ira Gamble, Dick Ginther, Bill Goodsene, William Goodwin, Steven C. Graham/A-C-D Museum, Mrs. Cynthia Haines, Charles Hilton, Biff Hitzeman, Dave Holcombe, Blaine Jenkins & Phil, Robert A. Jordan, Rod Lungstrom, Bob MacMillam, Skip Marketti, Mike Myers, Lee Muzzila, National Motor Museum, Beaulieu, England, Nikon Cameras, Pentax Cameras, Scott Pirsak, Gene Povinelli, George Sanders, Barney Smith, Less Sterling, Unique Color Lab, Ft. Wayne, Indiana, Gary & Sharon Vick, Tim Woods

Mirco De Cet would like to thank the following people and organizations for their help with picture research: Helen Gray at Ford Motor Co. Public Relations dept. Dearborn, Michigan. The Henry Ford Museum, Dearborn, Michigan. Linda Busse at the MVMA, Detroit, Michigan. Helen Early and James Walkinshaw at the Oldsmobile History Center, Lansing, Michigan. Lawrence Gustin at Buick Motor Div. Public Relations Dept., Flint, Michigan. Richard Scharchburg at the GMI Archives, Flint, Michigan.